XII Jornadas Iberoamericanas de Ingenieria de Software e Ingenieria del Conocimiento 2017 (JIISIC'17)

Held jointly with the Ecuadorian Conference on Software Engineering (CEIS'2017) and the Conference on Software Engineering Applied to Control and Automation Systems (ISASCA'2017)

Latacunga, Ecuador
17 – 18 August 2017

Editors:

Omar S. Gomez
Edison Espinosa

ISBN: 978-1-5108-4396-7

Printed from e-media with permission by:

Curran Associates, Inc.
57 Morehouse Lane
Red Hook, NY 12571

Some format issues inherent in the e-media version may also appear in this print version.

Printed by Curran Associates, Inc. (2017)

For permission requests, please contact Escuela Superior Politecnica de Chimborazo, ESPOCH and Universidad de las Fuerzas Armadas, ESPE-L at the address below.

Escuela Superior Politecnica de Chimborazo
Panamericana Sur km 1 1/2
Riobamba - Ecuador
Postal Code: EC060155

Phone: 593 (03) 2 998-200
Fax: (03) 2 317-001

http://www.espoch.edu.ec/

Universidad de las Fuerzas Armadas, ESPE-L
Ecuador, Cotopaxi – Latacunga
Calle Quljano y Ordonez y Hermanas Paez

Phone: (593) (3) 2810-206 / 2811-240
Fax: (593) (3) 2810-208

Marketing-el@espe.edu.ec
http://espe-el.espe.edu.ec/

Additional copies of this publication are available from:

Curran Associates, Inc.
57 Morehouse Lane
Red Hook, NY 12571 USA
Phone: 845-758-0400
Fax: 845-758-2633
Email: curran@proceedings.com
Web: www.proceedings.com

Preface

The Ibero-American Symposium on Software Engineering and Knowledge Engineering, known as JIISIC, represents a forum for the international meeting of scientists and professionals dedicated to the study and research of Software Engineering and Knowledge Engineering. Its fundamental purpose is to foster scientific and professional cooperation, as well as the transfer of technology in the Ibero-American context.

Since the first one in 2001, held in Buenos Aires, Argentina, an increasing number of attendees have convened at JIISIC. Previous editions have been held in Salvador de Bahía (Brazil), Valdivia (Chile), Madrid (Spain), Puebla (Mexico), Lima (Peru), Guayaquil (Ecuador), Merida (Mexico), Lima (Peru), Medellin (Colombia), Riobamba (Ecuador). This time, JIISIC remains in Ecuador, in the city of Latacunga, otherwise known as the delightful garden of the Andes.

JIISIC'2017 is carried out jointly with the Ecuadorian Conference on Software Engineering (CEIS'2017), and the Conference on Software Engineering Applied to Control and Automation Systems (ISASCA'2017).

In this edition, 82 manuscripts were received, and based on the reviews made by the members of the program committee, 31 manuscripts have been accepted; thus, having an acceptance rate of 38%.

The editors of this book of proceedings wish to thank those who chose JIISIC'2017 for their participation and the dissemination of their research work. We would also like to thank the members of the program committee for their valuable collaboration in the reviewing process. We are sure that their recommendations were positively valued by the authors of the accepted papers, as well as being positively valued by those authors whose works were not selected for this edition.

August 2017, Latacunga, Ecuador

Omar S. Gómez
Escuela Superior Politécnica de Chimborazo

Edison Espinosa
Universidad de las Fuerzas Armadas ESPE (Latacunga Unit)

Organizing Committee

JIISIC'2017 is organized by the Research Group on Biomedicine Applied Technologies (GITbio) from the Ecuadorian Army Force University (ESPE, Latacunga Unit) and by the Research Group on Software Engineering (GrIISoft) from the Technical University of Chimborazo (ESPOCH).

Steering Committee

Silvia Teresita Acuña. *Universidad Autónoma de Madrid* (España)
José Antonio Pow-Sang. *Pontificia Universidad Católica del Perú* (Perú)
Raúl Antonio Aguilar Vera. *Universidad Autónoma de Yucatán* (México)
Mónica Villavicencio. *Escuela Superior Politécnica del Litoral* (Ecuador)
Omar S. Gómez. *Escuela Superior Politécnica de Chimborazo* (Ecuador)

Local Committee

Edison Espinosa. *Universidad de las Fuerzas Armadas ESPE-L* (Ecuador)
Omar S. Gómez. *Escuela Superior Politécnica de Chimborazo* (Ecuador)

Program Committee

Acuña, Silvia Teresita. *Universidad Autónoma de Madrid* (Spain)
Aguilar Vera, Raúl Antonio. *Universidad Autónoma de Yucatán* (Mexico)
Aguileta, Antonio. *Universidad Autónoma de Yucatán* (Mexico)
Andaluz, Víctor H. *Universidad de las Fuerzas Armadas ESPE* (Ecuador)
Aranda, Alejandrina. *Universidad Politécnica de Madrid* (Spain)
Arcos, Gloria. *Escuela Superior Politécnica de Chimborazo* (Ecuador)
Aveledo, Marianella. *Universidad Simón Bolivar* (Venezuela)
Ayala, Claudia P. *Universidad Politécnica de Cataluña* (Spain)
Benalcazar, Marco. *Escuela Politécnica Nacional* (Ecuador)
Brandão, Alexandre. *Universidade Federal de Viçosa* (Brazil)
Carrizo, Dante. *Universidad de Atacama* (Chile)
Castro, John W. *Universidad de Atacama* (Chile)
Chavarriaga, Enrique. *Universidad Autónoma de Madrid* (Spain)
Condori-Fernández, Nelly. *Universidad Vrije de Amsterdam* (Netherlands)
Cortes, Karen. *Universidad Veracruzana* (Mexico)
Dieste, Óscar. *Universidad Politécnica de Madrid* (Spain)
Espinosa, Edison. *Universidad de las Fuerzas Armadas ESPE-L* (Ecuador)
Ferreira, Juan Marcelo. *Cámara de Senadores, Poder Legislativo de la República del Paraguay* (Paraguay)
Fonseca C., Efraín R. *Universidad de las Fuerzas Armadas ESPE* (Ecuador)
Gallardo, José. *Universidad Católica del Norte* (Chile)

Garcia-Martinez, Ramon. *Universidad Nacional de Lanus* (Argentina)
Garcia Peñalvo, Francisco José. *Universidad de Salamanca* (Spain)
Gómez, Omar S. *Escuela Superior Politécnica de Chimborazo* (Ecuador)
Lozoya Ponce, Ricardo Eliu. *Instituto Tecnológico y de Estudios Superiores de Monterrey* (Mexico)
Luna, Washington. *Escuela Superior Politécnica de Chimborazo* (Ecuador)
Macías Iglesias, José Antonio. *Universidad Autónoma de Madrid* (Spain)
Marín, Beatriz. *Universidad Diego Portales* (Chile)
Mon, Alicia. *Universidad Nacional de la Matanza* (Argentina)
Monsalve, Carlos. *Escuela Superior Politécnica del Litoral* (Ecuador)
Moreno, Silvana. *Universidad de la República* (Uruguay)
Ontañon, Luis J. *Universidad Autónoma de San Luis Potosí* (Mexico)
Ovalle, Demetrio Arturo. *Universidad Nacional de Colombia* (Colombia)
Panach Navarrete, José Ignacio. *Universidad de Valencia* (Spain)
Pardo, César. *Universidad del Cauca* (Colombia)
Pow-Sang, José Antonio. *Pontificia Universidad Católica del Perú* (Peru)
Rámos, Isidro. *Universidad Politécnica de Valencia* (Spain)
Roberti, Flavio. *CONICET* (Argentina)
Rodríguez, Francy. *Swissport* (Spain)
Rodríguez, Pilar. *Universidad de Oulu* (Finland)
Rodriguez-Elias, Oscar M. *Instituto Tecnológico de Hermosillo* (Mexico)
Rosero, Raúl H. *Escuela Superior Politécnica de Chimborazo* (Ecuador)
Solari, Martín. *Universidad ORT Uruguay* (Uruguay)
Triñanes, Jorge. *Universidad de la República* (Uruguay)
Ucán Pech, Juan Pablo. *Universidad Autónoma de Yucatán* (Mexico)
Vara, Juan Manuel. *Universidad Rey Juan Carlos* (Spain)
Villalobos-Abarca. *Universidad de Tarapacá* (Chile)
Villavicencio, Mónica. *Escuela Superior Politécnica del Litoral* (Ecuador)
Zapata Jaramillo, Carlos M. *Universidad Nacional de Colombia* (Colombia)
Zarate, Óscar. *Universidad de Guadalajara* (Mexico)

Table of Contents

Sponsors

- Ecuadorian Army Force University - Latacunga Unit (Universidad de las Fuerzas Armadas ESPE extensión Latacunga)
- Technical University of Chimborazo (Escuela Superior Politécnica de Chimborazo, ESPOCH)
- Ecuador Global

A Software Application for Collecting Usability Empirical Data about User Efficiency, Effectiveness and Satisfaction

Juan M. Ferreira[1], Silvia T. Acuña[2]

[1] Facultad Politécnica, Universidad Nacional de Asunción, CC 1439, San Lorenzo, Paraguay
jmferreira1978@gmail.com
[2] Universidad Autónoma de Madrid, Calle Tomás y Valiente 11, 28049 Madrid, España
silvia.acunna@uam.es

Abstract. This article presents a software application developed to collect empirical data in order to study and analyze the usability impact under the attributes of user efficiency, effectiveness and satisfaction. The application is endowed with functional usability features implemented as usability mechanisms, which are recommendations of the Human Computer Interaction community with a high impact in software design. The Abort Operation, Progress Feedback and Preferences usability mechanisms are implemented in this software application. In experimental execution, subjects are guided by this application to accomplish different tasks. The application collects quantitative and qualitative data about users' behavior while they are using this application with usability mechanisms being activated or deactivated. Data of time, number of clicks, percentage of completed task and answers to questionnaires are collected. Three experimental executions were carried out using this application and the collected empirical data have been proven to be useful in several researches by evidencing which usability mechanisms improve the user-system interaction. Finally, this software application contributes to the experimental software engineering research by allowing to collect empirical data for usability studies.

Keywords: usability, software Application, usability mechanism, usability metrics, empirical evidence, usability attributes.

1. Introduction

In Software Engineering (IS), usability is considered to be a quality attribute. Usability concerns have traditionally been treated as non-functional requirements due to their scarce influence on the system's functionality [1–3]. However, recent studies have shown that usability features have important implications on the system's functionality [4–8]. Over the last decade, usability concept has opened the challenge for the creators of quality standards [9]. Several professional uses gave rise to different definitions of usability inside ISO standards of ergonomics and software quality. As a consequence, the "quality in use" model of the ISO/IEC 25010 [10] defines usability as the degree to which a product or system can be used by specified users to achieve specified goals with efficiency, effectiveness and satisfaction in a specified context of use, avoiding negative consequences.

Considering the relevance of usability in software development, current software products still lack of usability aspects [3, 11–14]. Moreover, there is a shortage of empirical studies about the usability effect on the user performance under specific quality criteria, beyond the user interface [15]. In this sense, considering data collection tools for empirical usability studies, a recent state-of-the-art research has reported that most empirical data collection tools are proprietary paid software, user-interface focused, platform dependent and most of them are not powerful enough for research contexts related to the usability impact on quality attributes [16]. Therefore, the development of a software application has been proposed to collect empirical data in order to analyze the usability effect in terms of user efficiency, effectiveness and satisfaction.

The paper is structured as follows. In section 2 the usability metrics and functional usability features are described. The proposed solution is discussed in detail in section 3. Some experimental executions are discussed in section 4. Finally, in section 5, conclusions and future works of this solution are given.

2. Usability Metrics and Functional Usability Features

2.1. Usability Metrics

ISO/IEC 25010 [10] defines usability metrics where efficiency, effectiveness and satisfaction [17] are normally used as measures to evaluate the quality of a software product. The usability impact is measured as an increase of these three quality attributes, where the increase is for or against the application usability. Hence, the standard defines each attribute as:

- Efficiency: resources expended in relation to the accuracy and completeness with which users achieve goals.
- Effectiveness: accuracy and completeness with which users achieve specified goals.
- Satisfaction: degree to which a user is satisfied with their perceived achievement of pragmatic goals, including the results of use and the consequences of use.

In this software application, the usability metrics to be collected for each attribute are:

- Efficiency:
  a) User Speed: the time, measured in seconds, which a subject needs to complete a task [18].
  b) Interaction Degree: the number of clicks that a subject needs to complete a task [19, 20].
- Effectiveness: percentage of completed work in the task by a subject [21].
- Satisfaction: mean value of the answers to the questions of the post-task questionnaires. The questions have ordinal values of the Likert scale (one = strongly disagree to five = strongly agree) [22].

In the particular case of Efficiency as user speed, the collected data represent the task time of both reading and interpretation plus the time of doing it. Regarding Efficiency as an interaction degree, data collected are independent clicks, so a double click means two independent clicks made by the user. Additionally, subjective qualitative data are collected, especially additional user comments related to his/her behavior doing a task.

In summary, the quantitative and qualitative model to collect usability metrics is shown in Table 1.

Table 1. Quantitative and qualitative model for collecting usability metrics

	Metrics			
Data	**Efficiency**		**Effectiveness**	**Satisfaction**
Quantitative	Time	Clicks	% Completed task	Mean value of the answers the post-task questionnaires (s)
Qualitative	User comments related to their behavior while completing a task			

Time, clicks and % completed task are automatically collected during the experimental execution, while satisfaction data (responses and comments) are collected in post-task questionnaires.

2.2. Functional Usability Features

There are several recommendations developed by the Human Computer Interaction (HCI) community to improve the usability levels of software systems that suitably complement the IS community works [11, 23–27]. This proposal takes the HCI recommendations with high impact on software design [28]. These high impact recommendations, named as Functional Usability Features (FUFs), are shown in Figure 1.

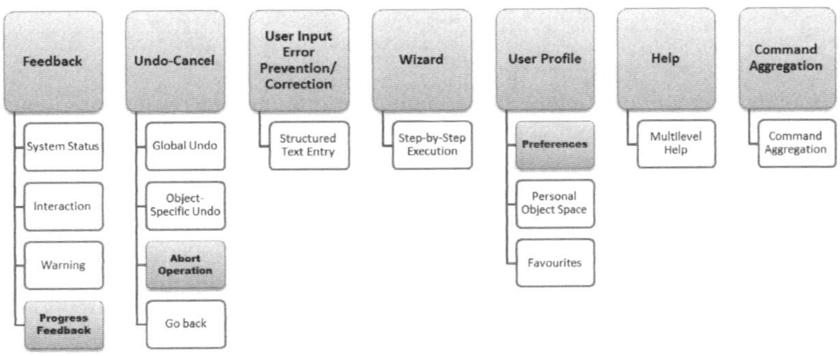

Fig. 1. Functional Usability Features (FUFs) and Usability Mechanisms (UM)

Each FUF is specialized in more detailed goals named as usability mechanisms (UM), where each mechanism involves the building of specific functionalities in software system in order to improve user-system interaction.

The usability mechanisms implemented in this software application are:

- **Abort Operation** (ABR-UM) from Undo-Cancel family. The purpose of this mechanism is "To cancel the execution of an action or the whole application".
- **Progress Feedback** (PFB-UM) from Feedback family. The goal of this mechanism is "To inform users that the system is processing an action that will take some time to complete."
- **Preferences** (PRF-UM) from User Profile family. The goal of this mechanism is "To record each of the user's options for using system functions".

The choice of these three mechanisms is based on the Juristo et al. research [28] where they emphasize that these three usability mechanisms can become critical because of their high impact on software design.

The implementation of these FUFs is based on the Rodríguez research [29–31]. She proposes different pattern-based artifact for including usability mechanisms in software development life cycle.

3. Proposed Solution

The goal of this solution is to build a software tool to allow collecting empirical evidence in order to study the effects of the usability mechanisms in a software system under the efficiency, effectiveness and satisfaction attributes using definitions and recommendations described in section 2.

For this, an interactive web application is developed in order to collect data about user's behavior while they are using a software system with usability mechanisms being activated or deactivated. The collected data are depicted in the quantitative and qualitative model of Table 1.

3.1. Software Application Features

QuickStore is an online store for ecommerce where users can search for a specific item, manage a shopping cart, etc. The store has several customizable categories where the different items sold by the store are organized. It has a section of information regarding guarantees (security, returns/refunds and privacy policies). In addition, a configuration option is provided where users can customize the store interface according to their preferences.

Both online-store user interface (UI) and experimental wizard are fully developed in Spanish because the target test population are Spanish speakers people, who are highly likely to have limited knowledge of other languages, such as English.

All tasks are designed following the scenario-oriented recommendations [32], in which a scenario is composed of several tasks to be sequentially executed. Each subject does all task assuming to be a store customer, that is, she/he interacts with the system UI doing non-administrative tasks.

The source code of the whole software application is available on github [33].

3.2. Tasks

The designed tasks in this software application are described in Table 2. Each task can be performed in different order according to the experimental design. Figure 2 shows a screenshot of a task description, in this case, the task involves the interaction with Abort Operation usability mechanism (ABR-UM).

Table 2. Tasks description for subjects

Task	Short Description
1. ABR-UM	subjects are asked to access their shopping cart in order to modify some data and then, to try to cancel the operation.
2. PFB-UM	subjects are asked to search for an item in the store.
3. PRF-UM	This task is broken up in two: □ Basic Task: subjects are asked to try to customize the application UI. □ Fictitious Task: After the basic task, subjects are asked to search for a specific information referring to deadlines for returns using the customized interface in basic task.

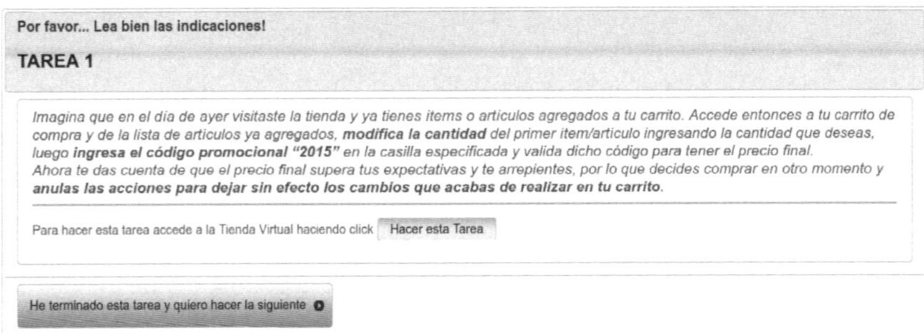

Fig. 2. Textual description of the ABR-UM task

3.3. Questionnaires

The two questionnaires to be used during the experimental execution are:

1. Familiarity questionnaire: this questionnaire is completed by the subject at the beginning of the experiment. Firstly the age, occupation, sex and languages of the subject is asked. Then, his/her relationship with computer science is asked. Finally, how they are using Internet is asked. The online form for collecting those data is shown in Figure 3.
2. Post-task questionnaires: this questionnaire is completed by the subject after each task. Note that this questionnaire collects the empirical data of user satisfaction. For example, the post-task questionnaire that collects satisfaction metrics data for ABR-UM is shown in Figure 4.

In addition to these two questionnaires, a SUS questionnaire [34] is provided at the end of the experiment to collect satisfaction global measures of the system.

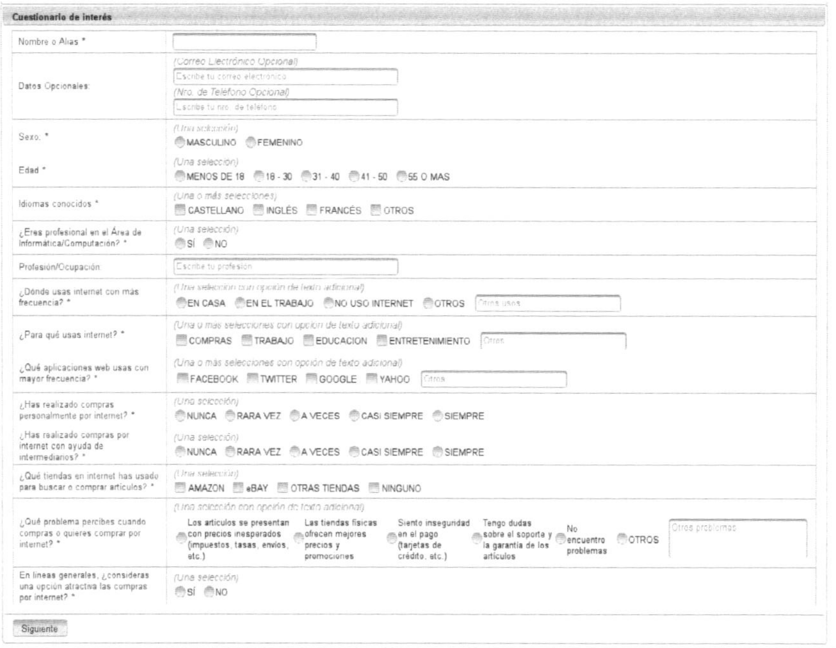

Cuestionario de interés

Nombre o Alias *	
Datos Opcionales:	(Correo Electrónico Opcional) Escribe tu correo electrónico (Nro. de Teléfono Opcional) Escribe tu nro. de teléfono
Sexo: *	(Una selección) MASCULINO FEMENINO
Edad *	(Una selección) MENOS DE 18 18 - 30 31 - 40 41 - 50 55 O MAS
Idiomas conocidos *	(Una o más selecciones) CASTELLANO INGLÉS FRANCÉS OTROS
¿Eres profesional en el Área de Informática/Computación? *	(Una selección) SÍ NO
Profesión/Ocupación:	Escribe tu profesión
¿Dónde usas internet con más frecuencia? *	(Una selección con opción de texto adicional) EN CASA EN EL TRABAJO NO USO INTERNET OTROS Otros usos
¿Para qué usas internet? *	(Una o más selecciones con opción de texto adicional) COMPRAS TRABAJO EDUCACION ENTRETENIMIENTO Otros
¿Qué aplicaciones web usas con mayor frecuencia? *	(Una o más selecciones con opción de texto adicional) FACEBOOK TWITTER GOOGLE YAHOO Otros
¿Has realizado compras personalmente por internet? *	(Una selección) NUNCA RARA VEZ A VECES CASI SIEMPRE SIEMPRE
¿Has realizado compras por internet con ayuda de intermediarios? *	(Una selección) NUNCA RARA VEZ A VECES CASI SIEMPRE SIEMPRE
¿Qué tiendas en internet has usado para buscar o comprar artículos? *	(Una selección) AMAZON eBAY OTRAS TIENDAS NINGUNO
¿Qué problema percibes cuando compras o quieres comprar por internet? *	(Una selección con opción de texto adicional) Los artículos se presentan con precios inesperados (impuestos, tasas, envíos, etc.) Las tiendas físicas ofrecen mejores precios y promociones Siento inseguridad en el pago (tarjetas de crédito, etc.) Tengo dudas sobre el soporte y la garantía de los artículos No encuentro problemas OTROS Otros problemas
En líneas generales, ¿consideras una opción atractiva las compras por internet? *	(Una selección) SÍ NO

Siguiente

Fig. 4. Familiarity questionnaire of the experiment

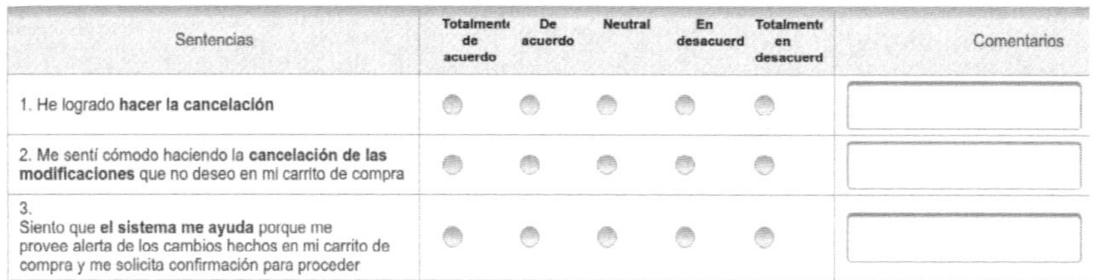

Sentencias	Totalmente de acuerdo	De acuerdo	Neutral	En desacuerd	Totalmente en desacuerd	Comentarios
1. He logrado **hacer la cancelación**						
2. Me sentí cómodo haciendo la **cancelación de las modificaciones** que no deseo en mi carrito de compra						
3. Siento que **el sistema me ayuda** porque me provee alerta de los cambios hechos en mi carrito de compra y me solicita confirmación para proceder						

Fig. 3. Post-task questionnaire for ABR-UM

3.4. Groups Assignment Matrix

The software application is configured on a Group Assignment Matrix (GAM). This matrix is built considering: 1) the different usability mechanisms, 2) the activation modes and 3) the order in which they will be showed at run time. This matrix is normally built following statistical experts recommendations and defines how the data should be grouped to be analyzed later. Basically, this matrix contains the different groups in which a subject can be assigned. A group define both the order in which the tasks will be performed and which usability mechanisms should be activated or deactivated. The default GAM for this software application is shown in Table 3.

Table 3. Default groups of the GAM

			First			Second			Third		
Treatment	**Group**	**Order**	**ABR**	**PFB**	**PRF**	**ABR**	**PFB**	**PRF**	**ABR**	**PFB**	**PRF**
A	**G1**	**O1**	0				0				1
	G2	**O2**	0					1		0	
	G3	**O3**		0				1	0		
	G4	**O4**		0		0					1
	G5	**O5**			1	0				0	
	G6	**O6**			1		0		0		
B	**G7**	**O1**	1				0				0
	G8	**O2**	1					0		0	
	G9	**O3**		0				0	1		
	G10	**O4**		0		1					0
	G11	**O5**			0	1				0	
	G12	**O6**			0		0		1		
C	**G13**	**O1**	0				1				0
	G14	**O2**	0					0		1	
	G15	**O3**		1				0	0		
	G16	**O4**		1		0					0
	G17	**O5**			0	0				1	
	G18	**O6**			0		1		0		
D	**G19**	**O1**	1				1				1
	G20	**O2**	1					1		1	
	G21	**O3**		1				1	1		
	G22	**O4**		1		1					1
	G23	**O5**			1	1				1	
	G24	**O6**			1		1		1		

The one values indicate that the mechanism is activated while the zeros mean deactivated. In this example, treatment A determines that only the PRF-UM will be activated in all six execution orders (O1...O6). Then, when a subject is assigned into the group G5, the software application will show each task as follow: First task with PRF-UM activated, second task with the ABR-UM deactivated and finally, the task with the PFB-UM deactivated.

3.5. Operation

At run time, the software application become a wizard, where the indications of each task are given. A questionnaire of familiarity is initially provided for the subject to collect additional information about its behavior. Then, this software application randomly assigns the subject to a group available in GAM (section 3.4) while maintaining the balanced groups' property. According to the GAM, the subject will do different tasks referring to each usability mechanism in different orders.

Time, clicks and % completed task are automatically collected during each task. Moreover, a post-task questionnaire is provided to collect satisfaction data after the task is completed.

Finally, the software application provides a SUS questionnaire [34] allowing the subjects to rate and comment their overall satisfaction regarding the usability of the system they have just tested.

4. Experimental Executions

Three experimental executions were carried out to collect empirical data using this software application. The experimental design information of this three experiments are out the scope of this article. For the purpose of this paper, just the experimental results of each one are presented. The first one [35] was carried out as a pilot in the context of the Master's Degree in Computer Engineering at the Universidad Autónoma de Madrid, Spain where 32 students have participated in an experimental session with a duration of approximately 30 minutes. The experimental design was a "Between Subjects" [36] with a GAM showing scenarios with logical sequences, where a task always starts with the PRF-UM activated or deactivated. The idea behind logical sequences is to allow a continuous block of logically ordered tasks. Eight possible groups have been built in the GAM. Efficiency and satisfaction are the usability attributes to be evaluated. The goal of this pilot has been to gather information to assess if the experimental design was correct. The results of the pilot have revealed that the presence of the usability mechanisms does not imply any improvement in the user efficiency and satisfaction. However, several important details to adjust the experimental design were detected. These adjustments are described in [35].

The second one was carried out at the Rodeira Institute in Galicia, Spain with 100 students of the electronics technician career. In this new adjusted design, all sequences are valid, not just the logical sequences. So, 24 groups have been built in GAM. Efficiency and satisfaction are again evaluated in this experiment. The results of this experimental execution [35] show an improvement of the usability system when usability mechanisms are activated, making users both to be more satisfied and to perform tasks more efficiently.

Finally, the third one has been carried out in two contexts: academic and professional. The results of this third experimental execution are still not available on web. The experimental design is the same as the previous one (Rodeira Institute) but the software application has been upgraded to collect effectiveness data in addition to efficiency and satisfaction data. 24 groups are available in GAM. 168 subjects have executed the experiment. The experimental results have revealed a positive effect when usability mechanisms are activated obtaining significant improvements in either efficiency, effectiveness, satisfaction or a subset of them. No negative effects were evidenced. In addition, the usability improvement seems to depend on the problem domain. In this sense, a specific usability mechanism could have a different effect in other contexts, so additional experiments are needed to gather more evidence and confirm these results.

5. Conclusions and Future Work

The features of a software application developed to collect empirical data have been presented in order to evaluate the impact of specific usability mechanisms considering the attributes of user efficiency, effectiveness and satisfaction.

The software application allows to automatically collect empirical usability data. Specifically, quantitative data of time, number of clicks and % completed task are collected. In addition, qualitative data of satisfaction are collected by post-task questionnaires. Thanks to embedded scenario-oriented tasks, no additional indications outside the software application are required. So, more control over the whole experiment is had.

The experimental design is pure random and the GAM randomly assigns a subject to a specific group in real time in order to do tasks. This avoids the problem of having to make groups of both test and control.

Incorporating others functional usability features, defining more tasks and other usability metrics are planned as a future work.

Finally, empirical studies are taking an increasing importance in IS by generating evidences that support the knowledge evolution in order to improve theories as a consequence of the empirical results. This software application addresses to this research line.

References

1. Lauesen, S., Younessi, H.: Six Styles for Usability Requirements. In: REFSQ'98. pp. 1–12 (1998).

2. Ferré, X., Juristo, N., Moreno, A.M.: Marco de Integración de la Usabilidad en el Proceso de Desarrollo Software Facultad de Informática. Universidad Politécnica de Madrid p. 273 (2005).

3. Golden, E.: Early-Stage Software Design for Usability PhD Thesis Human-Computer Interaction: Human-Computer Interaction Institute, Carnegie Mellon University p. 277 (2010).

4. Juristo, N., Moreno, A., Sanchez-Segura, M., Davis, A.: Gathering Usability Information through Elicitation Patterns. Investigación en Ingeniería de Software Empirica (GrISE). 1–9 (2005).

5. Juristo, N.: Impact of Usability on Software Requirements and Design. In: De Lucia, Andrea and Ferrucci, F. (ed.) Software Engineering. pp. 55–77. Springer-Verlag (2009).

6. Saxena, S., Dubey, S.K.: Impact of Software Design Aspects on Usability. International Journal of Computer Applications. 61, 48–53 (2013).

7. Laura Carvajal, Ana M. Moreno, Maria-Isabel Sanchez-Segura, Ahmed Seffah: Usability through Software Design. IEEE Transactions on Software Engineering. 39, 1582–1596 (2013) . doi: doi.ieeecomputersociety.org/10.1109/TSE.2013.29.

8. García, L.E.C., Sánchez-Capuchino, A.M.M.: Software Design Guidelines for Usability. In: Actas de las Jornadas de Ingeniería del Software y Bases de Datos (JISBD) 2011. pp. 67–76. SISTEDES, Sociedad de Ingeniería de Software y Tecnologías de Desarrollo de Software, Espa{ñ}a (2011).

9. Issa, A., Bong, C.H.: Measuring Software Quality in Use: State-of-the-Art and Research Challenges. ASQ. Software Quality Professional. 17, 4–15 (2015).

10. ISO/IEC 25010: Systems and Software Engineering - Systems and Software Quality Requirements and Evaluation (SQuaRE) - System and Software Quality Models. (2011).

11. Constantine, L.L., Lockwood, L.A.D.: Software for Use: A Practical Guide to the Models and Methods of Usage-centered Design. ACM Press/Addison-Wesley Publishing Co. (1999).

12. Ferré, X., Juristo, N., Windl, H., Constantine, L.: Usability Basics for Software Developers. IEEE Software. 18, 22–29 (2001) . doi: 10.1109/52.903160.

13. Seffah, B.A., Metzker, E.: The Obstacles and Myths of Usability and Software Engineering. Communications of the ACM. 47, 70–76 (2004).

14. Bias, R.G., Mayhew, D.J.: Cost-Justifying Usability: An Update for an Internet Age. Morgan Kaufmann Publishers (2005).

15. Abrahão, S.M., Insfrán, E., Fernandez, A.: Designing Highly Usable Web Applications. In: Topi, H. and Tucker, A. (eds.) Computing Handbook, Third Edition: Information Systems and Information Technology. p. 36: 1--14. {CRC} Press (2014).

16. Aveledo, M.: Identificación Empírica de Beneficios de Usabilidad Supervisor: Sánchez-Capuchino, A.M. Universidad Politécnica de Madrid p. 286 (2014).

17. Frøkjær, E., Hertzum, M., Hornbæk, K.: Measuring Usability : Are Effectiveness, Efficiency and Satisfaction Really Correlated? ACM CHI 2000 Conference on Human Factors in Computing Systems. 2, 345–352 (2000) . doi: 10.1145/332040.332455.

18. ISO 9241-11: Ergonomic Requirements for Office Work with Visual Display Terminals (VDTs)–Part II Guidance on Usability. (1998).

19. Hornbæk, K.: Current Practice in Measuring Usability: Challenges to Usability Studies and Research. International Journal of Human Computer Studies. 64, 79–102 (2006) . doi: 10.1016/j.ijhcs.2005.06.002.

20. Seffah, A., Donyaee, M., Kline, R.B., Padda, H.K.: Usability Measurement and Metrics: A Consolidated Model. Software Quality Journal. 14, 159–178 (2006) . doi: 10.1007/s11219-006-7600-8.

21. McFarlane, D.C.: Coordinating the Interruption of People in Human-Computer Interaction. In: Human-computer interaction, INTERACT'99: IFIP TC. 13 International Conference on Human-Computer Interaction. pp. 295–303. IOS Press (1999).

22. Sauro, J., Kindlund, E.: A Method to Standardize Usability Metrics into a Single Score. In: Proceedings of the SIGCHI Conference on Human Factors in Computing Systems. pp. 401–409. ACM (2005).

23. Tidwell, J.: Designing Interfaces. O'Reilly Media, Inc. (2010).

24. Nielsen, J.: Usability Testing. In: Usability Engineering. pp. 165–206. Morgan Kaufmann Publishers Inc. (1993).

25. Hix, D., Hartson, H.R.: Developing User Interfaces: Ensuring Usability Through Product & Process. John Wiley & Sons, Inc., New York, NY, USA (1993).

26. Mayhew, D.J.: The Usability Engineering Lifecycle: A Practitioner's Handbook for User Interface Design. Morgan Kaufmann Publishers Inc., San Francisco, CA, USA (1999).

27. van Welie, M., Mullet, K., McInerney, P.: Patterns in Practice: A Workshop for UI Designers. In: CHI '02 Extended Abstracts on Human Factors in Computing Systems. pp. 908–909. ACM, New York, NY, USA (2002).

28. Juristo, N., Moreno, A.M., Sanchez-Segura, M.-I.: Analysing the Impact of Usability on Software Design. Journal of Systems and Software. 80, 1506–1516 (2007) . doi: 10.1016/j.jss.2007.01.006.

29. Rodríguez, F.D.: Obtención y Uso de Patrones para la Implementación de Funcionalidades de Usabilidad en Aplicaciones Web Supervisors: Juristo, N & Acuña, S. E.T.S. de Ingenieros Informáticos (Universidad Politécnica de Madrid). (2014).

30. Rodríguez, F.D., Acuña, S.T., Juristo, N.: Design and programming patterns for implementing usability functionalities in web applications. Journal of Systems and Software. 105, 107–124 (2015) . doi: 10.1016/j.jss.2015.04.023.

31. Rodríguez, F.D., Acuña, S.T., Juristo, N.: Reusable Solutions for Implementing Usability Functionalities. International Journal of Software Engineering and Knowledge Engineering. 25, 727–755 (2015).doi: 10.1142/S0218194015500084

32. Nielsen, J.: Turn User Goals into Task Scenarios for Usability Testing, Retrieved from https://www.nngroup.com/articles/task-scenarios-usability-testing/.

33. Ferreira, J.M.: Source Code of Usability Test Software Application, Retrieved from https://github.com/ferremarce/TEST_USABILIDAD.

34. Brooke, J.: SUS - A quick and dirty usability scale. Usability evaluation in industry. 189, 4–7 (1996) . doi: 10.1002/hbm.20701.

35. Bouza Leirós, H.: Evaluación empírica de los mecanismos de usabilidad de preferencias, retroalimentación de progreso y abortar operación en un entorno Web Master Thesis. Supervisor: Acuña, Silvia T. Escuela Politécnica Superior, Universidad Autónoma de Madrid. p. 92 (2016).

36. Charness, G., Gneezy, U., Kuhn, M.A.: Experimental Methods: Between-Subject and Within-Subject Design. Journal of Economic Behavior and Organization. 81, 1–8 (2012) . doi: 10.1016/j.jebo.2011.08.009.

12 Ferrerira y Acuña, 2017

FAPS System: A prototype for Lean Manufacturing Scheduling in Footwear

John Reyes[1], Renato Urvina[1], Stalin Ramírez[1], Kevin Álvarez[1], Ricardo Pazmiño[1], Leonardo Sanchez[1], Marcos Benites[1], and Darwin Aldas[1]

[1] Universidad Técnica de Ambato, 180182 Ambato, Ecuador
{jpreyes, rurvina, dramirez8774, kalvarez0229, rpazmino5111, marcosrbenitez, darwinaldas}@uta.edu.ec
http://www.uta.edu.ec
[2] Universidad Tecnológica Indoamérica 180103 Ambato, Ecuador, 69042 Heidelberg, Germany
{leonardosanchez}@uti.edu.ec

Abstract. The research develops an industrial software application called FAPS System for the planning and scheduling manufacturing. It contains three modules used for planning and programming of resources, process management and Andon module focused on the use of lean manufacturing techniques for the notification, emission and display of contingencies presented during the production in real time. A case study is described in Ecuadorian footwear companies for the execution of experimental prototype efficiency tests. Through the unified modeling language diagrams, the requirements and functionalities of the software developed based on private and free technologies are defined. The planning module has a scheduling algorithm of days based on weighted standards that allows to estimate the delivery date of a production order, reprogram it and compare the planned quantity with respect to the capacity used. The Andon module is an Android application that consumes the information managed in the planning and process modules, thereby monitoring in real time the state of the plant and the production progress. The experimental results show that the system is adaptable to multiproduct orders and the scheduling allows to increase 6% the utilization percentage of the production processes.

Keywords: prototype system, scheduling, planning production

1 Introduction

Changing market conditions, variable demands and growing customer needs are some of the reasons why manufacturing companies create flexible and adaptable processes to meet their demands [1]. All companies are looking to implement a successful and sustainable continuous improvement process, and over time many companies have identified and documented best operating practices to meet their specific production objectives. Production scheduling has become a challenge [2].

The key to success or failure of a manufacturing company depends on good planning and the use of production systems like Lean Manufacturing (LM), the most successful philosophy in reducing waste during production processes without affecting performance [3]. Its main objective is to increase productivity, reduce lead time, manufacturing costs and improve the quality of the final product. Although, that companies are increasingly competing, yet some of them persist in obsolete management tools that do not allow them to achieve their goal, the main challenge is to have the right material, in sufficient quantity and at the right time, but the evidence shows that this challenge is not surpassed [4].

In recent years, industries in general have been evolving towards a systematic change in their manufacturing management, trying to find successful methods for excellent planning and production control [5]. During the change of paradigms, new tools and new planning methods were required, books were published and articles were written on the subject. It was during this period that computers were introduced into the manufacturing industries in order to support planning and control tasks [6]. It has been identified in the Footwear sector that planning and production control is increasingly complex but in many cases it is still being carried out manually. In addition, in the course of the manufacturing process there are often unexpected interruptions, which arise for different reasons related to machinery, personnel or breach of quality. The production lines stop automatically, which puts the production system in a state of emergency [7] and the time taken to detect the problem and take corrective measures to solve it is extremely excessive, causing delays and preventing the fulfillment of the scheduled production orders. The Lean Manufacturing methodology presents its tool called Andon which emits notifications or alerts in real time about abnormal events in production [8]. In this way, the industries are able to manage the interruptions quickly and efficiently which optimizes resources and reduces downtime [9].

In this context, making use of IT tools allows faster decision making and calculations for finite programming. Enterprise Resource Planning (ERP) has quickly become an indispensable system for integrating resource, commercial, after-sales, manufacturing and other functions into a system around a database. However, do not present an interface for real time monitoring of production.

According to the above, the need to develop software according to the requirements of the Ecuadorian footwear industry and the economic context of the country will imply an important contribution to Production Planning and Control in order to improve its productivity.

The present work proposes Footwear Advanced Planning and Scheduling System prototype based on web technology and developed with Open Source tools. This tool fuses the particularities of an advanced planning and scheduling system and an Andon system making it highly competitive, exclusive and unique in its scope, being able to respond to the demanding demands of the market. It's planning and process modules allow you to parameterize the resources (production lines, shift, processes) with which the work will be carried out, and graphically display the results. In addition, one of its main features is the Andon module for the monitoring of the different abnormalities that appear during the footwear production process through an application developed for Android.

2 Materials and Methods

The investigation begins by taking a sample for the collection data using Industrial Engineering tools in companies associated with the National Footwear Chamber (CALTU) in which the main models produced, production processes, operating strategies, planning, cycle times and product delivery are identified. These inputs allow the creation of software to define the modules to be developed. The project has two phases, the experimental phase that is developed in laboratory and the field testing phase. The experimental phase of the present work intends to validate the software development and to demonstrate the benefits that will be achieved when implementing the software in the planning and production control of footwear companies, while the field phase involves obtaining results of improvement productivity.

2.1 Lean Manufacturing and Technology of the information and communication

Conceptually, Lean principles and practices can be successfully carried out in a very simple way without using Information and Communication Technologies (TIC) or, on the contrary, achieving a high level of sophistication by supporting TIC. Companies with highly developed internal TIC achieve an automated flow of information among their internal processes that positively influences quality, delivery times and continuous improvement [10]. In essence, LM has several tools such as: just in time, total productive maintenance, visual factory, andon, value stream mapping among others, all aimed at eliminating the seven production wastes. The research uses an initial mapping of the processes in Ecuadorian footwear companies and obtains the cycle times, typical production orders and main characteristics of the production planning and control systems. From the previous study it is identified that the development of the processes during the day is dynamic and there are equipment failures which adversely affect the productivity of the plant that if not analyzed deeply the production can fall into a state of emergency [7]. Using LM, the implementation of Andon systems is proposed to counter this finding, it seeks to generate visual signals that allow the identification of the waste to intervene opportunely on the process that originates it and to reduce the reaction time of the workers.

2.2 System Modeling

The structural aspect of collaboration between production orders to carry out a business use case can be presented in an order diagram, where each order can be parameterized based on time-weighted standards that each model (Fig. 1).
Therefore, this diagram allows to express the process from the entrance of the demand, as well as the distribution in the different lines of production and shifts. In addition, it also allows you to display the daily scheduling of demand and it's scheduling at each shift.

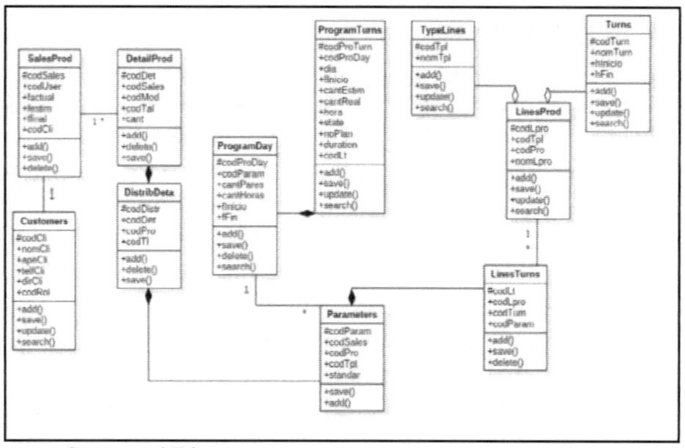

Fig. 1. FAPS System Command Diagram

The following diagram (Fig. 2) represents the entry and notification of each product registered for each production process. In addition, it expresses the relationship between the different alerts that will be issued in scheduling shifts based on the parameters calculated in the order diagram previously presented (Fig.1).

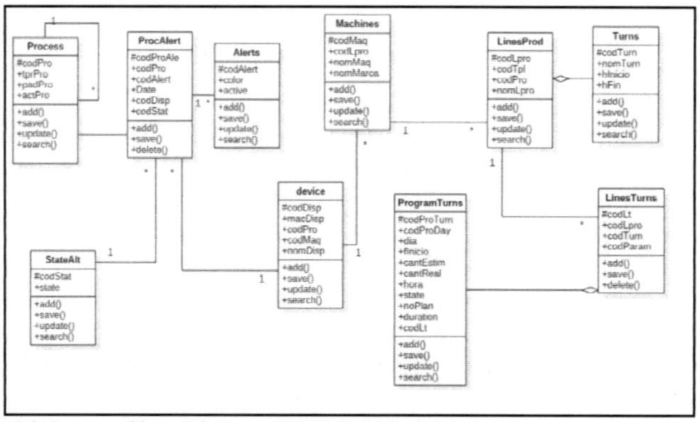

Fig. 2. FAPS System Class Diagram (ANDON Module)

3 Case Study

The footwear production process has three main macro processes: punching, trimming and assembly. The production planning is based on products with the make to order operation model and during the production day a mix of products is made because of the variety of models that are offered to the market. The prototype integrates information on manufacturing and failures from all processes in real time to generate indicators that allow making corrective decisions. The wireless connection interface provides flexibility for the mobility of Android devices throughout the entire industrial installation. The information boards located in each process allow you to visualize fault alerts and progress in planning relative to actual production to all staff to accelerate the cycle time and meet the targets set per shift.

3.1 Use Case Diagram

The identification of requirements is done for the purpose of achieving a good design, in addition to modeling and adequate results. Fig 3 defines the functionalities that Footwear Advanced Planning and Scheduling System (FAPS) must fulfill, in addition to its different actors. About users who will have access to Andon, will be restricted under a role that is assigned by the system administrator. In the case of processes and static entities, the system administrator will have the task of creating, assigning and configuring the capacities of the footwear manufacturing processes since this section is the basis for the system to be able to function effectively.

For the entrance to the software of the customers' demand, the data are collected like models of footwear, sizes and quantities to produce. Once this information is obtained, the weighted production capacities are generated to visualize the state of the productive plant (unattainable, available and committed) to face the multiple demands. Then a sequence of operations is configured with production lines, shifts and other specifications necessary for daily scheduling. Once the parameters have been configured, the system must visualize a distribution of the production based on the capacity and availability of the resources, production restrictions and deadlines. If this programming satisfies the production planner actor will proceed to validate for its later programming.

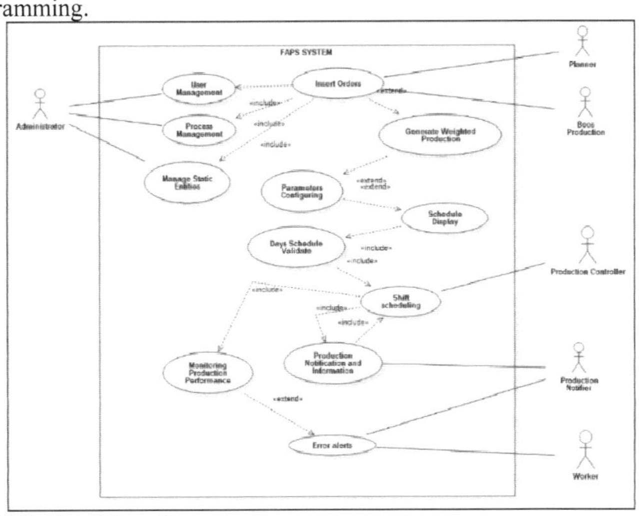

Fig. 3. FAPS System: Case of use

The control of production in shopfloor is realized with the use of the system Andon that visualizes the order with the different models and sizes that has been planned for the day and shift, being helped of a button for the respective notification of production. In addition, the option to change the order depending on the production, finish it and the ability to notify unplanned models. Abnormalities can be generated during production for which the interface has been implemented where it is possible to notify an alert depending on the type of fault encountered. This way, you can visualize in real time the current state of production and the alerts issued on the Andon board. One of the main characteristics of the ANDON system is the monitoring of the production performance by continuously monitoring and verifying the current status. In this sense, the system performs the comparison of the notified against the planned allowing to act quickly to deviations in the production.

4 FAPS System: Footwear Advanced Planning and Scheduling System

This project has developed FAPS System, a complete and complex software architecture with different web technologies. In Fig. 4, this architecture is presented, reflecting the internal modules such as: planning and programming (clients, orders and products), process management and the module corresponding to Andon. To integrate these modules is complemented the design with a database in charge of storing all the information that is generated in FAPS System. Data storage and management was performed with the PostgreSQL 9.5 Database Management System (DBMS) [11] on a Windows server platform. For the design of the entity - relationship model, static and dynamic data useful for implementing the application were considered.

Fig. 4. Architecture FAPS System

4.1 Planning and scheduling module (customers, orders and products)

When an order is received at the factory, the actors in charge of production enter the FAPS System database where all information about customers and products is collected. Once the order is entered the system automatically calculates the weighted production standard. The planning module is dedicated to the entry and storage of this data to manage each entry in the database. FAPS provides a user-friendly interface where there are a set of possible queries available. The information stored in the database is able to consider the individual characteristics of each order such as: expiration date, customer, start date, responsible for the order, model, size and quantity. To calculate the weighted standard (capacity to use available production resources), FAPS needs this information.

When comparisons are made between the quantities of each model, the system performs a query to the database of the process management module (explained in section 4.2) by selecting the maximum values of standard time (min / pair) for each product which belongs to the order. Then the objective function is applied between all these standards to obtain a weighted average between them, being this exclusive value of each order.

This result represents a fundamental input for the parameterization of production lines, work shifts and processes allowing the software to be completely configurable according to the needs of the user. Once this data is specified, FAPS System uses this information to generate the optimal daily production schedule by displaying it in a calendar as shown in Fig. 5. This result is stored in the database until the production planner decides to transfer the orders to the next module for the distribution phase at that time FAPS System will ask you to check if the quantity of products exceeds the daily capacity of production. This amount should also consider all items already scheduled that have not yet occurred due to breakdowns or the arrival of urgent orders. This decision usually depends on the experience and sensitivity of the planner.

In carrying out this configuration, the main objective is to have a module capable of reacting quickly to market needs in a flexible way.

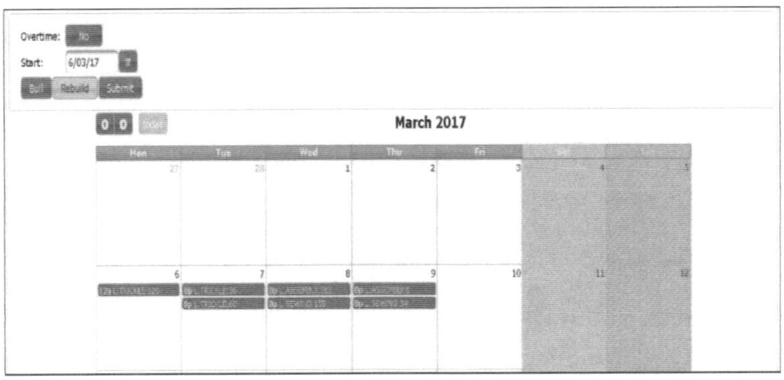

Fig. 5. Example of Production Order Scheduling

4.2 Process Management Module

The organization, productivity and quality of production is a fundamental part of each manufacturing company, this depends on the way in which they organize their processes and quantify them, allowing to measure the production capacity that each one develops [12]. The present module shows an intuitive web interface to manage these processes, allowing the design of the workflow by establishing time indicators for each process, converting this module as the basis of FAPS System to perform the above activities, see Fig. 6. In this module, the process structure is created in a hierarchical way, assigning parent processes (Processes) and child processes (Sub processes) as a fundamental component for the correct operation of the system. The time allocation (minutes / unit) for each model is stored in the database.

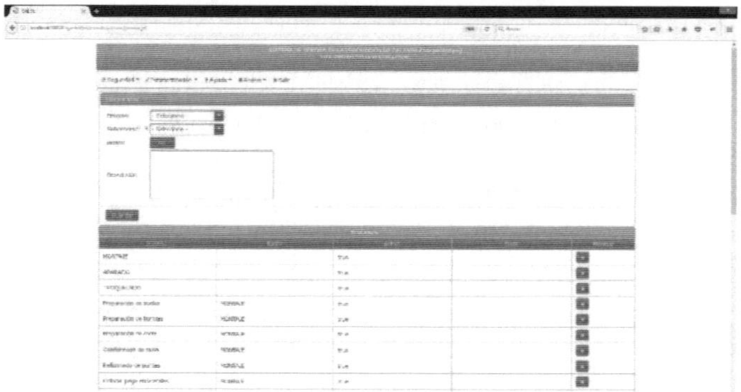

Fig. 6. Process manager

4.3 Management and Notification (Andon)

The Andon application in Fig. 7 has two supplementary modules, the first one is dedicated to production notification, while the second focuses on monitoring unplanned machine breakdowns that occur during the working day. From the notification module, the planned order will be displayed along with its different models and sizes, the operator must select the model and size to be produced by means of a button to add each produced pair.

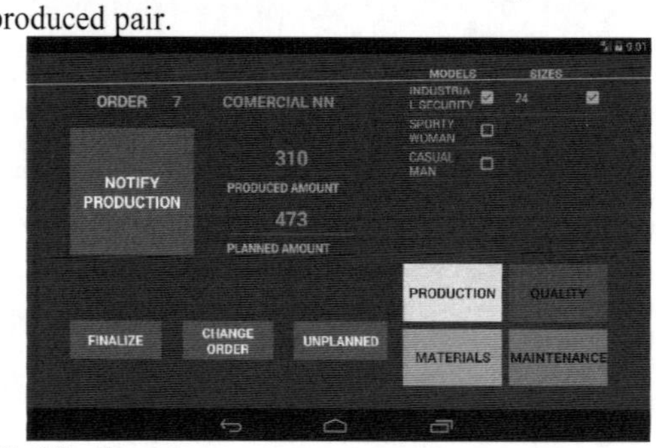

Fig. 7. Android Notification screen

In the unplanned breakdown monitoring module, 4 buttons are shown which are assigned to the different types of abnormalities that may occur during the production process: Production, Materials, Maintenance and Quality.

At the moment of issuing an alert internally a timer is started until the person in charge of resolving the abnormalities reaches the work station where the alert was issued, measuring the average reaction time. Another counter is started to account for the average time to repair that ends at the time the manager finishes making the corrections or respective maintenance to the machinery or raw material, this will depend on the type of alert that is issued.
The production control is carried out through a complementary display of the Andon of Fig. 8, which indicates the number of pairs produced in relation to the planned quantity. In addition, the screen displays the warnings due to faults that are generated during the shift, becoming an important tool for both supervisors and plant managers.

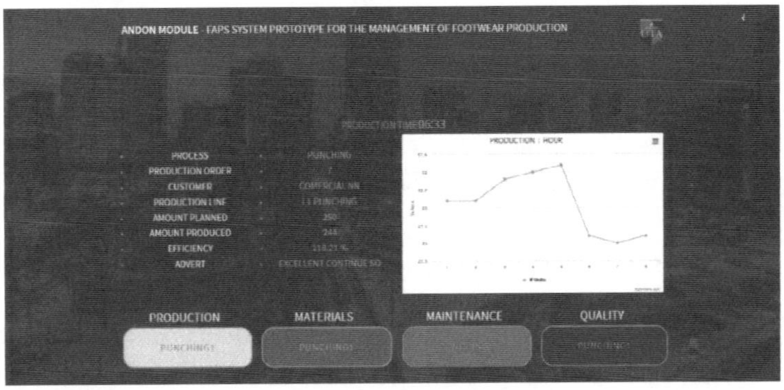

Fig. 8. Andon Display Screen

5 Discussion

In the experimental phase of the research, tests were carried out with several orders containing a mix of products and the scheduling obtained with the software was validated. With the data of the industrial engineering study the information was entered to the software verifying the operation of the orders module. It is identified that the input of data is a task that entails a considerable time and must be done by a person with complete knowledge of the production processes since these will depend on the internal calculations that the software performs. The interface of the software minimizes the percentage of error in the data entry since in making use of a table the typist can recognize each one of the parameters to enter and the order in which it must do it.
In the planning module, several typical production orders have been entered from Ecuadorian footwear companies and in each one the software correctly estimates the delivery date of the order, generating the days by process according to the distribution

algorithm in the structure of the software. In the test lab it has been proven that the times dedicated to the planning task are minimized since the software by simply selecting the production order for analysis generates the result in a matter of seconds.
The distribution module calculates a weighted production standard based on each model selected and verified in the laboratory the need to restrict the input of quantities above the standard, preventing the overuse of the process which allows the planner to scheduling orders according to the load of each process. During the experimental tests the connection between the software and the Android application was verified validating the correct operation of the sending of data. We simulated warnings due to quality, maintenance, production and material shortages, generating in each case the corresponding alerts and sounds, has been experimentally verified the functionality of the Andon and with the formation of a panel of experts of the footwear companies we get a good insight into the software and information displayed by the Andon display screen.
Based on data from a company belonging to the CALTU in which the initial stage for the field testing phase was executed, it has been determined that the average utilization percentage of the assembly process is 93% since it is programmed based on linear standard of 183 pairs without considering that each model has a different standard from Table 1. The same production orders were distributed in the software and it was determined that with the support of FAPS System the percentage of machine utilization increases by 6% since its characteristics allow to identify in real time the capacity of the machine.
On the other hand, the delivery date calculated with the software was informed to the footwear company that provided the production order samples, verifying an accuracy of 97% respect to the real delivery date.

Table 1. Scheduling with linear production standard VS Scheduling with software

MODEL	DEMAND	AVERAGE SCHEDULING BY SHIFT (LINEAR METHOD)	PRODUCTION STANDARD	PERCENTAGE USE OF PROCESS	AVERAGE SCHEDULING BY SHIFT (SOFTWARE)	PRODUCTION STANDARD	PERCENTAGE USE OF PROCESS
C	25	25	314	8%	25	314	8%
DM	81	81	279	29%	81	279	29%
S	111	50	139	36%	55	139	40%
SI	114	27	133	20%	30	133	23%
		183		**93%**	**191**		**99%**

To validate the usability of the system, a questionnaire of 6 questions is used (Table 2), which is given to those responsible for planning production in the companies associated with the CALTU, in which it is identified that 44% consider that the use of the system is easy and the messages on the screen are clear. Regarding the reports, 61% consider that the information they contain is very important and the production information is accurate. Regarding the sounds of the Andon module, 50% consider that they are necessary and 44% are not detectable, which increases the sound level of this module.

6 Conclusion and further development

The result of this research is a complete planning and scheduling system that provides the estimated delivery dates for each production order and allows the distribution based on the capacity of each process. In addition, the Andon module integrates the main parameters that must be controlled in the production and allows to shorten the reaction times, its interface provides the support that the supervisor needs for the production control since it integrates the worker with the production notification and machine failures.

Table 2. Results System Usability Questionnaire

What is your first reaction to manipulating the system?		How easy is the use of the system?	
Terrible	0%	Complex	0%
Regular	0%	Difficult	0%
Bad	0%	Normal	33%
Acceptable	50%	Easy	44%
Excellent	50%	Intuitive	22%
How clear are the messages on the screen?		**How useful is the information generated by the reports?**	
Confused	6%	Very important	61%
Complicated	0%	Important	28%
Extensive	11%	Relevant	11%
Clear	44%	Indifferent	0%
Concise	39%	Without importance	0%
How do you consider the sound emitted by the Andon module?		**How accurate is the production information in real time?**	
Annoying	0%	Imprecise	0%
Necessary	50%	Little accurate	0%
Strident	0%	Successful	33%
No detectable	44%	Concise	17%
Noisy	6%	Accurate	50%

The experimental phase of this research is the basis for future work in which the software is intended to be integrated into the production monitoring reports and the personnel need calculations for different demand scenarios. Future research is intended to introduce more complexity into the system, considering new parameters such as material transport, machine preparation times, material consumption and inventory level. It will also perform the phase field that involves testing the software in a real plant.

7 Acknowledgment

The authors thank the National Footwear Chamber of Ecuador and Technical University of Ambato (UTA) for the support provided during the execution of this work within the framework of the research project called "Operational optimization based on a lean dynamic system of alert of failures in the production processes for the footwear industry".

References

1. Zangiacomi, A., Zhijian, L., Sacco, M.: CR Boer.: Process planning and scheduling for mass customised shoe manufacturing. International Journal of Computer Integrated Manufactur ing, Vol. 17, No. 7. Taylor & Francis (2007) 613–621
2. Michalos, G., Makris, S., Mourtzis, D.: A web based tool for dynamic job rotation scheduling using multiple criteria. CIRP Ann Manuf Technol, Vol. 60, No. 1. Elsevier (2011) 453-456
3. Zakaria, N. H., Mohd, N., Nik, Z., Fadzil, M., Ab, F.: Lean manufacturing implementation in reducing waste for electronic assembly line. The 2nd International Conference on Automotive Innovation and Green Vehicle, Vol. 90 (2017)
4. Reyes, J., Álvarez, K., Vasquez, R.: Dynamic buffer management for raw material supply in the footwear industry. Journal of Industrial and Intelligent Information, Vol. 4, No. 1 (2016) 1–8
5. Harjunkoski, I., Maravelias, C., Bongers, P., Castro, P., Engell, S., Grossmann, I., Hooker, J., Méndez, C., Sand, G., Wassick, J.: Scope for industrial applications of production scheduling models and solution methods. Computers & Chemical Engineering. Vol. 62. Elsevier (2014) 161–193
6. Efthymiou, K., Michalopoulou, M., Sipsas, K., Giannoulis, C., Mourtzis, D., Chryssolouris, G.: On plant reconfiguration following a collaborative engineering and knowledge management approach. 14th International conference on modern information technology in the innovation processes of the industrial enterprises, Budapest, Hungary (2012)
7. García, M. P., Santos, J., Rico, M.: Desarrollo de una metodología de mapeo de procesos a partir del OEE para la mejora continua de las operaciones de manufactura. Revista Investigación Multidisciplinaria (2013) 31–40
8. Kotwal, A., Dhami, S., Singh, S.: Evaluation of Machine Downtime and Failure Analysis of Components in Paint Manufacturing Unit: Review Paper. International Journal of Mechanical and Industrial Technology, Vol. 3, No 1 (2015) 170–74
9. McKee, K. K., Forbes, G. L., Mazhar, I., Entwistle, R., Howard, I.: A Review of Machinery Diagnostics and Prognostics Implemented on a Centrifugal Pump. Eng. Asset Manag, (2011) 593–614
10. Moyano, J., Martínez, P. J., Maqueira, J. M., Bruque, S.: The role of IT in the search for efficiency: An analysis from Lean Production and the electronic integration of the supply chain. Cuadernos de Economía y Dirección de la Empresa, Vol. 15. Elsevier (2012) 105–116

11. Shebaro, B., Sallam, A., Karma, A., & Bertino, E.: PostgreSQL anomaly detector. In Proceedings of the 14th Annual Information Security Symposium. CERIAS-Purdue University (2013) 48–52
12. Jumbo, G.: Implementación del modelo de simulación kanban para mejorar las actividades de la fábrica de calzado femenino Covis. Univesidad Técnica de Machala, Machala, (2017)

26 Reyes et al., 2017

Usability Evaluation of Multi-Platform Mobile Applications: A Systematic Mapping Study

Efraín R. Fonseca C. [1], Sandra Velastegui[1], and John W. Castro[2]

[1] Departamento de Ciencias de la Computación, Universidad de las Fuerzas Armadas ESPE, Sangolquí, Ecuador
{erfonseca,svvelastegui}@espe.edu.ec
[2] Departamento de Ingeniería Informática y Ciencias de la Computación, Universidad de Atacama, Copiapó, Chile
john.castro@uda.cl

Abstract. —***Background:*** In recent years, the use of mobile devices has increased significantly so as to, among other things, afford people the ability to communicate and access to their data and services with ease from anywhere. Seen from this perspective, the usability of mobile apps plays a leading role on reaching this objective. Nevertheless, mobile apps still appear to have problems in that regard. **Aim:** to identify the mechanisms used for assess the usability on multi-platform mobile apps (MPMA), in order to establish better practices in this context. **Method:** We conduct a systematic mapping study (SMS). **Results:** From the information available on 42 primary studies, we find that there are very few mechanisms specifically designed to evaluate usability in MPMA; consequently, the existing attributes and metrics correspond to adaptations used to evaluate traditional web or desktop applications. **Conclusions:** The mechanisms used to evaluate the usability of traditional applications need to be reviewed, adapted or combined to cover aspects related to MPMA from the early stages of its development cycle, without neglecting the design of platform-independent interaction.

Keywords: usability tests, interaction design, mobile apps, systematic mapping study

1 Introducción

En los últimos años los dispositivos móviles han ganado importancia y protagonismo en la vida cotidiana de las personas, dado que representan la forma más sencilla de comunicación y acceso desde cualquier lugar a servicios considerados como básicos en la actualidad (por ejemplo, correo electrónico, internet, etc.). Desde la perspectiva del desarrollo de software, la construcción de aplicaciones orientadas a satisfacer la demanda actual, presenta cada vez nuevos desafíos, siendo uno de ellos la mejora constante de la usabilidad y la experiencia del usuario [17]. La usabilidad es considerada como un atributo de calidad del producto software [15]. Los factores principales que determinan la usabilidad son las condiciones y necesidades específicas del contexto de uso y los usuarios que utilizarán el sistema [15]. Por tal motivo, estos factores deberían ser catalogados como artífices en la definición de las condiciones idóneas para que un producto software sea considerado de calidad [15]. Desde esta perspectiva, podría ser recomendable realizar un diseño adecuado de la interfaz de usuario (IU) y la aplicación de técnicas de evaluación de la usabilidad, para determinar el grado en el que el sistema le permite al usuario realizar sus tareas [15].

No obstante, los mecanismos existentes para evaluar la usabilidad fueron creados para aplicaciones tradicionales de escritorio o web, lo que dificulta su aplicación en el desarrollo de aplicaciones móviles [37] Además, los mecanismos de evaluación de usabilidad se aplican generalmente en las últimas etapas del desarrollo, donde los problemas de usabilidad son más marcados y en numerosas ocasiones imposibles de superar [7].

Por otra parte, la evaluación de usabilidad por sí sola no es suficiente para determinar si un sistema es considerado como usable, ya que esta práctica no evidencia todos los problemas asociados al diseño de la IU [15]. La creación de la IU enfrenta el dilema de atender la filosofía de interacción propia de cada plataforma, o de crear un diseño común de interacción multi-plataforma [6]. En la actualidad existen únicamente directrices genéricas para el diseño de la interacción independiente de la plataforma [6].

En este sentido, la medición de la usabilidad de las aplicaciones móviles se ha convertido en un tema de interés para los investigadores [37], [20]. En nuestro caso particular, nos ha motivado conocer la situación actual del proceso de evaluación de la usabilidad de las Aplicaciones Móviles Multi-Plataforma (AMMP), para lo cual llevamos a cabo un Mapeo Sistemático de Literatura (SMS de sus siglas del inglés Systematic Mapping Study), el cual se delimitó por las siguientes preguntas de investigación (RQ de las siglas del inglés Research Questions):

RQ1: ¿Qué técnicas, métodos y modelos son comúnmente utilizados para evaluar la usabilidad de aplicaciones móviles?

RQ2: ¿Qué atributos y métricas son considerados en la evaluación de la usabilidad de aplicaciones móviles?

RQ3: ¿En qué medida se consideran los factores de usabilidad en el diseño de interacción de las aplicaciones móviles y cómo difiere este diseño entre las plataformas?

Habitualmente las RQ tienden a expresarse en formato PICOC [35], lo que puede resultar en mayor o menor grado una complicación. En este caso que estamos buscando una información específica en los artículos, expresar en formato PICOC las RQ es hasta cierto punto irrealizable, dado que PICOC ha sido definido típicamente para la comparación de dos tratamientos versus una salida.

Lo que resta del artículo está estructurado como sigue. En la Sección 2, se analizan los trabajos relacionados. La Sección 3 describe el SMS. En la Sección 4 se responden las RQ. En la Sección 5, se discuten los hallazgos obtenidos. Finalmente, en la Sección 6, se presentan las conclusiones.

2 Trabajos Relacionados

La evaluación de la usabilidad en aplicaciones móviles, plantea retos cada vez más complejos, dado que este tipo de aplicaciones operan en distintos entornos, sus características varían dependiendo de la plataforma en la que son implementadas, existe una gran variedad de tipos de usuarios y los mecanismos utilizados para su medición fueron concebidos originalmente para otro tipo de aplicaciones [36], [37]. Por lo tanto, la evaluación de la usabilidad en aplicaciones móviles en tales circunstancias, es propensa a que los resultados sean poco fiables [36]. Existen varios estudios que proponen diferentes alternativas de evaluación de usabilidad para aplicaciones móviles [25], [44]. Sin embargo, no hemos identificado propuestas capaces de cubrir todos los elementos de este tipo de aplicaciones, y sobre todo que sean independientes de la plataforma.

Por un lado, identificamos estudios que presentan un amplio marco teórico sobre usabilidad de aplicaciones móviles. Por ejemplo, los trabajos de Nayebi y otros [31] y Patel & Dalal [34], presentan definiciones genéricas de usabilidad y de los mecanismos de evaluación. Mientras que, De Lima Salgado & Pimenta Freire [13] realizan un SMS sobre los mecanismos de evaluación heurística más usados en los últimos años, su aceptación, entre otras características. Los resultados de este estudio muestran que los mecanismos de evaluación heurística ordinarios (evaluación de usabilidad basada en las heurísticas de Nielsen y Molich o heurísticas de IU) quizá no siempre son apropiados para evaluar todo tipo de interfaces móviles y posiblemente no sean capaces de cubrir características específicas de las aplicaciones móviles (por ejemplo, sus dimensiones reducidas, su sistema operativo que tiene sus particularidades en cuanto al manejo de la IU y su contexto de uso).

Por otro lado, encontramos diferentes estudios que reportan evaluaciones de usabilidad de distintas aplicaciones móviles aplicando técnicas usadas para aplicaciones tradicionales (escritorio o web). Por ejemplo: Faliagka y otros [14], reportan problemas de usabilidad encontrados en aplicaciones nativas de iOS luego de realizar una evaluación de laboratorio. Jadhav y otros [21] reportan la evaluación de la usabilidad de aplicaciones de mensajería instantánea (WhatsApp, Skype, etc), aplicando la técnica recorrido cognitivo. Los resultados de esta evaluación muestran varios problemas de usabilidad (por ejemplo, la funcionalidad ineficaz de "búsqueda") por lo que los autores sugieren que el diseño de interfaces móviles debe ser mejorado.

Entre las propuestas de frameworks de usabilidad, destaca el trabajo de Nayebi y otros [32], quienes proponen un conjunto de criterios para evaluar aplicaciones de la plataforma iOS. En este estudio los autores indican que la evaluación de la usabilidad debería ser adaptable a todos los sistemas operativos móviles. Sin embargo, actualmente esta adaptación es un tanto complicada, ya que cada plataforma móvil sigue sus convenciones para crear sus aplicaciones [6]. Barea [6] en su estudio sobre el diseño de interacción de la plataforma Android vs iOS, indica que actualmente en el desarrollo móvil se aplican guías genéricas de diseño de interfaz ya que no existe un modelo formal de principios o guía de interacción multi-plataforma para ser aplicado en la evaluación de la usabilidad y en el diseño de la interfaz de las AMMP [6].

En general, los estudios identificados en la literatura se basan en mecanismos de usabilidad de aplicaciones no necesariamente móviles, no muestran la situación actual del proceso de evaluación de la usabilidad de las AMMP y no brindan una vista integral de los progresos en cuanto a métodos de evaluación dentro de etapas tempranas y posteriores del ciclo de vida del producto software móvil. Por tanto, el objetivo del presente trabajo es identificar el estado del arte y de la práctica con respecto a la evaluación de la usabilidad de AMMP.

3 Mapeo Sistemático de Literatura

El método de investigación seleccionado fue un SMS. Seguimos los lineamientos propuestos por Kitchenham & Charters [24]. Un SMS permite resumir la evidencia existente referente a una tema de interés, e identificar cualquier vacío existente en una investigación en curso [24]. El protocolo planteado propone la definición de: (1) RQs, (2) estrategia de búsqueda, (3) criterios de inclusión y exclusión, (4) proceso de selección y, (5) extracción de datos.

3.1 Definición de las Preguntas de Investigación

La especificación de las RQ define al objetivo de la investigación como alcanzable, ya que plantean explícitamente lo que se desea encontrar (las RQ se detallan en la Sección 1). Por tanto, el SMS se enfoca en dar respuesta a las RQ [24].

3.2 Definición de la Estrategia de Búsqueda

El planteamiento del SMS precisa conformar una estrategia de búsqueda. Nuestra estrategia consta de las siguientes actividades: (1) Conformar un grupo de control de literatura, (2) construir una cadena de búsqueda y, (3) buscar estudios candidatos. La conformación del grupo de control permite formalizar y dar validez al proceso de localización de términos relevantes que conforman la cadena de búsqueda, a partir de estudios fiables cuyo objetivo esté relacionado directamente con el del SMS. El proceso inicia con una revisión de literatura básica de cada investigador que participa en el SMS. El resultado de esta actividad, es un grupo de estudios por investigador. La fiabilidad de dichos estudios no es descuidada en ningún momento en esta actividad. En este caso, únicamente fueron considerados estudios publicados en revistas y congresos de alto impacto, indexados en bases digitales bien conocidas (por ejemplo: SCOPUS, IEEE). Finalmente, se realiza una validación cruzada en un grupo de discusión para confirmar qué estudios conformarán el grupo de control (GC). Como resultado, el GC se conformó con 14 estudios.

La **construcción de la cadena de búsqueda** inicia con la revisión detallada de los estudios de control por al menos dos investigadores, para identificar términos explícitos específicos o comunes entre los estudios (y sus sinónimos), con la característica de que todos sean referidos al propósito del SMS. En este caso, se buscaron términos referidos a la evaluación de la usabilidad de AMMP. Para conformar la cadena de búsqueda los términos obtenidos de los estudios de control son combinados a través de operadores lógicos: OR para agregar sinónimos y AND para agregar nuevos términos.

Finalmente, la cadena establecida para la búsqueda fue:("method" OR "paths" OR "requirements" OR "techniques" OR "patterns" OR "framework" OR "principales"

OR "metrics" OR "model" OR "philosophy") AND ("evaluation" OR "evaluating" OR "study" OR "measuring") AND ("usability" OR "interaction design" OR "human-centered design process") AND ("mobile application" OR "mobile systems" OR "mobile interfaces" OR "mobile phone development" OR "smartphone applications" OR "Multiplatform mobile application" OR "mobile apps").

La **Búsqueda de Estudios Candidatos** marca el inicio de la ejecución del SMS. Se realiza en cuantas bases digitales sea posible, utilizando la cadena de búsqueda. Previo a la búsqueda, establecimos las siguientes consideraciones: (i) fuentes de información: tesis de magister, artículos y capítulos de libro aceptados en conferencias y revistas internacionales entre los años 2014 a 2016 dado que se requiere información actual, (ii) publicaciones escritas en inglés dado que las revistas y congresos internacionales aceptan artículos solo en este idioma, (iii) bases digitales consideradas: Springer, Scopus y ACM, que son a las que tenemos acceso, y (iv) adaptar la cadena de búsqueda a la sintaxis cada base digital.

Los estudios candidatos resultantes fueron: 368 en Scopus, 52 en ACM y 212 en Springer. Luego de una depuración (ver proceso en la sección 3.4), se obtuvieron 600 estudios candidatos.

3.3 Criterios de Inclusión y Exclusión

Los criterios de inclusión y exclusión constituyen un acuerdo entre los investigadores sobre los parámetros que deben cumplir los estudios candidatos para ser considerados, o no, como fuente primaria de información para la investigación. En este caso se establecieron los siguientes criterios.

Criterios de inclusión: El artículo: (i) Describe el proceso de evaluación de la usabilidad en aplicaciones móviles, (ii) se refiere a la importancia de medir la usabilidad en las diferentes etapas del proceso de desarrollo en aplicaciones móviles, (iii) detalla el mecanismo utilizado para evaluar la usabilidad en aplicaciones móviles, (iv) propone mecanismos para evaluar la usabilidad en aplicaciones móviles.

Criterios de exclusión: (i) Artículos que no hagan referencia a estudios de usabilidad de aplicaciones móviles, (ii) artículos sobre guías de diseño de interacción que se centren en el diseño de IU y que no consideren la usabilidad en aplicaciones móviles, (iii) artículos que no contengan información detallada de cómo realizaron la evaluación de usabilidad de aplicaciones móviles.

3.4 Proceso de Selección de Estudios Primarios

En este proceso de revisión se aplican como filtro los criterios de inclusión y exclusión de forma iterativa hasta establecer los estudios primarios. Para este caso, se plantearon las siguientes actividades: Depuración de estudios candidatos, selección de estudios y selección de estudios primarios. En la Depuración de Estudios Candidatos al menos dos investigadores depuran en consenso los estudios duplicados por base y entre bases, obteniendo un listado general de estudios candidatos.

La **Selección de Estudios** representa la primera iteración de filtrado de los estudios candidatos, donde se aplican los criterios de inclusión y exclusión a nivel de título, resumen y palabras claves, obteniéndose un listado de 206 estudios seleccionados y se descartaron 394 estudios candidatos.

La **Selección de Estudios Primarios** es la segunda iteración de filtrado realizada a los estudios seleccionados. La diferencia con la primera iteración radica en que los criterios de inclusión y exclusión se aplican a nivel del artículo completo, lo que implica que los estudios seleccionados deben ser descargados, de ser posible. La verificación del cumplimiento de los criterios de inclusión y exclusión dio como resultado un listado de 42 estudios primarios, se descartaron 160 estudios seleccionados y no fueron analizados 4 estudios seleccionados por la imposibilidad de conseguirlos.

3.5 Extracción de datos

Al menos dos investigadores realizan en consenso la extracción de las características generales de los estudios primarios y de la información relevante para responder las RQ. La extracción de la información representa un proceso exhaustivo de revisión de los estudios primarios, la cual se describe en la Sección 4. Con el único propósito de motivar la replicación de esta investigación, hemos publicado el detalle del proceso realizado en el siguiente enlace.

4 Resultados

Esta sección presenta los resultados obtenidos del SMS, los cuales están divididos en dos partes: Generalidades de los estudios primarios y las respuestas a las preguntas de investigación. La primera parte se resume en la Figura 1, en donde se muestra una visión sintética de los 42 estudios primarios identificados. En esta figura, los resultados se han segmentado en dos zonas. La primera (lado izquierdo), consiste básicamente en dos gráficos (parte superior e inferior) de dispersión XY con burbujas en las intersecciones de las categorías: (i) Tipo - Año de publicación, (ii) tipo - técnicas de evaluación más utilizadas. Los tipos de publicación son revistas, congresos y tesis de magister. El tamaño de cada burbuja está determinado por el número de estudios primarios que se han clasificado como pertenecientes a cada categoría. La segunda zona (lado derecho) de la Figura 1, muestra el número de estudios primarios por año de publicación. Además, la Figura 1 refleja que los estudios primarios han sido publicados principalmente en revistas (60%) y congresos (38%).

La segunda parte de esta sección presenta la síntesis del análisis de los estudios primarios, a partir del cual se respondieron las preguntas de investigación.

RQ1: ¿Qué técnicas y modelos son comúnmente utilizados para evaluar la usabilidad de aplicaciones móviles?

Identificamos diferentes técnicas y modelos que han sido usados y adaptados para evaluar la usabilidad en aplicaciones móviles, pero que originalmente fueron creados para evaluar aplicaciones tradicionales de escritorio. Numerosos autores combinan más de una técnica para evaluar la usabilidad. Las aplicaciones evaluadas al combinar técnicas están relacionadas con: salud [11], [38], [28], [29], [41], [33], [9], monitoreo de actividad física [40], aprendizaje[1], redes sociales [19], [27], y privacidad [5]. A continuación describimos brevemente algunas técnicas.

- **Evaluación Heurística:** Esta técnica evalúa la conformidad del diseño de la interfaz de la aplicación móvil con un conjunto de heurísticas [13], [4]. Aunque esta técnica está centrada en aplicaciones de escritorio, es adecuada para las características móviles específicas [45]. Esta técnica ha sido usada, por ejemplo para evaluar aplicaciones relacionadas con la salud [4] y el aprendizaje [20].

- **Test de Usabilidad en Laboratorio:** Esta técnica ha sido usada en aplicaciones nativas en iOS [14] y aplicaciones móviles de portales web [39]; en la cual los participantes son observados por un experto a lo largo de su rendimiento en tareas asignadas [40], quien registra (en vídeo) la comunicación no verbal relevante de los usuarios (por ejemplo, expresiones faciales confusas).

- **Cuestionarios:** Esta técnica fue usada en aplicaciones relacionadas con el aprendizaje [30] y la salud [18], [16], [23], [12], en la cual se presentan preguntas sobre la usabilidad percibida por el usuario y su grado de satisfacción con la aplicación [11]. Los cuestionarios más populares son SUS [42], SUMI [40] y PSSUQ [40].

- **Evaluaciones Automatizadas:** Identificamos dos propuestas: (i) AUT (Automated Usability Testing), que evalúa la usabilidad de aplicaciones iOS y cuenta con cinco tipos de técnicas: evaluación, inspección, cuestionario, modelos analíticos y simulaciones [25], e (ii) Inspección Automatizada, un framework disponible para aplicaciones de salud para Android [44].

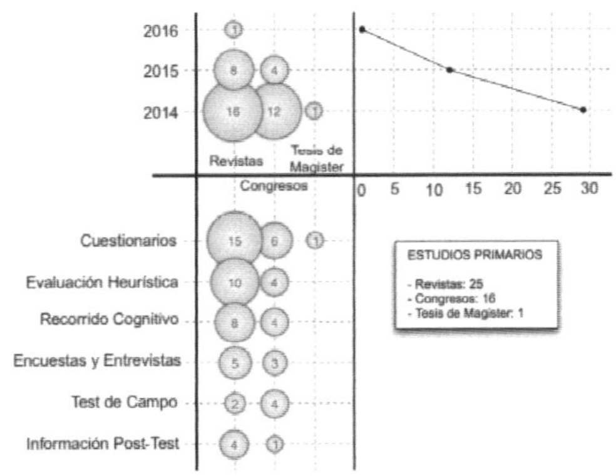

Fig. 1. Mapeo con la Distribución de Estudios Primarios según las técnicas usadas, Incluyendo Tipo y Año de Publicación

-**Evaluación de Usabilidad Basada en Modelos:** Son guías con lineamiento y atributos (como eficiencia y satisfacción) que deben ser medidos dentro de un proceso de evaluación. Identificamos que el modelo más conocido y usado es el de Nielsen [4], [22], [13], [27].

Otras técnicas de evaluación de la usabilidad que han sido utilizadas son: Test de Campo [26], entrevistas [2], recorrido cognitivo [28], pensar en voz alta [10] y estudio longitudinal [3], [43]. Estas dos últimas técnicas han sido usadas para evaluar aplicaciones de salud.

RQ2: ¿Qué atributos y métricas son considerados en la evaluación de usabilidad de aplicaciones móviles?

Identificamos que los cinco atributos más evaluados son: Eficiencia, errores, satisfacción, consistencia y estándares y control y libertad para el usuario. La Tabla 1 muestra los atributos más usados con sus respectivas métricas y los estudios primarios que los referencian.

Table 1. Atributos y métricas usados para medir la usabilidad

Atributo	Métrica	Estudios Primarios
Eficiencia	Tiempo invertido en realizar la tarea, clics requeridos para completar la tarea	[6], [7], [8], [9], [10], [11], [12], [13], [14], [15], [16], [18], [22], [26], [10]
Errores	% de tasa de errores, número de errores cometidos dos por tarea	[7], [8], [27], [15], [17], [18], [19], [10], [11], [20], [21], [19]
Satisfacción	Nivel de confort percibido por el usuario	[7], [9], [10], [11], [12], [13], [16], [17] [22], [23], [19], [22]
Consistencia y Estándares	% o nivel de cumplimiento de estándares	[6], [27], [15], [22], [10], [20], [44]
Control y libertad para el usuario	Posibilidad del usuario de reiniciar sus acciones	[6], [18], [19], [40], [15], [9], [12],

RQ3: ¿En qué medida se consideran los factores de usabilidad en el diseño de interacción de las aplicaciones móviles y cómo difiere este diseño entre las plataformas?

Los factores que determinan la usabilidad de un producto software (usuarios, tareas y contexto de uso) generalmente no son considerados en el diseño de la interacción de las AMMP, lo que podría reducir la productividad y aceptación de una aplicación móvil [26]. En 8 estudios primarios se consideran estos tres factores de usabilidad desde etapas tempranas del desarrollo de software, usando prototipos y primeros diseños con la participación de los usuarios en un entorno real [20], [18], [29], [41], [45], [42], [26], [3]. Por otra parte, en estos 5 estudios: [8], [33], [9], [27], [43], solamente fueron considerados los factores usuarios y tareas. En [27], crearon un primer prototipo, evaluaron su interfaz y usabilidad y luego, considerando los problemas o recomendaciones dadas por usuarios y expertos, crearon un nuevo prototipo con mejoras. En [9], crearon una aplicación móvil de manera iterativa (desarrollo-evaluación de usabilidad) con tareas preestablecidas que realizaban usuarios. En los demás estudios, se añaden tareas específicas a usuarios puntuales para predecir sus necesidades y comportamientos.

En los estudios se observa también que el diseño de interacción difiere en gran medida entre las plataformas, su efecto heterogéneo es evidente a pesar de que cada dispositivo es necesario que cumpla con principios de usabilidad independientes de la plataforma [14]. Este diseño de interacción distinto influye en la usabilidad de una aplicación, por ejemplo en el estudio [29] los participantes que son dueños del mismo tipo de dispositivo móvil y tienen previa experiencia con el mismo, incrementan su nivel de autoconfianza y realizan menos peticiones de ayuda mientras realizan las tareas del test de usabilidad. En cambio, quienes no tenían o era limitada su experiencia con este tipo de dispositivos, necesitaron más orientación [29].

5 Discusión

Para evaluar la usabilidad de las aplicaciones móviles se están usando técnicas creadas para evaluar aplicaciones tradicionales, es decir no existen técnicas específicas para evaluar AMMP. Las aplicaciones evaluadas en mayor medida son las relacionadas con la salud. Las técnicas de evaluación de la usabilidad más utilizadas son cuestionarios, evaluación heurística y recorrido cognitivo. Los cuestionarios son importantes para obtener opiniones significativas de los usuarios finales de las aplicaciones móviles, pero no capturan ciertos elementos que definen la usabilidad de una aplicación (por ejemplo, eficiencia, eficacia). La evaluación heurística es una técnica de inspección rápida, barata y fácil, que no considera a los usuarios finales en su evaluación, lo que sería ideal si se desean obtener datos más específicos. El recorrido cognitivo ha permitido identificar problemas de usabilidad a los que se enfrentan los usuarios novatos y experimentados, mientras se centra en tareas específicas.

Identificamos que dentro de la literatura, no existe una técnica de evaluación de la usabilidad automatizada con un enfoque multi-plataforma, solo encontramos escasas técnicas de evaluaciones automatizadas dependientes de las plataformas móviles. Los autores de los estudios deciden en numerosas ocasiones combinar más de una técnica de evaluación y adaptar los modelos existentes para abordar el enfoque móvil. Esto refleja que falta una técnica de evaluación integral que cubra todos los aspectos particulares de la usabilidad móvil. En cuanto a los factores que determinan usabilidad: usuarios, tareas y contexto de uso, observamos que no todos los autores los consideran tanto al desarrollar como al evaluar la usabilidad de las aplicaciones móviles. Con respecto al diseño de la interacción de las aplicaciones móviles y el efecto heterogéneo entre las plataformas existentes, no encontramos en la literatura una guía de diseño de la interacción independiente de la plataforma, lo que influye en la usabilidad de una AMMP, porque las expectativas y forma de usar una aplicación de los usuarios depende en gran medida de la plataforma que usen habitualmente.

Finalmente, identificamos posibles amenazas a la validez en este estudio: (i) cobertura de las RQ, (ii) sesgo hacia ciertas publicaciones, iii) calidad de la evaluación, y iv) desconocimiento del área. Es probable que las RQ planteadas podrían cubrir parcialmente la temática de estudio, lo que intentamos mitigar definiendo un objetivo de trabajo y planteando varias RQ en consenso, con el propósito de hacer alcanzable el objetivo. Es posible que en un SMS se tienda a encaminar el proceso hacia un grupo específico de estudios, lo cual evitamos conformando un grupo de control de literatura y planteando en consenso una cadena de búsqueda con términos de control explícitos. Es probable que la calidad de la evaluación de los estudios no sea la adecuada por desconocimiento del área de investigación, lo cual mitigamos incluyendo en el equipo de SMS a dos investigadores con experiencia en temas de usabilidad y realización de SMS.

6 Conclusiones

Este trabajo describe el estado actual del proceso de evaluación de la usabilidad de las AMMP. Encontramos un total de 42 estudios primarios referentes a esta temática. A pesar de que el rango de años que comprendió el SMS es relativamente corto, el número de estudios primarios identificados es importante, lo que sugiere el interés de la comunidad por las temáticas de investigación. Los principales hallazgos de nuestra investigación son tres. En primer lugar, existen diferentes técnicas y métodos para evaluar la usabilidad de las aplicaciones tradicionales (web y de escritorio). Sin embargo, son muy escasos aquellos creados exclusivamente para evaluar AMMP. Por tanto, los mecanismos existentes requieren ser revisados, adaptados o combinados para cubrir todos los aspectos inherentes a las AMMP (es decir: usuarios, tareas y plataforma). En segundo lugar, los factores que determinan la usabilidad de las aplicaciones móviles, comúnmente no son considerados para su evaluación; ni tampoco para diseñar la interacción con el usuario. En tercer lugar, el diseño de la interacción de las aplicaciones móviles generalmente sigue los lineamientos de cada plataforma, lo que incide de forma distinta en la usabilidad de una misma aplicación para cada plataforma.

Combinando un método de desarrollo con una técnica de evaluación de la usabilidad integral que capture los aspectos del contexto móvil, a través de un proceso iterativo de desarrollo-evaluación, es posible descubrir una amplia y detallada gama de problemas de usabilidad que pueden ser resueltos a tiempo, para producir una aplicación fácil de utilizar. En las aplicaciones móviles existe un factor que produce un impacto significativo en su usabilidad, este factor es la plataforma móvil. Esta característica puede afectar las experiencias y comportamientos de los usuarios, por lo que al crear el diseño de la interacción de las AMMP es importante aplicar guías de IU independientes de la plataforma móvil. La adopción de mecanismos automatizados para la evaluación de las usabilidad requiere de un mayor esfuerzo de investigación, para combinar más de una técnica y ofrecer un enfoque multi-plataforma, porque las técnicas existentes son únicamente para plataformas y aplicaciones específicas.

En el proceso de evaluación de la usabilidad móvil es recomendable: (i) considerar el contexto, (ii) evaluar las aplicaciones dentro del proceso de desarrollo de software considerando todos los principales factores de usabilidad (tareas, usuarios, y contexto de uso), (iii) crear y aplicar guías de IU independientes de la plataforma, (iv) estudiar los factores de usabilidad en el proceso de desarrollo del producto software, e (v) investigar la adopción de mecanismos automatizados para evaluar la usabilidad, combinando más de una técnica, y considerando un enfoque multi-plataforma.

Las dos principales limitaciones de nuestra investigación son el corto periodo de la búsqueda y el número de bases de datos consultadas. Como trabajos futuros proponemos: (i) ampliar el periodo de la búsqueda, así como también las bases de datos, (ii) construir un framework automatizado para evaluar la usabilidad de las aplicaciones móviles, considerando todos los factores de usabilidad (usuarios, tareas y contexto de uso) (ii) crear un conjunto de guías y lineamientos de IU común entre

AMMP, (iii) estudiar el contexto de uso dentro del proceso de desarrollo y la evaluación de usabilidad de las AMMP.

Agradecimientos. Este trabajo ha sido subvencionado por el proyecto de investigación denominado: "Laboratorio Industrial en Ingeniería del Software Empírica (LI2SE)" de la ESPE y además contó con la financiación del "Proyecto DIUDA 22316" de la Universidad de Atacama.

Referencias

1. Abdul, N., Hussain, A., Azida, Z.: A usability testing on jfakih learning games for hearing impairment children. In: ICT4M (2014)
2. Ahmad, N., Zainal, A., Razak, F., Wan Adnan, W., Osman, S.: User experience evaluation of mobile spiritual applications for older people. JTAIT (2015)
3. Angulo Cevallos, E.: Case study on mobile applications UX: effect of the usage of a crosss-platform development framework. Master's thesis, E.T.S.I.I., UPM (2014)
4. Arnhold, M., Quade, M., Kirch, W.: Mobile applications for diabetics: a systematic review. JMIR (2014)
5. Assal, H., Hurtado, S., Imran, A., Chiasson, S.: What's the deal with privacy apps? In: Proceedings of the 14th ICMUM. pp. 25–36 (2015)
6. Barea, A., Ferré, X., Villarroel, L.: Android vs. ios interaction design study for a student multiplatform app. In: Proceedings HCI International Conference (2013)
7. Bertholdo, A.P.O., Kon, F., Gerosa, M.A.: Agile Usability Patterns for User-Centered Design Final Stages, pp. 433–444 (2016)
8. Beul-Leusmann, S., Samsel, C., Wiederhold, M., Krempels, K., Jakobs, E., Ziefle, M.: Usability evaluation of mobile passenger information systems. In: HCI (8) (2014)
9. Biederer, M., Arguel, A., Liu, J., Lau, A.: From web-based to mobile: Experiences of developing a personally controlled health management system. EJHI 8(1) (2014)
10. Choi, M., Suk Lee, H., Ho Park, J.: Usability of academic electronic medical record application for nursing students' clinical practicum. HIR 21(3) (2015)
11. Cruz Zapata, B., Fernández-Alemán, J., Idri, A., Toval, A.: Empirical studies on usability of mhealth apps: A systematic literature review. JMS, 39(2):1 (2015)
12. Cruz Zapata, B., Hernández Niñirola, A., Idri, A., Fernández-Alemán, J., Toval, A.: Mobile phrs compliance with android and ios usability guidelines. JMS, 14
13. de Lima Salgado, A., Pimenta Freire, A.: Heuristic evaluation of mobile usability: A mapping study. In: HCI App & Services, V-8512 (2014)
14. Faliagka, E., Rigou, M., Sirmakessis, S.: A usability study of iphone built-in applications. JBIT, Volume 34(8) (2014)
15. Ferré, X., Juristo, N., Windl, H., Constantine, L.: Usability basics for software developers. Journal IEEE Software (2001)
16. Foo, E., McDonald, R., Savage, E., Floyd, R., Butler, A., Rumball-Smith, A., Connor, S.: Mobile task management tool that improves workflow of an acute general surgical service. ANZ Journal of Surgery (2015)
17. Giovanni, P.D., Romano, M., Sebillo, M., Tortora, G., Vitiello, G., Ginige, T., Silva, L.D., Goonethilaka, J., Wikramanayake, G., Ginige, A.: User centered scenario based approach for developing mobile interfaces for social life networks. In: First International Workshop UsARE. pp. 18–24 (June 2012)

18. Hsiu Ching, L.: Developing mobile application design of virtual pets for caring for the elderly. In: Human Aspects of IT for the Aged Population (2015)
19. Hussain, A., Hashim, N., Nordin, N.: mGQM: evaluation metric for mobile and human interaction. In: HCI International (2014)
20. Hussain, A., Saleh, A., Taher, A., Ahmed, I., Lammasha, M.: Usability evaluation method for mobile learning application using agile: A systematic review. Jurnal Teknologi, Vol 77, No 5 (2015)
21. Jadhav, D., Bhutkar, G., Mehta, V.: Usability evaluation of messenger applications for android phones using cognitive walkthrough. In: 11th APC-HCI (2013)
22. Joyce, G., Lilley, M., Barker, T., Jefferies, A.: Smartphone application usability evaluation: The applicability of traditional heuristics. In: IC-HCI (2015)
23. Kalz, M., Lenssen, N., Felzen, M., Rossaint, R., Tabuenca, B., Specht, M., Skorning, M.: Smartphone apps for cardiopulmonary resuscitation training and real incident support: A mixed-methods evaluation study. JMIR 16(3) (2014)
24. Kitchenham, B., Charters, S.: Guidelines for performing systematic literature review in software engineering. Tech. rep., Keele U. & U. of Durham (July 2007)
25. Kluth, W., Krempels, K., Samsel, C.: Automated usability testing for mobile applications. In: 10th ICWIST (2014)
26. López-Gil, J.M., Urretavizcaya, M., Losada, B.n., Fernández-Castro, I.: Integrating field studies in agile development to evaluate usability on context dependant mobile applications. In: Proceedings of the XV ICHCI (2014)
27. Luhur, H., Widjaja, N.: Location-based social networking media for restaurant promotion and food review using mobile application. In: ICASCE, V68 (2014)
28. Lyles, C., Sarkar, U., Osborn, C.: Getting a technology-based diabetes intervention ready for prime time: a review of usability testing studies. In: CDR 14(10) (2014)
29. Mirkovic, J., Kaufman, D., Ruland., C.: Supporting cancer patients in illness management: usability evaluation of a mobile app. JMIR Mhealth Uhealth (2014)
30. Nawi, A., Hamzah, M.I., Ren, C.C., Tamuri, A.H.: Adoption of mobile technology for teaching preparation in improving teaching quality of teachers. IJI; 8(2) (2015)
31. Nayebi, F., Desharnais, J., Abran, A.: The state of the art of mobile application usability evaluation. In: 25th IEEE CCE & CE (2012)
32. Nayebi, F., Desharnais, J.M., Abran, A.: An expert-based framework for evaluating ios application usability. In: 23Nd IWSM (2013)
33. O'Malley, G., Dowdall, G., Burls, A., Perry, I., Curran, N.: Exploring the usability of a mobile app for adolescent obesity management. JMIR (2014)
34. Patel, N.N., Dalal, P.: Usability evaluation of mobile applications. International Journal of Engineering Research and Technology (2013)
35. Petticrew, M., Roberts, H.: Systematic Reviews in the Social Sciences: A Practical Guide. Wiley-Blackwell (2008)
36. Rahmat, H., Zulzalil, H., Ghani, A.A.A., Kamaruddin, A.: An approach towards development of evaluation framework. In: 9th MySEC. pp. 178–182 (2015)
37. Rodriguez Molano, J., Sierra Yara, E., Jaramillo García, L.: Model for measuring usability of survey mobile apps. In: 10th CISTI (2015)
38. Skorin-Kapov, L., Dobrijevic, O., Piplica, D.: Towards evaluating the quality of experience of remote patient monitoring services. IJ M.H.C.I. (2014)
39. Tsiaousis, A.S., Giaglis, G.M.: Mobile websites: Usability evaluation and design. Int. J. Mob. Commun. (2014)
40. Van Der Weegen, S., Verwey, R., Tange, H., Spreeuwenberg, M., de Witte, L.: Usability testing of a monitoring and feedback tool. PPA Journal (2014)
41. Vélez, O., Boakye, P., Kanter, A., Bakken, S.: A usability study of a mobile health application for rural ghanaian midwives. JMWH (2014)

42. Wein, L.: Visual recognition in museum guide apps: Do visitors want it? In: Proceedings of the SIGCHI (2014)
43. Witt, S.: A set of quantitative user experience metrics for multi-modal dialog systems. In: Speech Communication; 11. ITG Symposium (2014)
44. Xu, J., Ding, X., Huang, K., Chen, G.: A pilot study of an inspection framework for automated usability guideline reviews. In: Proceedings of the WHNIH (2014)
45. Yáñez Gómez, R., Cascado Caballero, D., Sevillano, J.: Heuristic evaluation on mobile interfaces: A new checklist. TSWJ Volume 2014 (2014)

Comparation Between Free Software (Python) and Proprietary Software (Matlab) for Digital Image Processing, Processing Speed Measurement and Peripheral Board Control, Applied to the Monitoring of Pyroclastic Flows in Eruptive Processes

Christyan Mario Cruz Ulloa, Francisco Xavier Viteri Vargas, Kevin Iván Barrera Llanga, and Darío José Mendoza Chipantasi

Universidad de las Fuerzas Armadas ESPE, 171-5-231B,
Sangolquí, Ecuador
{cmcruz1, fxviteri1, kibarrera, djmendoza}@espe.edu.ec

Abstract. The digital image processing has its strength in the autonomy and robustness of a system to perform multitasks, as detect areas of interest or locate variables inside images and for that, there are different types of free software based on C ++ or private software, which offer different characteristics like programming times, execution times, processing speed of frames and number of features recognized in that processing, having advantages and limitations of one over other. These are the main reasons to develop a study that let to determine clearly which are the differences that exist between proprietary and privative software for the processing of images and control of outputs based on the analysis of pyroclastic flows of volcanic eruptions.

Keywords: python, matlab, digital image processing, eruptive process

1 Introducción

El uso de software libre ha sido potenciado debido a las contribuciones realizadas por la comunidad de programadores que comparten sus desarrollos, brindando de esta manera plataformas con una amplia gama de aplicaciones en diferentes ámbitos. Uno de estos ambientes es el procesamiento digital de imágenes, que adicionalmente con las librerías de OpenCV por ejemplo, permiten la ejecución de este tipo de aplicaciones. Por otra parte, se tiene software propietario, denominado de esta manera debido a que está disponible solo desde un único proveedor [1], siendo sus principales campos de aplicación la ingeniería, la ciencia y además la economía. Ambos softwares permiten realizar procesamiento digital de imágenes, pero además permiten la conexión de periféricos y plataformas para la adquisición de señales del medio físico, su procesamiento a través de programación y la emisión de señales a través de puertos y salidas para el control de actuadores o para realizar alguna acción correctiva [2].

Para el desarrollo de esta investigación se han realizado pruebas en base a videos e imágenes de erupciones volcánicas, las cuales han sido cargadas en programas desarrollados tanto en Python como Matlab, para obtener resultados concluyentes al momento de realizar la comparación del reconocimiento de variables. Se hace uso de dos plataformas para el control de periféricos y así poder realizar la comparativa: 1. Por un Arduino controlado y programado en Matlab, y 2. Los puertos de entrada y salida de propósito general controlados por su propia tarjeta Raspberry y cuyo control está programado desde Python, para que la Raspberry trabaje completamente de manera autónoma.

Las pruebas se realizarán en base a los tiempos de ejecución una vez detectado un flujo piroclástico, así como la estabilidad para el control de puertos [3].

En la sección 2 del presente manuscrito se muestran algunos de los proyectos y trabajos que actualmente se han desarrollado basados en el procesamiento digital de imágenes, así como los principales programas existentes y las tarjetas de control para accionamiento de periféricos.

En la sección 3 y 4, se podrán apreciar los algoritmos utilizados para el procesamiento de imágenes, así como los algoritmos para el control de periféricos tanto en Python como en Matlab, respectivamente en cada sección.

Para finalizar se muestran en la sección 5 imágenes, tablas y gráficos porcentuales de los resultados obtenidos en esta investigación, así como su interpretación, para finalmente presentar las conclusiones.

2 Análisis Bibliográfico y Literario

2.1 Software aplicado al procesamiento digital de imágenes

Principalmente el procesamiento de imágenes se realiza a través de matrices en un mayor porcentaje, pero también existen otros tipos de procesamiento como el de las imágenes térmicas o de ultrasonido.

Actualmente se vienen desarrollando proyectos en el ámbito de la visión por computadora con la finalidad de simplificar tareas, optimizar procesos y realizar monitoreos constantes [4]. En Argentina se desarrolla el Proyecto SoPI el cual está enfocado en agregar la gran capacidad de resolución que poseen las imágenes satelitales junto con tecnologías geoespaciales hacia las tareas profesionales de reconocimiento. Este programa se especializa en visualizar y procesar imágenes capturadas a través de sensores remotos, desarrollándose a la par mediante Windows - Linux [5].

ADCIS es otra compañía encargada del desarrollo y comercialización de sistemas de procesamiento de imágenes, caracterizándose por su innovación, donde el software Aphelion es su principal producto; entre los diferentes enfoques de esta compañía están el control de calidad, la biología, análisis de movimiento y seguridad (Figura 1).

Fig. 1. Detección de un Jet Euro Fughter 2000, en aplicación de seguridad por ADCIS

2.2 Software aplicado al control de periféricos

El control de dispositivos externos es necesario cuando se realiza tareas utilizando el procesamiento digital de imágenes, ya que permite tomar acciones de control sobre el medio físico en base a las referencias obtenidas del procesamiento realizado por el programa [6].

Entre las principales tarjetas para adquisición de datos y accionamiento de periféricos están:

- Arduino
- Raspberry Pi
- BeagleBone
- Nanode
- Wasomote

Estas tarjetas pueden ser acopladas y controladas por los diferentes tipos de softwares tales como: OpenCV, Python, Maltab, Visionscape, VisionPro, AIS. [3]

3 Algoritmos para procesamiento de imágenes

Los programas desarrollados en el ámbito del procesamiento digital de imágenes principalmente están enfocados en el mejoramiento de los fotogramas adquiridos por la cámara, esto se logra a través de la aplicación de operaciones morfológicas y de técnicas de filtrado cómo erosión y dilatación, cuyo resultado es la eliminación de ruido, además de la simplificación de información contenida en las imágenes, pero conservando sus principales características [7].

La detección del área de interés (flujos piroclásticos para esta comparativa), dentro de las imágenes es el resultado de la eliminación de ruido, administración de operaciones morfológicas y aplicación de filtros [8] para el reconocimiento de flujos piroclásticos mediante la segmentación de color en las capas específicas, este filtrado involucra determinar una gama de tonalidades, las cuales comprenden desde la emisión del flujo por el cráter, hasta su progresiva decoloración debido al descenso de temperatura mientras alcanza las faldas del volcán [9].

3.1 Software Libre (Python)

El proceso inicia al importar las librerías de OpenCV, estas permitirán realizar el procesamiento de imágenes [7]. Una vez cargada la imagen se establece un tamaño ideal para procesarlas a través de una interpolación. Las operaciones morfológicas aplicadas a la imagen son erosión y dilatación, luego pasa por un filtro de segmentación en función de tonalidades de color, las cuales permiten separar en una nueva imagen únicamente los flujos piroclásticos, en caso de existir.

Se considera un flujo piroclástico a la variable resultante del proceso antes descrito, cuya extensión sea mayor a 1000 píxeles, debido al escalamiento del volcán con respecto a los píxeles tratados [7].

La aplicación implementada está orientado a la determinación de flujos piroclásticos en erupciones volcánicas y se realiza mediante el siguiente código base ejecutado en Python.

```
import cv2
 frame1=cv2.imread('/home/pi/imagenes/vol8.jpg')
  height, width = frame1.shape[:2]
  frame=cv2.resize(frame1,(400,350),interpolation
  =cv2.INTER_AREA)
 hsv = cv2.cvtColor(frame, cv2.COLOR_BGR2HSV)
 auxil-
 iar=cv2.erode(hsv,cv2.getStructuringElement(cv2.MOR
 PH_RECT,(3,3)),iterations=1)
 auxil-
 iar=cv2.dilate(auxiliar,cv2.getStructuringElement(c
 v2.MORPH_RECT,(5,5)),iterations = 1)
 im=cv2.inRange(auxiliar,np.array((Hmin,Smin,Vmin)),
 np.array((Hmax,Vmax,Smax)))
     M = cv2.moments(im)
     if M['m00']>1000:
 cv2.circle(frame,(cx,cy),20,(0,255,0),2)
 cv2.putText(frame,'Alerta_erupcion_en_curso',(5,50)
 ,cv2.FONT_HERSHEY_SIMPLEX,0.8,(255,255,0),2,8)
     area = M['m00']
```

3.2 Software Propietario (Matlab)

Las tareas realizadas en el código desarrollado en Matlab tienen el mismo principio e igual finalidad que en de Python, la aplicación utiliza etapas de morfología, eliminación de ruido y aplicación de capas de matices para separación de zonas de interés [10].

Una vez finalizadas las operaciones de procesamiento, se marca el centroide del flujo piroclástico, el cual es el punto central de la distribución total de píxeles blancos [3]. En pantalla se mostrará la posición (X, Y) del punto central, con referencia a un sistema de coordenadas con origen en la esquina superior izquierda de la pantalla, para finalmente localizar el flujo piroclástico emitido encerrándolo en un rectángulo rojo (Tabla 1).

El reconocimiento y localización de flujos piroclásticos en procesos eruptivos se realiza mediante el siguiente código base en Matlab.

```
volcan=imread('C:\Users\imagenes\vol.jpg');
imagen = imsubtract(volcan(:,:,1), rgb2gray(volcan));
  imagen = medfilt2(imagen, [3 3]);
  imagen = im2bw(imagen,0.14);
  imagen = bwareaopen(imagen,300);
  im = bwlabel(imagen, 8);
  im = moments(im);
  stats = regionprops(im, 'BoundingBox', 'Centroid');
for flujo = 1:length(stats)
  bb = stats(flujo).Box;
  bc = stats(flujo).Centroid;
  rectangle('Position',bb,'EdgeColor','r',2)
  plot(bc(1),bc(2), '-m+')
  a=text(bc(1)+15,bc(2), strcat('X: ',
  num2str(round(bc(1))), ' Y: ',
  num2str(round(bc(2)))));
  set(a, 'FontName', 'Times', 'FontWeight', 'bold',
  'FontSize', 20, 'Color', 'red');
  imshow(imagen)
end;
```

4 Algoritmos para el control de periféricos

Los puertos para el accionamiento de actuadores son activados a través de comandos como 1 y True, respectivamente en Matlab y Python, de la misma manera estos puertos son desactivados con 0 y False [2]. La activación o desactivación de los puertos está en función del resultado del procesamiento y la detección de flujos, donde en caso de existir, se procederá a determinar su centroide y según esto se activará la respectiva alerta en pantalla, en conjunto con el accionamiento del sistema de potencia, Figura 4a y 4b, en donde los actuadores controlarán la rotación de derecha a izquierda de una cámara para que monitoree los flujos piroclásticos y lo mantenga siempre alineado con el centro de la imagen.

4.1 Software Libre (Python)

La Raspberry debe ser configurada en modo board para tener una concordancia entre la disposición de puertos y el número de los mismos, los puertos deben configurarse como salidas [11]. En caso de existir un área considerada como flujo piroclástico, se activa la respectiva salida de la tarjeta de control, siendo los pines (16, 32, 22) los que indiquen el destino del flujo (derecha, centro, izquierda), respectivamente, con referencia a los flancos del volcán .

La activación de puertos en la Raspberry basados en el destino de los flujos emitidos por un volcán, se realiza mediante el siguiente código implementado en Python.

```
import RPi.GPIO as GPIO
  GPIO.setwarnings(False)
  GPIO.setmode(GPIO.BOARD)
  GPIO.setup(16,32,22, GPIO.OUT)
    if(area >= 1000 ):
        if(cx < 400)
            GPIO.output(16, True)
        if(cx >= 400 && cx <= 500)
            GPIO.output(32, True)
        if(cx > 500)
            GPIO.output(22, True) [3]
```

4.2 Software Propietario (Matlab)

El uso de una tarjeta como medio de conexión físico para el exterior se inicia al cargar los programas de lectura en la tarjeta para la conexión con Matlab, seguido a esto se debe realizar el reconocimiento por parte del programa hacia el arduino. Una vez reconocida la tarjeta, el programa inicia con la declaración del arduino, declaración de puertos como salidas e inicialización en 0 (apagados) de los mismo [12]. La activación de los puertos, se realiza según la posición en X del centroide del flujo piroclástico detectado. Los pines (2, 3, 5) se accionarán respectivamente o en simultáneo indicando porque flanco del volcán descienden los flujos, (flanco derecho, centro, flanco izquierdo) respectivamente.

La declaración de la tarjeta de control (arduino), periféricos y activación de salidas, se realiza mediante el siguiente código ejecutado en Matlab.

```
a=arduino('COM3')
  a.pinMode(2,3,5,'output')
  a.digitalWrite(2,0);
  a.digitalWrite(3,0);
  a.digitalWrite(5,0);
 for object = 1:length(stats)
  if(Centroid.x < 400)
  a.digitalWrite(2,1); end;
  if(Centroid.x > 400 && Centroid.x > 500)
  a.digitalWrite(3,1); end;
  if(Centroid.x > 500)
  a.digitalWrite(5,1); end; end;
```

5 Resultados Obtenidos

Los datos presentados muestran una comparativa de la ejecución de los códigos tanto para el sistema de detección de flujos piroclásticos como para el control de periféricos, siendo la Tabla 1 los datos obtenidos en las pruebas realizadas para la verificación de los algoritmos.

5.1 Comparativa del procesamiento digital de imágenes

El conteo de píxeles referente a flujos piroclásticos dentro de las imágenes principales de volcanes, Tabal 1. (Columna denominada Imágenes principales), se realiza en base al histograma de cada imagen; para obtener este valor estándar de píxeles se utilizó la herramienta de Photoshop (Figura 2), Histograma (R, G, B), realizando el conteo de píxeles R comprendidos en un rango 30<R<250, relacionados con flujos piroclásticos [9], obteniendo así el número de píxeles mostrado en la Tabla 1 (Columna Imágenes principales, variable V(1)), para realizar las comparativas de eficiencia.

Fig. 2. Histograma de una imagen descompuesto en RGB, realizado en Photoshop

Por otra parte, para el conteo de píxeles en las imágenes resultantes (Tabla 1. Resultados Matlab/Python), se empleó la función "moments" para los códigos mostrados en la sección 3.1 y 3.2. La función "moments" utiliza la ecuación matemática (1) del teorema de Green para obtener el momento de inercia de contornos cerrados, según la documentación propia de OpenCV, y se basa en realizar la sumatoria de píxeles blancos en una imagen binaria [7].

$$M(2) = \int_{i}^{j} \int_{-g(x)}^{f(x)} \left(\frac{dP}{dy} - \frac{dQ}{dx}\right) dx\, dy \tag{1}$$

Donde *M(2)* es el total de píxeles resultantes (Mostrados bajo cada imagen en la Tabla 1, Columnas Resultados Matlab/Python); [$\frac{dP}{dx}$ y $\frac{dQ}{dx}$]son las derivadas parciales de la función generada por la zona blanca, mediante el comando moments en las imágenes binarias (Tabla 1); [i, j] son las dimensiones en píxeles de la imagen y [f(x), g(x)] son las funciones a trozos que conforman los contornos de la imagen blanca (Tabla 1, Resultados). Esta función de cálculo se utilizó, debido a que los bordes de los flujos piroclásticos son superficies cerradas, siendo aplicables en el cálculo del Teorema de Green.

Tabla 1. Toma de una muestra del banco de datos post-procesamiento de la aplicación de los respectivos algoritmos (Matlab-Python), donde se muestra la eficiencia medida en base a los píxeles M(2) con relación a los totales de los flujos de V(1).

Resultados Matlab	Imágenes principales	Resultados Python
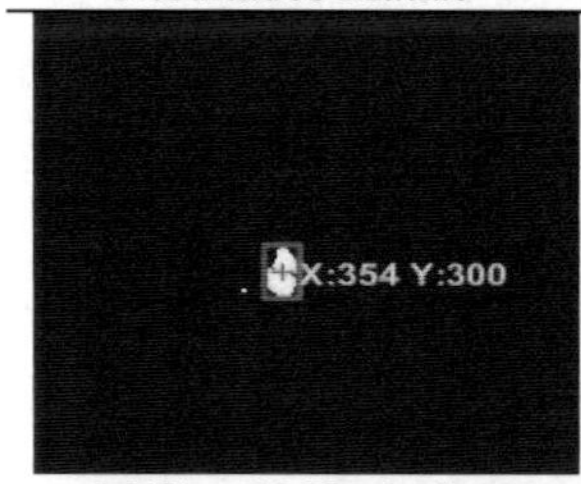		
M(2) = 1358 píxeles Eficiencia: 97%	V(1) = 1400 píxeles Resultado visual Matlab	M(2) = 1330 píxeles Eficiencia: 95%
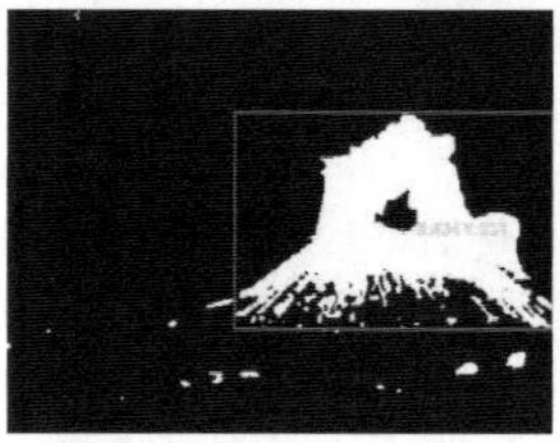	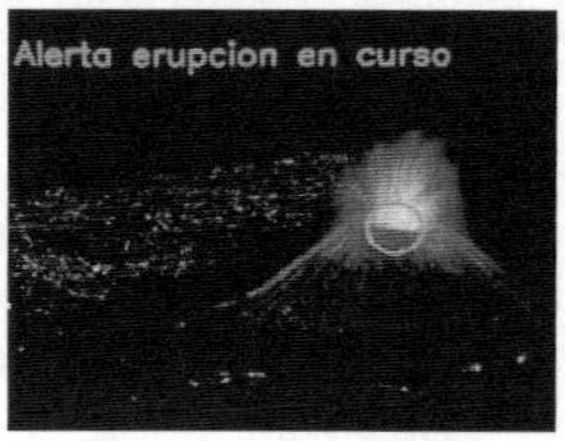	
M(2) = 17132 píxeles Eficiencia: 98%	V(1) = 17482 píxeles Resultado visual Python	M(2) = 16433 píxeles Eficiencia: 94%
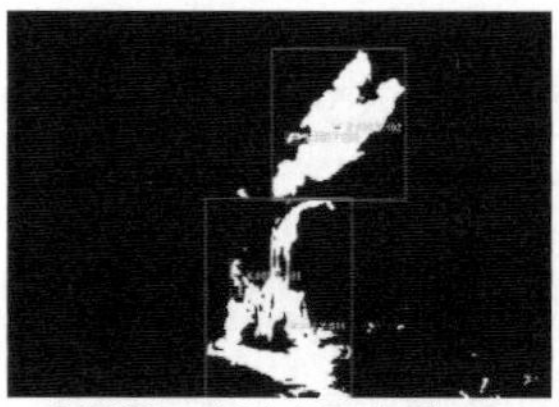		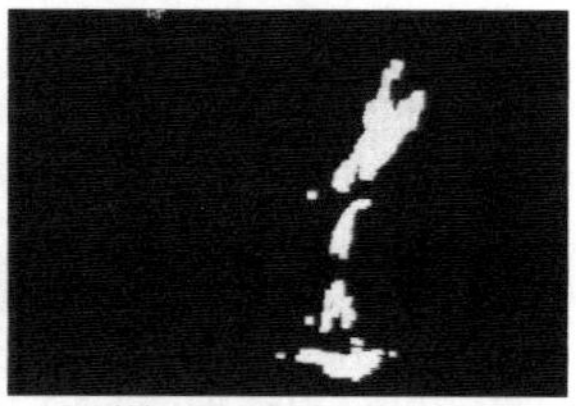
M(2) = 15149 píxeles Eficiencia: 99%	V(1) = 15303 píxeles Resultado visual Matlab	M(2) = 14537 píxeles Eficiencia: 95%
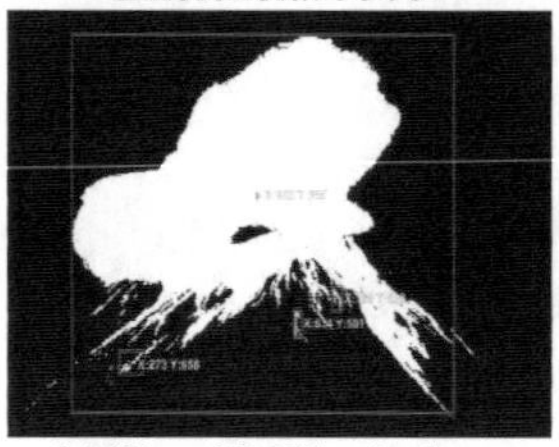		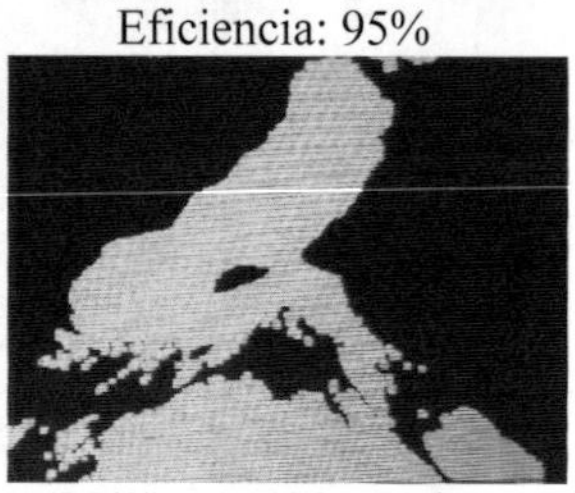
M(2) = 37651 píxeles Eficiencia: 98%	V(1) = 38420 píxeles Resultado visual Python	M(2) = 34578 píxeles Eficiencia: 90%

Tabla 1 (continuación). Toma de una muestra del banco de datos post-procesamiento de la aplicación de los respectivos algoritmos (Matlab-Python), donde se muestra la eficiencia medida en base a los píxeles M(2) con relación a los totales de los flujos de V(1).

Resultados Matlab	Imágenes principales	Resultados Python
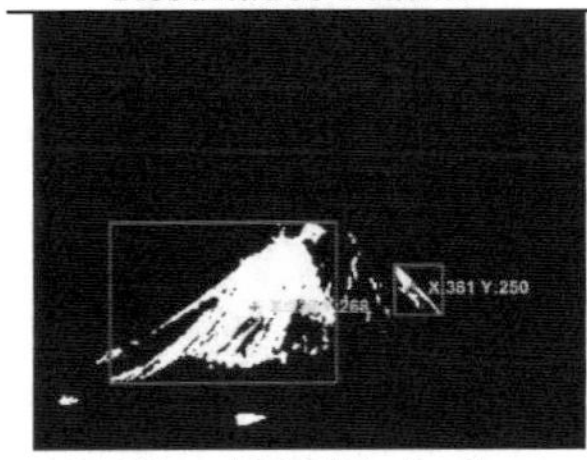		
M(2) = 123057 píxeles Eficiencia: 99%	V(1) = 12430 píxeles Resultado visual Matlab	M(2) = 12181 píxeles Eficiencia: 98%

El porcentaje de eficiencia de procesamiento en base a las pruebas realizadas en el algoritmo de Matlab es 98.2% (Figura. 3a), mientras que en Python es del 94.4% (Figura 3b), siendo Matlab un 3.8% más fiable que Python para este procesamiento, debiéndose principalmente a que Python es un lenguaje de propósito general, por otro lado Matlab es considerado como una herramienta matemática enfocada al procesamiento de matrices, donde para ambos casos el principal objeto a procesar son imágenes (matrices). **[13]**.

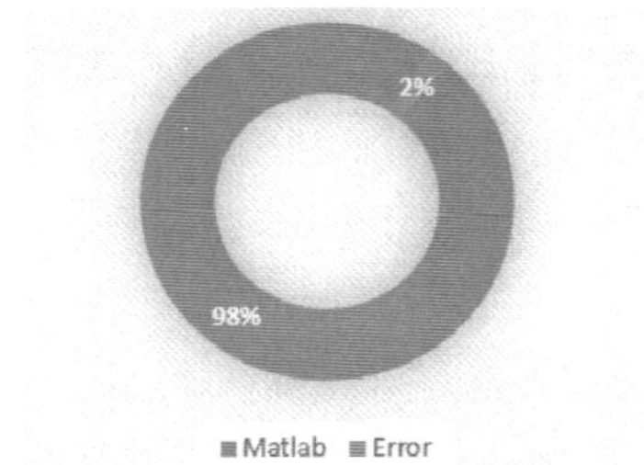

Fig. 3a. Eficiencia y error Matlab

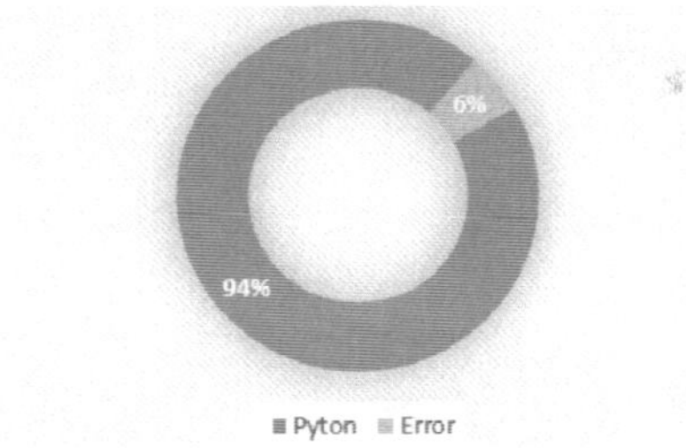

Fig. 3b. Eficiencia y error Python

5.2 Comparativa del Control de Salidas

El sistema de activación de alarmas tanto para sirenas y lámparas 1, 2, 3, es accionado por los puertos 2, 3, 5 (Figura 4 a) del arduino y en caso de la raspberry son los puertos 16, 32, 22 (Figura 4 b) siendo el circuito de potencia el mismo para ambas tarjetas. Los resultados de las pruebas son los tiempos de respuesta del accionamiento de periféricos en caso de erupción, estos tiempos serán medidos desde la detección de un flujo piroclástico hasta el accionamiento del sistema de potencia. Además se medirá el tiempo de ejecución con imágenes pre establecidas(Tabla 1, Imágenes principales), desde la ejecución del programa hasta la obtención de resultados (detección de flujos y dirección de los mismos con respecto al cono volcánico), estos resultados se detallan en la Tabla 2.

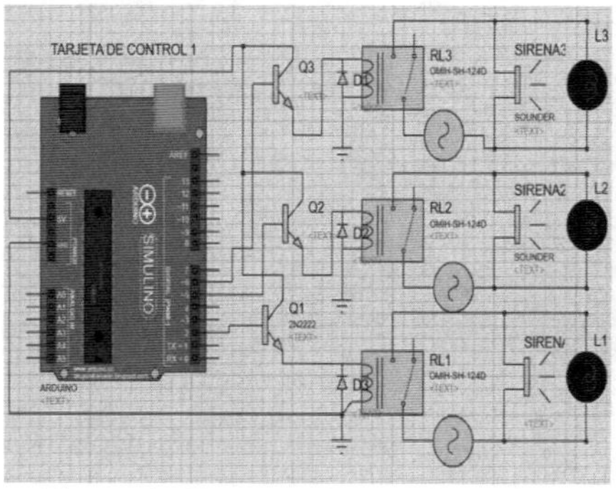

Figura 4a. Esquemas de conexión para Arduino

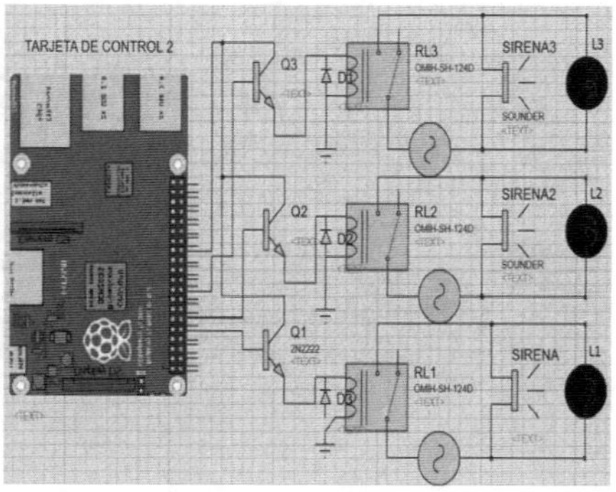

Figura 4b. Esquemas de conexión Raspberry

Tabla 2. Comparativa de velocidad de respuesta del accionamiento de periféricos de Arduino – Raspberry, fiabilidad y velocidad de procesamiento al determinar direcciones Centro, Derecha, Izquierda de flujos emitidos por el volcán. (Los resultados de las direcciones son basados en las imágenes obtenidas del procesamiento de la Tabla 1. y la base de pruebas realizadas Según los centroides del área de interés)

Test	Velocidad accionamiento puerttos Arduino	Velocidad accionamiento puertos Raspberry	Velocidad de procesamiento Matlab	Velocidad de procesamien Python
1	1.10 segundos	1.90 segundos	0.86 segundos	1.56Segundos
2	1.43 s	2.10 s	0.85 s	1.65 s
3	1.22 s	1.91 s	0.98 s	2.00 s
4	1.36 s	1.83 s	0.81 s	1.59 s
5	1.57 s	1.75 s	0.90 s	1.76 s
6	1.02 s	1.89 s	0.92 s	1.89 s
7	1.63 s	1.95 s	0.79 s	1.96 s
8	1.38 s	2.01 s	0.82 s	1.69 s
9	1.59 s	1.57s	0.91 s	1.99 s
10	1.03 s	1.64 s	0.89 s	1.81 s
Prom	1.33 seg	1.85 seg	0.87 seg	1.79 seg

El porcentaje de eficiencia de control basado en un tiempo óptimo de procesamiento de 1.3 segundos [14] para el accionamiento de periféricos, da como resultado en el arduino una eficiencia en tiempo de activación del 0.97%, mientras que para la Raspberry es de 0.703% (Figura 5). Por su parte de la velocidad de procesamiento se puede deducir que el tiempo de Python dobla al tiempo de Matlab para el mismo procesamiento.

5.3 Características de los procesadores empleados

Python fue ejecutado en Rasberry con Procesador quad-core ARMv8, 1.2GHz 64-bit, 1GB Ram, mientras Matlab en una PC Procesador Intel Core i3-2.6GHz 64 bit, 2 Ram (Figura 6).

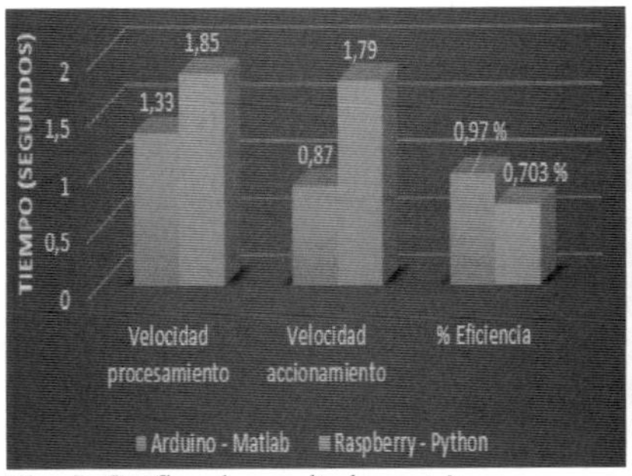

Fig. 5. Gráfica de resultados según las pruebas de Tabla 2

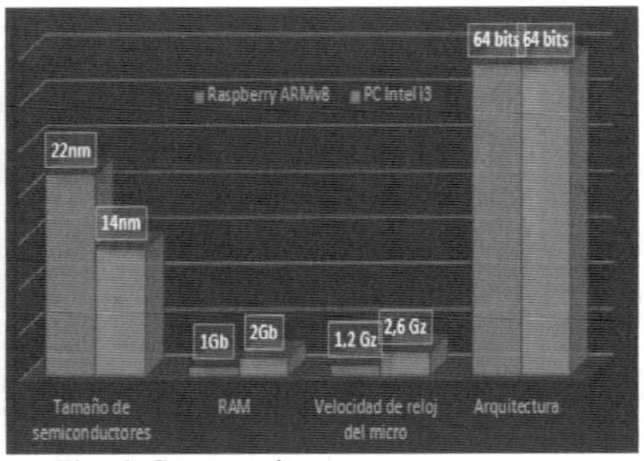

Fig. 6. Comparativa de los procesadores usados

Conclusiones

El arduino brinda un tiempo de respuesta de un 26.7% más eficiente con relación a la velocidad del accionamiento de periféricos de una raspberry, esto se debe a que en el arduino actúa únicamente como esclavo de una computadora, mientras la raspberry procesa el código y acciona los puertos de manera conjunta.

Por otro lado, para la obtención del tiempo de la velocidad de ejecución del programa hasta la obtención de resultados, fue en Matab promedio de 0.87 segundos, en comparación con Python que fue un promedio de 1.79 segundos. Siendo Matlab un 92% más rápido (Tabla 2).

El reconocimiento del área de interés (flujos piroclásticos) en Python tuvo un 94.4% de eficiencia, con relación al área total de interés de la imagen procesada, afectando principalmente el ruido y perturbaciones al momento de capturar la imagen. Mientras en Matlab el resultado de eficiencia fue de 98.2%, mostrados en la Tabla 1.

Para la obtención de los resultados expuestos existió mucha influencia del uso de funciones específicas mejor establecidas por Matlab que las que permite OpenCV, principalmente imsubstract y cv2.inRange para la extracción de áreas de interés respectivamente en cada lenguaje, donde la primera extrae la zona de interés en base a una gama de colores, mientras la segunda aplica un filtro de color dejando pasar los píxeles coincidentes. Aunque para la medición de la cantidad de píxeles se usa en ambos casos la función "moments".

Hay que tener en cuenta que Matlab se ejecuta en una PC con Procesador Intel Core i3 @2.6GHz 64 bit, 4RAM (Fig 5), mientras que Pytnon se ejecuta en una Raspberry con procesador Quad-core ARMv8 CPU, 1.2GHz 64-bit, 1 GB RAM (Fig 5.). Razón por la cual los tiempos de ejecución de Matlab doblan al de Python, debido al procesador del computador, además de que la Arquitectura Intel i3 posee semiconductores más reducidos.

En el resultado del procesamiento de las imágenes para análisis de una característica específica, en este caso el filtrado de una región por medio de su color (flujo piroclástico), la diferencia porcentual únicamente es de 4%, valor que significativamente no es muy alto, obteniendo entonces que Raspberry es una excelente opción con resultados comparables a la de unidades de cómputo muy superiores y que permite realizar proyectos bastante completos y complejos, brindando portabilidad, autonomía total para el procesamiento de imágenes, accionamiento de puertos y que necesita ser accionada únicamente con una fuente de 5 Voltios.

Agradecimientos

A la Universidad de las Fuerzas Armadas ESPE, por impartir la ciencia y el conocimiento necesarios para conllevar esta investigación, al Departamento de Energía y Mecánica, a la Carrera de Ingeniería Mecatrónica de la sede Latacunga y en especial al docente Ing. Darío Mendoza, mentor del proyecto.

Referencias

1. J. K. M. K. E. Fazel Sahraneshin Samani, «Features of free software packages in flow cytometry: a comparison between four non-commercial software sources,» *Annales de génétique et de sélection animale,* vol. 66, nº 10.1007/s10616-013-9609-8, p. 555–559, 2014.
2. R. H. E. A. Gregorio Bernabé, «Parallel implementations of the 3D fast wavelet transform on a Raspberry Pi 2 cluster,» *The Journal of Supercomputing,* nº 10.1007/s11227-016-1933-2, p. 1–14, 2016.
3. H. G. Dietmar Dietrich, «Embedded Vision System,» *EURASIP Journal on Embedded Systems,* vol. 12, nº 10.1155/2007/34323, 2007.
4. Ö. &. I. B. H. A. R. Erkent, «Artificial potential functions based camera movements and visual behaviors in attentive robots,» *Autonomous Robots,* vol. 32, nº 10.1007/s10514-011-9240-5, p. 15–34, 2012.
5. L. A. S. S. T. R. U. A. Elmer P, «Exploring compression impact on face detection using haar-like features,» *Scandinavian Conference on Image Analysis,* vol. 91, nº 10.1007/978-3-319-19665-7_5, p. 53–64, 2015.
6. I. M. V. A. Sethi, «Special section on artificial neural networks for machine vision,» *Machine Vision and Applications,* vol. 8, nº 10.1007/BF01211487, p. 261–261, 2009.
7. Y.-T. C.-T. H.-F. L.-J. Wang, «Image interpolating based data hiding in conjunction with pixel-shifting of histogram,» *The Journal of Supercomputing,* vol. 66, nº 10.1007/s11227-013-1016-6, p. 1093–1110, 2013.
8. S. K. T. V. P. P. I. M. Spiros V. Georgakopoulos, «Artificial Neural Networks and Principal Components Analysis for Detection of Idiopathic Pulmonary Fibrosis in Microscopy Images,» *International Conference on Engineering Applications of Neural Networks,* nº 10.1007/978-3-642-41013-0_30, pp. 292-301, 2013.
9. K. K. T. H., «Rise and flow of volcanic clouds observed from the ground and from satellites,» *Journal of Visualization,* vol. 3, nº 10.1007/BF03182442, p. 71–78, 2000.
10. D. R. O. T. Porwik Piotr, «The k-NN classifier and self-adaptive Hotelling data reduction technique in handwritten signatures recognition,» *Pattern Analysis and Applications,* vol. 18, nº 10.1007/s10044-014-0419-1, pp. 983-1001, 2015.
11. A. P. F. O. Vendittelli, «Vision-based maze navigation for humanoid robots,»

Autonomous Robots, vol. 41, nº 10.1007/s10514-015-9533-1, p. 293–309, 2016.

12. S. A.-K. Haitham Hasan, «Retraction Note to: Human–computer interaction using vision-based hand gesture recognition systems: a survey,» *Neural Computing and Applications,* vol. 28, nº 10.1007/s00521-017-2867-1, p. 849–849, 2017.
13. R. v. W. d. J. L. David, «Rethinking free, libre and open source software,» *Knowledge, Technology & Policy,* vol. 18, nº 10.1007/s12130-006-1001-y, p. 5–16, 2004.
14. V. B. M. Cruz Christyan, «Use of ICT´s to Generate Real-Time Alerts Based on the Automatic Analysis by the Artificial Vision System That Monitors Eruptive Processes,» *International Journal of Engineering, Malasia* 2016.

Use of neural networks to the detection of pyroclastic flows in Ecuador volcanoes.

Francisco Viteri[1], Christyan Cruz[1], Kevin Barrera[1], Darío Mendoza[1]

[1] Departamento de Ciencias de la Energía y Mecánica, Universidad de las Fuerzas Armadas ESPE, Sangolquí 171-5-231B, Ecuador.
{fxviteri1, cmcruz1, kibarrera, djmendoza}@espe.edu.ec

Abstract. Neural networks are oriented to provide solutions that require a complex computational solution and this answer must be precise, from they belong to a group of techniques grouped under deep learning, a branch that has proven to be effective in many tasks as image recognition and voice recordings in the last years. For this reason, a neural network was created for volcanic images recognition that allow presence of volcanic fluids detection, as well as their trajectory, to generate timely alerts when a volcanic phenomenon is present. For the algorithm implementation will be used open source computer vision libraries such as Open Computer Vision (OpenCV).

Keywords: neural network, pyroclastic flows, volcanoes

1 Introducción

En síntesis, las Redes Neuronales Artificiales (RNA) tratan de reproducir el procedimiento de solución de un problema, de una forma similar a como lo realiza el cerebro humano, el cual se basa en aplicar el conocimiento ganado a través de la experiencia de determinadas situaciones, de tal forma que una RNA aprende a tomar decisiones y realizar clasificaciones tomando como ejemplos problemas resueltos o también llamados patrones. [1]

Para realizar esta investigación se optó por la estructura perceptrón multicapa, la cual posee una capa de entrada, una o más capas ocultas y una capa de salida; todas las neuronas de una capa están conectadas a las neuronas de la capa antecedente, las señales fluyen en la misma dirección (hacia adelante); al realizar la operación entre las entradas y los pesos sinápticos se obtiene un escalar, que desde el punto de vista matemático se puede utilizar para la clasificación de problemas multiclase, debido a esto se dice que puede tomar como entradas valores continuos o discretos; generalmente tiene como función de activación la función sigmoidea. La fase de ejecución de un perceptrón multicapa es una operación computacional muy rápida que puede realizarse en tiempo real, para el monitoreo volcánico. [1, 2]

Este documento se ha organizado de la siguiente manera para facilitar su comprensión: la sección 2, describe los materiales y métodos utilizados. Las pruebas que se han realizado, así como también la discusión de los resultados obtenidos durante la investigación están en la sección 3. Las conclusiones de este proyecto basado en la experimentación con diversas fotos y videos de volcanes en erupción se presentan en la sección 4.

2 Materiales y Métodos

2.1 Estado del Arte

La manera de percibir y evaluar la actividad y riesgo que presenta un volcán, es a través de la observación y vigilancia sistemática utilizando diversos métodos instrumentales y visuales. Si estos métodos se aplican de manera anticipada a las fases previas que conlleva un proceso eruptivo, es posible, detectar de manera oportuna un cambio cuantitativo y cualitativo en la actividad de los volcanes que incluso pude conducir a una predicción a corto plazo de un proceso eruptivo inminente y poner en marcha el plan de emergencia establecido. La eficacia de estos sistemas se fundamenta en el conocimiento de la existencia de riesgos, los cuales han sido diseñados para avisar a la población de la proximidad de un evento destructivo, para que se pueden tomar medidas anticipadas y efectivas, que sirvan para minimizar o evitar la pérdida de vidas y daños materiales. Hecha la observación anterior, es importante conocer los riesgos que se presentan según el tipo de erupción, la cual estará determinada por la viscosidad del magma, pudiéndose mencionar los siguientes tipos de erupciones y sus características más relevantes:

Erupción Pliniana. Son las erupciones más violentas, la composición del magma es acida y tiene alto contenido de gases. Es una proyección violenta de gases en forma de columna, los materiales resultantes como cenizas y piedra pómez cubren grandes extensiones.

Erupción Peleana. Son erupciones violentas que se presentan de forma intermitente, presentan colapsos de domos que generan flujos de piroclásticos, formados por fragmentos de lava, cenizas y gases. Es una violenta explosión, resultado de la solidificación de un magma muy viscoso en la chimenea de un volcán.

Erupción Vulcaniana. Son erupciones explosivas en las cuales se emiten ceniza, y proyectiles balísticos, frecuentemente relacionados con la interacción del magma con agua lo que causa en el magma una fina fragmentación.

Erupción Hawaiana. Son erupciones caracterizadas por la emisión de lavas de composición basáltica, las cuales tienen un bajo contenido de gases. Se presenta una emisión de lava muy fluida que se derrama rápidamente en forma de coladas de gran extensión.

Erupción Estromboliana. Son erupciones debidas a pequeñas explosiones de materiales en estado fundido o pastoso, que suceden en pocos minutos u horas, acompañadas por derrames de coladas de lava.

Actualmente existe proyectos los cuales se basan en el uso de cámaras multiespectrales para desarrollar una nueva metodología para la vigilancia volcánica, entre ellos se pueden mencionar el diseño aerodinámico de un sistema aéreo no tripulado (UAS) para vigilancia volcánica en México [3], es una tecnología que se encuentra en desarrollo y se espera que al fusionarla con otros sistemas que se utilizan actualmente para el monitoreo volcánico (radar doppler meteorológico, cámara térmica, inclinómetros biaxiales, detectores de flujo, sismógrafos y diversos equipos para análisis químicos, mediciones geodésicas, determinación de las concentraciones de gases CO_2 y SO_2.) [4]

2.2 Sistema de Visión Artificial

La visión artificial es una rama de la inteligencia artificial cuyo objetivo es modelar la imagen digital suministrada por un sensor de tal forma que un ordenador este en capacidad de interpretarla y utilizarla para la toma de decisiones de un proceso. De forma más precisa, trata de la capacidad para deducir la estructura y las propiedades del mundo tridimensional a partir de imágenes bidimensionales. [5]

Dentro de un sistema de visión artificial están incluidas varias y diferentes técnicas, tales como el procesamiento de imágenes que trata de la captura, transformación, codificación de imágenes; o como el reconocimiento de formas, la cual se basa en la teoría estadística de decisiones y enfoques neuronales de aprendizaje enfocados a la clasificación de patrones [6]. Para llevar a cabo estos procesos, se realizan las etapas que se describen a continuación y están representadas en la Fig. 1.

Fig. 1. Etapas que conforman un sistema de visión artificial o visión por ordenador

Adquisición de imagen. Se usa una cámara, esta es la encargada de convertir las señales luminosas de la escena en señales analógicas para que puedan ser transmitidas. En otra etapa unos transductores proporcionan una señal con amplitud proporcional a la luminosidad de la escena y realizan la digitalización espacial completa que se realiza en dos dimensiones (líneas y columnas), pues se descompone la imagen en una matriz de puntos. [7]

Procesamiento de imagen. Se vuelve necesaria la transformación de la imagen original en otra imagen en la cual hayan sido eliminados o reducidos los problemas de ruido o de iluminación. Esto permite la adecuación de las imágenes digitales adquiridas en base a los requerimientos del sistema, es decir, la importancia del procesamiento de la imagen radica en el mejoramiento de la misma, de modo que el objeto y las formas contenidas tengan mayores posibilidades de éxito en la identificación. [7]

Segmentación. La segmentación es aquel proceso mediante el cual una imagen se descompone en regiones o varios conjuntos de píxeles que pueden corresponder a objetos, parte de objetos o contornos. Este proceso es el encargado de evaluar si cada pixel de la imagen genera una imagen binaria, es decir, se representa con 1 (blanco) los pixeles que pertenecen a dicho objeto y 0 (negro) a los que no corresponden. [7, 8]

Reconocimiento de objetos. Es importante que exista un reconocimiento de objetos en base a la obtención de patrones, en otras palabras, el reconocimiento y la localización de objetos van a la par, pues dependen entre sí uno del otro. Para realizar esta etapa es importante considerar las características representativas del objeto en la imagen como la intensidad, variación del valor de los píxeles, reflectancia, entre otros. [7, 8]

Interpretación de escena. Esta fase se relaciona con el campo de la inteligencia artificial, y se considera la relación existente entre los objetos de interés que han sido reconocidos y localizados con las reglas, el conocimiento de los eventos, parámetros o restricciones del mundo real que se tiene en cuenta para la toma de una decisión. [8]

Es evidente entonces que el procesamiento automático de imágenes permite extraer su contenido semántico en búsqueda de fenómenos de interés, ante la situación planteada se usó un sistema de visión artificial para adquirir y obtener información de imágenes volcánicas, en tanto que una red neuronal entrenada analizará esa información y determinará si existe algo fuera de lo normal (fenómeno volcánico), de modo que al existir anomalías en las imágenes se procedería a encerrar dicha anomalía, trazar su trayectoria y dar una alerta para que se analice y se determine de que se trata. Siendo todo este un proceso totalmente autónomo de monitoreo volcánico.

2.3 Transformada de Hotelling

Conocida también como Análisis de Componentes Principales (PCA), es una transformación que permite reducir la información redundante en las imágenes mediante la utilización de algoritmos estadístico-matemáticos presentes dentro del software libre. El objetivo de esta técnica es reducir toda la información innecesaria contenida en un conjunto original de N bandas, a un conjunto menor de nuevas bandas o componentes. Cualquier imagen se puede representar como una matriz en la que la intersección de una columna con una fila corresponde a un píxel. Teniendo presente esta característica, se pueden realizar sobre ella operaciones y transformaciones estadísticas y matemáticas, el análisis de componentes principales es reducir varias bandas sintetizando la información redundante. [9, 10]

3 Redes Neuronales Artificiales (RNA)

Es una estructura formada por varios procesadores simples llamados neuronas o nodos, que están conectados a través de canales de comunicación. Cada una de estas neuronas posee una memoria local, trabajando solo con sus datos locales y sobre las entradas que recibe a través de los canales de comunicación. Las RNA tienen asociado un entrenamiento o regla de aprendizaje que ajusta las conexiones acorde a los ejemplos proporcionados y muestran capacidad de generalizar más allá de esos datos mostrados.

En general las RNA presentan tres características principales: aprendizaje, generalización y adaptabilidad. El aprendizaje hace referencia a que la red neuronal posee la capacidad de almacenar conocimiento mediante un entrenamiento (aprendizaje). La generalización hace referencia a que se pueden obtener salidas razonables utilizando entradas diferentes a las usadas en el proceso de entrenamiento. Finalmente, la adaptabilidad se refiere a que una red neuronal se puede reentrenar para funcionar correctamente ante cambios en su medio ambiente. [11]

3.1 Estructura y Modelo de RNA

El algoritmo está compuesto por una RNA de tres capas que tienen como tarea identificar las formas contenidas en una región de interés (ROI), extraída de la etapa de procesamiento de imágenes, que es una imagen binaria con píxeles de color negro y blanco asignados con valores de 0.1 y 0.9 respectivamente; éstos valores se asignan, uno por uno, a cada neurona de la capa de entrada. El tamaño de la ROI depende de la imagen. [12]

La capa de arquitectura de la red neuronal que se implementó es similar a la que se observa en la Fig. 2, para llegar a ella se hicieron diferentes pruebas.

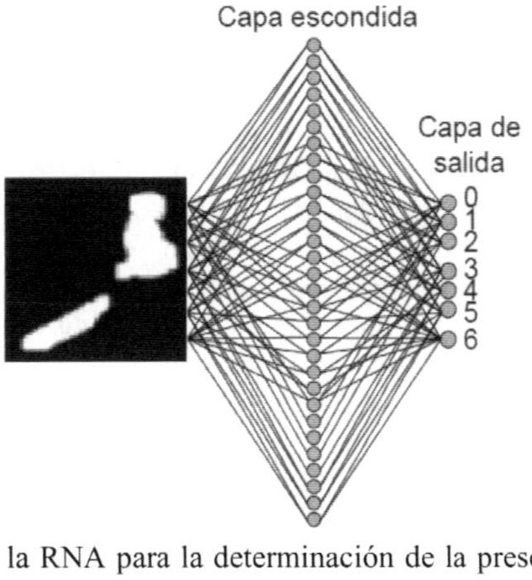

Fig. 2. Arquitectura de la RNA para la determinación de la presencia de flujos piroclásticos en conos volcánicos del Ecuador

3.2 Propagación de los patrones de entrada

Para un perceptrón multicapa con C capas ($C-2$ capas ocultas) y n_c neuronas en la capa c, para $c = 1,2,\dots,C$. Entonces $W^c = (w_{ij}{}^c)$ es la matriz de los pesos de las conexiones existentes en la capa c con la capa $c+1$ para $c = 1,2,\dots,C-1$., donde $w_{ij}{}^c$ pertenece al peso de conexión entre la neurona i en capa c con la neurona j en capa $c+1$; y $U^c = (u^c{}_i)$ que es el vector de umbrales de las neuronas que están en la capa c, para $c = 2, 3, \dots, C$. Donde $a^c{}_i$ pertenece a la activación de la neurona i en la capa c. Los cálculos de estas activaciones se muestran a continuación:

Activación de las neuronas de la capa de entrada ($a^1{}_i$): La capa de entrada se encarga de transmitir hacia la red las señales recibidas desde el exterior:

$$a^1{}_i = x_i \; para \; i = 1, 2, \dots, n_1 \tag{1}$$

siendo $X = (x_1, x_2, \dots, x_{n1})$ el patrón de entrada a la red.

Activación de las neuronas en la capa oculta ($a^c{}_i$): En la capa ocultas se procesa la información obtenida mediante la función de activación f a la suma de los productos de las activaciones que recibe por sus correspondientes pesos:

$$a^c{}_i = f\left(\sum_{j=1}^{n_c-1} w_{ij}{}^{c-1} a_j{}^{c-1} + u^c{}_i\right) para \; i = 1, 2, \dots, n_c \; y \; c = 2, 3, \dots, C-1 \tag{2}$$

siendo $a_j{}^{c-1}$ las activaciones en la capa $c-1$ de las neuronas.

Activación de las neuronas de la capa de salida ($a^c{}_i$): análogamente al caso de las capas ocultas:

$$y_i = a^c{}_i = f\left(\sum_{j=1}^{n_c-1} w_{ij}{}^{c-1} a_j{}^{c-1} + u^c{}_i\right) para \; i = 1, 2, \dots, n_c \tag{3}$$

siendo $Y = (y_1, y_2, \dots, y_{nc})$ el vector de salida de la red.

La función f utilizada es la función de activación. En este trabajo, se utilizó la función sigmoidal en la cual el valor de la salida viene dado por la función y es cercano a uno de sus valores asintóticos (0 y 1), por lo tanto, el valor de salida estará comprendido en la zona alta o baja del sigmoide; además es derivable en todo su intervalo, lo cual es importante para los algoritmos de aprendizaje de descenso por gradiente. [13]

$$f(x) = \frac{1}{1+e^x} \tag{4}$$

3.3 Algoritmo de Retropropagación

En el perceptrón multicapa se trata de un algoritmo de aprendizaje supervisado, se modifican los parámetros para minimizar el error entre la salida deseada y la salida producida por la red, es decir, $Min_W E$, en donde E es la función error y W es el conjunto de parámetros de la red. En general:

$$E = \frac{1}{N}\sum_{n-1}^{N} e(n) \tag{5}$$

donde N es el número de patrones y $e(n)$ es el error cometido por la red para el patrón n. Utilizando el error cuadrático medio, se obtiene:

$$e(n) = \frac{1}{2}\sum_{i=1}^{n_c}(s_i(n) - y_i(n))^2 \tag{6}$$

en donde $S(n) = (s_1(n), \dots, s_{nc}(n))$ y $Y(n) = (y_1(n), \dots, y_{nc}(n))$ son respectivamente los vectores de salida deseada para el patrón n y de salida de la red.
Pesos entre la conexión de la capa oculta $C-1$ con la capa de salida y umbrales de la capa de salida. [14]

Pesos:

$$w_{ij}^{C-1}(n) = w_{ij}^{C-1}(n-1) - \alpha\delta_i^{C}(n)\,a_j^{C-1}(n)\ para\ j = 1,2,\dots,n_{c-1}\ y\ para = 1,2,\dots,n_c \tag{7}$$

Umbrales:

$$u_i^{c}(n) = u_i^{c}(n-1) + \alpha\delta_i^{c}(n)\ para\ i = 1,2,\dots,n_c \tag{8}$$

Delta:

$$\delta_i^{C} = -(s_i(n) - y_i(n))y_i(n)(1 - y_i(n)) \tag{9}$$

4 Resultados Experimentales

Se han efectuado 2 pruebas, con estas pruebas se busca analizar 2 efectos principales: capacidad de reconocimiento de la red y rapidez del sistema, con estos resultados se comparó este sistema con otro que basa su funcionamiento en la detección de una gama de color rojo, cuando se detecta la presencia de un color dentro de esta gama en una imagen se aplican operaciones morfológicas para eliminar el ruido y hacer más fácil el reconocimiento del flujo piroclástico, logrando así obtener el contorno del flujo de lava para determinar la trayectoria mediante la transformada de Hotelling de acuerdo al área encerrada. [9]

Prueba 1: Modificación número de salidas de la red neuronal: Las redes neuronales creadas tienen 900 entradas (las imágenes empleadas en el aprendizaje se normalizaron a dimensiones de 30x30 pixeles). Para esta prueba se ha empleado un conjunto de 150 imágenes para el aprendizaje, divididas en 3 grupos: entrenamiento (65), validación (35) y test (50).

La activación de cada una de las 7 neuronas de la capa de salida se interpreta de la siguiente manera: las tres primeras (de la 0 a la 2) se utilizan para determinar el desplazamiento de la ROI en el eje horizontal, siendo la activación de la neurona 1 la que indica cuando la ROI se encuentra en el centro, las neuronas 0 y 2 se activan cuando existe una desviación de un píxel o más hacia la izquierda y la derecha respectivamente; las siguientes tres neuronas son empleadas para determinar el desplazamiento en el eje vertical, las desviaciones se distinguen hacia arriba (neurona 3), hacia abajo (neurona 5) y el centro (neurona 4); y la última neurona 6 se activa cuando dentro de la ROI esté cualquier otra forma que no corresponda a una erupción volcánica. Los errores de cada neurona se pueden observar en la Fig. 3.

Prueba 2: Impacto que genera el número de neuronas presentes en la capa oculta al número de ciclos de entrenamiento: Ahora se estudiará la influencia del número de neuronas en la capa oculta y la relación que tiene con en el rendimiento de la red neuronal. Es un factor importante, ya que, a mayor número de neuronas, mayor información disponible para el aprendizaje, pero mayor complicación del mismo y tiempo de proceso, estos resultados se muestran en la Fig. 4.

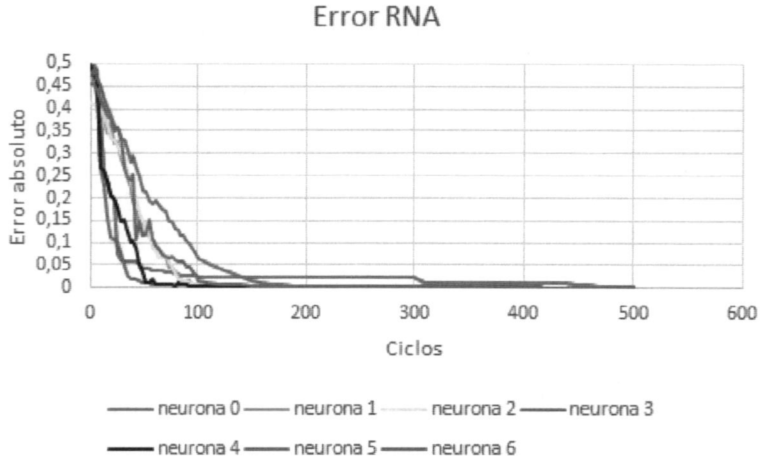

Fig. 3. Error presente en la capa de salida (en cada una de las neuronas) durante el entrenamiento de la red neuronal

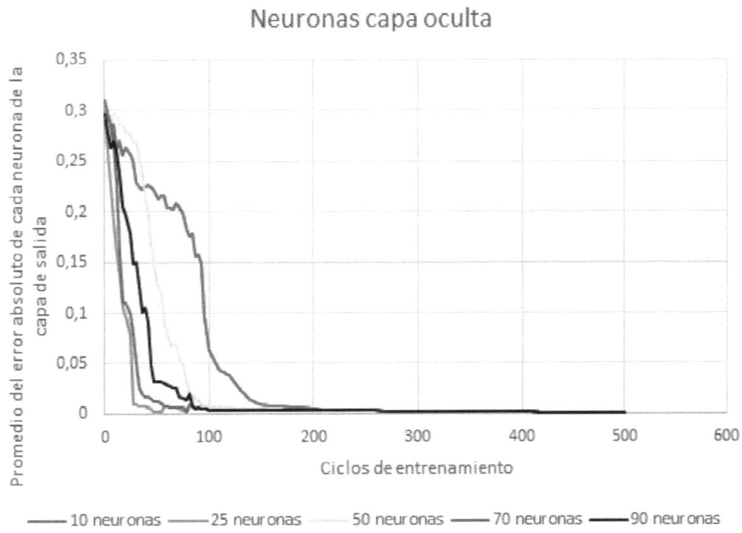

Fig. 4. Numero de iteraciones requeridas de acuerdo al número de neuronas presentes en la capa oculta

Un problema del aprendizaje de una red neuronal es el sobreentrenamiento, ya que se pierde la capacidad de generalización. La red se especializa demasiado en su propio conjunto de aprendizaje y no obtiene buenos resultados cuando se enfrenta a casos distintos [15]. En la Fig. 4 se aprecia una oscilación del error de test en función del número de iteraciones que se realizan. Un empeoramiento de los resultados e inestabilidad son producto del sobreentrenamiento.

Tabla 1. Evaluación del algoritmo con 50 imágenes de test que no pertenecen a las utilizadas en el entrenamiento de la red neuronal, dentro de ellas existen imágenes que varían en el tipo de erupción y se determina el tiempo que tardan en ser reconocidos los flujos piroclásticos

Reconocimiento	Tipo de erupción	Velocidad de detección [ms]
	Estramboliano	1140.141
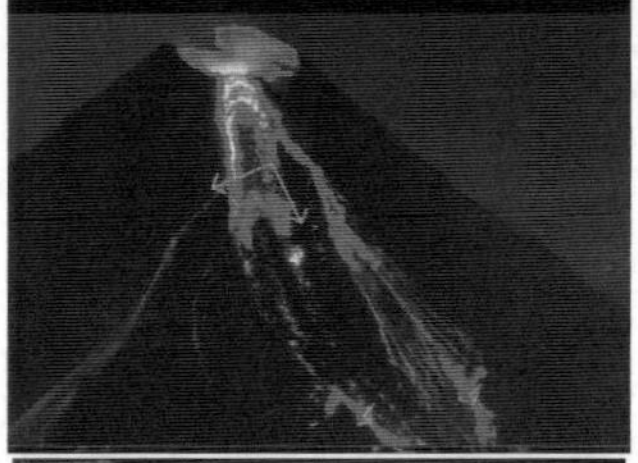	Hawaiano	914.236
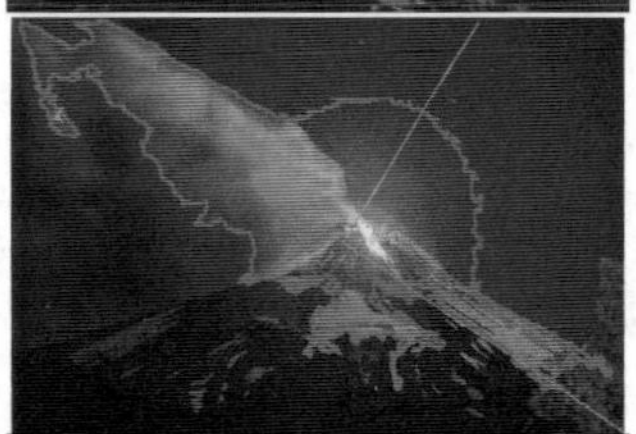	Vulcaniano	1587.326
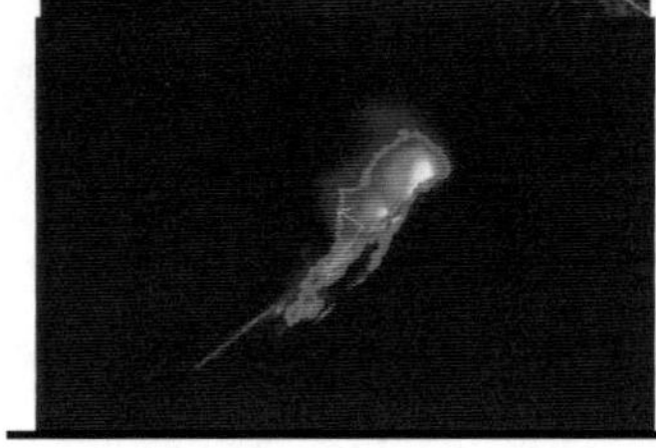	Peleano	1680.236

Tabla 2. Comparación de la red neuronal artificial con el algoritmo descrito anteriormente que detecta el color rojo y usa la transformada de Hotelling, para esta prueba se utilizarán las 50 imágenes de test que no pertenecen a las utilizadas en el entrenamiento de la red neuronal, además estarán presentes imágenes con diferentes tipos de erupción y se determina el tiempo de detección y el porcentaje de detección entre los algoritmos

Algoritmo usado	Porcentaje de detección $\%detección = \frac{\#img\ detectadas * 100\%}{50}$	Velocidad de detección [ms] (promedio)
Red Neuronal Artificial (RNA)	$\frac{46 * 100\%}{50} = 92\%$	1632.745
Detección de color mediante separación de elementos por capas	$\frac{38 * 100\%}{50} - 76\%$	925.632

Para evaluar el algoritmo desarrollado se comparó con el descrito anteriormente que detecta el color rojo y usa la transformada de Hotelling. Como se observa en la Tabla 2, la red neuronal presenta una tasa de detección mayor en comparación con el otro algoritmo, esto se debe a que no basa su funcionamiento solo en el color como el otro algoritmo, sino que puede generalizar a partir de su entrenamiento para detectar los diferentes fenómenos volcánicos. Con respecto a la velocidad de detección se puede observar que la red neuronal tarda más, esto se debe al número de neuronas presentes en la capa oculta ya que a mayor número de neuronas aumenta el costo computacional, pero a pesar de esto se ha obtenido una buena velocidad de detección que servirá para la generación de alertas.

5 Conclusiones

En la presente investigación se ha explorado la utilidad de las redes neuronales con arquitectura perceptrón multicapa como un método para la estimación de posibles erupciones volcánicas, obteniendo como resultado un algoritmo que permite una tasa de estimación de erupciones cercana al 92% para las 2 bases de datos (Mexican volcanoes database, Landsat) de prueba que se usaron en este trabajo y una velocidad de detección muy aceptable por lo cual la implementación de este algoritmo es el más adecuado para la aplicación que se ha descrito.

Se han encontrado errores en el reconocimiento mediante redes neuronales que son consecuencia de defectos en la segmentación de la imagen. Al tratarse de imágenes que son adquiridas en ambientes hostiles y presentan muchas interferencias que no permiten un procesamiento adecuado, y esto es un factor importante por lo complicado de elaborar algoritmos eficaces a la hora de separar correctamente cada característica.

A medida que se incrementan el número de neuronas de la capa oculta en una RNA se requiere menos tiempo de entrenamiento, pero, se incrementa el costo computacional del algoritmo. Se debe definir el número de neuronas en cada capa, en especial en la capa oculta ya que el incremento de neuronas reduce la velocidad de procesamiento para la obtención de datos en tiempo real, es decir, es necesario mantener un equilibrio entre el número de neuronas que cumplen el propósito y que no incrementen los cálculos de la red.

Para un funcionamiento correcto por parte de la RNA se necesita un entrenamiento supervisado, donde se va verificando que las neuronas de salida se comporten igual a los targets establecidos a partir de patrones conocidos, los cuales aparecen en una secuencia aleatoria. Para los entrenamientos se debe incluir una rutina de ruido para que los algoritmos de ejecución de la RNA sean robustos, es decir, respondan de una determinada forma ante entradas que no tienen relación con erupciones volcánicas.

Referencias

1. Kalchbrenner, Nal, Edward Grefenstette, and Phil Blunsom. "A convolutional neural network for modelling sentences." arXiv preprint arXiv:1404.2188 (2014).
2. Zare, Mohammad, et al. "Landslide susceptibility mapping at Vaz Watershed (Iran) using an artificial neural network model: a comparison between multilayer perceptron (MLP) and radial basic function (RBF) algorithms." Arabian Journal of Geosciences 6.8 (2013): 2873-2888.
3. Almaráz Sánchez, Edgardo Cristóbal. "Diseño aerodinámico de un sistema aéreo no tripulado (UAS) para vigilancia volcánica en México." (2017).
4. Marcillo, Pablo, Iván Bernal, and Carlos Macías. "Sistema para el Monitoreo y Cuantificación de Flujos de Lodo Basado en una Red Inalámbrica de Sensores." Revista Politécnica 35.1 (2015): 74.
5. Khaloo, A. and Lattanzi, D. "Extracting Structural Models through Computer Vision". Structures Congress (2015): 538-548.
6. Halfawy, M. and Hengmeechai, J. "Integrated Vision Based System for Automated Defect Detection in Sewer Closed Circuit Television Inspection Videos." J. Comput. Civ. Eng. (2014).
7. Behzad Nazarbakhsh, and Azizah Abd Manaf. "Image Pre-processing Techniques for En-hancing the Performance of Real-Time Face Recognition System Using PCA". Bio-inspiring Cyber Security and Cloud Services: Trends and Innovations (2014): 383-422
8. Gomes Samuel L., Rebouças Elizângela de S., Neto Edson Cavalcanti, Papa João P., Albu-querque Victor H. C., Rebouças Filho Pedro P., Tavares João Manuel R. S. "Embedded real-time speed limit sign recognition using image processing and machine learning techniques". Neural Computing and Applications (2016): 1- 12.
9. Viteri Francisco, Barrera Kevin, Cruz Christyan, Mendoza Darío. " Using Computer Vision Techniques to Generate Embedded Systems for Monitoring Volcanoes in Ecuador with Trajectory Determination ". Advanced Science Letters (2016).
10. Porwik Piotr, Doroz, Rafal, Orczyk Tomasz (2015). "The k-NN classifier and self-adaptive Hotelling data reduction technique in handwritten signatures recognition". Pattern Analysis and Applications (2015): 983-1001.
11. Spiros V. Georgakopoulos, Sotiris K. Tasoulis, Vassilis P. Plagianakos, Ilias Maglogiannis. "Artificial Neural Networks and Principal Components Analysis for

Detection of Idiopathic Pulmonary Fibrosis in Microscopy Images". 14th International Conference, EANN (2013): 292-301

12. Yeh, Wei-Chang, et al. "Forecasting wind power in the Mai Liao Wind Farm based on the multi-layer perceptron artificial neural network model with improved simplified swarm opti-mization." International Journal of Electrical Power & Energy Systems 55 (2014): 741-748.
13. Werner, Gabor Á., and László Hanka. "Tuning an artificial neural network to increase the ef-ficiency of a fingerprint matching algorithm." Applied Machine Intelligence and Informatics (SAMI), 2016 IEEE 14th International Symposium on. IEEE, 2016.
14. Burr, Geoffrey W., et al. "Experimental demonstration and tolerancing of a large-scale neural network (165 000 synapses) using phase-change memory as the synaptic weight element." IEEE Transactions on Electron Devices 62.11 (2015): 3498-3507.
15. Goyal, Vishal, Vinay Kumar Deolia, and Tripti Nath Sharma. "Robust sliding mode control for nonlinear discrete-time delayed systems based on neural network." Intelligent Control and Automation 6.01 (2015): 75

Secure Push notification service based on MQTT Protocol for mobile platforms

Carlos Silva[1, 2], Renato Toasa[1, 4], H. David Martinez[3], Jorge Veloz[2] and Cristian Gallardo[4]

[1]School of Technology and Management, Polytechnic Institute of Leiria, Portugal,
{2162317, 2162342}@my.ipleiria.pt
[2]Universidad Técnica de Manabí, Ecuador,
jveloz@utm.edu.ec
[3]Universidad de Guayaquil, Ecuador,
hector.martinezvi@ug.edu.ec
[4]Universidad Técnica de Ambato, Ecuador,
cmgallardop@gmail.com

Abstract. Push notification is conceptually an event-based mechanism where remote servers push events to smartphone client apps when these occur.
The communication between the MQTT client and the remote server has been performed via TCP by default, causing certain level of uncertainty in the obtaining data, which is necessary to enhance an adequate configuration of the server with the aim of generating security in the transmission and integrity of the data.
This paper present the secure MQTT services implement on android and iOS clients, developing a push notification service that can be used to solve the problem of instant pushing several messages on a company. It also details the different areas in which the MQTT protocol could be applied.

Keywords: push notification, service, secure, MQTT, android, iOS, SSL

1. Introduction

Smartphone adoption continues to permeate society, majority of people of the world now use a smartphone. The people are increasingly dependent on their mobile phones to get real-time messages, so instant messaging is particularly important, this comes in conjunction with push / notification systems [1].

Currently, the push/notification technology has become the most popular network of technology, many companies are aiming at the technology for research, and launched their own products, and apply this technology to many operating systems [2].

It is an irrefutable fact that in the last few years mobile phones have revolutionized the whole world, and part of this important world trend has involved changing the way people communicate with one another; one of the elements of this change has been instant messaging service, for developer push notification services is possible to use various protocol such as XMPP, Websockets, CoAP and MQTT. These protocols are used in each different situation. In particular, MQTT protocol was designed to work on low-power devices nicely as a light-weight protocol and has been used in many IoT devices and instant messaging systems [3].

MQTT protocol become our first choice because of its obvious advantages. It is an open, simple, lightweight messaging protocol and easy to implement. Initially it was designed to connect large numbers of remote sensors and control devices. The protocol has been applied in a variety of embedded systems. For example: hospitals use this protocol to communicate with pacemakers and other medical equipment supplier. Oil and gas companies use it to monitor oil pipeline thousands of miles away [4].

A mobile application that uses MQTT sends and receives messages by calling an MQTT library. Messages are exchanged through an MQTT messaging server. The MQTT client and server handle the complexities of delivering messages reliably to the mobile application and keep the price of network management under control [5]. Also, the goal of the protocol is to provide a reliable service that consumes few resources. So that's why in the protocol itself are only a few security mechanisms clearly specified. But in all implementations with Mqtt other security standards are used, like SSL/TLS for transport security, for this reason It can be stated that the data sent through Mqtt are protected[6].

MQTT applications run on mobile devices, such as smartphones and tablets. MQTT is also used in telemetry to receive data from sensors and to control them remotely. For mobile devices and sensors, MQTT offers a highly scalable publication / subscription protocol with secure delivery

In this paper, the secure service based on the MQTT protocol in android and iOS platforms is proposed to achieve instant messaging push. The process of subscription of the topic and the publication of messages in that topic is done in real time, in this way the message push / notification can be optimized and innovated.

The rest of the paper is organized as follows. Section II describes the context and state of the art. Section III presents the MQTT Protocol functionality, while the secure communication is shown in Section IV. Next, in Section V the Implementation of Mqtt Protocol is detailed, Next, in Section VI the applicable areas of Mqtt, in section VII the test and results and in section VIII the conclusions are presented.

2. Context and State of the Art

Currently there are few reports of MQTT usage to develop system based in mobile platform, the search for articles regarding this subject has revealed itself unsuccessful, but a wider search helped to find cases of MQTT, that are detailed below:

In the work [7] they created a system for acquiring and transmitting data via Bluetooth to an android mobile platform using the MQTT library for the communication with a remote server, where the data is stored in a database and visualization of Pulse Oximeter. In this work the client authentication via SSL was not implemented, the communication between the client and the remote server has been realized via TCP, so the security in the transmission and the medical data integrity is not warranted, causing a certain level of uncertainty in the obtaining data, because the information can be susceptible to capture and modification during the transmission process.

There are also some industry works on mobile push notification services. Currently the push notification service providers can be divided into two categories. Some of the services/products provide basic push notification service, and the other services/products provide enhanced push notification services [8].

The basic push notification service providers, such as Apple Push Notification Service [9], Microsoft Push Notification Services [11], can help users to deliver notifications through mobile devices. , these services only provide basic features for messaging service and cannot provide rich user experience. For example, Apple Push Notification Service only support the iOS platform. It makes the user inconvenient when the user need to push a notification to various platforms in most of the cases. However, the service Firebase Cloud Messaging [10], Amazon Device Messaging [12] and Facebook Push Notification [13] support pushing a notification to users with special context properties, these services support more one specific platform. MQTT can be implemented on platforms like android, iOS, python and other platforms and there is documentation on internet about the implementation and how to correct errors that occur during the addition to an existing project.

MQTT relies on TCP as transport protocol, which means by default the connection does not use an encrypted communication. To encrypt the whole MQTT communication, most many MQTT brokers allow to use TLS instead of plain TCP, when has been using the username and password fields of the MQTT connect packet for authentication and authorization mechanisms, the administrator should strongly consider using TLS in MQTT broker. Is the user's responsibility to address security issues for MQTT and MQTT-SN. In this direction, it is suggested to enable security for MQTT by envisaging SSL/TLS with certificates and session key management. [14].

3. MQTT Protocol functionality

MQTT protocol is the message push protocol released by IBM. It was designed to transfer a message reliably under the low-bandwidth network condition and long network delay. Currently, everything that is a web of things software company, Amazon IoT use MQTT protocol [4].

The MQTT push protocol defines the transmission Quality of Service (QoS) levels, which is an agreement between sender and receiver of a single message regarding the guarantees of delivery of message. There are three levels of QoS in MQTT [15, 16].

- QoS 0: At most once. Send a message at most once and do not guarantee to deliver a message.
- QoS 1: At least once. Send a message at least once and it is possible to deliver a message more than once.
- QoS 2: Exactly once Send a message exactly once with 4 way handshaking.

MQTT protocol consists of subscriber, publish and message broker. A client who wants to get the massage belong to certain topic subscribes topic to a message broker server. If another client publishes the message with the certain topic, then a message broker server republish the message to the subscriber who already subscribes with the certain topic. Topic is a message string to filter messages for each client and it consists of one or more topic levels. Each levels is distinguished by slash (/) and the structure looks like tree structure [17].

The Publishing/Subscribing Message Model. The design is based on publishing/subscribing messaging model. In this model, the publisher and subscriber are both clients, the message destination is called theme. By connecting to the message broker, they transfer data across the network. Publishers send a specific topic of messages to message broker, subscribers subscribe specific news topics to the message broker, and the connection between the subscriber and publishers managed by the message broker. When the message broker receives the published messages, it delivers the message to subscriber. Publishing/subscribing messaging model allows multiple providers to publish messages to the same topic. It also allows multiple users to subscribe messages with a subject [18]. Then the message broker will broadcast to different subscribers, the figure 1 show the publish - subscribe architecture

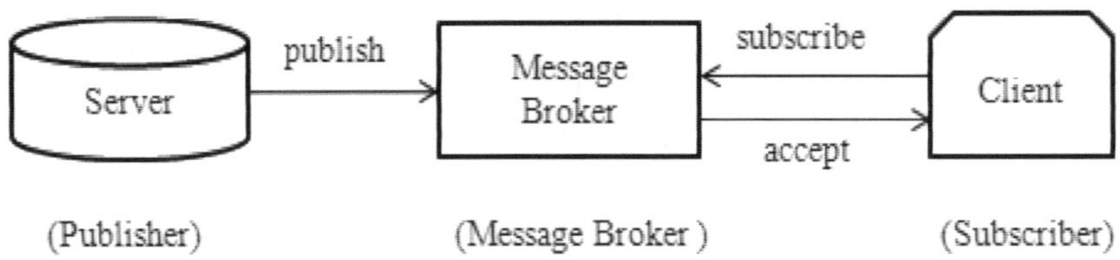

Fig. 1. Overall Architecture Diagram

As a message broker, it completes message routing function, receiving the message sent by the server, and then forwarded. Subscribers subscribe to the interesting topics, to submit information to the Message Broker, and to maintain a persistent connection. If publisher check into a new message, this message will be released by topic category. Depending on the topic, the Message Agent receives the message as well as the client's subscription, and releases this news to the corresponding phone, the figure 2 show the push process in the Mqtt protocol [17].

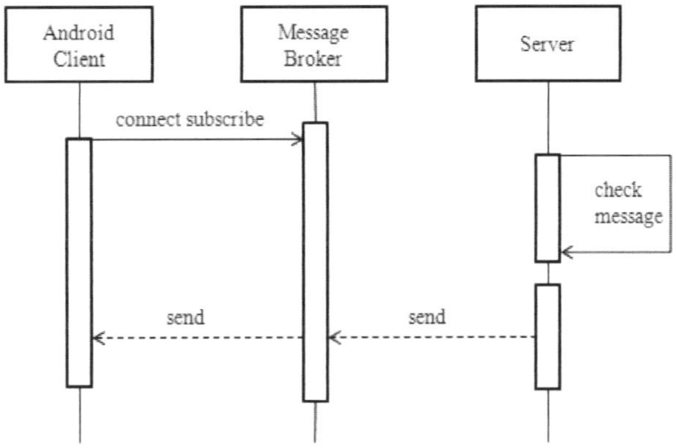

Fig 2. Push Process

The process in detail is: First, connecting MQTT. The client specifies the message broker host 's IP address and port number assigned by MQTT, establishes a connection and creates MQTT client object. MQTT object subscribes to a topic, requiring both subscription array parameter and service quality array parameter.

Second, releasing Information to the Agency. Interface server directly using the API functions provided by MQTT, requires theme, message, service quality and other parameters. Send push messages to the Message Broker.

Third, receiving a Message from the Agent. To make sure that the subscriber can receive messages, you must create a callback function and register in MQTT client. Callback function informs system that topic message has arrived at the client.

4. Secure communication

There is a drawback when using MQTT over TLS: security comes at a cost in terms of CPU usage and communication overhead. While the additional CPU usage is typically negligible on the broker, it can be a problem for very constrained devices which are not designed for compute intensive tasks. Techniques like Session

Resumption can drastically improve the TLS performance.TLS session resumption techniques allow to reuse an already negotiated TLS session after reconnecting to the server, so the client and server don't need to do the full TLS handshake again. It's important to note, that not all TLS libraries implement all session resumption techniques, some don't even implement any session resumption mechanism. [19]

The Port 8883 is standardized for a secured MQTT connection. The standardized name at IANA is "secure-mqtt" and port 8883 is exclusively reserved for MQTT over TLS.

Security in MQTT is divided in multiple layers. Each layer prevents different kind of attacks. The goal of the protocol is to provide a really lightweight and easy to use communication protocol for the internet of things. So that's why in the protocol itself are only a few security mechanisms clearly specified. But in all common implementations other security standards are used, like SSL/TLS for transport security [19].

4.1. Network Level

Using a physically secure network or VPN as foundation for any communication between clients and broker is one way to provide a secure and trustworthy connection. This would be suitable for gateway applications, where the gateway is connected to devices on the one hand and with the broker over VPN on the other side.

4.2. Transport Level

When the goal is to provide confidentiality in most cases TLS/SSL is being used for transport encryption. It provides a secure and proven way to make sure nobody can read along and even authenticate both sides, when using client certification authentication. We will also cover in detail the feasibility of TLS on constrained devices.

4.3. Application Level

On the transport level it can be ensured that the communication is encrypted and the identity is authenticated. The MQTT protocol provides a client identifier and username/password credentials, which can also be used to authenticate devices on the application level. These properties are provided by the protocol itself. When it comes to authorization or what each device is allowed to do, it lays in the hand of the broker implementation, how to handle it. Another possibility is to use payload encryption on the application level in order to make the transmitted information secure even without having a full-fledged transport encryption. [19]

Connections between the MQTT client and the queue manager are always initiated by the MQTT client. The MQTT client is always the SSL client. Client authentication of the server and server authentication of the MQTT client are both optional.

To implement SSL in MQTT brokers, it is necessary to perform the following actions:

- Generate the server certificates
- Configure SSL in MQTT Broker
- Configure MQTT Client for use SSL/TLS

4.4. MQTT Client configuration

To authenticate the MQTT client using SSL, the client connects to a telemetry channel using SSL. It must specify a TCP port that corresponds to a telemetry channel that is configured to authenticate SSL clients. For example, at the client:

```
MQTTClient mqttClient = new
MqttClient("ssl://www.example.org:8883","clientId1");
mqttClient.connect();
```

Add the digital certificate of the client, signed either using the private key of the client, or by a CA, to the password protected keystore on the client. If the certificate has a keychain, you can add the certificates from the keychain to the store. When the server verifies the client certificate, it uses the certificates sent by the client to match against certificates in its keystore. It is looking for the first match in the key chain with a certificate that it has. The remainder of the keychain is ignored. The MQTT client sends all the certificates in its keystore to the server. If the server authenticates any of the key chains the client sends, then the client is authenticated [4].

5. Implementation of Mqtt Protocol

5.1. General Architecture

The service proposed in this article allows the user to enter the server to be connected and define the port, this is done because some companies have their own servers and ports enabled, and do not require the free servers offered by Mqtt.

Once it is accessed, the user can subscribe the channel or topic in which the messages will be sent, and post messages in the defined channel. All these messages will be available; to be analyzed according to the needs of the people or companies that use the service. Figure 3 shows the service MQTT architecture and the push notification system.

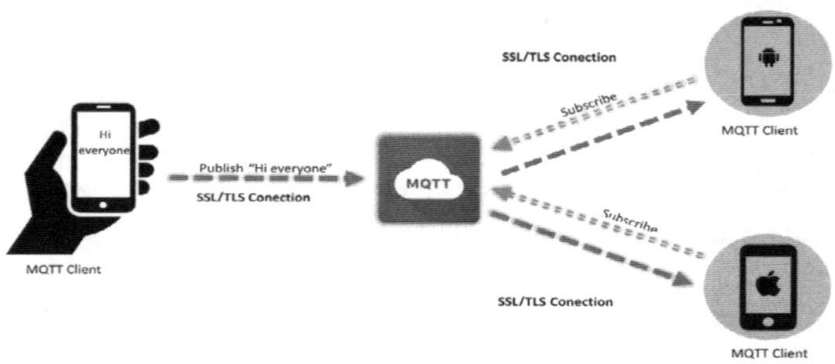

Fig. 3. Service MQTT architecture

5.2. Server Configuration

The server used is Ubuntu 16.04 of 32 bits, for install Encrypted Certificates we'll install the official client from an Ubuntu PPA, or Personal Package Archive with:

```
sudo add-apt-repository ppa:certbot/certbot
apt-get install certbot
```

Certbot needs to answer a cryptographic challenge issued by the Let's Encrypt API in order to prove we control our domain. It uses ports 80 (HTTP) and/or 443 (HTTPS) to accomplish this. We'll only use port 80, so let's allow incoming traffic on that port now:

```
sudo ufw allow http
```

Now run Certbot to get the certificate. Use the --standalone option to tell Certbot to handle the HTTP challenge request on its own, and --standalone-supported-challenges http-01 limits the communication to port 80. -d is used to specify the domain you'd like a certificate for, and certonly tells Certbot to just retrieve the certificate without doing any other configuration steps.

```
sudo certbot certonly --standalone --standalone-
supported-challenges http-01 -d localhost
```

When running the command, you will be prompted to enter an email address and agree to the terms of service. After doing so, you should see a message telling you the process was successful and where your certificates are stored.

To enable SSL encryption, we need to tell Mosquitto where our Let's Encrypt certificates are stored. Open up the configuration file we previously started:

```
sudo nano /etc/mosquitto/conf.d/default.conf
listener 1883 localhost
listener 8883
certfile /etc/letsencrypt/live/localhost/server.crt
cafile   /etc/letsencrypt/live/localhost/server.crt
keyfile /etc/letsencrypt/live/localhost/server.key
```

We're adding two separate listener blocks to the config. The first, listener 1883 localhost, updates the default MQTT listener on port 1883, which is what we've been connecting to so far. 1883 is the standard unencrypted MQTT port. Listener 8883 sets up an encrypted listener on port 8883. This is the standard port for MQTT + SSL, often referred to as MQTTS. The next three lines, certfile, cafile, and keyfile, all point Mosquitto to the appropriate Let's Encrypt files to set up the encrypted connections.

Since mqtt works with several users, it is necessary to configure Mqtt to handle connections by user and password, mosquitto includes a utility to generate a special password file called mosquitto_passwd.

```
sudo mosquitto_passwd -c /etc/mosquitto/passwd user
```

Now we'll open up a new configuration file for Mosquitto y add the next lines For use this password file to require logins for all connections

```
sudo nano /etc/mosquitto/conf.d/default.conf
allow_anonymous false
password_file /etc/mosquitto/passwd
```

Now mqtt allows connections by user and password, with encrypted messages. The operation is shown below:

```
mosquitto_sub -h localhost -t test -u "user" -P
"password"

mosquitto_pub -h localhost -t test -m "hello" -p
8883 --cafile /etc/ssl/certs/server.crt -u
"ipleiria" -P "ipleiria"

mosquitto_sub -h localhost -t test -u "user1" -P
"secretpassword"
hello
```

6. Applicable Areas

The applications for the MQTT protocol are infinite; here is a list of some applicable areas and their respective example:

6.1. Personal and Home(IoT)

The IoT is already connecting computing devices, appliances, humans and other living beings through the Internet. MQTT clients are very simple to implement.

MQTT can be used in this area as communication technology between devices, for example: it is possible to send information, in this case a power command to all devices in real time when a user arrives at the smart house, plus the flexibility of this protocol allows each device to be controlled individually because the MQTT architecture is based on publish subscribe architecture.

6.2. Wireless sensor networks

Wireless sensor networks (WSN), sometimes called wireless sensor and actuator networks (WSAN) are spatially distributed autonomous sensors to monitor physical or environmental conditions, such as temperature, sound, pressure, etc. MQTT protocol can be used in this field, and has many advantages over other protocols, because it is a protocol that consumes very little bandwidth and can be used in most embedded devices with few resources (CPU, RAM, etc.).

6.3. Health field

For example, in sensing and monitoring application, in health field is necessary the obtaining and presentation of medical data in real time. For example, the body sensors that have implemented an MQTT Client can emit information of the state of the patient to the devices of all doctors from different areas such as cardiology, allergology, infectology, neurology or only to a specific doctor, all this is possible because the MQTT protocol is light and based on a publisher / subscriber architecture.

6.4. Enterprise

In the companies can be used for the development of internal messaging application (Push notification), for real-time communication with company workers, especially in health care companies such as renal dialysis centers, intensive care centers , among others, in those places where notifying certain doctors about an event is very important issue when the time is a decisive factor.

6.5. Web and social Networks

The MQTT protocol can be used for the development of mobile applications that allow users to interact with each other through text messages, currently there are many instant messaging services such as facebook messenger, whatsApp, telegram and instagram, snapchat, among others, one of the problems they have is that messages and information from users using these services is stored in international companies, generating at some point less privacy for users.

7. Test and Results

In order to perform the tests of the service proposed in this research, two mobile applications prototype were developed, one for android platform and the other for iOS platform, the figure 4 show the interfaces of applications.

Functionality tests were performed on these platforms in order to verify the operation of the service or push / notification with Mqtt. Obtaining the following results:

The tests were performed in virtual machine in VMware Fusion 8.5.7 with the following characteristics:

CPU : 1 CPU virtual

RAM: 1 GB

Operating System: Ubuntu 16.04.2 LTS 32bits

The MQTT server used was mosquitto version 1.4.8.

7.1. Mobile Application

The first mobile application version has been developed for Android and iOS operating system, the iOS application has been developed in Xcode with Swift 3.0.2, Xcode is Apple's official integrated development environment (IDE), and uses the Swift programming language, which is focused on developing native applications for iOS and Mac OS X [20].Has been used the SwiftMQTT library for the application prototype [21]. The Figure 4 shows the main interfaces of the iOS application.

Fig 4. iOS application screens

The application for Android operating systems is developed in Android Studio 2.3 with JAVA programming language and is compatible with Android 4.1 (Jelly Bean) and above, has been used the Eclipse Paho libraries. The Paho Java Client is an MQTT client library written in Java for developing applications that run on the JVM or other Java compatible platforms such as Android.[22].The Figure 5 shows the main interfaces of Android application.

Fig. 5. Android application screens

The functionality test was performed on a local server with 15 users, subscribed to the same topic, and these made publications, the service worked correctly without delays or lost messages. The Mqtt protocol is designed to support thousands of connected users; this will depend on how the service is implemented.

Performance tests were performed on the mosquito server, sending messages to the server using certificates and not using it, showing that in a total 100.000 messages using certificates for communication between the client and the server decreases server performance between 60% and 65 % in the table 1 the results can be visualized.

During performance tests using certificates for communication between the MQTT server and the client, the server uses six times more CPU and twice the amount of RAM to perform the operations.

Table 1. Performance test on mosquito server

Quantity	Connection Type	Average message time	Total Time	Loss rate
100.000 messages	Normal	11 mls – 12 mls	20 min 3s 911mls	0.00%
100.000 messages	SSL	19 mls – 20 mls	33 min 16s 256mls	0.004%

8. Conclusions

Can be assured that MQTT is the protocol has used to provide new and revolutionary performance. It opens new areas for messaging use cases. As MQTT specializes in low-bandwidth, high-latency environments, it is considered an ideal protocol for machine-to-machine (M2M) communication. The MQTT design makes it appealing for the exponential emerging Internet of Things (IoT) market and new messaging systems.

During the implementation of the service, it is necessary to enhance an adequate configuration of the server with the aim of generating security in the transmission and integrity of the data because the information that is sent can be susceptible to capture and modification during the transmission process.

TLS is implemented properly on the client and server side, you make sure that no eavesdropper can intercept your communication and you get that additional layer of security that is important for application-level authentication and authorization.

When configuring an encrypted communication through certificates, it is necessary to verify the characteristics of the equipment, in an unencrypted communication the equipment does not consume many of its resources, but when an encrypted communication is used, the equipment increases the use of its means, making the equipment work slow.

References

1. Nielsen NewsWire, "State of the App-Nation—a Year of Change and Growth in US Smartphones," May 2012, [Online]. Available: www.nielsen.com.
2. H. C. Hwang, J. Park, and J. G. Shon, "Design and implementation of a reliable message transmission system based on mqtt protocol in IoT," Wireless Personal Communications, vol. 91, no. 4, pp. 1765–1777,2016. [Online]. Available: http://dx.doi.org/10.1007/s11277-016-3398-2
3. K. Tang, Y. Wang, H. Liu, Y. Sheng, X. Wang, and Z. Wei, "Design and implementation of push notification system based on the mqtt protocol," in International Conference on Information Science and Computer Applications (ISCA 2013), 2013, pp. 116–119
4. IBM. (2017, March) "Introduction to mqtt". [Online]. Available: https://www.ibm.com/support/knowledgecenter/SSFKSJ_7.5.0/com.ibm.mm.tc.doc/tc00000_.htm
5. K. M. Bell, D. N. Bleau, and J. T. Davey, "Push notification service,"Nov. 22 2011, uS Patent 8,064,896
6. HiveMQ, "Introducing the MQTT Security Fundamentals". [Online]. Available: http://www.hivemq.com/blog/introducing-the-mqtt-security-fundamentals
7. Barata, D., Louzada, G., Carreiro, A., & Damasceno, A. (2013). System of acquisition, transmission, storage and visualization of Pulse Oximeter and ECG data using Android and MQTT. Procedia Technology, 9, 1265-1272
8. Pan, Z., Liang, X., Zhou, Y. C., Ge, Y., & Zhao, G. T. (2015, June). Intelligent Push Notification for Converged Mobile Computing and Internet of Things. In *Web Services (ICWS), 2015 IEEE International Conference on* (pp. 655-662). IEEE.
9. Google, "Firebase Cloud Messaging (FCM) for Android, Available:"https://firebase.google.com/docs/cloud-messaging/l", 2017, [Online; accessed 24 March-2017].
10. Apple, "Apple Push Notification Service", Available:"https://developer.apple.com/library/content/documentation/NetworkingInternet/Conceptual/RemoteNotificationsPG/APNSOverview.html#//apple_ref/doc/uid/TP40008194-CH8-SW1, 2016, [Online; accessed 24-March-2017].
11. Microsoft, "Push notifications for Windows Phone 8", Available:"https://msdn.microsoft.com/en-us/library/windows/apps/ff402558(v=vs.105).aspx,2016, [Online; accessed 24-March-2017].
12. Amazon, "Amazon Device Messaging API," https://developer.amazon.com/device-messaging, 2017, [Online; accessed 24-March-2017].

13. Facebook, "Push Notifications", Available:"https://developers.facebook.com/blog/post/2016/04/12/facebook-analytics-for-apps-adds-push-notifications-deeper-insights/", 2017, [Online; accessed 24-March-2017].
14. Singh, M., Rajan, M. A., Shivraj, V. L., & Balamuralidhar, P. (2015, April). Secure mqtt for internet of things (IoT). In *Communication Systems and Network Technologies (CSNT), 2015 Fifth International Conference on* (pp. 746-751). IEEE.
15. IBM MQTT Protocol Specification. Access Dec 22, 2015, http://public.dhe.ibm.com/software/dw/webservices/ws-mqtt/mqtt-v3r1.html.
16. Lee, S., Jung, I., Kim, H., & Ju, H. (2013). The design of integrated mobile SNS gateway structure. In 2013 15th Asia-Pacific network operations and management symposium (APNOMS) (pp. 1–3).
17. Hunkeler, U., Truong, H. L., & Stanford-Clark, A. (2008, January). MQTT-S—A publish/subscribe protocol for Wireless Sensor Networks. In *Communication systems software and middleware and workshops, 2008. comsware 2008. 3rd international conference on* (pp. 791-798). IEEE.
18. Gero Mühl. Large scale content based publish subscribe systems: [PhD Thesis]. Darmstadt University of Technology, 2002.
19. HiveMQ, "Approach to security in MQTT", 2017, Available: "http://www.hivemq.com/blog/introducing-the-mqtt-security-fundamentals" [Online; accessed 25-March-2017].
20. A. Inc. "Apple developer". [Online]. Available: https://developer.apple.com/develop/
21. Adolfo Martinelli, "Swift MQTT", 2016, [Online]Available: https://github.com/aciidb0mb3r/SwiftMQTT
22. Lem, "Android MQTT", 2016, Available: [Online] https://github.com/bytehala/android-mqtt-quickstart.

Agile Management for Research Groups: An Exploratory Study

Gladys E. Carrillo[1], Mónica Villavicencio[1], Jhonny Pincay[1] and Edwin F. Boza[1]

[1] Escuela Superior Politécnica del Litoral, ESPOL, Facultad de Ingeniería en Electricidad y Computación, Campus Gustavo Galindo Km 30.5 Vía Perimetral,
P.O. Box 09-01-5863 Guayaquil, Ecuador
{gecarri, mvillavi, jvpincay}@espol.edu.ec,
eboza@fiec.espol.edu.ec

Abstract. Research groups in academic environments face many challenges when it comes to effectively managing the development of their projects, since they are mostly conformed by students and professors that commonly work in several projects at once. To mitigate the underlying difficulties and to improve the performance of research groups, the application of agile methodologies has been suggested to manage the development of research projects in the software development area. Contributing to get better insights about the specificities related to works exercised by research groups, this article presents the results of an exploratory study conducted at an Ecuadorian university. Specifically, the study focuses on identifying how they are formed, the methodologies and tools used, and the difficulties that researchers must cope with. Suggestions are offered in terms of concrete actions oriented to improve the performance of university research groups.

Keywords: roject management, research project, agile management, research group

1 Introducción

La generación y transferencia de conocimiento a través del desarrollo de proyectos de investigación, es parte fundamental de las actividades que deben cumplir los centros de educación superior del mundo. Estos proyectos se pueden realizar tanto dentro de centros de investigación, con estructuras jerárquicas y departamentales de tipo empresarial, como en pequeños grupos o laboratorios de investigación, usualmente conformados y dirigidos por uno o varios profesores que desean llevar a cabo proyectos propios en sus áreas de interés y que involucran a estudiantes de distintos niveles de formación superior.

Los proyectos de investigación y desarrollo en entornos académicos -por su propia naturaleza- presentan características particulares, tales como: 1) alta incertidumbre en la obtención de resultados; 2) cambios frecuentes en el rumbo del proyecto los cuales dependen de los resultados parciales obtenidos; 3) desarrollos por fases; 4) alta probabilidad de rotación del personal; y 5) periodos alternados de actividad dependiendo de la disponibilidad de investigadores interesados en el área específica [6].

Dado que las tres primeras características mencionadas rememoran aquellas de los proyectos desarrollados con metodologías ágiles, esto es: entorno de alta incertidumbre, aceptación de cambios en los requisitos y desarrollo por ciclos o fases, se han presentado propuestas de adaptación de metodologías ágiles para la administración de proyectos y grupos de investigación [1], [4], [5], [7]. Sin embargo, poco se ha aportado sobre la gestión de la rotación del personal y los periodos alternados de actividad.

Con frecuencia, los equipos de desarrollo de proyectos de investigación tienen entre sus miembros a estudiantes o investigadores visitantes. La presencia de estos participantes es temporal y genera un efecto de rotación del personal, lo que a su vez provoca una disminución en la productividad debido al tiempo que requiere un nuevo participante en aprender acerca del proyecto en curso.

Además, en proyectos de investigación abiertos -donde participan estudiantes escogiendo líneas de investigación de acuerdo a sus áreas de interés- se producen periodos de inactividad entre el momento en que un estudiante termina su ciclo y el momento en que se integra un nuevo estudiante interesado en continuar con dicha línea de investigación. Este lapso -en la mayoría de los casos- impide una transferencia de conocimiento adecuada de un estudiante al siguiente, acentuando el efecto negativo de la rotación del personal.

En el presente trabajo se muestran los resultados de un estudio exploratorio sobre la operación de tres grupos de investigación de una universidad ecuatoriana. A partir de los resultados obtenidos, se presentan recomendaciones a fin de mejorar la administración del conocimiento y mitigar los efectos de la alta rotación de personal y periodos de inactividad en el desarrollo de proyectos de investigación.

El resto del documento se organiza de la siguiente manera: en la Sección 2 se resumen los trabajos relacionados con la gestión de grupos de investigación y la adaptación de metodologías ágiles; a continuación, en la Sección 3 se detalla la metodología seguida en el desarrollo del estudio exploratorio; en la Sección 4 se exponen los resultados obtenidos; las Secciones 5 y 6 expone el análisis de los resultados y las conclusiones, respectivamente; el artículo finaliza con Sección 7 en la cual se presentan los posibles trabajos futuros.

2 Trabajos Relacionados

2.1 Gestión de Grupos de Investigación

La conformación de los equipos de desarrollo de proyectos de investigación depende -en gran medida- de la entidad a la que pertenecen y los tipos de proyectos a desarrollar. Los grupos de investigación formados por iniciativa de profesores, generalmente incluyen estudiantes que trabajan en un único proyecto a la vez. Por otro lado, los grupos que se forman en centros o laboratorios de I&D (investigación y desarrollo) suelen estar conformados tanto por estudiantes como por profesionales especialistas en alguna disciplina o herramienta, y con frecuencia participan en más de un proyecto a la vez [5]. Es habitual que un mismo profesor dirija más de un grupo de investigación, conformados por uno o varios miembros, quienes a su vez pueden participar en varios proyectos simultáneamente.

Omar y Ahmad [9] llevaron a cabo un estudio para medir cómo los factores de sobrecarga de trabajo, liderazgo en el equipo y el ambiente en el grupo de trabajo, influyen en la efectividad de un grupo de investigación en el ámbito académico. Las medidas que utilizaron para medir la efectividad fueron: 1) la productividad de la investigación, que se refiere al número de artículos terminados y aceptados para publicación y 2) las reacciones afectivas de los miembros del equipo, como son la satisfacción y la frustración. Los resultados de los cuestionarios aplicados a 292 miembros de grupos de investigación de cuatro universidades de Malasia revelaron lo siguiente: 1) una relación directa positiva entre el ambiente en el grupo de trabajo y la satisfacción del investigador, 2) que la sobrecarga de trabajo influye en la frustración del investigador, 3) que el liderazgo en el grupo de trabajo, influye positivamente en la satisfacción individual y únicamente ejerce un efecto mediador en la productividad del equipo de trabajo [9].

Según Henderson [3], los diferentes aspectos que se deben considerar para llevar a cabo un proyecto de investigación exitoso son: 1) la administración del riesgo, 2) la administración de los grupos de trabajo, y 3) el desarrollo de estrategias de comunicación. Henderson propone tomar en cuenta los riesgos presentes en los proyectos de investigación, entre los que se encuentra la salida de alguno de los miembros del grupo de investigación. Como parte de las acciones para disminuir este riesgo, recomiendan realizar reportes regulares sobre el proyecto y la capacitación a los otros miembros del grupo.

Lima et al. [5] mencionan los aspectos que afectaron negativamente al desenvolvimiento de los equipos de un laboratorio de investigación, luego de la aplicación de una metodología de gestión de proyectos, siendo estos: 1) la falta de compromiso en algunos miembros, al evitar colaborar en la resolución de los problemas de otros integrantes; 2) los errores en la estimación de las capacidades propias de algunos colaboradores -especialmente de los estudiantes- debido a su falta de experiencia en proyectos reales. Siendo éstos los principales factores que influyeron en los retrasos en la entrega de dos proyectos, los autores proponen las siguientes medidas para disminuir dichos riesgos: 1) realizar presentaciones tempranas y capacitaciones de la metodología a implementar; 2) realizar implementaciones piloto de la metodología; y 3) en base a la implementación piloto, evaluar los resultados obtenidos y realizar las adaptaciones necesarias en base a las características particulares propias de la organización.

Vom Brocke y Lippe [2] analizaron los diferentes aspectos relacionados a la administración de proyectos de investigación colaborativos. A través de una revisión sistemática de literatura, identificaron los principales desafíos que tienen estos proyectos y proporcionan un conjunto de guías y técnicas para afrontarlas. Relacionado a la administración del grupo de trabajo, sugieren -entre otras cosas- obligar a los investigadores a planificar definiendo tareas e hitos. También proponen que los investigadores monitoreen sus progresos para identificar desviaciones y corregirlas a tiempo.

Wang y Guan [11] estudiaron la importancia de la administración y generación del conocimiento dentro de los grupos de investigación y recomendaron: 1) establecer mapas o cadenas de conocimiento que permitan a los miembros acceder a la información que necesitan; 2) promover oportunidades de compartición de conocimiento (formales e informales), tales como reuniones o reportes periódicos; 3) alentar y estimular a los miembros a comunicarse y compartir conocimiento con sus pares; y 4) facilitar la obtención de ayuda de expertos externos cuando sea requerido por los miembros del grupo de investigación.

2.2 Adaptación de SCRUM para Administración de Proyectos de Investigación

El uso de metodologías ágiles por parte de profesores y tutores universitarios para el manejo de grupos de investigación, ha sido explorado previamente por Hicks y Foster [4] quienes proponen SCORE (Scrum for Research), una metodología de administración de grupos derivada de Scrum [12]. Las principales características de SCORE son: las reuniones de estado y las reuniones técnicas a demanda. En el primer caso, las reuniones de estado son similares a las reuniones diarias de SCRUM, pero con una menor frecuencia. En éstas participan todos los miembros del grupo de investigación, permitiendo así compartir el conocimiento adquirido entre los miembros que trabajan en distintos proyectos. En el segundo caso, las reuniones técnicas a demanda son organizadas cuando un miembro o equipo requiere discutir con mayor amplitud sobre temas específicos del proyecto en el que trabajan.

Los beneficios de esta propuesta se manifiestan no solo en la optimización del tiempo requerido por los profesores para mantener reuniones de seguimiento con los estudiantes, sino que además permite desarrollar entre los estudiantes un mayor sentido de pertenencia con el grupo. Las reuniones periódicas y frecuentes ayudan a los estudiantes a mantenerse informados sobre los diferentes proyectos que se están desarrollando en el grupo o centro de investigación, aumenta en ellos la empatía respecto a los progresos u obstáculos que encuentran sus compañeros y les permite afrontar de mejor manera los retos que encuentren en sus propios proyectos. Además, la compartición de conocimientos dentro de grupos de investigación facilita y promueve la creación de nuevos conocimientos [11].

Otra metodología basada en los principios de SCRUM es ARDev (Agile Research Development), propuesta por Bezerra et al. [1], que está dirigida específicamente al manejo de proyectos de investigación en tecnologías de software. Partiendo de la premisa de que los procesos de investigación, desarrollo e innovación (I+D+i) requieren producir conocimientos para aplicación inmediata. ARDev provee los lineamientos necesarios que permiten organizar las interacciones entre los participantes del proceso de investigación, promoviendo la comunicación constante y altos niveles de colaboración. ARDev define roles (Research Starter, ARDev Master, Research Team y Stakeholders), fases del proyecto (Concepción, Construcción y Evaluación), actividades, productos y modelos.

Los autores de ARDev evaluaron dicha metodología utilizando dos casos de estudio: un proyecto de investigación dentro de ámbito académico y otro proyecto desarrollado para el sector industrial. Algunos de los resultados obtenidos demuestran que la metodología: 1) puede ser aplicada en todas o parte de las etapas del proceso de investigación y desarrollo; 2) puede ser aplicada tanto en proyectos nuevos como en proyectos ya iniciados; 3) mejora la comunicación, compromiso y organización de los integrantes del proyecto; y 4) aumenta significativamente la documentación de acuerdo a la propuesta. Otra conclusión obtenida es que los grupos del entorno académico fueron mucho más receptivos a la implementación de la nueva metodología.

Marchesi et al. [7] presentan su experiencia del uso de la metodología SCRUM en el manejo de un proyecto de investigación. Proponen que SCRUM puede ser adaptado y utilizado en cualquier contexto en el que un grupo de personas requieran trabajar juntas para alcanzar una meta común. Los autores destacaron la flexibilidad del método, ya que este permite: 1) ser aplicado desde el inicio del proyecto o en una etapa posterior en la que se hayan presentado problemas de manejo del proyecto; y 2) ser utilizado en diferentes escalas organizacionales; por ejemplo, en niveles intra e intergrupales.

Lima et al. [5] también exponen su experiencia en el uso de una adaptación de la metodología SCRUM para el manejo de proyectos de software en un laboratorio de investigación y desarrollo. Analizando los cambios en la cultura organizacional requeridos para aplicar la metodología SCRUM, determinaron que existían dos situaciones de conflicto que demandaban adaptaciones en la mencionada metodología: 1) la imposibilidad de tener al representante del cliente como parte de los equipos de desarrollo; y 2) la dificultad de organizar las reuniones diarias en un mismo horario, debido a que una parte considerable de los miembros de los equipos de desarrollo son pasantes. Los cambios propuestos a la metodología SCRUM fueron: 1) en cada proyecto designar un "product owner" -el mismo que labora de manera permanente en las instalaciones del cliente- para suplir la presencia del cliente a tiempo completo junto al equipo de desarrollo; y 2) el horario de las reuniones diarias se define por consenso entre los miembros del equipo de desarrollo, tomando en consideración las limitaciones de horario de los pasantes.

3 Metodología de Investigación

De entre las diversas estrategias de investigación en Ingeniería de Software [10], se consideró que un "Estudio de campo" (Field Study) y más específicamente un estudio exploratorio, se ajusta de mejor manera para analizar la necesidad y la factibilidad de usar una metodología ágil para gestionar grupos de investigación que –como parte de sus actividades de investigación- desarrollan también software.

El alcance del presente trabajo comprende el análisis de la situación actual del manejo de proyectos de investigación en un entorno académico, incluyendo la medición de los niveles de aceptación o rechazo de los sujetos entrevistados, respecto a la adopción de métodos o herramientas que puedan ayudar a corregir los problemas a los que se enfrentan en los centros de investigación de la universidad.

Para el levantamiento de información, se seleccionaron seis grupos pertenecientes a tres centros de investigación de la Escuela Superior Politécnica del Litoral (ESPOL). Todos los grupos analizados realizan proyectos de investigación relacionados con diversas áreas de las ciencias de la computación como visión por computador, sistemas autónomos, uso de la tecnología en la educación, internet de las cosas; incluso, algunos llevan a cabo proyectos multidisciplinarios en conjunto con profesionales de otras áreas.

El levantamiento de información se realizó en dos fases: 1) Aplicar encuestas a los miembros de los grupos de investigación y 2) Entrevistar a los coordinadores de proyectos de investigación. Para la primera fase, se diseñó un cuestionario de 28 preguntas para recopilar la siguiente información:

- Conformación de grupos de investigación (perfil de los encuestados, tamaño del grupo, número de proyectos que se manejan).
- Uso de metodologías para manejo de proyectos de investigación que incluyan actividades de desarrollo de software.
- Uso de herramientas de manejo de proyectos, escritura de documentos y colaboración entre los miembros del equipo.
- Problemas recurrentes a los que se enfrentan.

Las preguntas del cuestionario y las alternativas de respuestas fueron redactadas en base a la literatura existente (ver Sección 2). En el caso específico de las preguntas relacionadas al uso de herramientas, se realizó una búsqueda para identificar aquellas que permiten la comunicación y colaboración entre los integrantes de un proyecto, que fueran aplicables a grupos de investigación, que fortalezcan las áreas de planificación de proyectos, que permitan crear repositorios de documentos y de código fuente generados durante la ejecución de los proyectos [8].

La segunda fase consistió en llevar a cabo entrevistas semiestructuradas con los coordinadores de proyectos de investigación, con el fin de validar los resultados obtenidos de las encuestas a los miembros de los grupos de investigación.

4 Resultados

En esta sección se describen los resultados obtenidos tanto de la encuesta como de las entrevistas. La encuesta fue respondida por 35 integrantes de grupos de investigación, y la entrevista fue realizada a dos coordinadores de centros de investigación.

4.1 Conformación de los Grupos de Investigación

Para este estudio en particular, los grupos tienen distintos tamaños, existiendo -incluso- grupos de más de 6 integrantes. Sin embargo, la mayor parte (51%) son grupos pequeños de entre 1 y 3 integrantes, como se muestra en la Fig. 1 (a). El 69.4% de los encuestados son de género masculino, mientras que el porcentaje restante (30.6%) son del género femenino.

En cuanto a la edad de los participantes del estudio, el 88% tiene entre 20 y 30 años, siendo la mayoría de ellos estudiantes. Específicamente, el 70% de los encuestados se encuentra cursando estudios de pregrado o postgrado, lo que incide en su tiempo de estadía en un grupo de investigación y podría ser una causa de la rotación de los integrantes de los grupos. Las tareas que normalmente realizan son: revisión de literatura, conducción de experimentos, análisis de resultados, desarrollo de aplicaciones y escritura de artículos científicos.

Aunque la mayoría de los integrantes (63%) trabajan en un único proyecto, el 27% trabaja en más de un proyecto de manera simultánea. Algunos miembros del grupo incluso se encuentran participando en 4 o más proyectos concurrentes (ver Fig. 1 (b)).

En la Fig. 1 (c) observamos que casi tres cuartas partes de los integrantes de los centros de investigación tienen solo formación de pregrado, lo que también se refleja en los años de experiencia reportados en la Fig. 1 (d); el 80% de los integrantes de los grupos de investigación tienen 2 años o menos realizando tareas de investigación, mientras que solo el 20% ha trabajado más de 3 años.

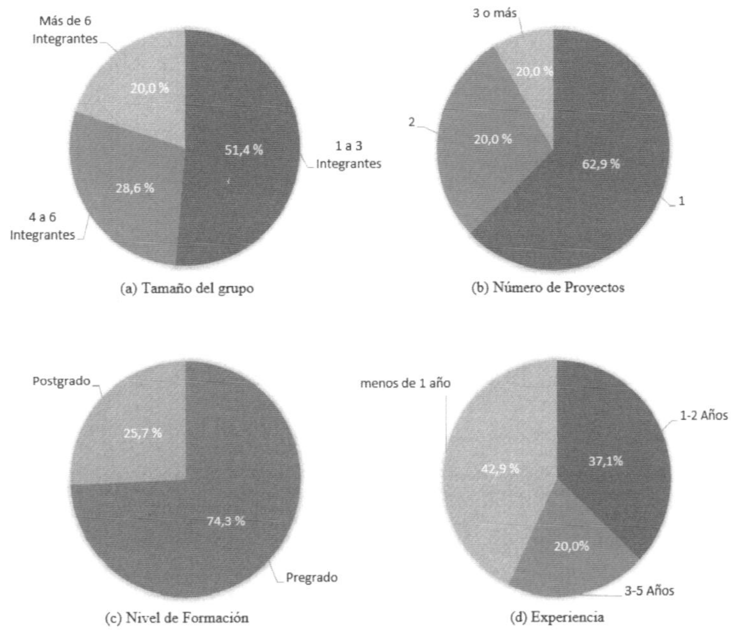

Fig. 1. Organización y conformación de los grupos de investigación

4.2 Uso de Metodologías

Se preguntó a los participantes si en sus grupos de investigación se empleaba alguna metodología para desarrollar sus proyectos de investigación –mayoritariamente proyectos que involucran desarrollo de software-. El 40% informó que no lo hacían, mientras que el 34,3% no estaba seguro de aquello; esto último pone en evidencia la falta de comunicación. Quienes afirmaron usar alguna metodología, indicaron en un 14,7% el uso de metodologías ágiles frente a un 8,8% de las tradicionales o combinación de metodologías.

Respecto al uso de metodologías para la gestión de grupos, el 17,1% de los participantes del estudio afirmó que empleaban alguna, mientras que el 40% aseveró que no lo hacían. De los encuestados que afirmaron usar alguna metodología, el 17% señaló que usaban metodologías tradicionales (p. ej. Cascada) y 8,6% metodologías ágiles.

Los miembros de los grupos de investigación que no usan metodologías fueron consultados respecto a su predisposición para adoptar alguna, ya sea sólo para gestionar los grupos o para desarrollar software. El 91.4% de los participantes señaló que estaría dispuesto a adoptar metodologías que permitan mejorar la gestión del grupo, a fin de mitigar los problemas que los aquejan. Por otra parte, el 97.1% indicó que estaría dispuesto a adoptar y aplicar metodologías de desarrollo de software para seguir un proceso definido que facilite su trabajo. Este alto porcentaje de predisposición (97,1%), podría deberse a que los participantes del estudio tienen formación en ciencias de la computación y están familiarizados con los beneficios que estas metodologías de desarrollo traen consigo.

4.3 Uso de Herramientas

La
Tabla 1 presenta las herramientas usadas por los miembros de los grupos consultados, para efectuar sus labores de investigación. Según reportaron los encuestados, las aplicaciones mayoritariamente empleadas son aquellas que permiten la escritura colaborativa de documentos, tales como Google Docs y Overleaf; estas herramientas les facilitan tareas como la elaboración de minutas de reuniones y artículos de investigación de los proyectos en los que trabajan.

Tabla 1. Herramientas empleadas por los grupos de investigación

Repositorios de código	**%**
Github	66.7%
Bitbucket	16.7%
Sistemas de versionamiento propios	25.0%
Otros	13.9%
Ninguno	11.1%
Escritura Colaborativa	**%**
Google Docs	86.1%
Overleaf	47.2%
Microsoft OneDrive	19.4%
Ninguna	2.8%
Repositorio de Documentos	**%**
Google Drive	72.2%
Dropbox	50.0%
Github	33.3%
Microsoft OneDrive	19.4%
Blogs	11.1%
Páginas Wiki	5.6%
Ninguna	8.3%

Otro tipo de herramientas comúnmente empleado por los miembros de los grupos son los repositorios de documentos; éstos les facilitan la compartición y distribución de la documentación de sus proyectos. Dentro de esta categoría, las aplicaciones que son usadas con mayor frecuencia son Google Drive y Dropbox. Plataformas para gestionar repositorios de código, tales como Github y Bitbucket, son también utilizadas por los encuestados, aunque su uso es menor en comparación con las herramientas para escritura colaborativa y repositorios de documentos.

4.4 Problemas Reportados dentro de los Grupos de Investigación

En la Fig. 2 se presentan los problemas que fueron reportados por los miembros de los grupos de investigación que participaron en este estudio. Como se puede observar, la falta de documentación alcanza el mayor porcentaje (20%), seguido por la excesiva carga de trabajo (17%) y falta de comunicación (15%). Los encuestados manifestaron que el tiempo dedicado a crear documentos necesarios para la correcta administración y ejecución del proyecto era casi nulo y no llegaba a más de dos horas semanales.

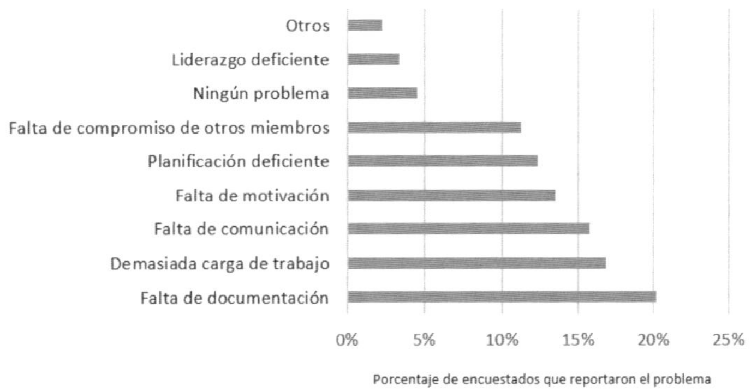

Fig. 2. Problemas reportados por los miembros de los grupos de investigación

Por último, a los participantes se les preguntó sobre las acciones que consideran necesarias para sobrellevar los problemas que enfrentan; la Tabla 2 resume sus respuestas. Según el criterio de los encuestados, mejorar la comunicación es la acción más relevante para enfrentar los problemas existentes.

Tabla 2. Acciones de mejora requeridas

Acciones	%
Mejorar la comunicación	66%
Uso de metodologías para gestionar grupos y desarrollar software	60%
Realizar reuniones periódicas	51%
Usar herramientas de control de proyectos	46%
Usar herramientas para repositorio de documentos	40%
Usar herramientas para repositorio de código	29%
Otro	3%
Ninguno (No hay problemas que resolver)	3%

4.5 Entrevistas a Coordinadores de Grupos

Los dos coordinadores de los Grupos de Investigación entrevistados, manifestaron que el mayor problema al que se enfrentan es la falta de documentación de los proyectos de investigación. Este problema es causado principalmente por la falta de hábito de documentar que tienen los estudiantes de pregrado.

Este problema se agrava más aún por la falta de comunicación que existe entre las personas que laboran en el centro. Este problema, según los coordinadores, se origina porque tanto los estudiantes como los profesores investigadores están sujetos a sus horarios de clases y exámenes, los cuales generalmente difieren. Además, reconocen que es necesario tener reuniones periódicas, a fin de suplir la falta de documentación y mejorar el problema de la comunicación.

Ambos coordinadores, también mostraron interés en aplicar metodologías para el manejo de sus grupos de investigación, incluso indicaron que han identificado herramientas para la planificación y seguimiento de los proyectos, las cuales piensan usar a corto plazo.

Con respecto a la carga de trabajo de los miembros de los grupos de investigación, uno de los coordinadores mencionó que dicha carga se ve afectada por los problemas económicos que en ocasiones enfrenta el centro al depender únicamente de ingresos provenientes del sector público. Ante esta realidad, es común que existan demoras en definir y aprobar proyectos, recibir la aprobación de los avances de proyecto en ejecución y recibir oportunamente la asignación de recursos económicos correspondiente. Esto trae como consecuencia la incertidumbre de contar con recursos económicos que permitan contratar nuevo personal o prolongar los periodos de contratación, obligando a los coordinadores a distribuir las tareas al personal que labora en el centro de investigación (p. ej. corrección de tareas de un proyecto terminado o por terminar, más las tareas de un nuevo proyecto).

El otro coordinador manifestó que en el caso del centro que dirige, se manejan proyectos públicos y privados. Coincide con el otro coordinador en que recibir los recursos que provienen del sector público a veces está fuera de su control, lo que ocasiona la excesiva carga de trabajo dentro del grupo de investigación, la falta de motivación y de compromiso para continuar en el proyecto o en el centro.

5 Análisis de Resultados

El estudio exploratorio reportado en este artículo muestra que tanto la estructura de los grupos de investigación como los problemas a los que se enfrentan, son similares a los expuestos en la literatura relacionada. De las encuestas realizadas, notamos que los grupos de investigación están conformados mayoritariamente por estudiantes o recién graduados, con pocos años de experiencia en tareas de investigación.

Los resultados obtenidos indican también que el uso de metodologías, tanto para manejar grupos de investigación como para desarrollar software, es mínimo; lo cual se refleja en los problemas reportados (falta de documentación, planificación deficiente y falta de comunicación).

Ante esta situación, es conveniente que los profesores investigadores adopten una metodología que permita la sistematización de la planificación, definición de hitos y monitoreo de avances de los proyectos de investigación que dirigen. Es importante recordar que cuando se realiza investigación, se debe promover el manejo adecuado del conocimiento, desde su generación hasta su difusión, incentivando la creación y validación de la documentación [2], [4].

Si bien la aplicación de metodologías de gestión de grupos no es una práctica común entre los encuestados, no ocurre lo mismo en cuanto el uso de herramientas. Repositorios de código, de documentos y aplicaciones para elaboración colaborativa de documentos, son herramientas utilizadas por los grupos de investigación. Sin duda alguna, estas herramientas facilitan las labores de investigación, pero quizás no son aprovechadas al máximo al no ser usadas bajo ningún esquema de trabajo o metodología.

Continuando con el análisis, observamos que existe consenso entre los coordinadores de los grupos de investigación y sus dirigidos respecto a los problemas que afectan el funcionamiento de los grupos. También, ambos muestran predisposición para adoptar metodologías que les permitan mitigar sus efectos. Dicha predisposición genera un entorno abierto a los cambios, que -según la literatura- facilita la implementación de metodologías de trabajo [1] y como consecuencia la reducción o mitigación de los problemas reportados.

Un aspecto mencionado por los coordinadores entrevistados es la falta de recursos y de financiamiento, lo que también causa problemas en el desarrollo de proyectos de investigación. Sin embargo, la solución a este problema, si existiese, está fuera del alcance del presente y futuros trabajos.

Con base en los resultados de este estudio exploratorio, podemos sugerir acciones concretas para optimizar el funcionamiento de los grupos de investigación dentro de la universidad, a fin de mejorar la administración del conocimiento y mitigar los efectos de la alta rotación de personal y periodos de inactividad:

a) Usar una metodología orientada a grupos pequeños: Sugerimos usar SCORE, en la cual se resalta una relación de tutelaje y acompañamiento, desde el profesor/coordinador hacia los estudiantes/integrantes de los grupos, facilitando así la gestión de los grupos de investigación. Según [2], [3], [9], para obtener un adecuado desempeño del grupo se requiere que exista liderazgo y tutoría de parte de los profesores y directores de los proyectos. Además, el uso de metodologías de manejo de grupos adaptadas al entorno académico ayuda a los profesores en el proceso de guiar a los estudiantes en el desarrollo de capacidades de investigación y autonomía [4], [6].
b) Conducir un caso piloto usando SCORE, para evaluar su efectividad en la gestión de grupos de investigación. En caso de ser necesario, se debe adaptar la metodología de acuerdo a las particularidades encontradas del grupo de investigación.
c) Incluir un control de documentación como parte de las reuniones de estado o como parte del ciclo semanal de SCORE. La revisión de documentación por parte de miembros del grupo que están trabajando en otros proyectos equivaldría a una revisión por pares y aumentaría la objetividad en la evaluación de la documentación generada.
d) Estandarizar y utilizar aplicativos (p. ej. repositorios de documentos y código, y herramientas para la escritura colaborativa) que soporten las acciones descritas en

los puntos anteriores. Si bien muchos miembros de los grupos los utilizan, se evidencia una diversidad de aplicativos y herramientas, lo cual puede ocasionar problemas al momento de encontrar archivos de un proyecto. Se recomienda también crear carpetas y archivos con nombres apropiados y correctamente versionados.

6 Conclusiones

Los centros de investigación en ciencias de la computación de la ESPOL están formados por grupos pequeños, integrados principalmente por estudiantes o graduados de carreras de pregrado. Los principales problemas que reportan estos grupos son la falta de documentación y planificación, una comunicación poco eficaz, entre otros. La causa principal de estos problemas es la escasa aplicación de metodologías de manejo de grupos. Existe consenso entre los integrantes de los grupos de investigación y sus coordinadores respecto a los problemas existentes. Además, existe predisposición para adoptar metodologías que faciliten la gestión de los grupos de investigación. Los principales problemas identificados en este estudio exploratorio son en cierta medida similares a los reportados en los estudios relacionados; lo que nos lleva a pensar de que pueden acogerse recomendaciones expuestas en los trabajos relacionados.

7 Trabajos Futuros

En el presente trabajo se realizó un análisis de la situación actual de la gestión de proyectos de investigación en un entorno académico. Si bien los resultados permiten identificar varias de las dificultades que los grupos de investigación enfrentan, es necesario levantar información considerando un número mayor de grupos. Una vez que los problemas y las características particulares de los grupos han sido identificados, se deben diseñar instrumentos que permitan medir de manera objetiva los efectos que la aplicación de una metodología ágil y herramientas de soporte trae consigo. Esto constituiría un primer paso hacia la formulación de artefactos y marcos de trabajo, que pudiesen contribuir a mejorar el desempeño de grupos de investigación que realizan sus labores en entornos restrictivos.

Referencias

1. Bezerra, D.R. et al.: ARDev: a methodology based on scrum principles to support research management on software technologies. In: Proceedings of 24th Annual International Conference on Computer Science and Software Engineering. pp. 363–366 IBM Corp. (2014).
2. vom Brocke, J., Lippe, S.: Managing collaborative research projects: A synthesis of project management literature and directives for future research. Int. J. Proj. Manag. 33, 5, 1022–1039 (2015).
3. Henderson, R.: Research Project Management Key Concepts. My Consult. Ltd. (2010).
4. Hicks, M., Foster, J.S.: Adapting Scrum to Managing a Research Group. (2010).

5. Lima, I.R. et al.: Adapting and Using Scrum in a Software Research and Development Laboratory. Rev. Sist. Informação FSMA9. 16–23 (2012).
6. Lugmayr, A.: Managing Creativeness in a Research Laboratory-Lessons Learned from Establishing NAMU Lab./EMMi Lab. 25th Beld eConference: eDependability: Reliable and Trustworthy eStructures, eProcesses, eOperations and eServices for the Future. Univ. Maribor. (2012).
7. Marchesi, M. et al.: Distributed Scrum in research project management. In: International Conference on Extreme Programming and Agile Processes in Software Engineering. pp. 240–244 Springer (2007).
8. McCue, R.: Research & Collaboration Tools for Students, Staff & Faculty: Creating a Modern Memex. (2012).
9. Omar, Z., Ahmad, A.: Factors Contributing to Research Team Effectiveness: Testing a Model of Team Effectiveness in an Academic Setting. Int. J. High. Educ. 3, 3, 10–26 (2014).
10. Stol, K.-J., Fitzgerald, B.: A holistic overview of software engineering research strategies. In: Proceedings of the Third International Workshop on Conducting Empirical Studies in Industry. pp. 47–54 IEEE Press (2015).
11. Wang, J., Guan, J.: The analysis and evaluation of knowledge efficiency in research groups. J. Am. Soc. Inf. Sci. Technol. 56, 11, 1217–1226 (2005).
12. Learn about SCRUM, https://www.scrumalliance.org/ why-scrum.

Processes Improvement for Software Quality Assurance based on Capability Maturity Model Integration (CMMI-DEV v1.3) for National University of Loja

Hernán Torres-Carrión[1], Lady Iñiguez-Carchi[1], René Guamán-Quinche[1]

[1] Facultad de Energía, las Industrias y los Recursos Naturales no Renovables, Universidad Nacional de Loja, Ciudadela Universitaria Guillermo Falconí Espinosa, La Argelia, Loja-Ecuador
{hltorres, ldiniguezc, rguaman}@unl.edu.ec

Abstract. This work consists on the development of a proposal for the process improvement in the Process and Product Quality Assurance Area (PPQA) based on the Capability Maturity Model Integration (CMMI-DEV v1.3) jointly with the IDEAL model and its phases (Beginning, Diagnosis, Establishment, Performance and Learning), as well as standards such as: BPMN to establish software processes development, IEEE 730 2002 to define the PPQA plan, IEEE 830-1998 for requirements specification, UML for use case specifications, ISO / IEC / IEEE 29119 -3:2013 for tests plans; additionally, the ISTQB norm to define policies, roles and responsibilities to Process and Product Quality Assurance in software department from Telecommunications and Information Unit (TIU) at National University of Loja.

Keywords: processes improvement, CMMI-DEV, PPQA, IDEAL, software quality

1 Introducción

En los últimos años la mayoría de organizaciones que desarrollan software se han preocupado por satisfacer las necesidades de los clientes y del mercado para obtener un producto de calidad basándose en diferentes procesos, procedimientos y reglas. Esto se debe a que las organizaciones buscan reducir costos y tiempo dedicado para la construcción de un software. La calidad de software ha ido mejorando de acuerdo a como ha crecido las exigencias de los clientes; es decir, a medida que los clientes se vuelven más selectivos y comienzan a rechazar software poco fiable nace la necesidad de implantar modelos de mejora de procesos que aseguren un producto de software de calidad.

El principal enfoque para garantizar la calidad de un producto de software es utilizar modelos, los cuales se basan en normas, estándares y procedimientos. Un modelo de proceso es una colección estructurada de elementos que describen características de procesos efectivos (aquellos que han demostrado por experiencia ser eficaces). [1]

La calidad de un software se basa en la calidad del proceso utilizado para desarrollarlo [2]. Es importante destacar que la calidad del software debe ser considerada en todos sus estados de evolución (especificaciones, diseño, código, etc.) no solo al terminar el producto.

La presente propuesta de mejora de procesos en el área de Aseguramiento de la Calidad del Proceso y del Producto, cuyo piloto de pruebas fue el módulo de Planificación y Desarrollo Institucional del Sistema de Información Académico Administrativo Financiero (SIAAF), tiene la finalidad de servir como base para el mejoramiento del desarrollo de futuros productos de software.

2 Antecedentes

2.1 Modelo de mejora de procesos

Para la propuesta de mejora de procesos planteada en este proyecto se realizó una comparativa entre diferentes modelos y normas considerados los más importantes y utilizados, entre ellos están: CMMI-DEV v1.3, ISO 9001, ISO/IEC 15504 y Six Sigma; luego de esta comparativa, se determinó que el modelo que predomina y el que más se acopla a los objetivos del Grupo de Desarrollo de Software de la Unidad de Telecomunicaciones e Información (UTI), es CMMI-DEV v1.3.

Estructura. CMMI-DEV v1.3 se ha estructurado de forma que las organizaciones logren mejoras tanto a nivel de madurez de la empresa (representación por etapas) como en la capacidad de los procesos (representación continua). A continuación en la Tabla 1 se detalla los dos tipos de representación.

Modelo de Capacidad de Madurez Integrada (CMMI-DEV v1.3). Es un modelo de evaluación y mejora de proceso de desarrollo de software en una organización. Se basa en evaluaciones que al ser aplicadas permiten definir las mejoras necesarias para alcanzar un nivel de capacidad o madurez. [3]

2.2 Metodologías, modelo y estrategia de mejora de procesos

CMMI-DEV v1.3 tiene componentes para una organización o un grupo pequeño de proyectos que quieran mejorar sus procesos implementando metas, practicas específicas y genéricas; pero no especifica cómo se debe hacer, por ello se requiere el uso de una metodología, modelo o estrategia, a continuación se describen algunas de ellas.

Tabla 1. Comparativa de modelos y normas de mejora de procesos

	VENTAJAS	DESVENTAJAS
CMMI-DEV v1.3	– Guía paso a paso para la mejora, a través de niveles de madurez y capacidad. [3] – Ayuda a las organizaciones a mejorar sus procesos de desarrollo y de mantenimiento, para los productos y servicios. [4] – Control continuo de los proyectos, en cuanto a: Riegos, Recursos, Esfuerzo, Costos, Plazos. [4]	– Requiere mayor inversión económica para implementarlo completamente. [3] – El proceso para lograr un nivel de madurez es largo y costoso, lo que puede significar varios años de esfuerzo. [5]
ISO 9001:2002	– Se acopla a los requerimientos de la organización sin importar su tipo, tamaño y producto suministrado. [6] – Libertad de implementación y de interpretación de los requisitos. [5]	– Si se desea obtener un rango más amplio en los objetivos de un sistema de gestión de la calidad se debe relacionar con la norma ISO 9004. [6] – Para integrar un sistema de gestión de la calidad propio de una empresa se debe alinear con la norma ISO 14001:1996. [6]
	VENTAJAS	DESVENTAJAS
ISO/IEC 15504	– Permite asegurar una mejora mediante niveles de madurez. [7] – Primer modelo de procesos de dos dimensiones independientes para los procesos y la capacidad. [4]	– Hace uso de algunas de las prácticas definidas en la norma ISO/IEC 12207. [7] – El costo de implantación es más costoso que otros modelos. [3] – Se considera inapropiado aplicar dicha certificación en organizaciones con menos de veinte (20) personas. [7]
SIX SIGMA	– Produce en las empresas resultados económicos muy notables. [8] – Cuenta con herramientas de software que hacen las estadísticas cada vez más fáciles. [8]	– Tiene un alto grado de dificultad para entender. [9] – Se debe tener conocimientos generales de investigación de operaciones, arquitectura de sistemas e ingeniería concurrente. [9]

Tabla 2. Representación del modelo CMMI-DEV v1.3 [10]

Nivel	Representación continua Niveles de capacidad	Representación por etapas Noveles de madurez
Nivel 0	Incompleto	
Nivel 1	Realizado	Iniciado
Nivel 2	Gestionado	Gestionado
Nivel 3	Definido	Definido
Nivel 4		Gestionado cuantitativamente
Nivel 5		En optimización

PDCA. El ciclo de mejora continua PDCA está constituido por cuatro fases: "Planificar", "Desarrollar", "Verificar" y "Actuar" [11], en la Fig 1 se muestra el detalle de la misma con cada una de sus fases y tareas a realizar.

Fig. 1. Ciclo continuo del modelo PDCA [11]

DMAIC. Su propósito es para mejorar procesos existentes en una organización, se basa en el ciclo de calidad PDCA, constituido por 5 fases: "Definir", "Medir", "Analizar", "Mejorar", "Controlar" [12], en la Fig 2 se muestra el detalle de la misma con cada una de sus fases a realizar.

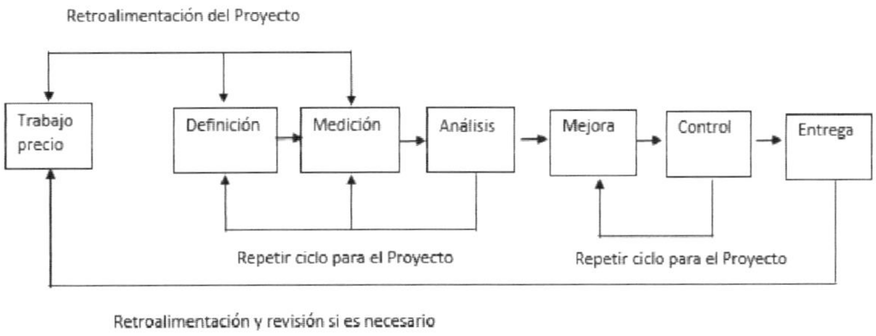

Fig. 2. Ciclo continuo de DMAIC [13]

DFSS. Se utiliza cuando se requiere diseñar un nuevo proceso e introducirlo en una organización, consta de 5 fases: "Definir", "Medir", "Analizar", "Diseñar", "Verificar", y conjuntamente con DMAIC pertenecen al modelo Six Sigma. [12]

IDEAL. Integra planes para iniciar y administrar un programa de SPI (Software Process Improvement), consta de 5 fases: "Inicio", "Diagnóstico", "Establecimiento", "Actuación", "Aprender", el mismo que fue desarrollado por el Software Engineering Institute (SEI), para adoptarlo con CMMI [14], en la Fig 3 se indica a detalle sus fases y las tareas a realizar en cada una de ellas.

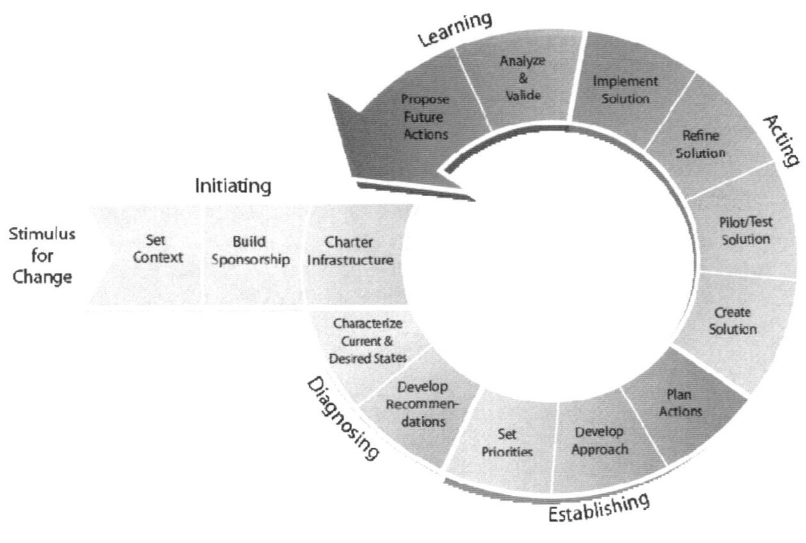

Fig. 3. Ciclo continuo del modelo IDEAL [15]

3 Resultados

Dentro de las metodologías, modelo y estrategia de mejora de procesos analizados, la que cumple con las necesidades requeridas para la propuesta de mejora de procesos en el área del aseguramiento de la calidad es: IDEAL (Initiating, Diagnosing, Establishing, Acting, Learning), el mismo que está desarrollado para el modelo CMMI por el Software Engineering Institute (SEI) con la ventaja de acoplarlo a los objetivos de cada organización, a diferencia de las metodologías DMAIC y DFSS que su implementación es un proceso largo y costoso y que además se debe tener conocimientos generales de arquitectura de sistemas o de ingeniería concurrente convirtiéndose en unas de las metodologías más complejas, por su parte la estrategia PDCA tiene una estrecha relación con la ISO 9001 la que garantiza de igual manera mejoras a largo plazo y la misma se debe comenzar de forma experimental.

IDEAL dentro de cada fase propone objetivos, los mismos que se detallan a continuación:

3.1 Fase Inicio

Los objetivos de esta fase son:

- Establecer el patrocinio por parte del GDS de la UTI para el SPI.
- Conocer de forma general la estructura y funcionamiento del GDS de la UTI.
- Conformar el grupo de mejora de procesos software referente al área PPQA.

Patrocinio por parte de la Organización. Se determinó la factibilidad que tiene la propuesta y de los objetivos a cumplir para la mejora de procesos en el área de PPQA con todos los interesado y específicamente con las máximas autoridades de la Unidad de Telecomunicaciones e Información, definiendo que mejoras se realizan y estableciendo un compromiso mutuo de todas las personas involucradas en el desarrollo de software.

Estructura Organizacional. La UTI actualmente consta con un organigrama de forma muy general, donde se divide en un primer rango la Dirección de la UTI y en un rango inferior los departamentos de Desarrollo de Software, Redes y Equipos Informáticos y por último el departamento de Electrónica y Telecomunicaciones.

Tabla 3. Comparativa de metodologías, modelo y estrategia de mejora de procesos

	Ventajas	Desventajas
IDEAL	– Garantiza que la introducción de nuevas tecnologías, productos respondan a necesidades de los clientes y al deseo de mejorar continuamente. [16] – IDEAL ayuda a fomentar una cultura de mejoras continuas en la organización. [16] – Aporta un mecanismo para reunir lecciones aprendidas en cada actividad y poder acceder a ellas cuando se inicie un nuevo ciclo de mejora. [16]	– IDEAL es altamente recomendado como modelo secuencial, sin embargo en la práctica es casi imposible seguir una secuencia ya que algunas actividades se realizan en forma paralela. [17]
DMAIC y DFSS	– DMAIC y DFSS se enfoca en las necesidades y los requerimientos de los clientes. [18] – Se la puede implantar en el desarrollo de proyectos simples hasta los más complejos. [18] – DMAIC y DFSS se requiere hacer uso de herramientas estadísticas apropiadas que conducen a soluciones válidas y efectivas. [19]	– No se puede aplicar DMAIC sin antes haber aplicado DFSS. [18] – DFSS es un proceso a largo plazo y costos. [19] – Tanto para DFSS y DMAIC se debe tener conocimientos generales de investigación de operaciones, arquitectura de sistemas e ingeniería concurrente.[19]
PDCA	– Es un método efectivo y rápido para implementar la mejora continua. [20] – El ciclo PDCA se puede aplicar a todas las actividades de una organización. [20]	– El ciclo PDCA garantiza mejoras a largo plazo. [20] – Difícil implantación incluso para los que tienen conocimientos acerca de la metodología. [20]

Conformar el grupo de SPI. Se define un grupo de personas quienes son los encargados de cumplir con las fases del proyecto para encaminarlo hacia la mejora y cumplir con el aseguramiento de la calidad.

Tabla 4. Grupo de SPI

Asesor del Proyecto	Ing. Hernán Torres
Asesores de SPI	Ing. Edison Coronel Ing. Lissette López
Equipo de trabajo	Lady Iñiguez

3.2 Fase Diagnóstico

Los objetivos de esta fase son:

- Determinar el estado actual del GDS respecto al aseguramiento de la calidad del software.
- Realizar la categorización y prioridad de los problemas encontrados.

Determinar la situación actual de la Organización referente al aseguramiento de la calidad. Por medio del Director de la UTI se obtuvo documentación formalizada como son el "Manual de Descripción, Valoración y Clasificación de Puestos de la Universidad Nacional de Loja" donde se evidenció que los roles existentes en el mismo son Subdirector de Desarrollo de Software y Analista 1 y 2 quedando en descubierto que no existen todos los roles pertinentes como Líder de proyecto, Líder de Aseguramiento de la Calidad del Proceso y del Producto o Tester quienes garantizaran la calidad de los productos software, también fue entregada la normativa "Las Políticas de Telecomunicaciones, Desarrollo de Software y Redes " evidenciando la no existencia de políticas que garanticen la calidad del software.

Categorización y priorización de los problemas encontrados. Los resultados obtenidos de esta priorización se utilizaron como guía para determinar qué acciones tomar en el proceso de mejora. Los criterios tomados para la clasificación de los problemas es la siguiente:

Alto = 3; Medio = 2

Tabla 5. Criterios de priorización

Prioridad (puntos)	Razón
3	Problemas que de forma directa sean parte de la solución a este proyecto o que a su vez estén dentro de mis alcances
2	Problemas que estén fuera de mi alcance es decir problemas que se generan por cuestiones externas al GDS

Tabla 6. Priorización de problemas

PROBLEMAS	PRIORIDAD
Escasa documentación formalizada de procesos y estándares.	3
Inexistencia de un plan PPQA.	3
Que no se detecten errores a tiempo en el producto.	2
Conocimiento limitado en la fase de PPQA.	2
Falta de personas encargadas del PPQA.	2
Falta de personal para las diferentes etapas del ciclo de vida de un proyecto.	2
Poca aplicación de pruebas finales.	2
Desconocimiento del personal en metodologías y modelos de mejora de procesos.	3
Carencia de presupuesto.	2
Inexistencia de una estructura orgánica.	2
Personal no calificado en herramientas tecnológicas para el aseguramiento de la calidad.	3
Carencia de un plan de capacitación.	2

Mediante esta clasificación se considera que el problema central en el GDS es que el "Producto Software no cuenta con la calidad esperada".

3.3 Fase Establecimiento

Mediante la revisión sistemática se determinó los aspectos necesarios para proponer roles y responsabilidades para el área de PPQA, políticas de calidad, procesos, plantillas y herramientas para el aseguramiento de la calidad.

Roles y responsabilidades para el Aseguramiento de Calidad. Definir políticas, roles y responsabilidades para los distintos miembros que conforma un grupo de PPQA (Líder de Proyecto, Líder de PPQA, Tester) es de vital importancia para iniciar con el plan de SPI, para los mismos se tomó como base la información proporcionada por el Comité Internacional de Cualificaciones de Pruebas de Software (ISTQB).

Líder de Proyecto. El Líder del Proyecto tiene las siguientes responsabilidades:

- Planifica las actividades del proyecto.
- Define la organización y estructura del proyecto.
- Administra recursos necesarios para cumplir los plazos establecidos.
- Organiza el equipo de trabajo para lograr el objetivo definido.
- Estudia la viabilidad de los requisitos en unión con el Analista.
- Revisa junto al Líder de PPQA los avances de acuerdo al plan de PPQA.
- Informa sobre el estado actual del proyecto a los clientes y a la alta Gerencia.

Políticas para el PPQA. La definición de políticas está enfocada en las metas de la organización en este caso se ajustan a la Unidad de Telecomunicaciones e Información (UTI) de la Universidad Nacional de Loja.

- Establecer un plan de PPQA para un proyecto ajustándose al mismo.
- Se pasará a producción un proyecto si el Líder de PPQA aprueba la funcionalidad.
- El Líder de PPQA planificará los casos de prueba dependiendo de las pruebas a realizar.
- El grupo de PPQA deberá documentar las no-conformidades encontradas durante todo el proceso de AQ.

Procesos de desarrollo de software. Los procesos son desarrollados en base a las metas y prácticas específicas proporcionadas por el modelo CMMI-DEV v1.3, los mismos que son:

- Desarrollo de software.
- Plan de aseguramiento de la calidad del proceso y del producto.
- Validar documentación.
- Plan de pruebas.
- Control de calidad.

En la Fig. 5 se observa el proceso para definir el plan de PPQA constando con roles como: Líder de proyecto y Líder de PPQA, los procesos han sido desarrollados en base al estándar Modelo y Notación de Procesos de Negocio (BPMN) el que describe la lógica de los pasos de un proceso de negocio.

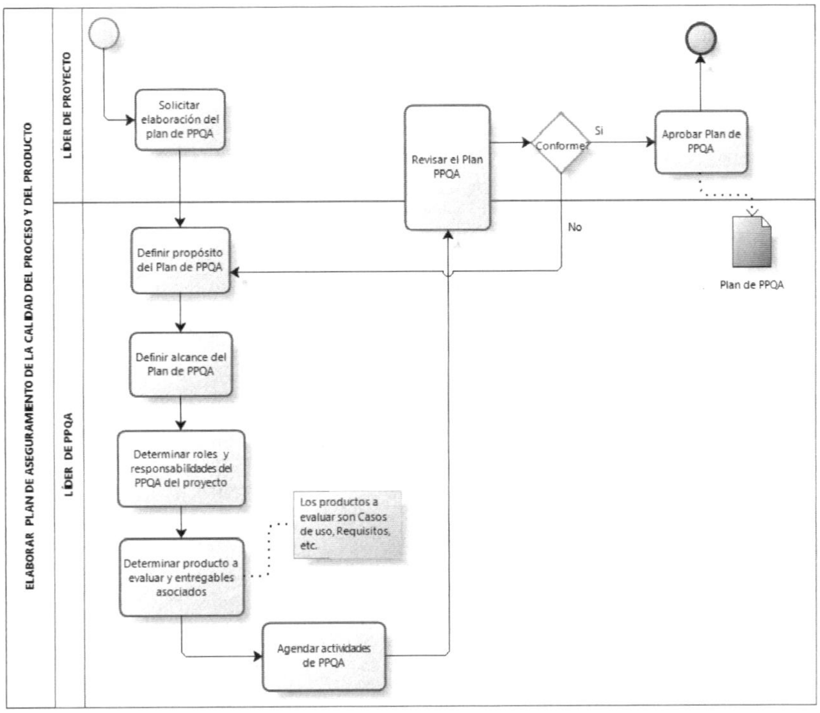

Fig. 5. Proceso para definir el plan de PPQA

Plantillas para el Aseguramiento de la Calidad. El levantamiento de plantillas se realizó de acuerdo a los procesos planteados, dentro del conjunto de plantillas tenemos:

- Plan de aseguramiento de la calidad del proceso y del producto, ref. estándar IEEE 730-2002.
- Checklist de validación de requisitos, ref. estándar IEEE 830-1998.
- Checklist de validación de prototipo.
- Checklist de validación de casos de uso, ref. estándar UML.
- Informe de no conformidades.
- Plan de pruebas e Informe de errores ref. ISO/IEC/IEEE 29119-3:2013.
- Informe de aprobación.

	UNIDAD DE TELECOMUNICACIONES E INFORMACIÓN MODELO DE CAPACIDAD DE MADUREZ INTEGRADA (CMMI V1.3) Aseguramiento de la Calidad del Proceso y del Producto (PPQA)

PROYECTO	<Nombre del Proyecto>
LÍDER DE PROYECTO	<Nombre>
FECHA DE INICIALIZACIÓN	<dd/mm/aaaa>

NOMBRE DE DOCUMENTO	Plan de Aseguramiento de la Calidad del Proceso y del Producto
VERSIÓN	1.0

ELABORADO POR:	<Nombre> <Cargo>	
	FECHA:	<dd/mm/aaaa>
REVISADO POR:	<Nombre> <Cargo>	
	FECHA:	<dd/mm/aaaa>
APROBADO POR:	<Nombre> <Cargo>	
	FECHA:	<dd/mm/aaaa>

Contenido

Fig. 4. Plantilla del Plan de Aseguramiento de la Calidad del Proceso y del Producto

3.4 Fase de Validación y Aprendizaje

Definir el tipo de prueba a realizar. Existen distintos niveles de prueba a menudo con diferentes intereses, uno de los criterios más habituales para clasificar las niveles de prueba se basa en el ciclo de vida del software, teniendo niveles de pruebas: Unitarias, Integración, Sistema, Implantación y Aceptación.

De acuerdo a la etapa de desarrollo en la que se encuentre el "Modulo de Planificación y Desarrollo Institucional" se determinó que en nivel de pruebas a realizar es el nivel de Sistema el mismo que permite verificar los requisitos funcionales y no funcionales, estableciendo que las pruebas que se realizaran en dicho nivel son pruebas funcionales, de seguridad a nivel de aplicación y rendimiento las mismas que son importantes cuando se realiza en un ambiente de trabajo parecido al de producción, permitiendo identificar y corregir errores que puedan ser demasiado costosos de reparar en fases posteriores.

Seleccionar las herramientas de prueba. Para el proceso de selección de una herramienta es necesario considerar factores como que tipos de pruebas se va a realizar y el alcance de dichas pruebas, con base a estos requisitos se seleccionó las herramientas que se utilizan para llevar a cabo las pruebas de funcionalidad y rendimiento, las mismas que son Testlink y Jmeter, las que se acoplan a las especificaciones del módulo a evaluar.

Pruebas del módulo.

Prueba Funcional. Se realizó mediante el uso de la herramienta Testlink, misma que más se acopló a la técnica de caja negra, enfocándose en determinar el cumplimiento o no de los requisitos planteados en la fase de análisis, la siguiente figura muestra el grupo de casos de prueba detallando la prioridad, la versión y el resultado obtenido.

Caso de Prueba	Prioridad	V 1.0	V 1.1	[Última Build] V 1.1	Última Ejecución
Suite de Pruebas: ADMINISTRAR ACCIONES (generado automáticamente desde espec. req.) (1 Item)					
MPDI-6:Gestionar Acciones [1]	Media	Fallado [v1]	Pasado [v1]	Pasado [v1]	Pasado [v1]
Suite de Pruebas: ADMINISTRAR INDICADORES (generado automáticamente desde espec. req.) (1 Item)					
MPDI-7:Gestionar Indicadores [1]	Media	Fallado [v1]	Pasado [v1]	Pasado [v1]	Pasado [v1]
Suite de Pruebas: ADMINISTRAR METAS (generado automáticamente desde espec. req.) (1 Item)					
MPDI-8:Gestionar Metas [1]	Media	Fallado [v1]	Pasado [v1]	Pasado [v1]	Pasado [v1]
Suite de Pruebas: ADMINISTRAR OBJETIVOS ESTRATÉGICOS (generado automáticamente desde espec. req.) (1 Item)					
MPDI-2:Gestionar OE [1]	Media	Pasado [v1]	No Ejecutado [v1]	No Ejecutado [v1]	Pasado [v1]
Suite de Pruebas: ADMINISTRAR OBJETIVOS OPERATIVOS (generado automáticamente desde espec. req.) (1 Item)					
MPDI-5:Gestionar OO [1]	Media	Fallado [v1]	Pasado [v1]	Pasado [v1]	Pasado [v1]
Suite de Pruebas: ADMINISTRAR PLANES ESTRATÉGICOS INSTITUCIONALES (generado automáticamente desde espec. req.) (1 Item)					
MPDI-1:Gestionar PEDI [1]	Media	Fallado [v1]	Pasado [v1]	Pasado [v1]	Pasado [v1]

Fig. 5. Caso de prueba funcional

Prueba de Seguridad a nivel de aplicación. Permitió asegurar que el módulo tenga los controles necesarios, verificando que el actor en este caso Administrador de PDI tenga acceso a las funciones y datos que su rol le permite.

Tabla 7. Caso de prueba de seguridad a nivel de aplicación

REGISTRO DE CASOS DE PRUEBA				
Módulo de Planificación y Desarrollo Institucional				
Rol	Versión	Tipo de prueba	Fecha de creación	Fecha de culminación
Administrador de PDI	V1.0	Seguridad a nivel de Aplicación	28/12/2016	28/12/2016
Funciones		Acciones autorizados		Resultado obtenido
Administrar PDI		Crear PDI		Exitoso
		Editar PDI		Exitoso
		Buscar PDI		Exitoso
		Eliminar PDI		Exitoso
Administrar Objetivos Operativos		Crear Objetivos Operativos		Exitoso
		Editar Objetivos Operativos		Exitoso
		Buscar Objetivos Operativos		Exitoso
		Eliminar Objetivos Operativos		Exitoso

Prueba de Rendimiento. Se realizó mediante el uso de la herramienta Jmeter la que permite determinar la velocidad de respuesta de una petición https, al momento de acceder a la información por parte del usuario. La Tabla 5 describe seis escenarios distintos de la prueba de rendimiento con un número de peticiones distintas para cada escenario, y con un tiempo de petición variante entre 1 y 2 segundos, teniendo como resultado dentro de un rango aceptable una latencia mínima que va entre 6,5 y 4,8 segundos con un 0% de error.

Tabla 8. Conjunto de escenarios de casos de prueba de rendimiento

Escenario	Número de peticiones	Tiempo de envió de peticiones (segundos)	Latencia mínima (segundos)	Error	Resultado
Escenario 1	100	1	38,139	3%	Fallido
Escenario 2	90	2	61,126	0%	Exitoso
Escenario 3	200	1	35,600	47.50%	Fallido
Escenario 4	185	1	37,708	32.97%	Fallido
Escenario 5	10 - en un bucle de 10 veces	1	6,559	0%	Exitoso
Escenario 6	10 - en un bucle de 20 veces	2	4,859	0%	Exitoso

Entrega de resultados.

Socializar resultados. Se socializaron los resultados obtenidos con el fin de dar a conocer todo el proceso realizado para la implementación de la mejora de procesos, inmiscuyendo los procesos levantados, las plantillas propuestas y todo el proceso de pruebas.

Entregar documentación. En esta etapa final se hizo la entrega de la documentación generada durante todo el proceso de aseguramiento de la calidad, donde se documentó todos los productos de trabajo utilizados y generados en cada una de las fases del desarrollo y evaluación del módulo, los cuales son: plan de PPQA, validación de documentación (requisitos, casos de uso y prototipo), informe de no conformidades para (requisitos, prototipo y casos de uso), plan de pruebas, informe de errores e informe de aprobación; los que permitirán controlar las versiones al momento de volver a evaluar el software por algún cambio en su funcionalidad.

A continuación en la Tabla 9. Se proporciona una comparativa del estado actual en el que se encuentra el GDS de la Unidad de Telecomunicaciones e Información y la mejora realizada indicando la decisión tomada y el cumplimiento de cada una de las metas y practicas especificas propuestas en el Área de Aseguramiento de la Calidad del Proceso y del Producto (PPQA) del modelo CMMI-DEV v1.3.

Tabla 9. Comparativa de lo que se tiene y lo que se propuso

Estado actual	Decisión tomada	Implicación	Meta cumplida de CMMI-DEV v1.3
Carencia de políticas de Aseguramiento de la Calidad.	Definición de políticas de Aseguramiento de la Calidad. – Utilización de la norma del Comité Internacional de Cualificaciones de Pruebas de Software (ISTQB)	Formalización de las políticas.	SG 1. Evaluar objetivamente los procesos y los productos de trabajo. (En contraste a los procesos, estándares y procedimientos definidos). – SP 1.1 Evaluar objetivamente los procesos. – SP 1.2 Evaluar objetivamente los productos de trabajo.
No consta con todos los roles para cubrir cada fase del ciclo de vida de un proyecto.	Determinar roles y responsabilidades. – Utilización de la norma del Comité Internacional de Cualificaciones de Pruebas de Software (ISTQB)	Formalización de roles y responsabilidades.	
No existen procesos definidos.	Establecimiento de nuevos procesos con los involucrados de la UTI. – Utilización del estándar Modelo y Notación de procesos de Negocio (BMPN)	Cambio de procesos.	
Estado actual	Decisión tomada	Implicación	Meta cumplida de CMMI-DEV v1.3
Documentación nula en el proceso de desarrollo de software.	Levantamientos de plantillas. – Plan de PPQA ref. estándar IEEE 730-2002. – Checklist de validación de requisitos, ref. estándar IEEE 830-1998. – Checklist de validación de casos de uso, ref. estándar UML. – Plan de pruebas e Informe de errores ref. ISO/IEC/IEEE 29119-3:2013.	Hacer uso de las plantillas propuestas.	SG 2. Proporcionar una visión objetiva. (Informar las no conformidades y establecer registros). – SP 2.1 Comunicar y resolver las no conformidades. – SP 2.2 Establecer los registros.
Ciclo de pruebas poco fiable.	Propuesta de herramientas para asegurar la calidad. – Uso de herramientas Testlink y Jmeter	Hacer uso de herramientas que ayuden al aseguramiento de la calidad.	

Referencias

1. M. A. Muñoz Mata, "Análisis de estándares y modelos de referencia de mejores prácticas", Tesis doctoral, Departamento de Lenguajes y Sistemas Informáticos e Ingeniería de software, UPM, Madrid, 2007.
2. F. Scalone, "Estudio comparativo de los Modelos y Estándares de Calidad del Software". Tesis magistral, Facultad Regional Buenos Aires, UTN, Buenos Aires, 2006.
3. "Modelos de Evaluación y Mejora de Procesos: Análisis Comparativo", Ministerio de Ciencia y Tecnología del proyecto CICYT, España, 2004 [Online]. Available: http://rabida.uhu.es/dspace/bitstream/handle/10272/8773/Modelos_de_evaluacion.pdf?sequence=2. [Accedido: 03-jun-2017]
4. G. Solarte, L. Muñoz y B. Arias, "Modelos de Calidad para procesos de software", *Redalyc,* vol. XV, pp. 375-379. [Online]. Available: http://www.redalyc.org/articulo.oa?id=84916714069. [Accedido: 03-jun-2017]
5. F. Ramos, O. Torres, N. Sánchez y M. Alba, "Implementación de CMMI nivel de madurez 2 en una pyme", *Revista Española de Innovación, Calidad e Ingeniería del Software*, vol. 6, pp. 35-46. [Online]. Available: http://www.redalyc.org/articulo.oa?id=84916714069. [Accedido: 03-jun-2017]
6. ISO Quality management systems – Requirements, ISO 9001 [Online]. Available: http://www.fbioyf.unr.edu.ar/evirtual/pluginfile.php/106579/mod_resource/content/0/ISO%209001-2000%20%28ESP%29.pdf. [Accedido: 03-jun-2017]
7. A. Alarcón, J. Gonzáles y S. Rodríguez, "Guía para pymes desarrolladoras de software, basada en la norma ISO/IEC 15504", *Revista Virtual Universidad Católica del Norte*, pp. 285-313, 2011 [Online]. Available: http://revistavirtual.ucn.edu.co/index.php/RevistaUCN/article/viewFile/339/651. [Accedido: 03-jun-2017]
8. "Seis Sigma: una herramienta estratégica para la calidad", Petrotecnia, Bariloche, Argentina, 2004 [Online]. Available: http://biblioteca.iapg.org.ar/ArchivosAdjuntos/Petrotecnia/2004-3/SeisSigma.pdf. [Accedido: 03-jun-2017]
9. J. M. García Camús, "Lean Six Sigma Startup Methodology: una metodología general de innovación de la calidad aplicada a los sectores de la producción y servicios", tesis doctoral, Univ. Rey Juan Carlos, 2015 [Online]. Available: https://eciencia.urjc.es/bitstream/handle/10115/13660/Tesis_L6SSM_JM_Garcia_Camus.pdf?sequence=
1&isAllowed=y. [Accedido: 20- mar-2017]
10. Software Engineering Institute, CMMI para Desarrollo, Versión 1.3 [Online]. Available: http://www.sei.cmu.edu/library/assets/whitepapers/Spanish%20Technical%20Report%20CMMI%20V%201%203.pdf. [Accedido: 20- mar-2017]
11. T. Rodríguez, *Guía de calidad y mejora en las administraciones públicas,* Pamplona, España: 2005 [Online]. Available: https://www.navarra.es/NR/rdonlyres/9B1AE1C6-4635-40E7-9DB4-2309D9946B86/320708/GuiadeCalidady
MejoradelasAAPP.pdf. [Accedido: 22-mar-2017]
12. Seis sigma: un enfoque teórico y aplicado en el ámbito empresarial basándose en información científica, Universidad de la Salle, Colombia, 2011 [Online]. Available: http://repository.lasallista.edu.co/dspace/bitstream/10567/515/1/13.%20223-242.pdf. [Accedido: 21- mar-2017]
13. R. Herrera, T. Fontalvo, "Seis Sigma Métodos Estadísticos y sus Aplicaciones", Colombia: 2011 [Online]. Available: http://biblioteca.utec.edu.sv/siab/virtual/elibros_internet/55821.pdf. [Accedido: 22-mar-2017]
14. B. Mendoza Ortiz, "Definición de planes de acción como resultado de las evaluaciones de proceso software en las pequeñas y medianas empresas software", tesis de Licenciatura,

Univ. Tecnológica de la Mixteca, 2009 [Online]. Available: http://jupiter.utm.mx/~tesis_dig/10722.pdf. [Accedido: 23-mar-2017]
15. IDEAL. A User's Guide for Software Process Improvement, CMU/SEI-96-HB-001 [Online]. Available: http://www.sei.cmu.edu/reports/96hb001.pdf. [Accedido: 23-mar-2017]
16. "Adaptación rápida a los cambios empleando el modelo de mejora IDEAL", Library ABB, California del Norte, EE.UU, 2009 [Online]. Available: https://library.e.abb.com/public/4594359b89217581c12575eb005695ca/58-63%202M974_SPA72dpi.pdf. [Accedido: 23-may-2017]
17. R. Klendauer, A. Hoffmann y M. Berkovich, "The use of the IDEAL Model in a small software enterprise", IEEE Xplore, pp. 66-72 [Online]. DOI: 10.1145/337180.337492. [Accedido: 23-mar-2017]
18. F. Scalone, "Estudio comparativo de los modelos y estándares de calidad del software", tesis de magister, Univ. Tecnológica Nacional Buenos Aires, [Online]. Available: http://laboratorios.fi.uba.ar/lsi/scalone-tesis-maestria-ingenieria-en-calidad.pdf. [Accedido: 03-may-2017]
19. M. Sokovic, D. Pavletic y K. Pipan, "Quality Improvement Methodologies – PDCA Cycle, RADAR Matrix, DMAIC and DFSS", *Journal*, vol. 43, pp. 476-483 [Online]. Availablehttps://www.researchgate.net/profile/Mirko_Sokovic/publication/49600834_Quality_improvement_methodologies_-_PDCA_cycle_RADAR_matrix_DMAIC_and_DFSS/links/0912f50ec1328b1a57000000/Quality-improvement-methodologies-PDCA-cycle-RADAR-matrix-DMAIC-and-DFSS.pdf. [Accedido: 03-may-2017]
20. J. Puche y J. Costas, "Entender el ciclo PDCA de mejora continua", Revista mensual de la Asociación Española para la Calidad, pp. 55-58, 2010 [Online]. Available: https://www.aec.es/c/document_library/get_file?p_l_id=64199&folderId=195586&name=DLFE-7137.pdf. [Accedido: 03-may-2017]

"Learning by playing", the Logic of Programming from a more fun perspective

Hussein Rahman[1], Franklin Mayorga[2], Clay Aldas[3]

[1] Universidad Técnica de Ambato, Ambato – Ecuador (hrahman3599@uta.edu.ec)
[2] Universidad Técnica de Ambato, Ambato – Ecuador (fmayorga@uta.edu.ec)
[3] Universidad Técnica de Ambato, Ambato – Ecuador (clayaldas@uta.edu.ec)

Abstract. Educational video games have proved to be excellent tools for developing psychological, cognitive, physical and / or social qualities and / or abilities, and have been incorporated as little complements of the learning process. The traditional teaching is obsolete, nowadays it is very common to use this type of tools to accelerate learning in different areas. This article presents the development of an educational video game, with the purpose of supporting the development of learning in the area of programming logic, through the "learn by playing" philosophy where the player will learn the educational content implicit in the game while being satisfied Their expectations of fun and motivation.

Keywords: android, Unity3D, educational video game, programming logic, EGameFlow

1 Introducción

Una de las grandes tendencias educativas globales actualmente consiste en enseñar la programación en edades tempranas ya que varias investigaciones confirman que el aprender lógica de programación ayuda a mejorar la capacidad de atención, concentración, mayor interés por la experimentación y la capacidad de cálculo y de lógica. Al apreciar que muchas habilidades, destrezas y capacidades son desarrolladas a través del aprendizaje de la programación, hoy en día muchas empresas e instituciones públicas y privadas de todo el mundo están enfocadas en mejorar los métodos de transmisión de conocimiento y desarrollo de destrezas en el área de programación dando como resultado que a través de los videojuegos educativos los niños presentan un mayor grado de captación, ya que los videojuegos despiertan mayor interés por el grado de diversión y el reto causado en los jugadores para repetir una y otra vez el mismo nivel hasta completarlo exitosamente, éstos videojuegos son creados con el objetivo de motivar aprendizaje de la lógica de programación [1].

A nivel mundial existen muchos videojuegos profesionales enfocados al aprendizaje de la lógica de programación, entre uno de estos proyectos se encuentra el de Danny Yaroslavski quien desarrolló el videojuego educativo Lightbot para el aprendizaje de conceptos de programación de software [2]. También podemos apreciar el proyecto mundialmente conocido desarrollado por MIT MEDIA LAB, quienes desarrollaron un lenguaje de programación visual diseñado para introducir las habilidades de programación en niños de 5-7 años de edad. Mediante la creación de proyectos con ScratchJr, los niños pequeños pueden aprender a pensar de forma creativa y razonar de forma sistemática [3].

En conjunto a los proyectos realizados tanto a niveles personales como Institucionales, se aprecia una propuesta por parte de los estudiantes del "Instituto Superior Politécnico José Antonio Echeverría" ubicado en Cuba desarrollaron un videojuego en 3D para el aprendizaje de conceptos de la programación, su proyecto se enfoca para los estudiantes de la carrera de Informática de los primeros niveles [4].

Al analizar los proyectos Lightbot y el Laberinto 3D los cuales comparten el mismo objetivo en común el cual es generar aprendizaje, sus diferencias radican en el enfoque dado para generar este aprendizaje. El primer proyecto oculta el contenido de aprendizaje utilizando al videojuego como un intermediario del proceso de aprendizaje siguiendo el modelo planeado por *Vygostky* [5], mientras el segundo proyecto se enfoca directamente en el contenido educativo lo que a corto plazo causa aburrimiento y la pérdida de motivación en el jugador.

Como resultado de lo anteriormente expuesto, y si bien existen diversos juegos multimedia cuyo objetivo es enseñar de forma lúdica, lo cierto es que dichas propuestas no terminan de satisfacer las expectativas de ocio/diversión de los jugadores, ya que no existe un proceso de juego y los alumnos pierden la motivación asociada al ocio y a la diversión [6].

Como propuesta para resolver los problemas citados con anterioridad se presenta el desarrollo de un videojuego educativo que ayuda al aprendizaje de la *Lógica de Programación* ofreciendo características nunca antes vistas en videojuegos similares, dichas características refuerzan el aprendizaje al ocultar el contenido educativo y mostrar únicamente lo que el jugador desea ver en un videojuego, la diversión.

Esta propuesta presenta la siguiente estructura. sección 2 *Caso de estudio*. En la sección 3 *Desarrollo del videojuego*, luego en la sección 4 se presenta la *Interfaz de usuario en el aprendizaje*. Sección 5 *Experiencia de usuario*, luego en la sección 6 *Resultados* y en la Sección 7 se finaliza la propuesta mostrando las *Conclusiones*.

2 Caso de estudio

El caso de estudio del presente artículo es el videojuego *"Hello Remi"*, desarrollado por el autor del mismo, cuyo objetivo es promover el aprendizaje indirecto de la *Lógica de Programación* mediante el uso comandos de acciones sobre un escenario tridimensional donde los niveles se generan aleatoriamente para generar diferentes posibilidades de problemas para el jugador.

La propuesta planteada busca generar aprendizaje de una forma divertida para los usuarios que están entrando al mundo de la programación en edades tempranas y encuentran dificultades para comprender los conceptos básicos de la *Lógica de Programación.*

3 Desarrollo del videojuego

Desarrollar un videojuego es una tarea ardua que requiere de herramientas apropiadas para el correcto funcionamiento de cada uno de los elementos que conformarán el videojuego. A continuación, se detalla a breves rasgos las herramientas utilizadas:

- **Unity 3D.** - Es un framework y motor para desarrollo de videojuegos, multiplataforma creado por Unity Technologies. Unity está disponible como plataforma de desarrollo para Microsoft Windows, OS X y Linux [7].
- **Blender.** - Es un programa informático multiplataforma, dedicado especialmente al modelado, iluminación, renderizado, animación y creación de gráficos tridimensionales, Actualmente es compatible con todas las versiones de Windows, Mac OS X [8].
- **Android SDK.** - El SDK (Software Development Kit) de Android, incluye un conjunto de herramientas de desarrollo [9].

3.1 Metodología DAV

DAV (Desarrollo Ágil de Videojuegos) fue la metodología utilizada para el desarrollo del videojuego, esta metodología nace con la unión de las características de SCRUM y XGD (Extreme Game Development), con la finalidad de proporcionar una estructura que permita la creación de videojuegos de forma técnica y sencilla. Esta metodología se compone de los siguientes elementos: valores, prácticas, roles, reuniones, fases, artefactos y herramientas [10].

4 Interfaz de usuario en el aprendizaje

Desarrollar un videojuego es una tarea ardua que requiere de herramientas apropiadas para el correcto funcionamiento de cada uno de los elementos que conformarán el videojuego. A continuación, se detalla a breves rasgos las herramientas utilizadas las cuales se dividen en dos grupos (codificación y diseño gráfico).

4.1 Escenario 3D

El contacto visual potencia la adquisición de nuevo conocimiento al ofrecer una forma rápida e interactiva de aprendizaje, lo menciona la *Dr. Anne Bamford* [11], también indica que el 85% de los niños en su estudio prefieren aprender viendo lo que están haciendo y un 15% prefiere escuchar lo que aprende.

De acuerdo al párrafo anterior, el 3D es un elemento muy importante para el aprendizaje, motivo por el cual el videojuego descrito en este artículo fue totalmente implementado en un espacio tridimensional permitiendo al jugador una inmersión total dentro del juego mejorando el aprendizaje mediante los elementos 3D y facilitando la comprensión de las acciones, dicho escenario se presenta en la **Fig. 1**.

Fig. 1. Escenario 3D del videojuego "Hello Remi"

4.2 Influencia del color en la memoria

Aprender la Lógica de programación requiere memorizar y dominar los diferentes conceptos que se incluyen en esta área. La psicología de los colores influye directamente en la memoria, tal y como lo describe *Mariam Adawiah Adawiah* [12] en su artículo. Un estudio de marketing ha encontrado que los colores aumentan el reconocimiento de una marca hasta en un 80% [13]. La mayoría de los anuncios publicitarios utilizan colores como elementos importantes para influir en la atención de la gente.

De acuerdo al estudio anterior existen 4 colores que se utilizan para un aprendizaje más efectivo, estos colores se utilizaron para la interfaz de usuario (UI) y los diferentes objetos que se encuentran dentro del mundo, de tal forma que el jugador pueda memorizar las acciones de los botones de acuerdo a su color, creando una mayor agilidad en el proceso de aprendizaje.

El la **Fig. 2** se puede apreciar los diferentes matices de colores utilizados para los botones de acciones del bloque condicional, cada color aporta de una manera diferente en el proceso de aprendizaje.

Fig. 2. Significado de los colores en la interfaz

5 Experiencia de usuario

5.1 Acciones visuales

De acuerdo a lo descrito en la **subsección 4.1**, la mejor forma de aprender es mediante un aprendizaje visual, la Lógica de Programación llega a ser compleja para ciertas personas ya que no logran visualizar que están haciendo o que quieren hacer cuando están empezando a conocer los conceptos de (secuencias, ciclos y decisiones) [14].

El siguiente ejemplo muestra un pequeño enunciado que puede ser resuelto con algoritmos informales [14], Problema: Un peatón tiene que cruzar una calle que tiene una distancia de 5 pasos, un poste de luz se encuentra a la misma distancia con un largo y ancho de 1 paso, Solución: Caminar 5 pasos hacia adelante luego girar hacia la izquierda dar un paso, girar hacia la derecha y dar un paso más.

La solución anterior aparentemente es correcta, leyendo nuevamente el párrafo anterior, el peatón se olvidó del poste que se encontraba a 5 pasos al frente, por lo que tendría que dar únicamente 4 pasos para evitar colisionar con él poste. Estos errores son muy comunes al tratar de resolver un enunciado cuando no existe un apartado visual que permita entender el contexto del problema.

La **Fig. 3** muestra el siguiente Problema: El jugador debe obtener el ítem blanco, Solución: El problema se lo puede resolver mentalmente y existen tres soluciones para el mismo problema, algo muy diferente a las posibilidades de solución del primer problema.

Fig. 3. Ejercicio desde la perspectiva del videojuego

De esta forma se ha demostrado las facilidades que brindan los elementos visuales en la experiencia del usuario, obteniendo una mejor percepción del problema para la solución requerida.

5.2 Aprendizaje indirecto

Muchos videojuegos educativos prefieren ir por la enseñanza directa, es decir mostrar el contenido educativo desde el inicio hasta el final, lo que a corto plazo causa aburrimiento y se pierde la motivación del jugador, por otro lado, está el modelo planteado por Vygostky [5] en el cual se utiliza al videojuego como un intermediario en el proceso de aprendizaje.

Dicho de otro modo, en el videojuego planteado desde el inicio se pretende divertir al jugador ocultando el contenido educativo en los aspectos jugable, en su storyboard, en los personajes y objetivos del mismo, de esta forma el jugador no siente la presión u obligación de aprender, enfocando su atención en otros elementos del videojuego.

6 Resultados

Para realizar la evaluación del videojuego se utilizó el modelo de evaluación de juegos EGameFlow [15], el cual es considerado una técnica para evaluar el uso y la aceptación por parte del usuario, enfocándose principalmente en el aporte del conocimiento y la jugabilidad. En base al modelo se ha tomado el criterio "Mejora de conocimiento" para realizar un cuestionario enfocado a los 3 conceptos más importantes de la Lógica de Programación (secuencias, ciclos y condiciones) [14].

Las preguntas se basan en los desafíos proporcionados por los diferentes niveles de dificultad del videojuego. A continuación, se detallan las preguntas con sus respectivas opciones de respuesta, un análisis de la respuesta correcta y su aporte en el conocimiento de la Lógica de Programación.

Los comandos mostrados en las preguntas del cuestionario son referentes a los utilizados en el videojuego en el "modo pro", para más información sobre los comandos y su forma de uso se puede consultar el manual localizado en la página donde se encuentra publicado el videojuego [16].

Pregunta 1

Al ejecutar el siguiente conjunto de comandos: **"go{move.1,turn.right}"**, ¿qué tipo de movimientos realiza el personaje?.

Opciones:

a) <u>El personaje realiza movimientos secuenciales.</u>
b) El personaje realiza movimientos repetitivos.
c) No realiza ninguna acción

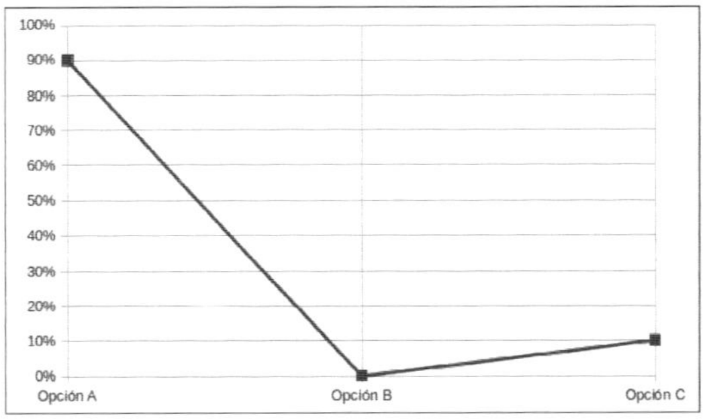

Fig. 4. Porcentaje de acierto de la pregunta 1

Análisis de la respuesta. - La respuesta correcta es la "a", ya que la sentencia indica movimientos secuenciales. Un mayor porcentaje de acierto indica que los jugadores diferencian entre sentencias secuenciales y cíclicas.

Pregunta 2

¿Qué sucede al ejecutar las siguientes acciones: **"go{move.1,use.portal"** ?.

Opciones:

a) El personaje dará un paso hacia adelante, usará el portal y girará a la izquierda.
b) El personaje dará un paso hacia adelante y luego girará en círculos.
c) <u>No se ejecutará ninguna acción.</u>

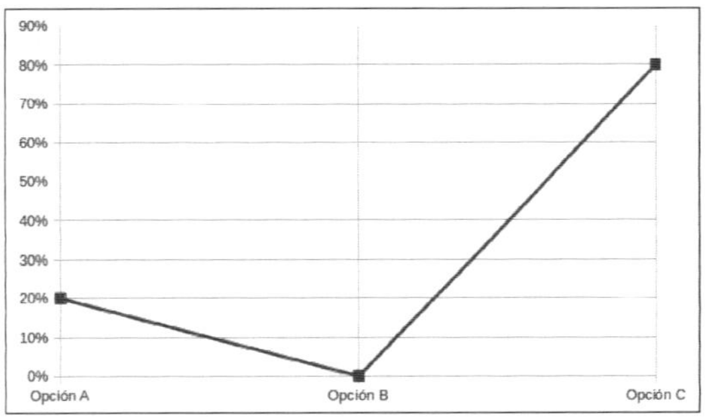

Fig. 5. Porcentaje de acierto de la pregunta 2

Análisis de la respuesta. - La respuesta correcta es la "c", ya que falta el comando "end" para finalizar el bloque. Un mayor porcentaje de acierto indica que los jugadores comprenden que las sentencias a ejecutarse deben tener un inicio y un fin.

Pregunta 3

El personaje necesita obtener las 3 calaveras y regresar a su posición inicial, ¿qué conjunto de acciones es correcto para realizar esta tarea?

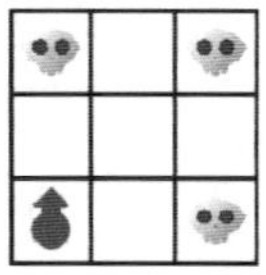

Opciones:

a) repeat(3){move.2,turn.right}
b) repeat(4){turn.right,move.2}
c) repeat(4){move.2,turn.right}

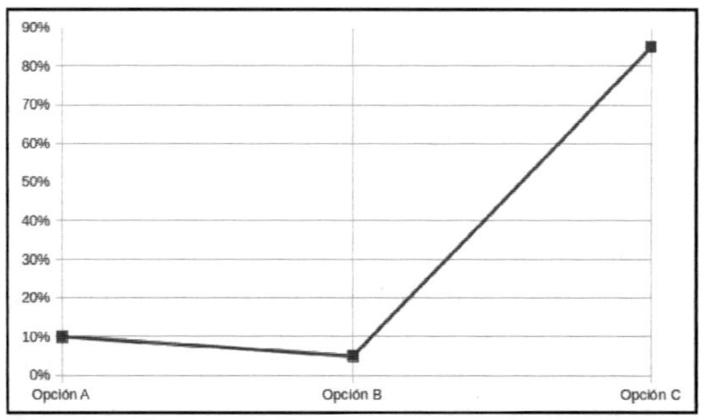

Fig. 6. Porcentaje de acierto de la pregunta 3

Análisis de la respuesta. - La respuesta correcta es la "c", ya que para obtener las tres calaveras y regresar a la posición inicial se recorren los cuatro lados del cuadrado avanzando 2 casillas y girando hacia la derecha. Un mayor porcentaje de acierto indica que los jugadores comprenden el uso de las sentencias cíclicas para repetir un grupo de acciones en base a una condición.

Pregunta 4

El personaje debe girar 3 veces hacia la derecha, ¿qué conjunto de comandos es la mejor opción?

Opciones:

a) repeat(3){turn.right}.
b) go{turn.right,turn.right,turn.right}.
c) Ninguna de las anteriores.

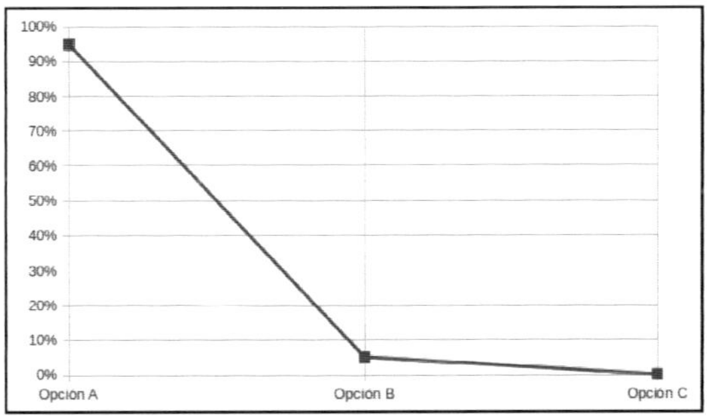

Fig. 7. Porcentaje de acierto de la pregunta 4

Análisis de la respuesta. - La respuesta correcta es la "a", ya se utiliza menos acciones y se realiza la tarea asignada. Un mayor porcentaje de acierto indica que los jugadores comprenden el concepto de repetir una misma tarea, en lugar de realizar la misma tarea varias veces, demostrando el aprendizaje de las sentencias cíclicas.

Pregunta 5

¿Qué acciones se realizarán al ejecutar el siguiente bloque de comandos: **"if(enemy.light)then{magic.dark}else{magic.light}"** ?.

Opciones:

a) Si el enemigo es blanco, usar magia negra, caso contrario usar magia blanca.
b) Si el enemigo es blanco, usar magia negra y también magia blanca.
c) Los comandos están ordenados incorrectamente.

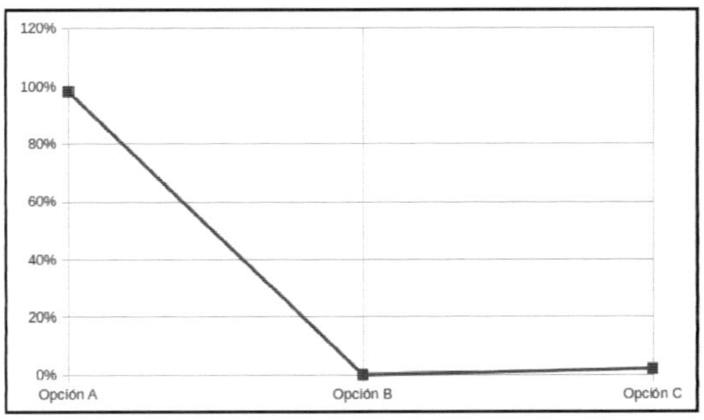

Fig. 8. Porcentaje de acierto de la pregunta 5

Análisis de la respuesta. - La respuesta correcta es la "a", ya que cumple con la sentencia propuesta. Un mayor porcentaje de acierto indica que los jugadores comprenden el concepto de las sentencias condicionales y que solo se puede tomar un camino dependiendo de la condición.

Pregunta 6

Frente al jugador puede aparecer un enemigo negro, ¿cuál opción es correcta para llegar a la casilla B?

Opciones:

a) if(enemy.dark)then{turn.left,move.1,turn.right,move.1,turn.right,move.1} else{move.2}
b) if(enemy.light)then{move.1,magic.dark,turn.right,move.1,turn.right,move.1} else{move.2}
c) Ninguna de las anteriores.

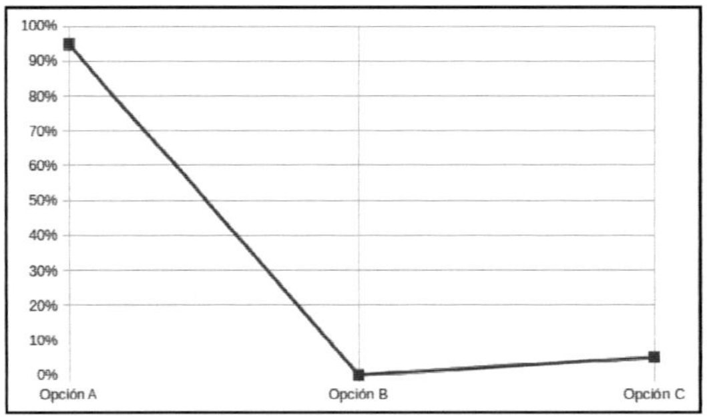

Fig. 9. Porcentaje de acierto de la pregunta 6

Análisis de la respuesta. - La respuesta correcta es la "a", ya que si aparece un enemigo el personaje rodeará al enemigo hasta llegar a la casilla B, caso contrario solo tendrá que avanzar 2 casillas para llegar a su destino. Un mayor porcentaje de acierto indica que los jugadores comprenden el concepto de las sentencias condicionales y la ayuda que brindan para tomar decisiones en determinadas situaciones.

6.1 Comparativa del aprendizaje tradicional vs videojuegos educativos

Se realizó un análisis comparativo del porcentaje de acierto al resolver el cuestionario del apartado anterior, usando los conocimientos aprendidos del libro "La esencia de la Lógica de Programación" [14] y los conocimientos obtenidos después de jugar el videojuego, el tiempo necesario para entender los conceptos por medio del videojuego fueron 10 a 15 minutos, mientras que el tiempo para captar los conceptos básicos del libro fue de 1 hora.

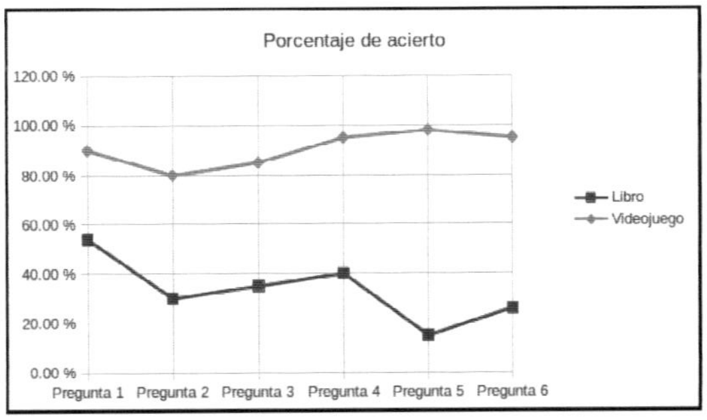

Fig. 10. Comparativa del aprendizaje tradicional vs videojuegos educativos

7 Conclusiones

En este artículo se ha demostrado que los videojuegos educativos pueden ser excelentes herramientas para incentivar al aprendizaje de conocimientos de áreas técnicas como la Lógica de Programación, ya que los videojuegos enfocados como propuestas divertidas logran captar la atención del jugador, motivándolo a solucionar los problemas planteados mientras indirectamente está aprendiendo un nuevo conocimiento.

Los resultados obtenidos son bastante aceptables al tratarse de un proyecto independiente, se logró captar la atención de una gran cantidad de jugadores sin conocimientos en el área de la programación. Se espera que en el futuro más desarrolladores propongan ideas similares para que a largo plazo existan más videojuegos educativos que se enfoquen en el aprendizaje indirecto.

El análisis de los resultados indica que se cumplió el objetivo del videojuego, ya que se generó aprendizaje sin que los jugadores se dieran cuenta, personas totalmente ajenas al área de la Informática aprendieron conceptos de la lógica de programación (secuencias, ciclos, condiciones) que nunca antes habían visto. De esta forma queda demostrado que los procesos de aprendizaje han cambiado y los videojuegos desde el enfoque educativo pueden llegar a ser herramientas muy útiles para los niños, adolescentes y adultos.

Referencias

1. ElMundo.es.: Enseñar a niños a programar es lo más 'in': Las mejores herramientas. http://www.elmundo.es/economia/2015/07/09/559d4c7222601de4208b45b1.html (2015).

2. J. Biggs.: Light-Bot Teaches Computer Science with A Cute Little Robot and Some Symbol-Based Programming". https://techcrunch.com/2013/06/26/light-bot-teaches-computer-science-with-a-cute-little-robot-and-some-symbol-based-programming (2015).
3. Cbsnews.com.: Coding for kindergarteners: App teaches kids computer basics. 2014. http://www.cbsnews.com/news/scratch-jr-app-teaches-kindergarteners-the-basics-of-computer-coding (2014).
4. E. Cisneros.: Videojuego Educativo como apoyo a la enseñanza de la Algoritmia para los estudiantes del Programa Nacional de Formación en Sistemas e Informática. (2010).
5. C. Money.: Theories of Childhood: An Introduction to Dewey, Montessori, Erikson, Piaget and Vygotsky, Redleaf Press. (2013).
6. A. McFarlane.: An exploration by TEEM of the contribution which games can make to the education process. http://questgarden.com/84/74/3/091102061307/files/teem_gamesined_full.pdf (2016).
7. Unity3D.com.: Unity - Game engine, tools and multiplatform. https://unity3d.com/es/unity (2017).
8. B. Foundation.: Blender | Free and open 3d creation software. https://www.blender.org/about (2017).
9. Develover.Android.com.: Android Studio y SDK Tools. https://developer.android.com/studio/index.html (2017).
10. M. Barreno.: Adaptación de las metodologías ágiles Scrum y Extreme Game Development en una metodología para el desarrollo de videojuegos en Android. Caso práctico. http://dspace.espoch.edu.ec/handle/123456789/2711 (2013).
11. A. Bamford.: The 3D in Education. (2011).
12. M. Adawiah.: The Influence of Colour on Memory Performance. (2013).
13. J. Morton.: Why color matters. (2010).
14. O. Trejos.: La esencia de la Lógica de Programación. (2010).
15. F. Fong, EGameFlow: A scale to measure learners enjoyment of e-learning games. (2010).
16. H. Rahman.: Hello Remi - Gamejolt, http://gamejolt.com/games/hello-remi/209204 (2017).

Cloud Services: The Good, the Bad, and the Ugly

Efraín R. Fonseca C.[1], John W. Castro[2], Cristina Pesántez[1], Margarita Aucancela[3], Christhian Chamba[1], and Tatiana Suntaxi[1]

[1] Departamento de Ciencias de la Computación, Universidad de las Fuerzas Armadas ESPE, Sangolquí, Ecuador
[2] Departamento de Ingeniería Informática y Ciencias de la Computación, Universidad de Atacama, Copiapó, Chile
[3] Facultad de Administración de Empresas, Escuela Superior Politécnica de Chimborazo ESPOCH, Riobamba, Ecuador
{erfonseca, rcpesantez1, ccchamba, tgsuntaxi}@espe.edu.ec
john.castro@uda.cl
maucancela@espoch.edu.ec

Abstract. —***Background:*** The hiring of cloud services is the current trend of companies and even people, mainly due to it avoids spend money in complex infrastructures implementation, maintenance and staff recruitment. However, there is uncertainty about the information confidentiality handled outside the context of their owners. ***Aim:*** To investigate the conditions under which cloud services are supplied, specially regarding the service level agreement (SLA) included in the providers' offering in terms of: confidentiality, security and information privacy. ***Method:*** A systematic mapping study was carried out in order to inquire about SLA's confidentiality, privacy and security offered by cloud service providers. ***Results:*** From the information available on 20 primary studies we found that each cloud service provider offers a different SLA, which are based on standards and existing best practices. Additionally, we found that the cloud service provider's security level is determined by metrics established through trust models. ***Conclusions:*** The SLA of cloud service providers is diverse, which forces the user to know different parameters to select the service that best suits their needs, always prioritizing the security, data privacy and services availability.

Keywords: cloud services, cloud computing, systematic mapping study, information security, service level agreement

1 Introducción

En la actualidad los servicios en la nube (SeN) tienen gran demanda en las organizaciones que carecen de infraestructuras tecnológicas complejas [4]. Los beneficios de los SeN se miden en términos de eficiencia [13], aceleración de la innovación [25], ahorro de costos [11], elasticidad y escalabilidad [13] y eliminación de las limitaciones geográficas para el flujo de datos [25]. Esto ha provocado que muchas organizaciones opten por contratar estos servicios, como evidencia el reporte de Gartner, el cual predice que la inversión en el mercado de los SeN superará los 244 mil millones de dólares para el año 2017 [19].

Los SeN representan un modelo de prestación de servicios tecnológicos, donde el usuario accede a un catálogo de opciones, basado en tres modelos definidos: *(i) Software as a Service (SaaS),* donde el consumidor usa las aplicaciones del proveedor a través de una interfaz, pero no administra o controla la infraestructura de la nube o las capacidades individuales de una aplicación; *(ii)Plataform as a Service (PaaS),* donde el consumidor despliega las aplicaciones de la nube usando lenguajes de programación, bibliotecas, servicios y herramientas soportadas por el proveedor, pero tampoco administra o controla la infraestructura; e *(iii) Infrastructure as a service (IaaS)*, donde el consumidor posee capacidad de procesamiento, almacenamiento, redes y otros recursos de computación, pero no administra o controla la infraestructura implícita de la nube [19].

A pesar de los evidentes beneficios que brindan los SeN, gran parte de las organizaciones aún son escépticas en encomendar a un tercero sus sistemas de gestión de información confidencial [19]. La desconfianza al parecer radica en temas de seguridad (ataques maliciosos), fallas de infraestructura (cortes del servicio) e incumplimiento del acuerdo de nivel de servicio (*SLA de las siglas del inglés Service Level Agreement*) [19]. De acuerdo a una encuesta realizada por Intel Security en el 2015, el 88% de un total de 1.200 directivos de Tecnologías de la Información (TI), señalaron que sus organizaciones confían hoy más en los SeN que hace un año. No obstante, sólo el 9% afirmo confiar completamente en proveedores de los SeN para mantener seguros datos sensibles [20].

En virtud de esta información, nos nace la inquietud de conocer si ¿Es posible contratar un SeN que realmente brinde seguridad? y ¿Cuán acertados son los aspectos que consideran los proveedores de SeN al momento de establecer su SLA? Estos cuestionamientos nos han motivado a llevar a cabo un estudio exploratorio de carácter empírico con el propósito de identificar los factores que determinan la calidad de los servicios ofertados en la nube, referidos a la Seguridad de la información, disponibilidad del servicio y cumplimiento de SLA. Para contextualizar la problemática identificada, se plantearon las siguientes preguntas de investigación (*RQ de las siglas del inglés Research Question*):

RQ1: ¿Qué parámetros de calidad consideran los SLA ofertados por los proveedores de SeN?
RQ2: ¿Con base a qué modelos y atributos se miden los niveles de Seguridad que ofertan los proveedores de SeN?
RQ3: ¿Qué tipo de información se está migrando a la nube y cuáles son los servicios más utilizados?
RQ4: ¿Cuáles son las principales amenazas a la confidencialidad de los datos al usar los SeN?

Con el objetivo de dar respuesta a las preguntas de investigación, se realizó un Mapeo Sistemático de Literatura (SMS de las siglas del inglés systematic mapping study). De la información contenida en los 20 estudios primarios resultantes del SMS, encontramos que los proveedores de SeN aplican distintos modelos (por ejemplo: evaluación del riesgo) para dar fiel cumplimiento a los SLA que ofertan.

Lo que resta del artículo está estructurado como sigue. En la Sección 2, se analizan los trabajos relacionados. La Sección 3 describe el SMS. En la Sección 4 se responden las RQ. En la Sección 5, se discuten los hallazgos obtenidos. Finalmente, en la Sección 6, se presentan las conclusiones.

2 Trabajos Relacionados

Actualmente los SeN se han convertido en una tendencia tecnológica dadas las facilidades que ofrecen [8]; probablemente porque, entre otras cosas, evitan la compra y mantenimiento de infraestructuras complejas y el soporte técnico inherente [3]. Sin embargo, a pesar de todas estas bondades, muchas empresas aún están renuentes a encomendar su información a terceros, fundamentalmente por temas de seguridad [6] y por políticas impuestas por los proveedores de SeN sobre la confidencialidad, disponibilidad e integridad de los datos y la delimitación entre las responsabilidades del usuario y del proveedor [24]. Por ejemplo, se esperaría que el SLA de los proveedores de SeN especifique los valores más altos en lo que respecta a: Disponibilidad, rendimiento, seguridad / privacidad de los datos, espectativas de recuperación de desastres, entre otros [28].

Luego de realizar una revisión inicial de literatura encontramos que existe una discusión intrincada en torno a los SLA de los proveedores de SeN, con énfasis en los mecanismos utilizados para su cumplimiento [21]. Wang Minchao & otros [29] proponen un sistema que permite evaluar la fiabilidad de un proveedor mediante su reputación. Además, ofrecen una plantilla de SLA que gestiona una negociación más equitativa entre proveedor y usuario.

Melaños [12] analiza los riesgos, amenazas y vulnerabilidades de la Seguridad en los SeN. De igual forma, examina el cumplimiento normativo necesario para la implantación de modelos de SeN, y resalta la preocupación que tienen los usuarios en cuanto a la seguridad e integridad de los datos ya que esto podría provocar graves inconvenientes a sus organizaciones como: paralización de sus actividades, dañar su imagen y reputación, entre otros.

Wang Ning & otros [15] presentan una arquitectura de SeN para facilitar y colaborar en la integración de los datos entre diferentes centros de datos. Además, analizan la migración de datos de muchas organizaciones hacia los SeN. Con el modelo propuesto ofrecen acceso fácil y eficiente a los datos que los usuarios comparten. Sin embargo, en esta investigación no se menciona el tipo de información que las organizaciones están migrando a los SeN.

En el estudio de Rejón [18], se describen las bondades de los SeN, sus principales ventajas así como la reducción de costos que significa su adecuada implementación. Además, se mencionan las principales limitaciones de los SeN como son: Licenciamiento, portabilidad de datos, restricciones legales de contratos y contratación con la administración pública. El autor se focaliza principalmente en las aplicaciones de los SeN en los sectores de: Agroindustria, turismo, eficiencia energética e industrias culturales.

León y Rosero [9] mencionan los aspectos que se deben considerar antes de contratar un SeN y analizan como deben definirse los servicios que una empresa necesita. Los autores concluyen que gracias a los SeN, las organizaciones pueden dedicarse a cumplir sus objetivos sin preocuparse por la infraestructura tecnológica que deben adquirir para que sus operaciones de TI funcionen normalmente. El estudio realizado por Shaikha y Sasikumarb [23] representa una aproximación a parte de los interrogantes que queremos resolver en la presente investigación, ya que en él se analizan las técnicas que adoptan ciertos proveedores para brindar calidad en sus servicios, algunos de los modelos de confianza válidos y las dimensiones que deben tomarse en cuenta para medir la seguridad. Estos autores concluyen que al usar un modelo de confianza un proveedor puede tener un punto de referencia sobre sus deficiencias y elaborar mejoras.

En resumen, la discusión en torno a los SeN es muy variada y controversial. Por un lado, la confianza en los SeN tiende a ser extremista, mientras que en otros casos hay mucho escepticismo sobre su uso. Por lo tanto, el panorama entorno a las pautas que deben considerarse para abordar de forma adecuada una negociación con un proveedor de SeN es incierto. No se conoce: (i) Cuales son los niveles de seguridad mínimos que deben ofrecer los SeN, (ii) el tipo de información que se encuentra en la nube, (iii) los principales riesgos de la información y (iv) los parámetros de calidad que se deben considerar a la hora de escoger un proveedor de SeN. Todos estos aspectos nos han motivado a realizar la presente investigación sobre lo bueno, lo malo y lo feo de los SeN.

3 Mapeo Sistemático de Literatura

Un SMS es un método de investigación secundario que está diseñado para dar una visión general de una temática de investigación específica a través de la clasificación y el conteo de los estudios relacionados con la misma [17,7]. Basados en las guías de Petersen & otros [17] y Kitchenham & Charters [7], se planteó la realización de las siguientes fases dentro del SMS: (1) Definición de las preguntas de investigación, (2) planteamiento de la estrategia de búsqueda, (3) establecimiento del proceso de selección y, (4) extracción de datos.

3.1 Definición de las Preguntas de Investigación

La definición de las RQ tiene como propósito establecer de forma explícita el alcance del objetivo de la investigación, ya que plantean claramente lo que se desea encontrar (las RQ se detallan en la Sección 1). Por tanto, el SMS se enfoca en dar respuesta a las RQ [7].

3.2 Definición de la Estrategia de Búsqueda

Para realizar el SMS es necesario definir una estrategia de búsqueda. Para este caso, se establecieron las siguientes actividades: (1) Definir los criterios de inclusión y exclusión, (2) crear el grupo de control (GC) de literatura, (3) construir la cadena de búsqueda y, (4) buscar los estudios candidatos.

Antes de ejecutar la búsqueda en las bases digitales es necesario definir los criterios de inclusión y exclusión, que establecen las condiciones que deben satisfacer los estudios para ser considerados o no, como relevante para la investigación. En nuestro caso se establecieron los siguientes criterios por consenso:

Criterios de inclusión. El artículo: (i) Se refiere a los niveles de Seguridad ofrecidos por los SeN, (ii) reporta los parámetros que consideran los SLA, (iii) enumera el tipo de información que se almacena en la nube, (iv) menciona los servicios más utilizados por los usuarios en la nube, y (v) describe las amenazas a la confidencialidad de los datos al usar los SeN.

Criterios de exclusión. El artículo: (i) Discute temas generales de Seguridad de los SeN, (ii) describe temas de SLA de forma general y no detalla su estructura ni características, (iii) no considera las amenazas a las que están expuestos los datos al usar los SeN, (iv) reporta la información que se está migrando a la nube de forma general y no determina los servicios más utilizados, (v) discute la parte meramente tecnológica de la implementación de los SeN.

Una vez definidos los criterios de inclusión y exclusión, es posible la creación del GC, a través del cual se identifican los términos afines al objetivo del SMS, que conformarán la cadena de búsqueda. El establecimiento del GC se realizó en dos etapas. En la primera, se conformó un GC preliminar por cada investigador que participó en el SMS. Los investigadores conformaron sus GC preliminares basados en los criterios de inclusión y exclusión y en su experticia de búsqueda. Como resultado de esta etapa se obtuvieron 20 estudios. En la segunda, se realizó una validación cruzada de los estudios de los GC preliminares. La validación consistió en la revisión detallada de los 20 estudios por cada uno de los investigadores. Finalmente, se sometió a votación la permanencia o no de los estudios revisados, obteniendo 8 estudios que conformaron el GC definitivo.

La construcción de la cadena de búsqueda es un proceso detallado en el que fundamentalmente se realizan actividades de revisión de los estudios del GC y adquisición y filtrado de términos generales, comunes y específicos afines al objetivo de investigación. El proceso consta de cuatros etapas. En la primera etapa, cada investigador busca términos referentes al objetivo de la investigación y en consenso se define un listado general de términos. En la segunda etapa, apoyados de herramientas de gestión de información documental (por ejemplo Atlas.ti), se realiza un conteo de términos comunes en cada estudio de control y entre estudios. En la tercera etapa, se realiza un filtrado y categorización de términos, con base en un mapeo de los términos identificados en la etapa 1, con respecto a los términos ubicados en la etapa 2. La categorización se realiza en términos de relevancia; es decir, son filtrados los términos que más se repiten en cada estudio y entre los estudios y que además fueron identificados por la mayoría de investigadores.

Finalmente, en la cuarta etapa se realizan pruebas iterativas para ajustar la cadena de búsqueda en una base digital relevante (de preferencia en SCOPUS, ya que cubre a otras bases digitales), utilizando los términos obtenidos en la etapa anterior y los conectores lógicos OR para unir sinónimos y AND para agregar términos distintos. La cadena seleccionada será capaz de recuperar: (i) la mayoría de los estudios del GC, (ii) en lo posible un número razonable de estudios, y (iii) estudios cuyos títulos respondan al objetivo del SMS. La cadena que cumplió estas características es:
("cloud service" OR "cloud computing" OR "cloud") AND ("privacy" OR "confidence" OR "trust") AND ("security" OR "security risks") AND ("SLA guarantees" OR "assurances") AND ("user" OR "customers" OR "providers") AND ("Quality" OR "quality of service") AND ("SLA").

La búsqueda de estudios candidatos se realiza a partir de la cadena de búsqueda, en las bases digitales seleccionadas: Springer, ACM, ScienceDirect e IEEE Xplore. Es preciso mencionar que para la búsqueda de estudios candidatos, se consideró adicionalmente en cada base digital lo siguiente: (i) estudios publicados en actas de congreso, revistas internacionales u otros representativos, (ii) publicaciones escritas en inglés y (iii) adaptación de la cadena de búsqueda a la sintaxis de la base. Con base en las consideraciones indicadas, los estudios candidatos fueron: 3 en Springer, 19 en ACM, 157 en ScienceDirect y 158 en IEEE Xplore. Luego de depurar estos estudios se obtuvieron *337 estudios candidatos*.

3.3 Proceso de Selección de Estudios Primarios

Los estudios primarios se obtienen luego de aplicar iterativamente los criterios de inclusión y exclusión a los estudios candidatos. El proceso de selección consta de las siguientes actividades: (i) Depuración de estudios candidatos, (ii) Selección de estudios y, (iii) selección de estudios primarios.

La depuración de los estudios candidatos es realizada en consenso por dos investigadores, eliminando los duplicados por base y entre bases. El resultado de la depuración es un listado de *estudios candidatos*. La selección de estudios se realiza aplicando los criterios de inclusión y exclusión al título, resumen y palabras claves de los *estudios candidatos*. Como resultado obtuvimos un total de *158 estudios seleccionados* y se descartaron *179 estudios candidatos*. La selección de estudios primarios es realizada aplicando por segunda ocasión los criterios de inclusión y exclusión, esta vez a los estudios seleccionados, con la diferencia de que en esta iteración los criterios son aplicados sobre los artículos completos, para lo cual es necesario descargar los *estudios seleccionados*. Finalmente, obtuvimos un total de *20 estudios primarios*, descartando *138 estudios seleccionados*.

3.4 Extracción de datos

El proceso de extracción de la información necesaria para responder las RQ a partir de los estudios primarios, fue realizado en consenso por dos investigadores. Este proceso consiste de una revisión exhaustiva de los *20 estudios primarios*, lo cual se reporta en la Sección 4. Con el único propósito de motivar la replicación de esta investigación, hemos publicado el detalle del proceso realizado en el siguiente enlace.

4 Resultados

En esta sección se presentan los resultados del SMS divididos en dos partes: (i) Generalidades de los estudios primarios y (ii) respuestas a las RQ. La Figura 1 resume la primera parte a modo de una visión sintética de los 20 estudios primarios identificados, la cual se presenta en dos regiones. En la primera (lado izquierdo), se despliegan dos gráficos de dispersión XY (parte superior e inferior), los cuales muestran burbujas en las intersecciones de las categorías: Tipo - año de publicación y tipo - amenazas a la confidencialidad de los datos. Los tipos de publicación son revista, congreso, workshop y coloquio. El número de estudios primarios clasificados como pertenecientes a cada categoría determina el tamaño de las burbujas. En la segunda región (lado derecho) de la Figura 1, se muestra el número de estudios primarios publicados por año. Como se observa, los estudios primarios han sido publicados en su mayoría en revistas (53%) y congresos (35%).

A continuación se detallan las respuestas dadas a las RQ a partir de la síntesis de los estudios primarios.

RQ1: ¿Qué parámetros de calidad consideran los SLA ofertados por los proveedores de SeN?

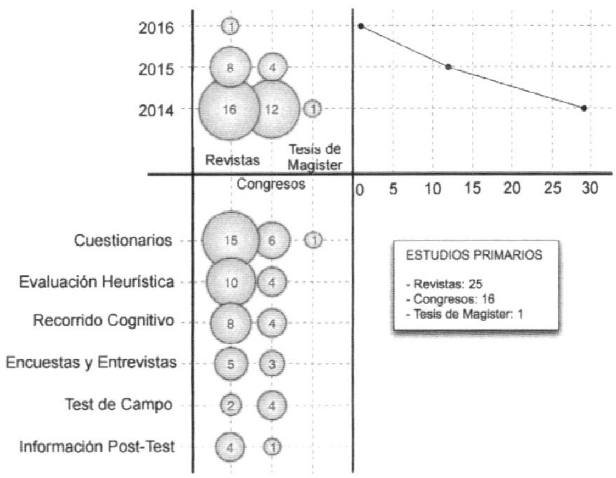

Fig. 1. Mapeo con la Distribución de Estudios Primarios según las Amenazas a la Cofidencialidad de los datos, Incluyendo Tipo y Año de Publicación

Dentro del modelo de confianza que propone Shaikha y Sasikumarb [23], los parámetros de calidad que un SeN debe contemplar son los siguientes:

- Gestión de identidades: Incluye la creación, el almacenamiento y la gestión del ciclo de vida de la identidad de los usuarios de la nube.
- Autenticación: Mide el procedimiento proporcionado por un SeN para comprobar la autenticación de usuario.
- Autorización: Se requiere autorización por parte de los usuarios para poder realizar cualquier tarea sobre los datos almacenados.
- Mecanismo de protección de datos: Mide la confidencialidad, integridad y disponibilidad de los datos.
- Confidencialidad: Evalúa el medio dado por un proveedor de SeN para brindar confidencialidad a la comunicación entre el usuario y el proveedor a través de distintos mecanismos (por ejemplo canales seguros de encriptación).
- Intensidad de la comunicación: Mide el rendimiento del SeN al momento de acceder a los datos o cuando se está transmitiendo información.
- Virtualización: Mide la seguridad en la capa de virtualización de una arquitectura de computación en la nube.
- Cumplimiento: Define el grado en el cual el proveedor cumple con los parámetros de calidad considerados en este modelo, sin dejar de lado las regulaciones impuestas por los organismos de control autorizados.
- Servicio administrado en la nube: Específica el tipo de servicio, el proveedor de servicio y el número de usuarios registrados para ese servicio. %e información contable.
- Confianza del modelo: El evaluador de la confianza usa los datos de servicio para calcular el valor de la confianza en función de parámetros estáticos y dinámicos.

- Registro de Servicio: Es la base de datos que registra la información de un servicio en la nube. Se compone de registros de entrada, de utilización del servicio, del número de transacciones exitosas y fallidas, tiempo de respuesta y demás parámetros relacionados con la prestación del servicio.
- Feedback sobre la seguridad: Investigación dinámica en la Web en la que se incluyen las fuentes de retroalimentación, principalmente los comentarios de los usuarios, para obtener conclusiones acerca de la seguridad del SeN.

Según Huang & Nicol [5], es preciso considerar la cadena de confianza establecida entre el proveedor, el servicio, el usuario, el corredor y el auditor de SeN. Dentro de esta cadena, los criterios a evaluar son: Acreditación, auditoría de cumplimiento de políticas, atributos (evaluados o certificados), auto evaluación e información reveladora y la reputación / recomendación.

RQ2: ¿Con base a qué modelos y atributos se miden los niveles de seguridad que ofertan los proveedores de SeN?

Trapero & otros [27], indican que entre los modelos empleados para medir los niveles de seguridad, se encuentran las: Técnicas de evaluación continua, metodologías de evaluación continua del riesgo y el monitoreo continuo de los proveedores de SeN para medir el cumplimiento de los acuerdos de seguridad y privacidad en sus servicios. Por un lado, los proveedores de SeN pueden usar los resultados de la evaluación continua para mejorar sus servicios. Mientras que los clientes, pueden optar por el proveedor que más les convenga, tomando como referencia el resultado de las evaluaciones [27].

De acuerdo con el estudio de Alia & otros [2], los niveles de seguridad en los SeN vienen dados en función de los siguientes atributos de seguridad: confidencialidad, integridad, autenticidad, autorización, no repudio y privacidad. Cada proveedor de SeN usa su propio mecanismo de seguridad para proteger los datos de sus clientes [27,10], para lo cual podrían implementarse diferentes algoritmos criptográficos que dependerán de la oferta del servicio de los proveedores [22,16].

Las garantías de seguridad y la confianza son dos requerimientos importantes que demandan los usuarios de la nube [22]. Por lo que se puede mencionar que la confianza en los SeN es el resultado de la interacción entre la seguridad, la privacidad y el riesgo [27,16]. No debemos olvidar que los monitores de SLA de servicios juegan un rol protagónico en la determinación de los niveles de servicios.

RQ3: ¿Qué tipo de información se está migrando a la nube y cuáles son los servicios más utilizados?

La oferta principal de los SeN incluye la sincronización y compartición de información, independiente de su tipo. Sin embargo, las empresas y las personas prefieren migrar a la nube información de uso cotidiano que no represente mayor consumo de recursos, cuya gestión sea sencilla y principalmente no sea muy confidencial (por ejemplo: documentos, fotos de baja definición) [30].

Los servicios más demandados en la nube están relacionados con la virtualización de recursos físicos [26], principalmente para evitar: el incremento de infraestructura física (por ejemplo servidores, clusters de almacenamiento) [16], la complejidad de la arquitectura, pérdida de control sobre las configuraciones, entre otros [22]. La virtualización, debería considerar la seguridad de la información gestionada, así como también la colaboración, la creación y gestión de contenidos, el almacenamiento y el flujo de trabajo [1]. De la mano de la seguridad de la información, los proveedores de SeN incluyen en su oferta alta disponibilidad de sus servicios, la cual es posible gracias a la redundancia de su infraestructura [30,22].

RQ4: ¿Cuáles son las principales amenazas a la confidencialidad de los datos al usar los SeN?

En determinadas ocasiones los SeN han sido víctimas de ataques y vulneraciones de su seguridad y privacidad, principalmente por trasgresión de los protocolos de seguridad establecidos. Por ejemplo, en ciertas ocasiones los proveedores de SeN se ven obligados a permitir el acceso a los datos de sus usuarios, a las agencias de control gubernamental; o en su defecto, son descuidadas las vulnerabilidades de seguridad que todo el tiempo se están presentando [27]. A continuación se especifican las principales amenazas que podrían afectar a los SeN:

1. Las brechas de datos: Las organizaciones cuya información confidencial está en riesgo por la presencia de brechas de seguridad, corren el peligro de perder su prestigio e inclusive dejar de funcionar [1].
2. Autenticación: la inadecuada gestión y manejo de los datos para la autenticación crean vulnerabilidad ante los ataques; ante lo cual el proveedor de SeN debe implementar mecanismos de prevención, por ejemplo diseñando algoritmos adecuados de encriptación [16,2].
3. Aprovisionamiento: se da cuando la administración de cuentas se delega a diferentes proveedores y c/u tiene una gestión de identidad diferente [16].
4. Privacidad: Es importante definir con los proveedores de SeN la propiedad de la información y el sitio donde es almacenada, ya que el uso de la información por parte del proveedor podría no estar claramente definida en los términos del servicio o contrato, permitiendo usarla para sus propósitos o venderla a un tercero [1, 27].

En un estudio realizado por Monteiro y Vasconcelos [14] se encontró que las principales preocupaciones que tienen las organizaciones y las personas a la hora de elegir un proveedor para migrar sus servicios a la nube son: el rendimiento del servicio, la disponibilidad, la seguridad, la privacidad de los datos y la pérdida de información; es decir, las preocupaciones son principalmente a nivel operativo.

5 Discusión

La contratación de los SeN y la permanencia de los clientes con un proveedor de SeN determinado, se basan en una relación de confianza, la cual fundamentalmente está representada por el SLA que oferta el proveedor de SeN y el nivel de cumplimiento que se da al mismo [22]. En la práctica, la confianza se basa en factores como: la reputación, la auto-evaluación, el cumplimiento de políticas y las certificaciones y la aplicación de modelos de confianza [23] del proveedor de SeN [5]. Estos factores estructuran un modelo de confianza que actúa como un patrón de referencia y clasificación para medir en términos generales: la seguridad, confidencialidad, integridad y disponibilidad de la información que brinda el proveedor de SeN [23].

A su vez, el SLA que ofertan los proveedores de SeN, representa un factor de confianza adicional para los clientes, dado que este documento: detalla la calidad del servicio que oferta el proveedor, guía al usuario en caso de fallos y especifica características de interés del usuario (por ejemplo, el porcentaje de disponibilidad del servicio contratado). Más específicamente, los SLA están orientados a determinar los aspectos contractuales entre el proveedor y el cliente de SeN. La mayoría de estos aspectos se basan en estándares y mejores prácticas existentes. Por el lado del cliente, paralelamente a la elección del SLA más adecuado, es preciso determinar: (i) Qué aplicaciones o cargas de trabajo llevará a la nube, (ii) necesidades actuales de infraestructura, (iii) requisitos de seguridad, (iv) nivel de portabilidad de la información, (v) uso de la nube pública o privada y, (vi) características idóneas del SLA, para elegir el más adecuado.

A pesar de que la prestación de los SeN se encuentra determinada por el SLA que oferta el proveedor de SeN, sería importante que el cliente priorice la protección de sus datos, para lo cual se recomienda el uso de mecanismos de autenticación basados en software o hardware. Otro aspecto a considerar, es la encriptación de los datos y la obtención de un respaldo diario de la información. Además, las organizaciones podrían contar con políticas que detallen el uso adecuado de las credenciales de los clientes, y establezcan servicios controlados, de tal manera que cada transacción sea personal.

Finalmente, es preciso indicar que este trabajo presenta como posibles **amenazas a la validez:** (i) la cobertura de las RQ, (ii) el sesgo hacia ciertas publicaciones, iii) la calidad de la evaluación, y iv) el desconocimiento del área. Es posible que las RQ planteadas cubran parcialmente la temática bajo estudio, lo que procuramos reducir planteando un objetivo de investigación y varias RQ consensuadas y alineadas con tal objetivo. Es probable que en un SMS exista la tendencia de direccionar el proceso hacia un conjunto particular de estudios, lo que evitamos creando en consenso un GC y una cadena de búsqueda generada a partir de dicho GC. También es probable que la calidad de la evaluación de los estudios no sea la idónea, debido al desconocimiento del área de investigación, lo que intentamos reducir al incluir a dos investigadores con experiencia en contratación de SeN y ejecución de SMS.

6 Conclusiones

Esta investigación consideró como objetivo la identificación de los aspectos que podrían condicionar la calidad de los SeN, en cuanto a la seguridad de la información que los usuarios migran, la disponibilidad de los SeN y el adecuado cumplimiento de los SLA por parte de los proveedores de SeN. Para cumplir con este objetivo se llevó a cabo un SMS, del cual se obtuvo un total de 20 estudios primarios relacionados con la temática de interés. Del análisis de estos estudios, determinamos que las principales características referentes a la seguridad de la información son la: confidencialidad, integridad y disponibilidad. Al respecto, los usuarios aún muestran preocupación por entregar información confidencial de sus organizaciones a los proveedores de SeN, pese a existir una tendencia marcada en el uso de estos servicios.

Previo a contratar un SeN, los clientes podrían apoyarse en modelos de confianza para evaluar o medir los servicios ofertados por los proveedores. Los criterios comunes a ser evaluados son: disponibilidad, confidencialidad, autenticidad, autorización, privacidad, aislamiento y cumplimiento legal. Dar al cliente un modelo de confianza base para elegir a un proveedor de SeN específico, permite la libre competencia entre los proveedores existentes y les obliga a mejorar sus servicios con base en la cantidad de prestaciones detalladas en su SLA, siempre y cuando sean alcanzables. En la medida en que los proveedores de SeN no hagan público su SLA a los clientes, automáticamente generarán incertidumbre e inseguridad en su contratación. Consideramos que transparentar la infraestructura mediante la cual el proveedor de SeN prestará el servicio, ayudará a afianzar los lazos de confianza entre ambas partes (cliente-proveedor).

Como trabajo futuro nos planteamos la construcción de un marco de trabajo que ayude al cliente a contratar un proveedor de SeN. Dicho marco de trabajo será construido a partir de las características de seguridad y SLA identificadas en los estudios primarios, de tal manera que permita evaluar las ofertas de proveedores de SeN y recomendar la más adecuada.

Agradecimientos. Este trabajo ha sido financiado por el proyecto: "Laboratorio Industrial en Ingeniería de Software Empírica (LI2SE)" del Departamento de Ciencias de la Computación de la Universidad de las Fuerzas Armadas ESPE.

Referencias

1. Adjei, J.K.: Explaining the role of trust in cloud computing services. info 17(1), 54–67 (2015)
2. Alia, M., Lacoste, M., He, R., Eliassen, F.: Putting together qos and security in autonomic pervasive systems. In: Proceedings of the 6th ACM Workshop on QoS and Security for Wireless and Mobile Networks. pp. 19–28 (2010)
3. Armbrust, M., Fox, A., Griffith, R., Joseph, A.D., Katz, R., Konwinski, A., Lee, G., Patterson, D., Rabkin, A., Stoica, I., Zaharia, M.: A view of cloud computing. Commun. ACM 53(4), 50–58 (Apr 2010)
4. Chinyao, L., Yahsueh, C., Wu, M.: Understanding the determinants of cloud computing adoption. Emerald Group Publishing Limited (2011)
5. Huang, J., Nicol, D.M.: Trust mechanisms for cloud computing. Journal of Cloud Computing: Advances, Systems and Applications 2(1), 9 (2013)
6. Hussain, S.A., Fatima, M., Saeed, A., Raza, I., Shahzad, R.K.: Multilevel classifica- tion of security concerns in cloud computing. Applied Computing and Informatics 13(1), 57 – 65 (2017)
7. Kitchenham, B., Charters, S.: Guidelines for performing systematic literature review in software engineering. Tech. rep., Keele U. & U. of Durham (July 2007)
8. Krishna, B.H., Kiran, S., Murali, G., Reddy, R.P.K.: Security issues in service model of cloud computing. Procedia Computer Science 87, 246–251 (2016)
9. León-Velandia, B., Rosero-Muñoz, M.: Recomendaciones para contratar servicios en la 'nube'. Revista Facultad de Ingeniería 23(37) (2014)

10. Li, S., Fu, J.: User revocation for data sharing based on broadcast cp-abe in cloud computing. In: Communications Security Conference. pp. 1–8 (May 2014)
11. Marston, S., Li, Z., Bandyopadhyay, S., Zhang, J., Ghalsasi, A.: Cloud computing the business perspective. Decision Support Systems 51, 176–189 (2011)
12. Melaños, C.: Análisis de los Riesgos Técnicos y Legales de la Seguridad en Cloud Computing. Master's thesis, ETS de Ingenieros de Telecomunicación (2013)
13. Mell, P., Grance, T.: The NIST Definition of Cloud Computing. National Institute of Standards and Technology (2011)
14. Monteiro, L., Vasconcelos, A.: Survey on important cloud service provider attributes using the smi framework. Procedia Technology 9, 253–259 (2013)
15. Ning, W., De, X., Baomin, X.: Collaborative integration and management of community information in the cloud. In: 2010 International Conference on E-Business and E-Government. pp. 1406–1409 (May 2010)
16. Patil, S., Ade, R.: Cloud data security for goal driven global software engineering projects. Procedia Computer Science 46, 548 – 557 (2015)
17. Petersen, K., Vakkalanka, S., Kuzniarz, L.: Guidelines for conducting systematic mapping studies in software engineering: An update. Information and Software Technology 64, 1 – 18 (2015)
18. Rejón, I.: Cloud computing aplicado a los sectores de la agroindustria, eficiencia energética, industrias culturales y turismo. Tech. rep., Everis (November 2012)
19. Rjaibi, W.: Obtenga confianza sobre la seguridad de los datos en la nube
20. Samani, R., Reavis, J.: Blue skies ahead?: The state of cloud adoption. Tech. rep., Intel (June 2015)
21. Sandoval, Y., Gallizo, G., Curiel, M.: Evaluation of monitoring tools for cloud computing environments. In: Conferencia Latinoamericana En Informática (CLEI). pp. 1–10 (Oct 2012)
22. Shaikh, R., Sasikumar, M.: Security issues in cloud computing: A survey. Intern. Journal of Computer Applications 44(19), 4–10 (April 2012)
23. Shaikh, R., Sasikumar, M.: Trust model for measuring security strength of cloud computing service. Procedia Computer Science 45, 380 – 389 (2015)
24. Sharma, M., Davies, P., Newell, D., Moore, P., Sidhu, C.: Text mining terms and condition to provide a confidence factor for the use of cloud services. In: 2015 10th International Conference on P2P (3PGCIC). pp. 108–115 (Nov 2015)
25. Smith, B.: Building confidence in the cloud. Available at http://ec.europa.eu/justice/news/consulting_public/0003/contributions/ (Last visited: March 21, 2017)
26. Srinivasan, M.K., Sarukesi, K., Rodrigues, P., Manoj, M.S., Revathy, P.: State-of-the-art cloud computing security taxonomies. In: Intern. Conf. on Advances in Computing, Communications and Informatics. pp. 470–476. ICACCI '12 (2012)
27. Trapero, R., Luna, J., Suri, N.: Quantifiably trusting the cloud: Putting metrics to work. IEEE Security Privacy 14(3), 73–77 (May 2016)
28. Trappler, T.: If it's in the cloud, get it on paper: Cloud computing contract issues. EducaUseReview (June 2010)
29. Wang, M., Wu, X., Zhang, W., Ding, F., Zhou, J., Pei, G.: A conceptual platform of sla in cloud computing. In: IEEE Int. Conf. on D.A.S.C. pp. 1131–1135 (2011)

30. Zhygmanovskyi, A., Yoshida, N.: Distributed cloud bursting model based on peer-to-peer overlay. In: Conf. on Future IoT and Cloud. pp. 823–828 (Aug 2015)

Proposal of a mechanism of customization of metamodels Ecore

Santiago P. Jácome-Guerrero[1], Mayra C. Salazar-Grandes[1], Alexandra Corral[1], José Luis Carrillo-Medina[1], Nancy Jacho-Guanoluisa[1], Patricio Espinel[1], Ivone Arias-Almeida[1], Juan M. Ferreira[2], Edison P. Bedón-Salazar[3]

[1] Universidad de las Fuerzas Armadas ESPE, Av. General Rumiñahui s/n, 171-5-231B Sangolquí, Ecuador
{psjacome,mcsalazar,macorral,jlcarrillo,npjacho, pgespinel,giarias}@espe.edu.ec
[2]Facultad Politécnica, Universidad Nacional de Asunción, CC 1439 San Lorenzo, Paraguay
jmferreira1978@gmail.com
[3]Universidad Técnica de Cotopaxi, Av. Simón Rodríguez, Latacunga, Ecuador
edison.bedon@utc.edu.ec

Abstract. Model-Driven Engineering (MDE) is considered as the evolution of the software development process, using models to develop software rather than the typical programming languages. The models before the occurrence of MDE were considered only as "documentation" that after the implementation were discarded. A model is specified through a well-defined language with precise syntax and semantics. In MDE this syntax is defined through a metamodel. There are scenarios that require the modification of existing meta-models, such as those of KDM or DD of the OMG, which require the extension of certain elements according to norms described in natural language and not implemeted in tools. In order to solve this problem, this article proposes a mechanism that allows the establishment of personalization guidelines (rules) for Ecore metamodels through the implementation of an Eclipse plug-in.

Keywords: Model-Driven Engineering, customization, Ecore, MDE, DSL

1 Introducción

Durante el desarrollo de software se utiliza un gran abanico de modelos que se los emplea para representar las diferentes vistas de la arquitectura de un sistema de software [1]. Se pueden tener modelos para representar los elementos constitutivos de un sistema, tales como: datos, procesos, eventos e interfaces. Se puede elegir construir modelos con cierto grado de libertad, como utilizar cajas dibujadas a mano sobre papel [2], o con cierto grado de sofisticación como utilizar diagramas UML (Unified Modeling Language) complejos, producidos con herramienta de modelado automático. Para ser procesables de manera automática los modelos deben estar descritos de manera precisa. La sintaxis abstracta de un modelo se encuentra descrita por un metamodelo (modelware) y/o gramáticas libres de contexto (grammarware) que contienen las clases, atributos y referencias que pueden usarse en los modelos, así como restricciones de integridad que los modelos han de cumplir. Definido el metamodelo, las herramientas de modelado permiten a los ingenieros de software crear modelos conformes a dicho metamodelo [3].

A pesar de que las tareas de modelado se encuentran reguladas por el metamodelo correspondiente, actualmente no existen mecanismos comúnmente aceptados que regulen la personalización (llámese también: modificación, adaptación, extensión) de metamodelos . Existen ocasiones en las cuales es común diseñar metamodelos con el propósito de que deben ser extendidos por otros desarrolladores [4]. Por ejemplo, OMG[1] considera metamodelos estándar para ser utilizados mediante la extensión de algunas parte del metamodelo. Este es el caso de los metamodelos estándar como KDM[2] (Knowledge Discovery MetaModel) y DD (Diagram Definition)[3] . Su empleo requiere la extensión de ciertas clases a través de reglas expresadas en lenguaje natural. Situación que puede introducir errores, más cuando no existe un mecanismo automatizado que permita verificar las extensiones. Por tanto, se considera que deben existir mecanismos que admitieran establecer reglas para la correcta extensión de un metamodelo, así como la gestión de dichas reglas por medio de herramientas automatizadas.

Para cambiar esta situación, en el presente artículo se considera un enfoque para la definición de reglas o directivas para la personalización de metamodelos , así como una herramienta que permita su extensión de acuerdo a las directivas definidas. La herramienta se ha desarrollado como un plug-in de Eclipse/EMF (Eclipse Modelling Framework). La herramienta fue validada al ser aplicada en los estándares señalados, así como en varios casos específicos.

El artículo se organiza de la siguiente manera. La sección 2 describe el escenario donde el mecanismo de personalización de metamodelos resulta de utilidad, lo cual ha motivado su desarrollo. La sección 3 describe el mecanismo propuesto para la personalización. La sección 4 presenta un ejemplo de utilización de la herramienta desarrollada. La sección 5 compara la propuesta con trabajos relacionados. Finalmente la sección 6 termina con las conclusiones y líneas de trabajo futuro.

2 Escenario de uso

Como se señaló, existen escenarios en las que se diseñan metamodelos con el propósito de que sean extendidos. Como los metamodelos de KDM y DD, así como también metamodelos aplicados a otros dominios, como el señalado en la sección 4, aplicado a un proceso de desarrollo de software.

---

[1] http://www.omg.org/
[2] http://www.omg.org/spec/KDM/
[3] http://www.omg.org/spec/DD/1.0/Source/10-05-01.pdf

KDM se considera como un estándar de modelado en el entorno de modernización de software. Su intención es representar como modelos, los artefactos de las aplicaciones heredadas, como puede ser el código fuente. Una vez que se tiene su representación en forma de modelos, estos son tomados como base para la modernización de la aplicación con tecnologías más recientes. De acuerdo al estándar, KDM puede extenderse para representar elementos y relaciones específicas del lenguaje [5].

Mientras que DD permite la creación de sintaxis gráficas para metamodelos de manera estándar. La arquitectura de DD distingue dos tipos de información gráfica dependiendo de si los usuarios del lenguaje tengan control sobre ésta (posición de nodos y puntos de enrutamiento de líneas) o no (forma y estilos de línea definidos por los estándares del lenguaje) [6].

3 Mecanismo de personalización

En esta sección se describe los parámetros del mecanismo de personalización de metamodelos Ecore propuesta.

3.1 Perfiles de usuario del mecanismo de personalización

El mecanismo de personalización de metamodelos considera dos perfiles de usuario para realizar el proceso. Un perfil asignado al experto de modelado o ingeniero de software *(perfil 1)*, para que defina las reglas o directivas de personalización. Por lo cual se debe proveer al experto de modelado una herramienta automatizada que le permita especificar las modificaciones que se podrían aplicar al metamodelo base (original), sin que el metamodelo pierda su esencia básica, es decir, que el metamodelo mantenga su semántica. El experto de modelado podría disponer de un repositorio de metamodelos a personalizar, seleccionar uno de ellos y definir las directivas de personalización que correspondan. Una vez definido el modelo de personalización del metamodelo, éste podrá ser abierto y utilizado por otra persona, pudiendo ser el experto del dominio *(perfil 2)*, para que a través de la utilización de interfaces gráficas de usuario intuitivas pueda ejecutar las modificaciones especificadas en el modelo de personalización.

Las interfaces, permitirían ejecutar únicamente las directivas de personalización especificadas en el modelo de personalización. Es decir, se establece un margen limitado (filtro) al experto del dominio para que pueda ejecutar la personalización requerida, como se señala en la Figura 1.

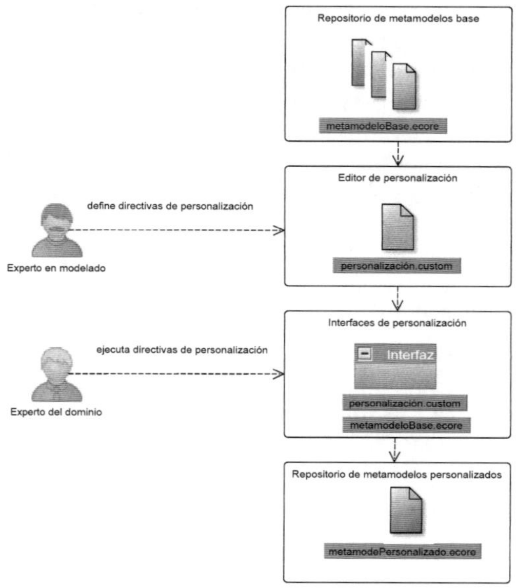

Fig. 1. Perfiles de usuario del mecanismo de personalización de metamodelos

Una vez realizadas las modificaciones sobre el metamodelo base, el metamodelo personalizado podrá ser almacenado en un repositorio diferente. Cabe señalar que se pueden tener varias versiones del modelo de personalización sobre un mismo metamodelo a personalizar, lo que genera varias versiones modificadas del metamodelo base. Como resultado de aplicar las directivas de personalización al metamodelo base se genera un metamodelo modificado completamente funcional, que se ajusta a los nuevos requerimientos del usuario.

El enfoque de personalización propuesto, considera criterios tales como:

- *Generalidad:* es decir que el proceso pueda ser aplicado a cualquier metamodelo.
- *No invasivo:* en el sentido de que sea opcional la posibilidad de modificar directamente el metamodelo base o trabajar sobre éste sin modificarlo.
- *Persistencia del modelo de personalización*: al poder almacenar las operaciones de personalización que se aplican sobre el metamodelo base.
- *Facilidad de uso del proceso de personalización:* para que pueda ser entendido y utilizado rápidamente.
- *Dinamicidad y sincronización del proceso de personalización:* partiendo del hecho de que los cambios sobre el metamodelo se reflejan en tiempo de ejecución de la aplicación.

3.2 Estructura del mecanismo de personalización

La estructura del mecanismo de personalización propuesto (Figura 2), parte del diseño de un metamodelo de personalización denominado *"custom.ecore"*, el cual especifica las operaciones que se pueden realizar sobre el metamodelo base (a personalizar). Para el presente proyecto se han considerado varias operaciones para ser aplicadas sobre el metamodelo base, esto no quita que el metamodelo de personalización pueda ser ampliado en el futuro. Las operaciones que se pueden realizar sobre el metamodelo en términos generales son: (a) extensión de EClass (herencia), (b) redefinición de EReferences, (c) eliminación de EClass, (d) actualización de EClass y (e) creación de nuevas EClass.

Posteriormente se instancia el metamodelo de personalización, es decir, se crea un modelo de personalización (archivo con extensión *.custom) utilizando un editor tipo árbol. El modelo de personalización especifica los elementos del metamodelo susceptibles de ser modificados. Para ello, el modelo de personalización se *"engancha"* desde un repositorio de metamodelos al metamodelo a personalizar (fichero con extensión *.ecore). Una vez definido el archivo de personalización (fichero con extensión *.custom), se procede a ejecutar las directivas de personalización a través de las interfaces gráficas de usuario.

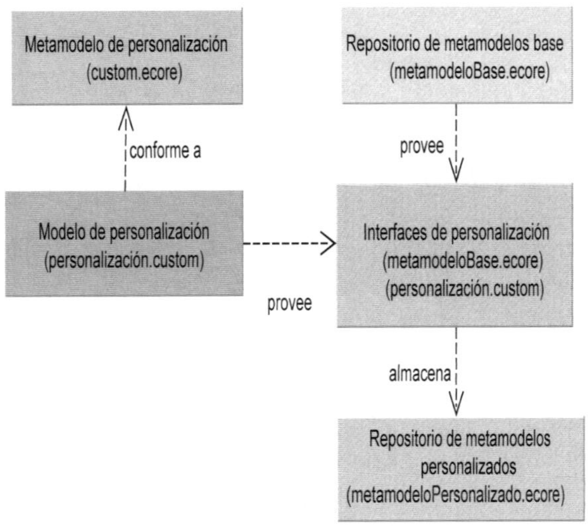

Fig. 2. Estructura del mecanismo de personalización

El metamodelo de personalización es un metamodelo creado en ECore, un fragmento del metamodelo de personalización se muestra en la Figura 3. El metamodelo de personalización se enlaza (import) al metamodelo de Ecore para que a través de este pueda acceder a todos los elementos del metamodelo a personalizar, es decir, puede acceder a EClass, EReferences, EAttriutes, etc. A través de este metamodelo de personalización se definen las directivas para poder adaptar/extender el metamodelo.

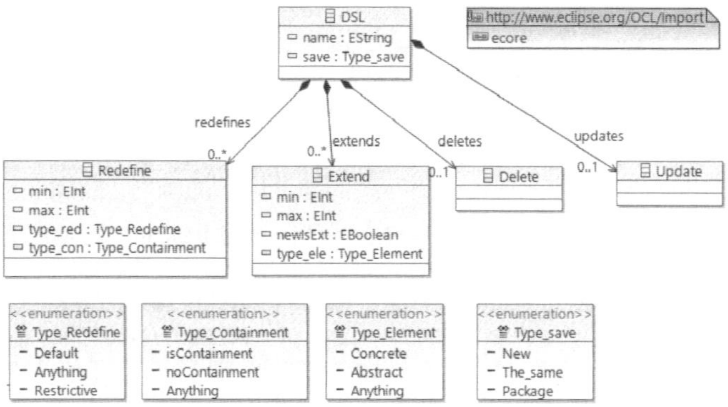

Fig. 3. Extracto del metamodelo de personalización de metamodelos

3.3 Directivas de personalización permitidas

A continuación se describen las directivas que se pueden ejecutar para realizar el proceso de personalización de metamodelos :

3.3.1 Directiva: Extend EClass (extensión de una clase)
Descripción: Esta directiva permite *extender* una EClass que se deriva de la EClass seleccionada. Extender una EClass considera crear una relación de herencia, es decir se puede crear una sub-EClass de una EClass base. Se puede especificar ciertas propiedades de extensión, tales como:

- Que una EClass tenga que ser extendida obligatoriamente como máximo una vez. Obligatoriedad a 1 → [1..1].
- Que una EClass tenga que ser extendida obligatoriamente una o más veces. Obligatoriedad a muchos → [1..N].
- Que una EClass pueda ser extendida como máximo una vez. Opcionalidad a 1→ [0..1].
- Que una EClass pueda ser extendida cero o más veces. Opcionalidad a muchos → [0..N].
- Que la EClass sea abstracta, concreta o ninguna (el usuario posteriormente lo decidirá).

3.3.2 Directiva: Redefine EReference (redefinición de una referencia)

Descripción: Esta directiva permite *redefinir* una EReference entre dos EClass. Redefinir un EReference considera que al extender una EClass se pueda definir EReferences entre las Sub-EClass extendidas. Se debe especificar ciertos aspectos:

- Que se puede hacer un Redefine por cada EReference de cada EClass.
- Que se puede especificar si la EReference es contenedora o no.
- Que cuando se tenga que extender una EClass se puede redefinir una EReference de la EClass base (EClass padres).

De esta manera se consideran tres tipos de *cardinalidad* cuando se redefine una EReference:

- **Tipo D** (Default - Defecto): Por ejemplo, si la EReference base tiene cardinalidad [1..2], se configura Extend del tipo Default de [1..3] y de tipo isContainment. Como resultado, la cardinalidad del ERedefine solo puede tomar valores de entre [1..2] (cardinalidad de la EReference base), será de tipo contenedor, pero solo se puede redefinirse de entre 1 a 3 veces.
- **Tipo R** (Restrictive - Restrictivo): Por ejemplo, si la EReference base tiene cardinalidad [1..2], se configura Extend del tipo Restrictive de [1..3] y de tipo noContainment. Como resultado, la cardinalidad del ERedefine pueden tomar solo los valores comprendidos entre [1..3], es decir [1..1],[1..2], [1..3], [2..3] y [3..3] y será de tipo no contenedor, pero solo se puede redefinir de entre 1 a 3 veces.
- **Tipo A** (Anything - Cualquiera): Por ejemplo, si la EReference base tiene cardinalidad [1..2], se configura un tipo de Extend del tipo Anything de [1..3] y de tipo noContainment. Como resultado, la cardinalidad del ERedefine pueden tomar cualquier valor (no considera para nada la cardinalidad de la EReference base) y será de tipo no contenedor, pero solo se puede redefinir de 1 a 3 veces.

3.3.3 Directiva: Delete EClass (eliminación de una clase)

Descripción: Esta directiva permite eliminar del metamodelo una EClass, siempre y cuando la EClass a eliminar no se encuentre referenciada por otra EClass.

3.3.4 Directiva: Udpate EClass (actualización de una clase)

Descripción: Esta directiva permite agregar nuevos EAttributes y EReferences a una determinada EClass del metamodelo. Con la finalidad de no afectar la semántica del metamodelo base, se ha limitado a la herramienta para que no permite eliminar EAttributes y EReferences.

3.3.5 Directiva: New EClass (creación de una nueva clase)

Descripción: Si el modelo requiere una nueva EClass, esta directiva permite crear una EClass independiente de las demás EClass, con sus propios EAttributes y EReferences. También es posible realizar herencia múltiple (que una EClass pueda admitir heredar de más de una EClass).

4 Ejemplo de utilización de la herramienta

A continuación se ilustra las capacidades de personalización en el ámbito del Modelado de Procesos. La Figura 4 muestra el metamodelo base (Modelado de Procesos) y la Figura 5 el metamodelo personalizado (Modelado de Procesos Software). Las clases *TipoActividad* y *TipoRecurso* deben ser extendidas obligatoriamente con una clase abstracta. La referencia *TipoActividad.necesita* debe ser redefinida una o más veces con cualquier cardinalidad. En la extensión realizada, se ha redefinido 3 veces en la clase *ActividadIngenieriaSoftware*, modelando que las tareas de ingeniería del software tienen cero o más *entradas* que son *artefactos*, una o más *salidas* que también son *artefactos* y son llevadas a cabo (*realizadoPor*) uno o más *personas*. El destino de cada una de estas tres referencias (*Artefacto*, *Persona*) es compatible con el destino de la referencia *necesita (TipoRecurso)*. Esta redefinición hace que la referencia *necesita* se pueda ver como una referencia derivada, resultado de la unión de las referencias *entradas*, *salidas* y *realizadoPor*.

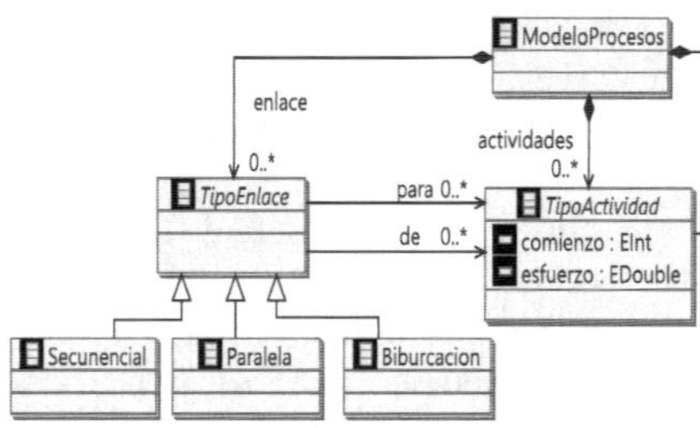

Fig. 4. Metamodelo base (a personalizar)

El editor del modelo de personalización permite especificar las directivas de personalización (algunas especificadas en la Tabla 1) a realizar sobre el metamodelo base (Modelo de Procesos), para crear su metamodelo personalizado (Modelo de Procesos de Ingeniería de Software).

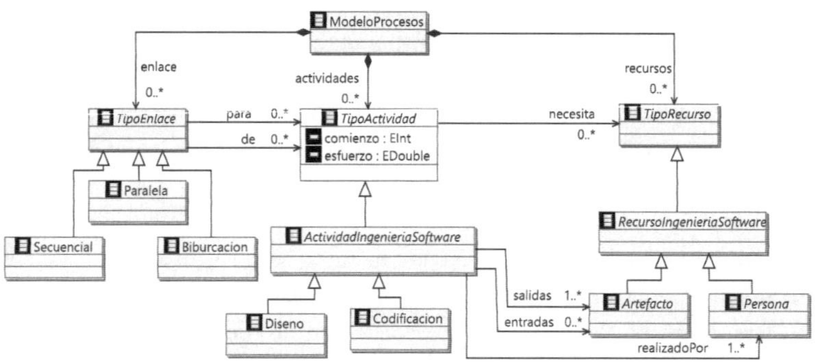

Fig. 5. Metamodelo personalizado

Tabla 1. Directivas de personalización de Extensión y Redefinición

Modelo de personalización			Metamodelo personalizado
Directiva de personalización		Valor	Resultado de su aplicación
Extensión (1)	custom_extend type_ele min max	TipoActividad Abstract 1 1	Clase abstracta *ActividadIngenieriaSoftware* creada.
Redefinición (1)	custom_redefine type_red type_con min max	necesita Anything noContainment 1 -1 (n)	Redefinición de la referencia *necesita* entre las clases *TipoActividad* y *TipoRecurso* a la referencia *entradas* y *salidas* entre las clases *ActividadIngenieriaSoftware* y *Artefacto*, y la referencia *realizoPor* entre las clases *ActividadIngenieriaSoftware* y *Persona*.

Las directivas de personalización de la Tabla 1, son definidas en el modelo de personalización a través de un editor gráfico (tipo árbol), como se muestra en la Figura 6.

Directiva de personalización: Extend (1)

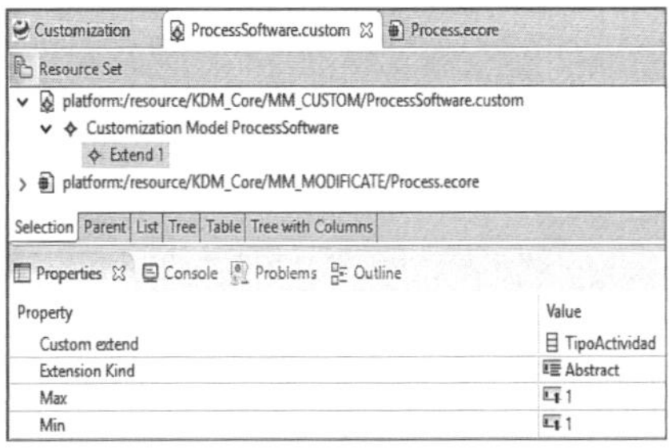

Directiva de personalización: Redefine (1)

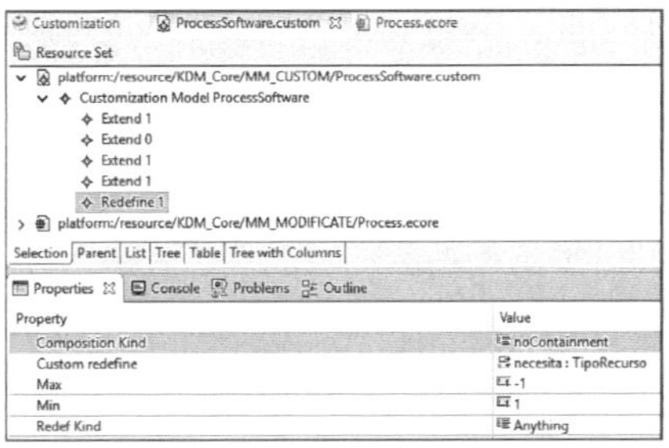

Fig. 6. Definición de las directivas de personalización en el modelo de personalización

Una vez definidas las directivas de personalización sobre el metamodelo base, se procede a aplicarlas a través del plug-in de Eclipse que implementa varias interfaces gráficas de usuario (Fig. 7).

Fig. 7 (a). Interfaz principal de personalización

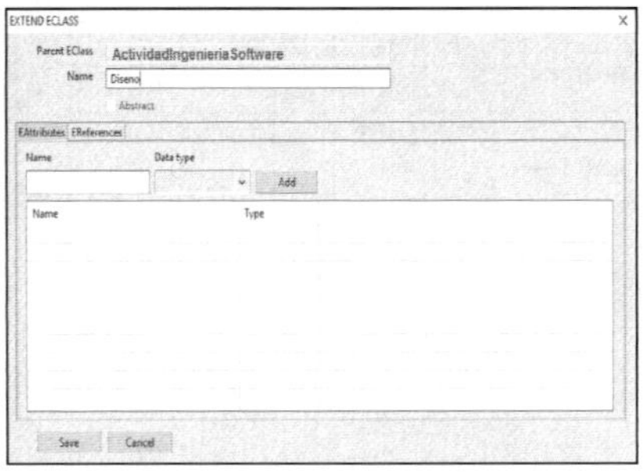

Fig. 7 (b). Extensión de EClass

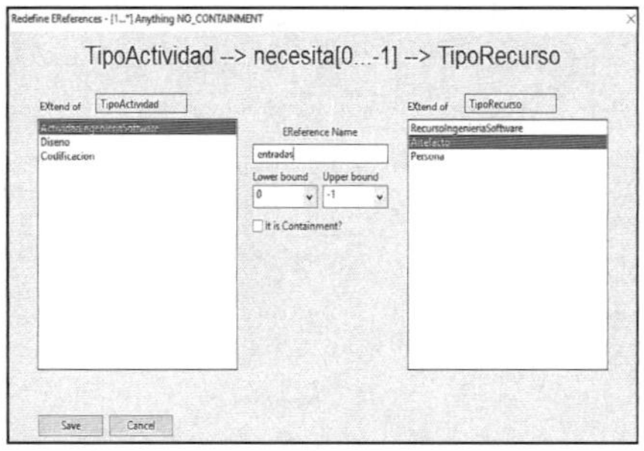

Fig. 7 (c). Redefinición de EReferences

Una vez definidas las directivas de personalización (Tabla 1) para el metamodelo base (Figura 4) en el modelo de personalización (Figura 6) y ejecutadas en la herramienta de personalización (Figura 7), se obtiene como resultado un metamodelo personalizado (Figura 5) completamente funcional. Cabe señalar, que la herramienta ha sido evaluada en varios escenarios de personalización de metamodelos estándar como KDM, así como en metamodelos de otros dominios.

5 Trabajos relacionados

El objetivo del presente trabajo ha sido proponer un enfoque que permita controlar la personalización de metamodelos. A continuación se compara con algunos trabajos relacionados.

En [7] se plantea la adaptación de metamodelos a través de un lenguaje de dominio específico textual. Los procesos son creados como anotaciones en el mismo metamodelo. Se puede crear y modificar clases, también es permite establecer relaciones entre las clases. Nuestro mecanismo propuesto se puede considerar como no invasivo, debido a que al metamodelo a personalizar no se debe incluir anotaciones y código complementario para realizar la personalización.

En [8] se señala que los perfiles de UML proporcionan un medio valioso para la adaptación de los metemodelos existentes hacia plataformas específicas. Los perfiles son un mecanismo de extensión de peso ligero (lightweight), donde es posible la extensión del metamodelo sin sobrescribir los elementos originales [9]. Los perfiles permiten extender los metamodelos a través de estereotipos, restricciones y valores etiquetados. Nuestro enfoque se centra en metamodelos Ecore, utilizados en la definición de un lenguaje de dominio específico.

En [10] se proporciona una clasificación para los mecanismos de extensión y considera el concepto de *enganche*, a la posibilidad de dejar partes abiertas de un programa para definirlas y especificarlas posteriormente mediante la inserción de código [11]. Otras partes del programa permanecen fijas, denominadas como *puntos conge-*

lados en [12]. Nuestro enfoque permite que un usuario no especialista pueda insertar, modificar o eliminar ciertas secciones del metamodelo a través de una herramienta intuitiva.

En [13] se propone dos tipos de mecanismos de extensión de metamodelos y los define como mecanismo *controlado* y mecanismo *no controlado*. El controlado permite que cualquier modificación debe derivarse del metamodelo original. El no controlado permite agregar elementos arbitrariamente al metamodelo original. Nuestro enfoque implementa los dos mecanismos de extensión, el controlado cuando el usuario únicamente puede ejecutar las directivas de personalización definidas en el modelo de personalización, y el no controlado, cuando el usuario puede incluir nuevas clases que no están especificadas en el modelo de personalización.

6 Conclusiones y trabajos futuros

El desarrollo de software desde su aparición ha evolucionado, tratando de hacer cada vez más fácil y rápida la generación de aplicaciones. Desde hace algunos años han aparecido varias propuestas, una de ellas MDE, que se ocupa de la utilización sistemática de modelos de software para mejorar la facilidad, productividad y calidad del desarrollo de software.

Un modelo expresado con un DSL se encuentra definido por su sintaxis abstracta (elementos y relaciones que tendrá cada modelo) y su sintaxis concreta (visualización textual o gráfica de los modelos), así como por su semántica (significado del modelo).

La sintaxis abstracta es definida a través de un metamodelo por lo general expresado en el lenguaje de metamodelado Ecore. Muchas ocasiones, el metamodelo debe ser personalizado (modificado), es decir, se debe poder adaptar, extender, eliminar o cambiar ciertas características. Por ejemplo, como se hace con metamodelos estándar como KDM de la OMG.

Las herramientas propuestas establecen una guía para realizar la personalización de metamodelos a través de la automatización de las directivas (reglas) de personalización, tratando de que no se introduzcan errores accidentales debido al uso de lenguaje natural. Actualmente, se está trabajando en la mejora de la herramienta, así como en mejorar la expresividad de las directivas de personalización.

Agradecimientos. Al Doctor Juan de Lara, profesor investigador de la Universidad Autónoma de Madrid, por su guía y apoyo en el desarrollo del presente trabajo de investigación.

Referencias

1. Jácome Guerrero, S., *Descripción de las actividades de una propuesta de Metodología de Desarrollo de Software Dirigida por Modelos*, 2013.

2. Mohagheghi, P. and V. Dehlen. *A metamodel for specifying quality models in model-driven engineering*. in *Proc. The Nordic Workshop on Model Driven Engineering*. 2008.
3. García, J., et al., *Desarrollo de Software Dirigido por Modelos: Conceptos, Métodos y Herramientas*.2013. 586.
4. Lara, J.D., E. Guerra, and J.S. Cuadrado, *When and how to use multilevel modelling*. ACM Transactions on Software Engineering and Methodology (TOSEM), 2014. 24(2): p. 12.
5. *Knowledge Discovery Meta-Model™ (KDM). Version 1.3* 2011; Available from: http://www.omg.org/spec/KDM/1.3/PDF/.
6. *Diagram Definition™ (DD™)*. 2015; Available from: http://www.omg.org/spec/DD/.
7. Bruneliere, H., et al. *On Lightweight Metamodel Extension to Support Modeling Tools Agility*. in *European Conference on Modelling Foundations and Applications*. 2015. Springer.
8. Braun, R. *Towards the state of the art of extending enterprise modeling languages*. in *Model-Driven Engineering and Software Development (MODELSWARD), 2015 3rd International Conference on*. 2015. IEEE.
9. Rumbaugh, J., I. Jacobson, and G. Booch, *Unified modeling language reference manual, the*2004: Pearson Higher Education.
10. Braun, R. *Behind the scenes of the bpmn extension mechanism principles, problems and options for improvement*. in *Model-Driven Engineering and Software Development (MODELSWARD), 2015 3rd International Conference on*. 2015. IEEE.
11. Birsan, D., *On plug-ins and extensible architectures*. Queue, 2005. 3(2): p. 40-46.
12. Kulesza, U., et al. *Improving extensibility of object-oriented frameworks with aspect-oriented programming*. in *International Conference on Software Reuse*. 2006. Springer.
13. Schleicher, A. and B. Westfechtel. *Beyond stereotyping: Metamodeling approaches for the UML*. in *System Sciences, 2001. Proceedings of the 34th Annual Hawaii International Conference on*. 2001. IEEE.

Using Multi-Sensorial Augmented Reality in a Museum's Exhibition Environment

Juan J. Tustón, S. Manzano, F. Fernández-Peña

Universidad Técnica de Ambato, FISEI, Ambato, Ecuador
{jtuston0358,victorsmanzano,fo.fernandez}@uta.edu.ec

Abstract. Augmented reality actually impacts the development of interactive environments in museums and general learning environments. This paper presents the results in the design of a multi-sensorial augmented reality experience. The novelty of the proposal resides in the capacity of interpreting the reality through the activation of electronic actuators. The software was encoded using Unity3D and the hardware includes the use of a mobile with Bluetooth communication with an Arduino. The so called app RACIE was implemented as a free open source solution which is described in this paper. An experiment was carried out for evaluating the acceptance of RACIE by using the Technology Acceptance Model. The results were satisfactory. In opinion of potential users, the proposal would increase interest in learning by visiting museums with this technology. Nevertheless, results are not conclusive and more research is needed since sociological point of view is determinant in this research.

Keywords: augmented reality, enriched user experience, arduino, electronic actuators management

1 Introducción

Con frecuencia, cuando se piensa en un Centro de Exposición de las Artes, se crea el imaginario de un lugar que jamás prioriza las sensaciones del visitante; observar y escuchar son básicamente las dos actividades que se realizan en el recorrido de un museo. Esta es una metodología anticuada que necesariamente debe ser innovada, si se desea potenciar los centros patrimoniales de arte y cultura.

Tradicionalmente, esta trayectoria consiste en la transmisión de conocimientos de un interlocutor hacia un grupo de personas, contando la historia casi de memoria y recitando el mismo discurso repetitivamente. Por lo tanto, la poca afluencia de visitantes internos y externos ocasiona que la sociedad pierda el significado del valor cultural e histórico que estos encierran [1] [2].

Lo cierto es que los centros culturales no solo compiten entre sí, sino que también se enfrentan con la preferencia de otros atractivos turísticos; ya que evidentemente, el interés de visitar un museo y conocer su colección de piezas arqueológicas ha decrecido; esta reflexión se acentúa especialmente en los jóvenes [3]. En consecuencia, la sociedad moderna ya no se siente atraída por la didáctica tradicional poco satisfactoria que ofrecen los museos.

La realidad aumentada en ámbitos de enseñanza – aprendizaje se desempeña como una herramienta innovadora que logrará captar la atención y enriquecer al usuario con información real, contextualizada, formativa y entretenida, al mismo tiempo que se involucra en el campo tecnológico, revolucionando la experiencia de los visitantes de centros de arte y cultura.

Al realizar el estudio del estado del arte, se han encontrado artículos que proponen el desarrollo de aplicaciones con realidad aumentada [5-10] y estudios dedicados a la integración con una placa electrónica [11-13]. Sin embargo, no se han encontrado trabajos que vinculen ambas propuestas. La hipótesis que se plantea es que a través de un híbrido de estas dos propuestas se estará en condiciones de crear museos con interactividad multisensorial que atraigan clientes y enaltezca la labor educativa de este tipo de centro cultural.

El museo de Montreal, ubicado en Canadá, pretende integrar en el año 2017, una aplicación de realidad aumentada con soporte para Android y IOS, que permitirá acceder a contenidos históricos de la Universidad de Concordia [15].

En ciudades italianas como Florencia, Roma y Venecia existen monumentos, palacios históricos y centros de arte, alrededor de las cuales se ofrece una aplicación con realidad aumentada que enriquece el proceso de aprendizaje de usuarios interesados en la cultura. El usuario de esta aplicación es capaz de obtener datos desde el pasado hasta el presente, acorde a la disponibilidad de información [2].

El Museo Estatal del Hermitage en San Petersburgo, Rusia presenta colecciones de petroglifos para inspirar interés en el público, convirtiendo espacios de exposición tradicionales en el espacio aumentado con modelados 3D que proporcionan el desarrollo cultural en la Edad del Bronce [14].

Por su parte, el Museo de Arte y Ciencia de Filadelfia tiene un proyecto que lo reinventa con un ambiente de aprendizaje interactivo del sigo XXI para el patrimonio cultural y ciencias tecnológicas, automatizando la gestión de la experiencia en entornos interactivos de aprendizaje, revitalizando el museo con el uso de realidad aumentada [4].

El presente trabajo tiene como objetivo mostrar los resultados de la evaluación de la aceptación de la tecnología propuesta, utilizando como caso de estudio el Museo de la Unidad educativa Bolívar de Ambato (UEB). El ambiente real del museo fue enriquecido con animaciones digitales que aparecen ante el visitante y la interacción con estas animaciones le permiten al usuario activar componentes físicos que estimulan sus sentidos. A este tipo de experiencia se denomina Realidad Aumentada Multisensorial (RAM).

Este artículo se encuentra estructurado de la siguiente manera. En la sección 2 se describe el sistema implementado. En la sección 3 se describe la metodología seguida para la evaluación experimental de la aceptación de la tecnología propuesta. En la sección 4 se discuten los resultados obtenidos y, en la sección 5, se arriba a conclusiones.

2 Descripción del Sistema

La aplicación que se desarrolló para este proyecto se denomina "RACIE", que significa: Realidad Aumentada con Interacción Electrónica. La arquitectura del sistema multisensorial, está formado por tres capas principales: realidad aumentada, comunicación inalámbrica e interacción electrónica. Tal y como se ilustra en la figura 1, la capa de realidad aumentada está relacionada con la capa de presentación e interacción con el usuario. A través de los botones virtuales, se establece una comunicación inalámbrica con los actuadores. Finalmente, los actuadores enriquecen la experiencia de usuario en el medio real en que ocurre la interacción.

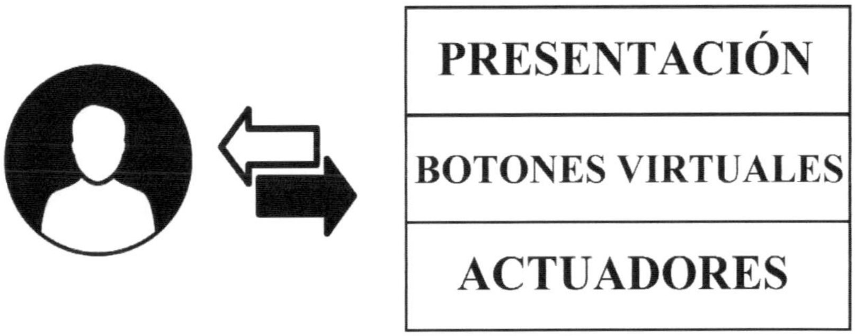

Fig. 1. Arquitectura del sistema multisensorial, el usuario interactúa directamente con la aplicación mediante botones virtuales poniendo en acción la presentación del entorno conjuntamente con los actuadores

2.1 Realidad Aumentada

Marcador. Entre los distintos SDK (Software Development Kit) existentes para el desarrollo de elementos con realidad aumentada, se destaca Vuforia, por características como el rápido tiempo de reconocimiento de imagen, teniendo un rastreo robusto el que no se perderá fácilmente, incluso cuando el dispositivo se mueva y que permite la detección de múltiples marcadores. En la Tabla 1. Se indica la comparativa del tiempo de reconocimiento del marcador con otros SDK's.

En el portal Vuforia Develop, se generó el paquete descargable, que contiene la base de datos de las imágenes, que actuará como marcador, donde se utilizó una imagen basada en código HRQR, optimizando el tiempo de respuesta en el reconocimiento de imagen.

Las animaciones serán sobrepuestas después que el marcador impreso sea reconocido por el lente de la cámara del dispositivo móvil, lo cual se logra analizando la imagen de la cámara a través de los *frame* de la cámara con el fin de encontrar coincidencias en la base de datos que almacena una colección de marcadores para ser reconocidos.

Table 1. Comparación de los SDK [7]

SDK	*Tiempo de reconocimiento en segundos*
Vuforia	*0.0030*
Metaio	*0.0133*
AR Toolkit	*0.0131*

Dispositivo de Realidad Aumentada. Los teléfonos inteligentes de gama media poseen características mínimas: 1.2GHz de procesamiento, 1GB de memoria RAM [16]; estas características permiten la generación de gráficos tridimensionales que, mezclados con el contenido visualizado a través de la cámara de video integrada, que poseen, permiten la creación de una experiencia de realidad aumentada [6]. Este es el principio sobre el que se diseñó la propuesta evaluada a través de este trabajo.

La aplicación desarrollada puede ser compilada para sistema Android y IOS. Con la inserción de scripts desarrollados en C# se incorporaron funciones específicas dedicadas a la renderización de figuras tridimensionales.

Al momento que, a través de la cámara, se reconoce determinado marcador, se muestra la animación 3D que corresponde. Los experimentos se realizaron con un elefante y un león descargados de la Asset Store [18]. Con botones virtuales superpuestos a marcadores, el usuario envía órdenes a la placa electrónica previamente programada. Unity3D [17] es el entorno de desarrollo que permitió integrar todos estos aspectos de programación de una realidad aumentada con interacción electrónica, tal y como se observa en la figura 2. Con un editor visual intuitivo, esta herramienta permite importar modelos 3D, texturas, imágenes y sonidos con gran facilidad.

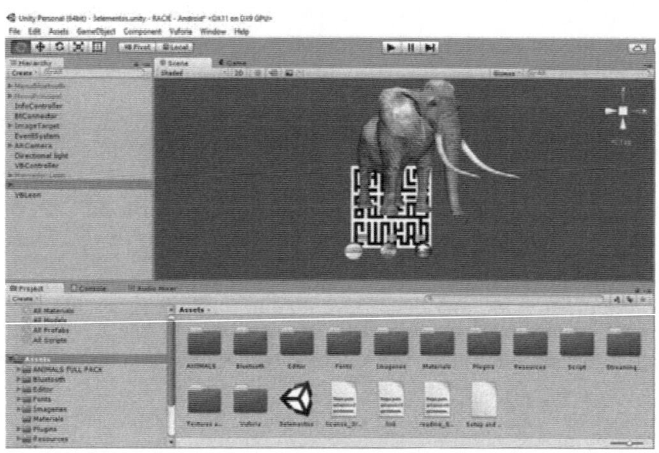

Fig. 2. Entorno de trabajo en Unity 3D, editor sencillo y potente que consta de 5 vistas principales: explorador *(lista de todos los elementos del proyecto)*, inspector *(Muestra y define las propiedades de los elementos del proyecto)*, jerarquía *(Lista jerárquica de los elementos de la escena)*, escena *(Diseño y maqueta del proyecto completo)* y juego *(Visualiza el proyecto a distintas resoluciones)*

Para la utilización del visor de realidad aumentada como puede ser Cardboard [19], se incluyó el Google VR SDK para Unity 3D, lo que permitió llevar la aplicación al formato de salida adecuado al visor de realidad aumentada. Esto quiere decir que, la aplicación se despliega en un teléfono inteligente, el que se monta en el visor de realidad aumentada y queda todo integrado como una única pieza tecnológica, tal y como se puede observar en la figura 3.

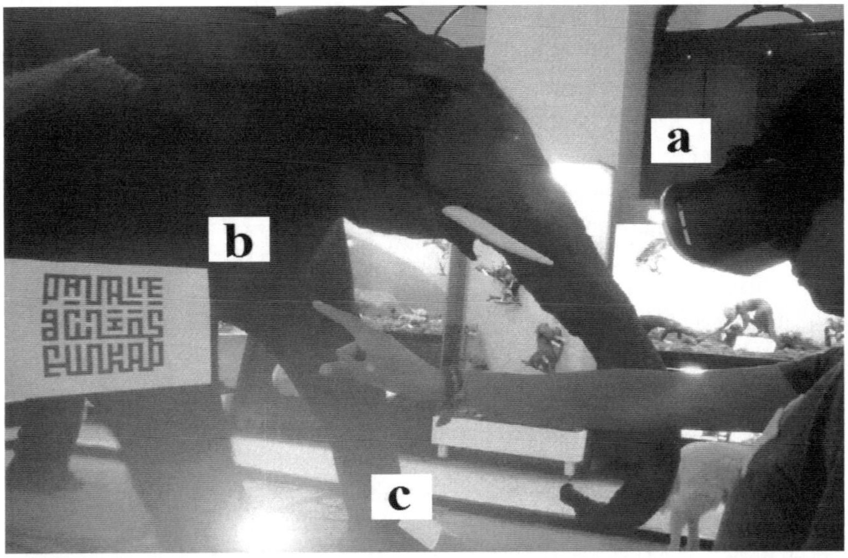

Fig. 3. Entorno de realidad aumentada donde *a (visor de realidad aumentada)* permite mezclar el entorno real con información virtual mientras que *b (marcador puesto en el entorno real)* es identificado por la cámara y sobreimprime la información y *c (reflector)* actuador activado o desactivado según la selección del escenario a visualizar

2.2 Comunicación Inalámbrica

La aplicación utiliza la capacidad de comunicación inalámbrica del teléfono inteligente. Utilizando Bluetooth 2.0, se establece la comunicación con una placa Arduino. De esta forma se envían las órdenes a los actuadores en tiempo real. Para la incorporación de conectividad Bluetooth se ocupó el paquete Android & Microcontrollers/Bluetooth, el que brinda los plugins y scripts necesarios para adherir conexión serial Bluetooth entre dispositivos Android o IOS y dispositivos con capacidad Bluetooth (en este caso el Arduino). El esquema de conexión inalámbrica entre el dispositivo móvil Android y el Arduino se ilustra en la figura 4.

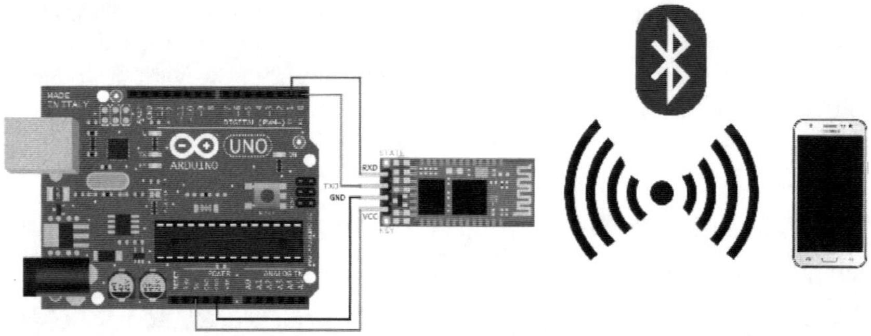

Fig. 4. Esquema de conexión inalámbrica entre la placa arduino y el teléfono móvil Android. En la placa arduino se hace uso del módulo bluetooth HC-05, en el teléfono se utiliza el módulo bluetooth integrado en el propio dispositivo mediante el uso de plugins

2.3 Interacción Electrónica

El proyecto utiliza Arduino Uno, incorporado al módulo HC-05 [12]. Ello permite accionar actuadores remotamente (luces, aspersores, parlantes, aire acondicionado, máquina de humo, etc.) ubicados en el entorno para generar un ambiente multisensorial [13].

El módulo HC-05, recibe las ordenes enviadas a través de los botones virtuales, ubicados en el entorno de realidad aumentada para activar un reflector o la reproducción de sonidos, en dependencia a la situación de interés para el usuario.

Activado RACIE, se visualiza una interfaz de emparejamiento con el Arduino, a través de una conexión Bluetooth, la que se visualiza en la figura 5. Se debe presionar el botón "Buscar" para visualizar los dispositivos Bluetooth disponibles, seleccionar HC-05 como el módulo que se encuentra conectado al Arduino y presionar "Conectar" para establecer la conexión.

Fig. 5. Interfaz de presentación de RACIE, pantalla principal de la aplicación para el emparejamiento con el módulo bluetooth de la placa arduino

Una vez establecida la comunicación, se despliega el visor de realidad aumentada, ya sea usando el dispositivo móvil directamente o montado en el visor de realidad aumentada (ver figura 6). Posteriormente, se procede a enfocar el marcador para sobreponer la imagen animada del elefante con los botones virtuales.

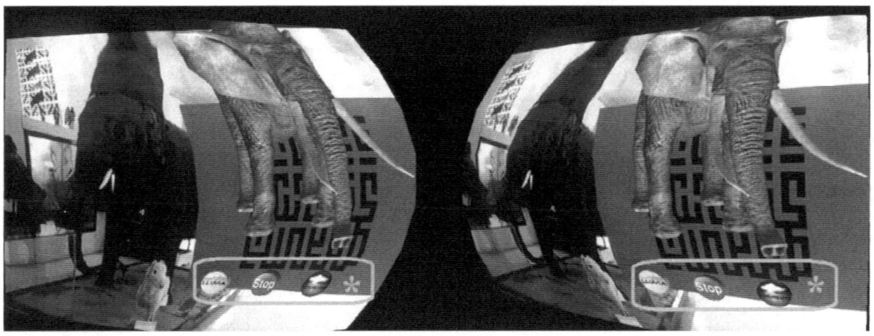

Fig. 6. Adecuación del formato de imagen para el uso de la aplicación con visor de realidad aumentada. * *(Ubicados en el marcador)* botones virtuales para interacción electrónica, según se visualiza en cada ojo del usuario

En la figura 6 se destaca la ubicación de los botones virtuales, que permiten: reproducir el sonido del ambiente y un audio narrativo con la información sobre la vida del elefante; visualizar un texto descriptivo del animal y accionar el reflector mediante Arduino, emulando un ambiente virtual con sonido y luz. El ejemplo en el caso de estudio es la simulación de una tormenta en la que se describe el comportamiento del animal que está en exhibición en el museo.

2.4 Diseño de Experimento

Para evaluar la pertinencia del uso de la RAM en museos se trabajó en conjunto con el personal del Museo del UEB. En el transcurso de dos horas se entrevistó a los usuarios que visitaron el lugar. Un total de seis personas fueron entrevistadas, cuyas edades estuvieron entre los 48 y 65 años de edad, dos locales y cuatro turistas nacionales.

El personal del museo argumenta que los jóvenes son el sector más deprimido en las visitas a la institución, contrario al interés educativo de la labor que desarrollan. Teniendo en cuenta la poca afluencia de público al museo, se montó un entorno de realidad aumentada en la Facultad de Ingeniería en Sistemas, Electrónica e Industrial (FISEI), de la Universidad Técnica de Ambato y se diseñó un experimento para evaluar en qué medida los jóvenes estarían interesados en visitar el museo una vez que se esté utilizando la tecnología de realidad aumentada multisensorial.

La **pregunta de investigación** que se intenta responder con el presente estudio es: ¿la creación de una experiencia de RAM en el entorno museístico del UEB gozará de la aceptación de tecnología de usuarios potenciales de este tipo de instalación?

Un total de 18 personas, entre estudiantes y docentes, fueron escogidos al azar para participar en el experimento. El tamaño de muestra para el experimento se decidió en función de que solo se contaba con un kit de realidad virtual para la experimentación y que el experimento se debía llevar a cabo teniendo en cuenta la disponibilidad de tiempo en el calendario académico. Se buscó un espacio adecuado para el trabajo con un estudiante a la vez, de forma tal que las respuestas de un usuario potencial no influyeran en las de cualquier otro usuario.

Del total de estudiantes involucrados en el experimento, el 50% fueron hombres. En cuanto a la edad, el 5.6% eran menores de 17 años, el 61.1% jóvenes entre 18 y 25 años y el 33% mayores de 26 años, pero menores de 45 años.

En el transcurso del experimento se llevó a cabo una evaluación cualitativa de la experiencia de usuario utilizando criterio de experto. Para ello, se convocó a dos docentes de las carreras de Ingeniería Electrónica y Sistemas Computacionales, con experiencia en el diseño interactivo de hardware y software, respectivamente.

Al concluir el experimento, se aplicó una encuesta de usabilidad (anexo 1) que está basada en el Modelo de Aceptación de Tecnología (TAM, del inglés *Technology Acceptance Model*). El cuestionario tuvo en cuenta el propuesto por González *et al.* [21].

En la encuesta se midieron los criterios de usabilidad percibida, facilidad de uso percibida, actitud de uso e intención de uso. La cantidad de preguntas asociadas a cada uno de estos criterios fue 5, 5, 2 y 2, respectivamente. Cada pregunta se evaluó utilizando una escala Likert con valores de 1 a 5. El objetivo de esta encuesta fue corroborar el nivel de aceptación de la tecnología propuesta por parte de los estudiantes involucrados en el experimento.

El diseño de la encuesta estuvo inspirado en el resultado de trabajos de evaluación de TAM previos [21] y los resultados de su aplicación fueron validados oportunamente. El valor de Cronbach-Alpha que se obtuvo al analizar las respuestas obtenidas fue de 0,92, lo cual evidencia una excelente consistencia interna de los datos. Del mismo modo, un Análisis de Componentes Principales permitió corroborar que las respuestas a las preguntas del cuestionario se agruparon de acuerdo a los criterios TAM a evaluar.

3 Resultados

Los resultados de las entrevistas realizadas a seis personas en la Unidad Educativa Bolívar arrojaron que el 83.3% de personas encuestadas consideran que el empleo de RAM en entornos expositivos y museísticos contribuiría de manera significativa al aprendizaje. Este resultado rompe con el criterio de que existan barreras tecnológicas para el uso de estas tecnologías por parte de personas de mayor edad. Se considera que es un proceso muy asequible ya que solo necesitan instalar la aplicación en el dispositivo móvil. En general, consideran que la Realidad Aumentada es un aporte en los museos que podría servir de estímulo al público para visitarlo con más frecuencia.

Del procesamiento de la encuesta aplicada se obtuvo como resultado un alto índice de aceptación de la tecnología. En solo un caso y en solo una pregunta, la evaluación por parte del usuario fue la de menor satisfacción (pregunta 9, relacionada a usabilidad). No obstante, en sentido general, los índices de usabilidad, facilidad de uso, actitud de uso e intención de uso son altamente satisfactorios, como se puede observar en la figura 7. Vale destacar que, según TAM, estos son los criterios que determinan la aceptación de una tecnología [21].

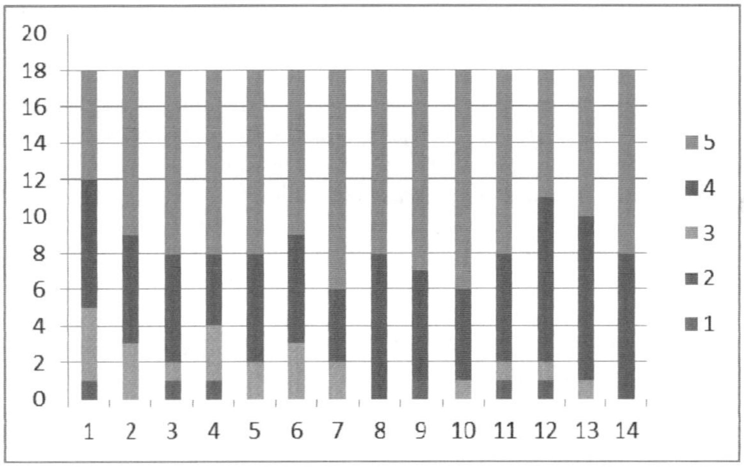

Fig. 7. Estadísticas de la encuesta aplicada

Por su parte, las limitantes del uso de RACIE, determinadas por los expertos en usabilidad que asistieron a la realización del experimento, están asociadas fundamentalmente a:

- Para la detección idónea del patrón de referencia, el marcador debe estar perpendicular al visor de la cámara del móvil.
- La distancia entre el marcador y el dispositivo móvil debe limitarse a tres metros máximo. Al sobrepasar esta distancia la lectura del marcador no se realizará de forma oportuna.
- Detectado el patrón de referencia, el movimiento del visor no debe ser inferior a los 30 grados de azimut respecto al plano del marcador; debido a que la cámara perderá el patrón de referencia.
- Al hacer uso de la tecnología Bluetooth, solo un equipo podrá comunicarse en un instante de tiempo dado.

Si bien estas limitantes no afectan el resultado para el tipo de producto que se diseñó, sí deberán ser tenidas en cuenta para la extensión de los resultados a entornos de enseñanza en general.

4 Conclusiones

De acuerdo a los resultados obtenidos, la creación de una experiencia de RAM en el entorno museístico del UEB gozará de la aceptación de tecnología de usuarios potenciales de este tipo de instalación. La hipótesis de este trabajo fue comprobada al evaluar satisfactoriamente la aceptación tecnológica de la propuesta. Se validó que, en sentido general, museos que utilicen RAM atraerán clientes y enaltecerán la labor educativa de este tipo de centro cultural.

RACIE es novedoso en el entorno de los sistemas de realidad aumentada al incorporar la capacidad de interacción electrónica. Unity 3D permitió generar el entorno de la aplicación con la inclusión de Vuforia SDK, una biblioteca Bluetooth y un paquete con la información de los marcadores. Se enriqueció la experiencia de usuario, tal y como corrobora la evaluación experimental que se llevó a cabo.

El manejo de la aplicación parte del uso de un dispositivo móvil, con el que el usuario interactúa y que permite la comunicación con la tarjeta Arduino que manipula los actuadores electrónicos, los que han de ser ubicados estratégicamente. La integración de nuevos recursos tecnológicos en entornos museísticos motiva la participación de los visitantes, logrando que vivan una experiencia enriquecida, percibida a través de los sentidos, con la lectura de un marcador.

La tecnología RAM permitió al usuario involucrarse activamente en el contexto de la exposición e incrementa la participación activa del usuario al encender o apagar dispositivos electrónicos utilizando botones virtuales. Basados en los resultados del experimento, es de suponer la aceptación de RAM, y que el interés y preferencia del público hacia museos que utilicen estas tecnologías aumente. No obstante, los resultados obtenidos no son concluyentes. Se requiere extender el estudio por más tiempo para evaluar si el interés y preferencia son sostenibles o se deben a la curiosidad que despierta una nueva tecnología.

Referencias

1. Areti Damala, Nenad Stojanovic.: Tailoring the Adaptive Augmented Reality (A2R) Museum Visit: Identifying Cultural Heritage Professionals Motivations and Needs. IEEE International Symposium on Mixed and Augmented Reality - Arts Media and Humanitie, 71-80 (2012).
2. Alessandro Bellini, Cinzia Luddi, Simone Naldini, Carlo Ghetti, Emanuele Bellini, Giovanni Bergamin.: The application is designed to offer an immersive. Signal-Image Technology & Internet-Based Systems (SITIS), 358-363 (2013)
3. R. Monistrol.: Evolución y aplicación del marketing cultural en los museos. Bid Facultat de Biblioteconomia i Documentació, (2009).
4. Glen Muschio, Jichen Zhu, Aroutis Foster.: Revitalizing Peale's Museum as a digital interactive learning environment. Digital Heritage, (2015).
5. Moisés Ramírez, Erik Ramos, Omar Cruz, Jorge Hernández, Esperanza Pérez-Cordoba, Monica Garcia.: Design of interactive museographic exhibits using Augmented reality. Electronics, Communications and Computing (CONIELECOMP), 1-6 (2012).
6. Sasithorn Rattanarungrot, Martin White.: A service-oriented mobile augmented reality architecture for personalized museum environments. Virtual Systems & Multimedia (VSMM), 277-284 (2014).
7. Carlos F. Perea-Tanaka, Isidro Moreno, Edmond C. Prakash, Andrés A. Navarro-Newball.: Towards tantalluc: Interactive mobile augmented reality application for the Museo de América in Madrid. Computing Colombian Conference (10CCC), 164-1771 (2015).
8. Athanasios Kakarountas, Stamatis Dragoumanos, Konstantinos Kakarountas.: Extending visitor's reality at museums. Information, Intelligence, Systems and Applications(IISA), 196-200 (2014).
9. Thomas Chatzidimitris, Evangelia Kavakli, Maria Economou, Damianos Gavalas.: Mobile Augmented Reality edutainment applications for cultural institutions. Information, Intelligence, Systems and Applications (IISA), 1-4 (2013).
10. Antonie Ferreira, Ana M. Bernardos, Luca Bergesio.: ARTHE_ experiencing projected Augmented Reality with things of the Everyday. International Conference on and 10th International Conference on Autonomic and Trusted Computing (UIC/ATC), 495-501 (2013).
11. Chi-Fu Lin, Pai-Shan Pa, Chiou-Shann Fuh.: Mobile application of interactive remote toys with augmented reality. Signal and Information Processing Association Annual Summit and Conference (APSIPA), 1-6 (2013).
12. AquiHayApuntes, http://www.aquihayapuntes.com/indice-practicas-pic-en-c/bluetooth-hc-05.html, accedido: 2016/04/29.
13. Fabiano Amorim Vaz, João Lucas de Souza Silva, Rafael Sol dos Santos.: KinardCar: Auxiliary Game in Formation of Young Drivers, Utilizing Kinect and Arduino Integration. Virtual and Augmented Reality (SVR), 139-142 (2014).
14. Nikita Pikov, Maxim Rumyantsev, Mariia Vishniakova, Inna Kizhner, Daria Hookk.: Touching an ancient stone: 3d modeling and augmented reality techniques for a collection of petroglyphs from State Hermitage Museum. Digital Heritage, (2015).
15. Miao Song, Serguei A. Mokhov, Sudhir P. Mudur, Jean-Claude Bustros.: Demo: Towards historical sightseeing with an augmented reality interactive documentary app. Games Entertainment Media Conference (GEM) 2015 IEE, 1-2 (2015).
16. About en español, http://celulares.about.com/od/Smartphones/ss/Parametros-Reales-Para-Identificar-Gamas-De-Los-Celulares.htm, accedido: 2016/06/01.
17. Unity3d, http://unity3d.com/es/unity, accedido: 2016/03/15.

18. AssetStore, https://www.assetstore.unity3d.com/en/#!/home, accedido: 2016/04/13.
19. Cardboard, https://vr.google.com/cardboard/get-cardboard, accedido: 2016/05/18.
20. Developer.vuforia, https://developer.vuforia.com/downloads/sdk, accedido: 2016/04/25.
21. L. González, M. Valdivia.: Posibilidades para el uso del modelo de aceptación de la tecnología (TAM) y de la teoría de los marcos tecnológicos para evaluar la aceptación de nuevas tecnologías para el aseguramiento de la calidad en la educación superior chilena. Revista electrónica Educare, 19 (2), 181-196 (2015).

Anexo

Realidad Aumentada con Interacción Electrónica

Está encuesta tiene como finalidad medir el conocimiento e impacto del uso de realidad aumentada aplicada en entornos expositivos y museísticos.

Las respuestas a las preguntas de evaluación de aceptación de tecnología se dan en una escala lineal de **1** a **5**, donde **1** significa NO EN ABSOLUTO y **5** COMPLETAMENTE DE ACUERDO.

*Obligatorio.

INFORMACIÓN DEMOGRÁFICA:
Género (Hombre / Mujer) *
Edad (12-17, 18-25, 26-en adelante) *
EVALUACIÓN DE ACEPTACIÓN DE TECNOLOGÍA
1. El uso de los botones virtuales es intuitivo. *

2. Está satisfecho con el diseño y calidad técnica de la aplicación. *

3. El diseño de interfaz de la aplicación la hace fácil de utilizar. *

4. La interfaz facilita el entendimiento de la información consultada. *

5. La interfaz facilita el acceso a la información requerida. *

6. Está satisfecho con el diseño de la aplicación móvil. *

7. La aplicación es fácil de utilizar. *

8. El contenido de la aplicación tiene utilidad. *

9. La aplicación ayuda a incrementar la cultura general del usuario. *

10. El medio de comunicación con el usuario es adecuado. *

11. La aplicación le da control al usuario en todo momento. *

12. La aplicación es eficiente en el procesamiento de información. *

13. Utilizaría este tipo de aplicación. *

14. Tiene intención de utilizar este tipo de aplicaciones. *

Automated System of Storage and Recovery (AS/RS), through artificial vision for Flexible Manufacturing Systems for educational purposes

Fausto Acuña[1], Eddie Galarza[1], Carlos Capilla[2], José Pulloquinga[2]

[1] Universidad de las Fuerzas Armadas ESPE, Departamento de Energía y Mecánica, Sangolquí, Ecuador
fvacunia@espe.edu.ec, eegalarza@espe.edu.ec
http://www.espe.edu.ec/
[2] Universidad de las Fuerzas Armadas ESPE Extensión Latacunga, Carrera de Ingeniería Mecatrónica, Latacunga, Ecuador
ccapilla@espe.edu.ec, jlpz.mecatronica@gmail.com

Abstract. Storing raw material and retrieving finished products, in Flexible Manufacturing System (FMS) is one of the essential elements. The FMS systems have problems like the high costs of the equipment and maintenance, a lot of space for storing, more people included in the processing system, not easy to change the system and others. These reasons make necessary to find a solution that must be able to eliminate the disadvantages that the non-automatic systems have. The work presented in this paper is the description of the design and implementation of a prototype for automating the storage and retrieval system AS/RS that uses computer vision technics. The system consists of an aluminum structure divided into shelves where the items contained in pallets will be stored, the manipulation will be done by a cartesian robot with 4 axes X, Y, Z and B. This system was implemented at the Manufacturing Flexible Cell of the CNC Laboratory of the University of the Army Forces at Latacunga Ecuador. The implemented system is able to store and to retrieve mechanical manufacturing items in an automated way.

Keywords: storage and recovery, artificial vision, education

1 Introducción

El almacén es un componente fundamental en la cadena de suministro cuyas actividades incluyen: recepción, transferencia, almacenamiento, selección de pedidos, acumulación, clasificación, cruzamiento y envío [1]

n y repetibilidad del sistema, se utilizó la norma ISO 9283 aplicados a robots producto terminado como de la materia prima, para ello se utiliza la técnica JIT [2], disponer de materiales y productos en cantidad, calidad, en el momento y lugar preciso. Algunas de las ventajas de los sistemas AS/RS sobre los sistemas tradicionales de almacenamiento son: optimización de los espacios, reducción de los costes laborables y mejor control del inventario [3].

Un AS/RS (Automated Storage/Retreival System), es un sistema que realiza operaciones de almacenamiento y recuperación con velocidad y precisión, consiste en un conjunto de estanterías y pasillos, un mecanismo de almacenamiento y recuperación (S/R) que se mueve entre estanterías, y un único punto donde se deposita o se recoge el material llamado Pickup and Deposit (P&D). Para la entrada de material, el sistema asigna una ubicación al elemento que se va almacenar, luego determina la secuencia de operaciones del S/R para realizar el almacenamiento y la recuperación con el fin de optimizar el desplazamiento global, que se denomina política de entrelazado. [4]

Estudios sobre sistemas AS/AR proponen una serie de modelos de apoyo a la decisión de la operación de almacén [1, 5, 6, 7]. En este artículo se describe el diseño y la construcción de un prototipo de sistema AS/RS, con la aplicación de la visión por computadora [8] para la recepción de la mercadería y la tecnología robótica para la transferencia, almacenamiento, selección y envío del producto, con propósitos educativos.

2 Diseño Mecatrónico

Para el diseño de un AS/RS se debe considerar varios factores como: tipo de sistema, tamaño y tipo de carga, frecuencia de movimiento, flujo de trabajo, tipo de control, tipo de HMI [9], se consideró algunos factores que se describen en la Tabla 1.

Tabla 1. Parámetros de diseño del prototipo

Característica	Valor
Tipo	AS/RS Unit Load
Carga	Materiales blandos y livianos
Volumen y peso de carga	$1x10^{-3}$ m^3 y 26 N
Capacidad	36 unidades
Tamaño estimado	1538x1519x638 mm^3
Tamaño estanterías	160x716.2x188 mm^3
Grados de libertad	4: X, Y, Z, B
Velocidad lineal máxima	200 mm/seg
Medida máxima de carga	100x100x100 mm^3
Estructura mecánica	Rígida y liviana de aluminio

Conforme a los requerimientos se establece el diseño de un sistema tipo Unit Load [10], de tres ejes prismáticos X, Y, Z con robot cartesiano y un eje rotacional B alrededor del eje Y, con acceso directo al sistema de transporte y sin utilizar estaciones P&D. El robot cartesiano tendrá 4 grados de libertad, Fig. 1, el eje X estará compuesto por cuatro guías cilíndricas, dos sobre las cuales se desplazan el robot y dos que sirven de apoyo durante el movimiento longitudinal.

La transmisión de movimiento en los ejes X, Y y Z son del tipo Lineal Omega comprendido por una banda sincrónica, dos rodillos tensores, y una polea motriz.

Para la estructura se empleó aluminio aleado 6061 T4 (Sy=145 MPa.) [11], por su apariencia agradable, bajo peso, buena resistencia a la corrosión, facilidad relativa de formado y maquinado.

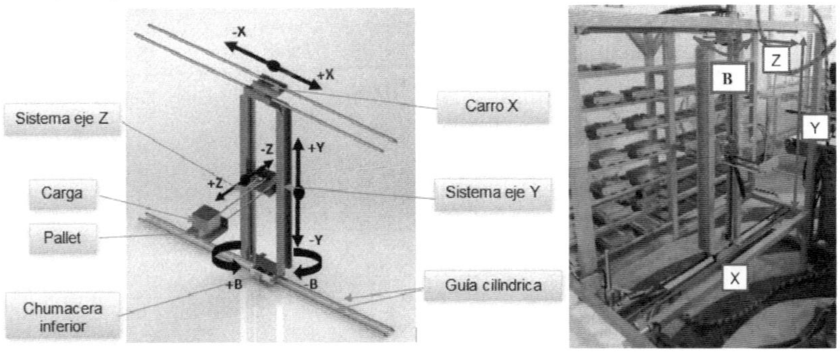

Fig. 1. Disposición de ejes de la máquina S/R

2.1 Módulo de almacenaje

La función del módulo de almacenaje Fig. 2, es contener las cargas a transportar y permitir su manipulación mediante la máquina S/R. Los datos para su diseño son: carga de 26,84 N y madera de pino (Sy=96 MPa) como material de construcción. Está sometido a esfuerzo normal por flexión, el momento crítico es de 397,20 N-mm.

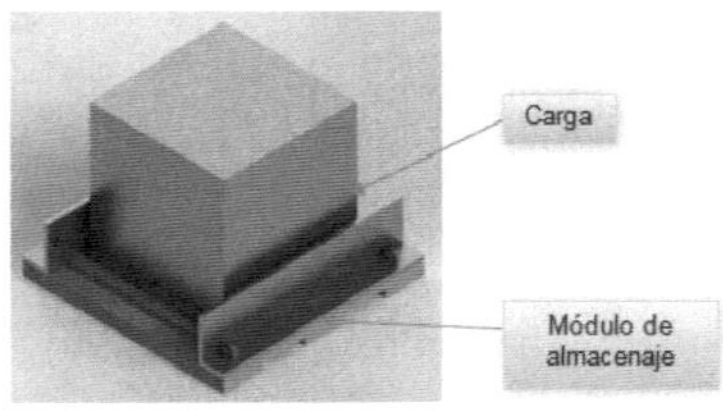

Fig. 2. Módulo de almacenaje con la carga a transportar

El cálculo del espesor se obtiene aplicando la Ec. 1.

$$h=\sqrt{(6*Mmax)/(b*\sigma D)}=1,57 \text{ mm} \quad (1)$$

Para su construcción se eligió un espesor de 2 mm, con factor de seguridad de 2,41 comprobando el diseño

2.2 Diseño de las horquillas.

Las horquillas de transporte Fig. 3, deben tomar y depositar la carga desde y hacia el sistema AS/RS. Los parámetros para su diseño son: carga de 27.18 N, aluminio 6061-T4 (Sy=145MPa) como material y un factor de diseño de 1,5 [11]. Las horquillas están sometidas a esfuerzo normal por flexión y tensión directa, debido a la carga ubicada a 75mm de su apoyo. El momento máximo es de 1019.25 N-mm. El espesor se obtiene aplicando la Ec. 2.

$$Sy/1{,}5 * b * h^2 - F * h - 6 * M = 0 \qquad (2)$$

El espesor calculado es 0.91 mm, se utilizó 1 mm, con un factor de seguridad de 1.77, comprobando el diseño.

Fig. 3. Horquillas de transporte y carro X sobre guías cilíndricas

2.3 Diseño del eje "Z"

El eje Z, Fig. 4, está constituido por dos guías cilíndricas paralelas unidas por una placa de aluminio y las horquillas de transporte, su función es movilizar la carga de forma horizontal sobre el carro YZ.

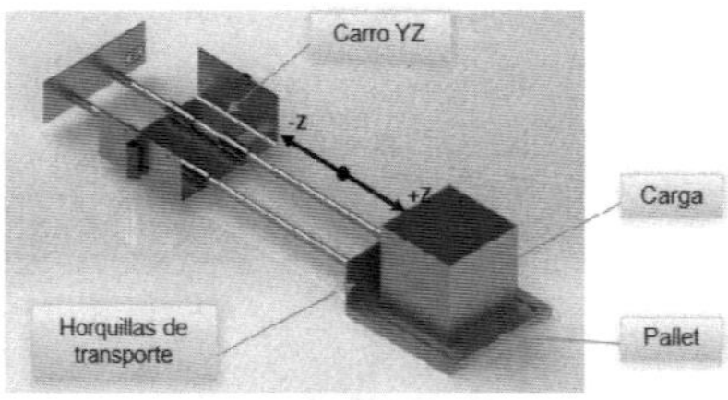

Fig. 4. Eje Z con carga a transportar

Para el diseño se utilizó una carga de 28,03 N ubicada a 75,54 mm, acero AISI 1018 (Sy=370 MPa) como material y un factor de seguridad de 2. Las guías están sometidas a esfuerzo normal por flexión, el momento resultante de trasladar mediante el principio de sistema fuerza-par es 2117,95 N-mm. El momento crítico es 6242,67 N-mm. Para calcular su diámetro se utilizó la Ec. 3.

$$d = \sqrt[3]{((64 * Mmáx) / (\pi * Sy))} = 7mm \qquad (3)$$

Para su construcción se utilizó un eje de 8 mm por disponibilidad en el mercado, alcanzado un FS de 1.99.

2.4 Diseño del eje "Y" con su correspondiente eje rotacional "B"

Este sistema permite el desplazamiento vertical y rotacional, está constituido por dos guías cilíndricas paralelas, de acero, unidas mediante láminas de aluminio horizontales y dos perfiles de aluminio verticales, Fig. 5

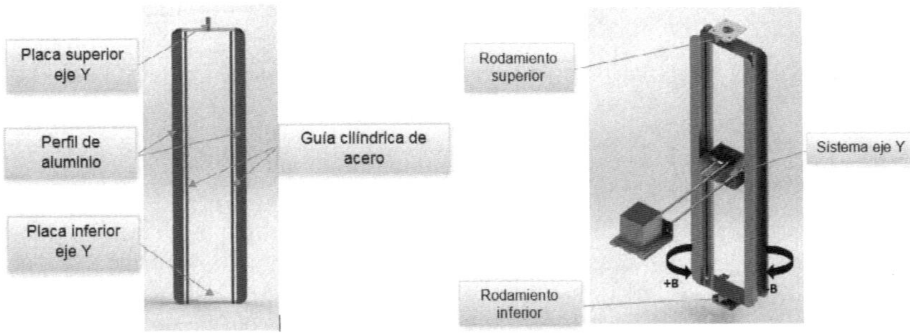

Fig. 5. Eje Y y eje rotacional B, con sus elementos

Para su diseño se tomó la carga de 18N, el momento producido fue 6756,62 N-mm, acero AISI 1018 (Sy=370MPa) como material y factor de seguridad de 2. Aplicando el principio de superposición [12], se determinó el esfuerzo a compresión necesario para calcular el diámetro de las guías aplicando la Ec. 4.

$$\pi * d3 * (Sy / N) - 4 * d * F - 32 * M = 0 \quad (4)$$

El diámetro obtenido fue de 7,19 mm, se utilizó 7,5 mm y se obtuvo un factor de seguridad de 2,26.

Sobre el eje Y rota el eje B, conseguido por un sistema de dos rodamientos cónicos [11] con sus respectivas bases como muestra la Fig. 5.

2.5 Diseño del eje "X"

El carro X es el encargado de transportar la carga sobre las guías cilíndricas, en sentido longitudinal, está compuesto por una base de aluminio sujeta por 4 bocines de bronce a las guías cilíndricas Fig. 6. Se considerarán como cuatro guías cilíndricas paralelas de acero, ancladas a la estructura de almacenamiento.

Para el diseño se utilizó la teoría de flexión máxima con carga de 81.71 N y un momento producido en el eje Z de 13528.29 N-mm. Para determinar la flexión máxima en máquinas de precisión moderada se aplicó la Ec. 5.

$$Yd = 0{,}0005 * L \quad (5)$$

Con una longitud del eje de 1.5 m, se obtuvo una flexión de 0.6 mm. Con el módulo de elasticidad de 207 GPa para el acero AISI 1018, se aplicó la Ec. 6 de vigas biempotradas para determinar el diámetro del eje, dando como resultado 15,5 mm.

$$d = \sqrt[4]{((64 * P * L^3) / (192 * \pi * E * Ymax))} \quad (6)$$

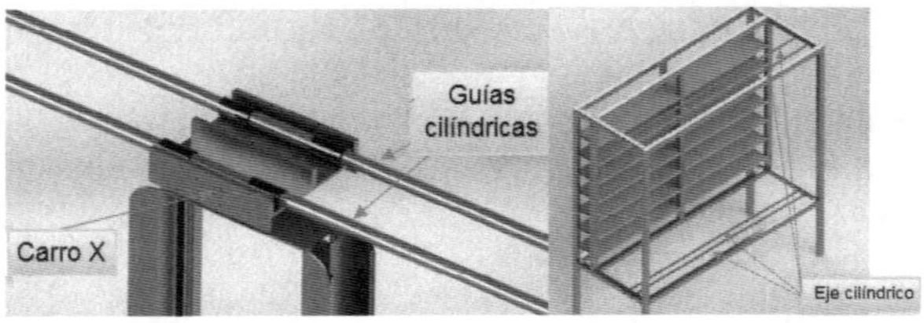

Fig. 6. Carro X sobre guías cilíndricas y estructura de almacenamiento

2.6 Selección de motores

Para determinar la potencia [13] de los motores se analiza el eje Y por manejar una carga suspendida. La Fig. 7 muestra las fuerzas implicadas en el movimiento.

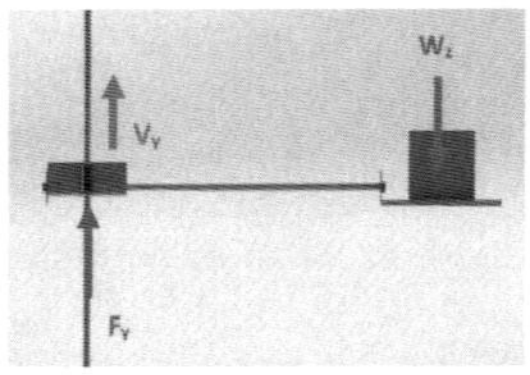

Fig. 7. Fuerzas en el movimiento del eje Y.

Aplicando la Ec. 7, con: Carga *Fy* de 36N, Velocidad *Vy* de 200 mm/s, Eficiencia de transmisión ε de 95%, Factor de servicio F.S. de 1,25, se obtiene una potencia de salida de 7,57W

$$P = (Fy * Vy) / \epsilon \quad (7)$$

Aplicando la Ec. 8, se obtiene una potencia de diseño de 9,47W, por lo cual se selecciona un motor 131:1 Metal Gearmotor ofertado por Pololu [14].

$$PD = F.S. * P \quad (8)$$

2.7 Transmisión Mecánica

Para este sistema se ha seleccionado una transmisión por correas dentadas [15] ancladas a los ejes, accionadas mediante una polea motriz y dos rodillos tensores fijos en los carros de movimiento Fig. 8.

Fig. 8. Omega Linear Motion Belt

Para este tipo de transmisión se debe seleccionar el perfil de la correa dentada [15] y el diámetro de la polea en base a la potencia y velocidad del actuador. Con una velocidad angular máxima de 15 r.p.m. y una potencia de 9,47 W, se selecciona el perfil T5. Para los ejes X e Y de 1.5 m de longitud tipo 10 T5-1500-FT-ML y para el eje Z de 0,5 m de longitud tipo 10 T5-500-FT-ML.

3 Diseño Eléctrico y Electrónico

El sistema de control debe cumplir con algunos requerimientos como: control de posición y velocidad de cada eje, registro de materia prima y producto terminado, reconocimiento y categorización de perfiles mediante procesamiento digital de imagen, señales de entrada para la solicitud de materia prima, indicador de producto terminado de calidad y defectuoso, e ingreso de producto terminado, señales de salida para indicar materia prima lista, limitación de recorrido de cada uno de los ejes, aro de emergencia. Fundamentado a los parámetros anteriores, el sistema de control se realizará en base a un ordenador, por medio de una aplicación HMI se realizará comunicación mediante protocolo RS-232 con una tarjeta principal encargada de realizar cambios en la posición de los motores, control de entradas/salidas digitales y finales de carrea. El control de posición se realizará por medio de controladores de servomotores, el diagrama de bloques del sistema se observa en la Fig. 9.

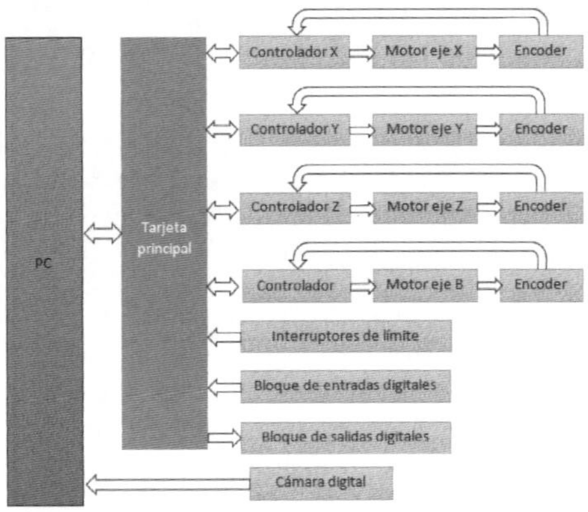

Fig. 9. Diagrama de bloques del Sistema de Control

3.1 Selección de controladores y tarjeta principal

Luego de analizar diversas tarjetas de control existentes en el mercado se selecciona Roboclaw 2x15A [16] por el control simultaneo de 2 motores mediante algoritmos PID para carga variable, mientras que la tarjeta principal será Arduino Uno por su fácil comunicación tanto con los controladores de los motores, así como con el PC, cuenta con 20 pines digitales que pueden actuar como entradas o salidas digitales.

3.2 Aplicación HMI

La aplicación debe tener 3 modos: **Modo Manual.-** El usuario controla el posicionamiento en los ejes X, Y, Z y B. **Modo Automático.-** Atiende las solicitudes de materia prima y almacena los productos terminados. A la falta de materia prima detiene el proceso para que el usuario la ingrese, además, supervisa que estanterías están vacías y cuales llenas. **Modo de ingreso/salida.-** Se puede ingresar materia prima para que el sistema analice y categorice su forma y lo almacene, el usuario puede ingresar materia prima o despacho de producto terminado de forma manual.

4 Implementación y Pruebas

Una vez seleccionada la tarjeta principal y los controladores se procede a la implementación de acuerdo al diagrama de la Fig. 10 cuyo resultado físico se muestra.

Fig. 10. Diagrama eléctrico y Tablero de Control compuesto por: 1.-Luz piloto verde, 2.-Luz piloto roja, 3.-Selector principal, 4.-Paro de emergencia, 5.-Controladores, 6.-Tarjeta principal, 7.-Módulo de salidas digitales, 8.-Fuente 12V, 9.-Fuente 5V, 10.-Portafusible

4.1 Algoritmo de reconocimiento de materia prima

El reconocimiento de patrones mediante visión artificial [8] menciona: una imagen capturada por un sensor se expresa como una función continua f (X, Y) de dos coordenadas en el plano, la digitalización de imágenes asigna a cada muestra un valor entero, el intervalo de la función continua de imagen f (X, Y) se divide en K intervalos. Utilizando el método de sustitución lineal, para fortalecer el gradiente de contraste y mejorar las características de borde de la imagen, suponiendo que el alcance de la gradación de la imagen de entrada f (X, Y) es [a, b] y la gradación de la imagen de salida g (X, Y) es [m, n], entonces el gradiente de contraste puede ser representado:

$$g(X,Y) = \begin{Bmatrix} \left[\frac{(n-m)}{(b-a)}\right][f(X,Y)-a]+m \\ m \\ n \end{Bmatrix} \begin{Bmatrix} a \le f(X,Y) \le b \\ f(X,Y) < a \\ f(X,Y) > b \end{Bmatrix}$$

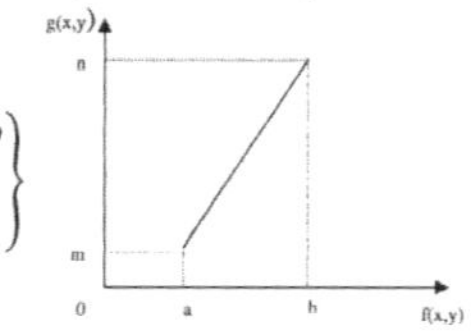

Fig. 11. Fortalecimiento del gradiente de contraste

Para cumplir con la relación anterior se desarrolla mediante la herramienta IMAQ de LabVIEW, patrones para identificar las clases rectángulo, cuadrado y cilindro.

4.2 Algoritmo para almacenamiento y/o recuperación S/R

Para el almacenamiento y/o recuperación de la materia prima como del producto terminado, se aplicó [12] que expresa: son sistemas influenciados por factores como las políticas de almacenamiento / recuperación, los modos de operación y el punto de partida / parada (HOME), compuestos por m filas y n columnas, separados una distancia Dij entre dos cubos Pi = (Xi, Yi) y Pj = (Xj, Yj) expresado como:

$$Dij = \max\left(Xr * (|Xi - Xj|),\ Xc * (|Yi - Yj|)\right)$$

Dónde: Xr es la distancia central entre dos contenedores adyacentes en una fila y Xc distancia central entre dos contenedores adyacentes en una columna.

4.3 Aplicación HMI en LabVIEW

La interfaz HMI, permite al usuario supervisar y administrar los recursos a través de un diseño estructurado e intuitivo, la Fig. 12 muestra sus componentes generales.

Fig. 12. Aplicación HMI: 1.-Asigna un puerto de comunicación con Arduino UNO, 2.- Exhibe error en la configuración del puerto, 3.- Indica fallo en la conexión con la base de datos, 4.- Señala la posición en pulsos de cada motor, 5.- Muestra la velocidad de los motor en RPM, 6.- Lleva a la máquina S/R a su posición de inicio y encera las posiciones de los motores, 7.- Módulo de salidas digitales, 8.- Detiene el HMI luego de cerrar el puerto de comunicación y finalizar la escritura/lectura de la base de datos

En la Fig. 13 se muestran los componentes del modo ingreso/despacho

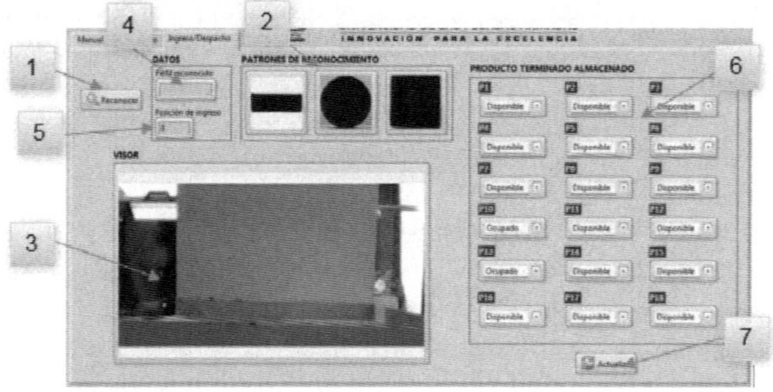

Fig. 13. Modo Ingreso/Despacho: 1.- Inicia el procesamiento digital de imagen para determinar el tipo de materia prima colocado, 2.- Presenta los patrones de búsqueda con los que se realiza el reconocimiento de materia prima, 3.- Indica la materia prima colocada, 4.- Indica el tipo de perfil reconocido, 5.- Exhibe la posición donde se almacenará el perfil de materia prima, 6.- Muestra/ modifica el estado de las estanterías para el producto terminado, 7.- Actualiza el estado de producto terminado en la estructura de almacenamiento

4.4 Pruebas y análisis de resultados

Para determinar la precisión y repetibilidad del sistema, se utilizó la norma ISO 9283 aplicados a robots cartesianos, con 26 N de carga, 200 m/s de velocidad, sobre un cubo de 1285x820x310 mm a razón de 30 ciclos. La Fig. 14, muestra el comportamiento del error en el eje X, con valores que varían entre -1,40 mm. y 1,50 mm., en el eje Y entre -1,60 mm. y 1,10 mm. y en el eje Z entre -1,60 mm. y 1,00 mm.

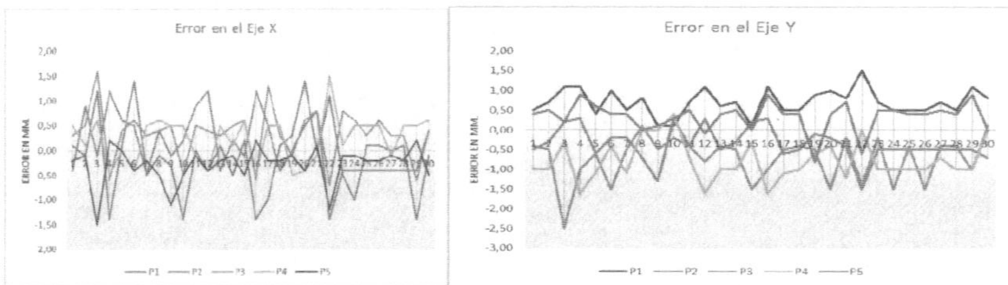

Fig. 14. Error de precisión en los ejes X e Y

Las pruebas anteriores dan como resultado un rango de precisión de ±0,50 mm para todo el sistema. El eje B se desempeña con una repetibilidad promedio de 1,0336°. En la Tabla 2 se resumen las características técnicas obtenidas del sistema AS/RS.

Tabla 2. Características técnicas del sistema

	Posicionamiento	Orientación
Precisión	0,7147 mm	-0,3133° +0,2033°
Repetibilidad	2,1704 mm	1,0336°

4.5 Eficiencia del sistema

Pruebas realizadas al sistema con una muestra de 50 operaciones determinan una eficiencia del 78% en la entrega del material y un 72% en la recepción, esto debido a ciertos factores como pérdidas mecánicas por fricción y pérdidas por carga inductiva que afectan el posicionamiento correcto del sistema, a esto se debe descontar un 28% de error provocado por las cintas transportadoras de la celda de manufactura.

4.6 Reconocimiento de materia prima

Debido a la capacidad de almacenamiento del sistema se selecciona una muestra de 20 piezas de materia prima, se realiza el reconocimiento de perfiles y se obtiene una eficiencia del 84% para perfiles rectangulares, 78% para perfiles circulares, 86% para perfiles cuadrados, esto debido a la luz ambiental, la calidad, complejidad del perfil, la orientación, resolución de la cámara y la posición del módulo de reconocimiento.

5 Conclusiones

Se diseñó y construyó un Sistema Automatizado de Almacenamiento/Recuperación (AS/RS), cuya máquina S/R es un robot cartesiano de 4 ejes X,Y,Z,B para el manejo de materia prima y producto terminado, la misma que es controlada por un micro controlador Atmega328 desde una aplicación HMI en LabVIEW, con una precisión de ±0,50 mm y una eficiencia del 78%.

Las pruebas de funcionamiento se realizaron aplicando la norma ISO 9283, las pruebas del software se realizaron con una muestra de la capacidad mensual de producción de la celda de manufactura.

El Sistema AS/RS fue implementado en el Laboratorio CNC de la Universidad de las Fuerzas Armadas ESPE Extensión Latacunga, permitiendo a los docentes y discentes realizar aplicaciones de manufactura flexible a pequeña escala y consecuentemente mejorar el compendio de esta disciplina tecnológica.

Referencias

1. De Koster R. Le-Duc T. and Roodbergen K.J: Design and control of warehouse order picking: A literature review. European Journal of Operational Research. (2007) 182, 481–501.
2. Hiroyuki Hirano: JIT Implementation Manual. Second edition. Volume 1. CRC Press. USA, (2009). pp. 1 a 12.
3. Chen L. Langevin A. Riopel D: The storage location assignment and interleaving problem in an automated storage/retrieval system with shared storage. Int. Jou. of Production Research. (2010). 48, 4, 991-1011.
4. Mikell P. Groover. Automation, Production Systems and Computer Integrated Manufacturing. Prentice Hall. Third edition (2007).

5. Gu J. Goetschalckx M. e McGinnis L. F. Research on Warehouse Operation: A Comprehensive Review, European Journal of Operational Research. (2007). 177(1), 1–21.
6. Cormier G. Operational research methods for efficient warehousing. em Langevin A. e Riopel D. (Eds.). Logistics Systems: Design and Optimization, Springer, New York, (2005). 93–122.
7. Van den Berg J. P. e Zijm W. H. Models for Warehouse Management: Classification and Examples, International Journal of Production Economics. (1999). 59, 519–528.
8. C. Yu, S. Jianzhu, U. Jinan, L. Zhao, N. Xu and S. Li: Study of Computer Vision and Robot Control Technology in AS/RS. Automation and Logistics. IEEE International Conference on, Jinan, vol. 6, (2007). pp. 876-879.
9. M. Gamberi, R. Manzini and A. Regattieri: Analytical and Numerical Modeling of AS/RS Cycle Time in Class-Based Storage Warehousing. Warehousing in the Global Supply Chain: Advanced Models, Tools and Applications for Storage Systems. London. (2012). pp. 261-283
10. Heungsoon F.L. and Schaefer S.K.: Retrieval sequencing for unit-load automated storage and retrieval systems with multiple openings. Int. J. Prod. Res. Vol 34, No 10. (1996) 2943-2962.
11. Mott R.L.: Diseño de elementos de máquinas. Cuarta Edición. University of Dayton. Pearson Educación. (2004).
12. Krishnaiah O. and Sarveswar M.: Genetic algorithms for studies on AS/RS integrated with machines. The International Journal of Advanced Manufacturing Technology. London (2003). Vol. 22, Issue 11-12 pp 932-940.
13. Shigley J. and Mitchell L.: Diseño en Ingeniería Mecánica. Mexico. (1999). McGraw-Hill.
14. Pololu.: Servomotor 12V. Available: http://www.pololu.com/product/1447. Retrieved 17/09/2014.
15. Megalinear: Available: http://www.megabelt.sk/files/katalog megalinear_2010.pdf. Retrieved 3/09/2014.
16. Motion Control.: Available: http://www.ionmc.com/RoboClaw-2x15A-Motor-Controller_p_10.html. Retrived 17/09/2014

Methodological Proposal for Ethnographic Research in Software Engineering: A Case Study

Dante Carrizo[1], and Andres Alfaro[1]

[1] University of Atacama, Computer Science Department, Ave. Copayapu 485, Copiapó, Chile
{dante.carrizo, andres.alfaro}@uda.cl

Abstract. To guide an investigative process, it is necessary a methodology of work focused on the type of research that is intended to be carried out. In software engineering, there is little experience in the use of ethnography as a research technique, probably due to the lack of knowledge on how to proceed in these types of studies. This article presents a methodology, with a practical approach, that was used to execute a research on Chilean software developers. For this, the methodological proposal of ethnographic research, based on a qualitative approach, consists of 5 stages: Definition, Field, Collection, Proposal and Evaluation. This experience demonstrated that this methodology helps to guide and order the investigative process, preventing confusion and mismatches in the search for knowledge. Although it has only been tested in a study, this proposal represents an important contribution for researchers to carry out this type of research in different areas of software engineering.

Keywords: ethnography, software engineering, empirical research

1 Introducción

Para la búsqueda de soluciones a problemas que surgen en un proceso investigativo, los investigadores se ven en la necesidad de tomar una serie de decisiones [1]. En este contexto, se hace necesario contar con una metodología de investigación, que contenga decisiones que un investigador toma para alcanzar sus objetivos, tales como: estrategias a utilizar, diseño de la investigación, muestra, métodos para la recolección y análisis de datos [2].

En la actualidad, la búsqueda del conocimiento se ha polarizado en básicamente dos enfoques o paradigmas; Cuantitativo y Cualitativo. Para un enfoque cuantitativo, se busca resolver preguntas tales como: ¿Cuántos?, y ¿Con qué frecuencia?, a través de la recolección de datos y su análisis, confiando en la medición y uso de estadísticas con el objetivo de probar una hipótesis. A su vez, el enfoque cualitativo busca responder preguntas tales como: ¿Por qué? y ¿Para qué?, a través de la observación, desarrollando una descripción cercana a la realidad que se investiga [3].

Según [4], la elección del paradigma está íntimamente relacionado con el contexto de la investigación, y a su vez condiciona el procedimiento de estudio que sigue una investigación. Cuando se quiere conocer el estilo o forma de vida de un grupo de individuos, la etnografía es una técnica que nos permite insertarnos, aprender su lenguaje, conocer sus costumbres y comportamientos. De esta manera, se podrán realizar adecuadas interpretaciones no solo del grupo de estudio, sino además de los acontecimientos que suceden [5].

A la hora de realizar una investigación cualitativa, no solo es necesario tener en claro el objetivo de la investigación, sino además preparar y planificar las intervenciones. Según [5], además de exponer la importancia que tiene la etnografía en la investigación pedagógica, nos da una serie de reseñas y particularidades que nos permiten tener una base o guía a la hora de realizar un estudio de este tipo. Además, explica que la etnografía no es una fotografía del momento con detalles externos. Se trata de ir más atrás, de profundizar en el grupo, a través de una serie de acciones, técnicas y métodos que facilitan conocer de forma más detallada al grupo de investigación.

Si bien la etnografía, es utilizada como técnica a la hora de educción de requisitos ya sea entrevistas, observaciones, entre otras. No es utilizada comúnmente como técnica de investigación en la ingeniera de software [6]. Esto lleva a proponer este trabajo como guía para realizar investigaciones cualitativas en el plano de la ingeniería de software, utilizando como técnica la etnografía. Este enfoque metodológico, se extrajo y sintetizó en base a la experiencia de un estudio, que tiene como objetivo, conocer cómo trabajan las empresas de desarrollo de software en Chile, además de identificar factores de riesgo, fracaso y éxito de la industria.

El resto del artículo sigue de la siguiente forma. En la sección 2, se describirán con más detalle algunos conceptos que ayudarán a entender de mejor forma el enfoque metodológico. Luego, en la sección 3 se presentará la metodología propuesta, con sus etapas y tareas. En la sección 4 se expone un estudio de caso, donde se demuestra la utilización de esta metodología de investigación; esto sirve además como guía para aplicar esta propuesta en otras investigaciones. En sección 5, se realiza una breve discusión sobre las ventajas y desventajas, experiencia y recomendaciones a la hora de aplicar la metodología propuesta. Finalmente, en la sección 6, se presentan las conclusiones sobre este trabajo.

2 Antecedentes y Trabajo Relacionado

Esta propuesta metodológica está basada en un paradigma cualitativo. Este enfoque sirve para comprender la realidad social donde no hay leyes generalizadas, sino pensamientos e historias de los actores sociales que son captadas en testimonios [2]. El paradigma cualitativo sirve para el estudio de fenómenos de carácter dinámico y continuo en el tiempo. Para [7], la investigación cualitativa es válida para explorar relaciones y procesos que transcurren en una organización. Además, a través de este paradigma, podremos responder preguntas tales como: ¿Qué piensan las personas sobre una situación en particular?, ¿Cómo sería su participación, en determinadas situaciones? Estas preguntas requieren de información cualitativa sobre las vivencias, percepciones, sentimientos de los participantes de un entorno [3].Y por último, los datos son considerados ricos y profundos debido a que se pueden extraer con más detalles gracias a la cercanía entre el investigador y el problema a estudiar [7].

Debido a lo anteriormente expuesto, este paradigma encaja perfectamente en el contexto de estudio de esta investigación, que como se mencionó en apartados anteriores, su objetivo es conocer cómo trabajan las empresas desarrolladoras de software chilenas, pero de una forma más interna, comprendiendo sus métodos, procesos y estilos de trabajo contados por sus propios trabajadores. A su vez, este paradigma cualitativo proporciona una serie de alternativas o técnicas a los investigadores para tener un mayor conocimiento en situaciones más concretas. Es así como dentro de las diferentes técnicas para esta metodología de investigación se consideró la etnografía, debido a que es ideal para estudios de campo con carácter cualitativos [3].

En [3], se describe la Etnografía como "una forma particular de articular la experiencia de campo y el trabajo analítico, los dos son parte inseparable de un mismo proceso"; "técnica para recolectar, analizar y presentar datos (observación participante, entrevista abiertas, análisis cualitativo, descripciones narrativas)". La etnografía, permite descubrir el conocimiento cultural que poseen miembros de un grupo o comunidades y a su vez trata de conocer la cultura "no estudiando a la gente", sino "aprendiendo de ella" [3]. En relación a la recolección y posterior análisis de datos, [8] nos habla sobre la importancia de la elección de los métodos de recolección y análisis de datos, destacando la observación, que se caracteriza por la recopilación de detalles descriptivos en la interacción de los individuos. Junto con ello, es útil la entrevista, donde la mayoría de las preguntas son de carácter abierto, y pueden variar desde la más informal, hasta una más estructurada. A su vez, están los cuestionarios que tiene la finalidad de recolectar datos puntuales sobre el grupo de estudio. Según [6], nos dice que la finalidad de la etnografía es presentar la mirada de las personas estudiadas y no la forma que el investigador está viendo el grupo de estudio, proporcionando una visión a las personas interesadas. Además, describe un conjunto de trabajos donde se utiliza el conocimiento tácito, para lograr extraer información. Y por último, muestra una guía para aplicar la etnografía, según sea el caso, manera o forma cono se quiere utilizar. Otra guía es la descrita en [9], que nos proporciona una serie de recomendaciones a la hora de realizar un proceso etnográfico en la ingeniería de software. A pesar de que [6] y [9] son guías en las cuales se describen recomendaciones o formas de cómo abordar un proceso etnográfico en la ingeniería de software, en ninguna de ellas se puntualizan etapas bien definidas o concretas para llevar un proceso investigativo. Además, no señalan alguna forma de procesamiento de datos o herramientas que ayuden a desarrollar este tipo de trabajos empíricos.

Debido a estas razones, se desarrolla esta propuesta que tiene como objetivo ser la base y guía de un proceso investigativo, que incorpore estas recomendaciones y a su vez proponga una serie de etapas, pasos y herramientas a seguir, para ayudar a los investigadores en estos estudios empíricos.

3 Metodología de Investigación

Como se mencionó anteriormente, esta Propuesta Metodológica (Figura 1) tiene como base un enfoque cualitativo, con una técnica etnográfica como centro, lo que nos permitirá desarrollar la investigación y obtener conclusiones asertivas.

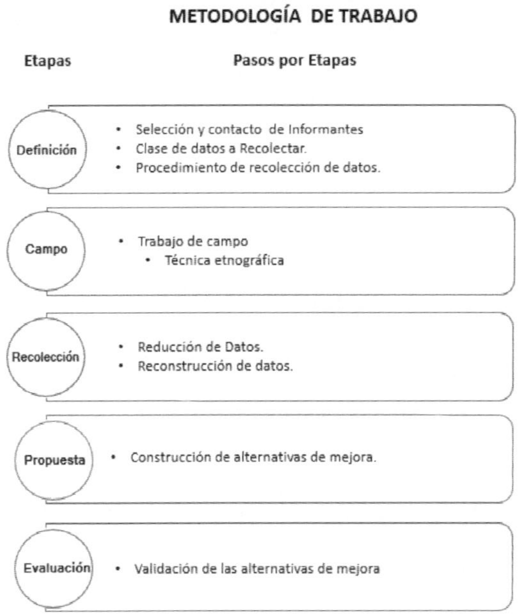

Fig. 1. Estructura de la propuesta metodológica

3.1 Definición

En esta fase, como tareas sugeridas, están: Selección y contacto de informantes, Clase de datos a Recolectar, y Procedimientos de recolección de datos. Estas tareas buscan explicar y describir cómo se selecciona la población o el grupo a estudiar, y además, cómo se realizaron los contactos para poder cumplir la inmersión en estos grupos. Y por último, qué información o datos se buscará recolectar y la forma o técnica a utilizar para recoger estos datos. El contacto puede ser a través de diferentes medios, contactándose personalmente con el grupo de estudio o a través de organismos o contactos que ayuden a un acercamiento con el grupo. En relación a la información que se quiere recolectar, puede ser guiada por medio de diferentes técnicas, tales como: preguntas abiertas, entrevistas, preguntas claves (¿qué?, ¿cómo?, ¿por qué?), mapas de trayectoria [10] (sirven para mejorar el entendimiento de procesos por medio de experiencias), entre otras.

3.2 Campo

Bajo el nombre de "Campo", se comienza el estudio empírico de la población o grupos seleccionados. Para ello se utiliza la técnica de etnografía, junto con las preguntas de entrevistas que en conjunto ayudarán a la extracción de información. Estos datos, información, comentarios, relatos, etc. pueden ser recolectados a través de videos, audio, notas de campo, documentación, etc., en general, cualquier medio que ayude a retener y almacenar esta información, que luego será procesada en la siguiente etapa.

3.3 Recolección

En la tercera etapa de "Recolección", están como tareas: La Reducción y Reconstrucción de datos, esto quiere decir, el análisis de los datos. A través de la trascripción de las notas, audios, documentos de campo, además de una clasificación y categorización de los mismos hallazgos y conclusiones, esta etapa puede ser realizada a través de murales colaborativos utilizando técnicas como: saturar y agrupar, trascripción gráfica de los mapas de trayectoria, o clasificación de conceptos [10]. A través de lo anterior, se obtiene una información procesada y lista para ser utilizada de diferentes maneras, ya sea para responder a las hipótesis planteadas o comprender el funcionamiento social del grupo de estudio.

3.4 Propuesta

Esta fase tiene como tarea sugerida la Construcción de Alternativas de Mejoras, esto quiere decir que frente a la obtención de la información procesada se extraen diferentes posibilidades u opciones que busque mejorar en diferentes ámbitos el grupo o población seleccionada. Para proponer mejoras, es de suma importancia, tener en cuenta las limitaciones que tiene el o los grupos de estudio, de esta manera no se propondrán ideas o mejoras alejadas de la realidad de la muestra. Para esto, se pueden intercambiar algunas propuestas de mejora ya realizadas por los grupos de estudio, además de la revisión y selección de la literatura que sugiera alternativas de mejora según, como ya se mencionó anteriormente, la realidad del o los grupos de estudio.

3.5 Evaluación

En esta etapa se busca validar las propuestas realizadas en la etapa anterior, ya que tiene como tarea sugerida la Validación de las Alternativas de Mejora. Esto busca no solo obtener una retroalimentación, sino además evaluar la efectividad de las propuestas o si fuese necesario replantearlas o re-estructurarlas. Para esto, se pueden enviar las propuestas de mejora a un grupo pre-seleccionado de participantes en el estudio, para que evalúen y entreguen una retroalimentación sobre las propuestas, de esta manera se podrán, mantener, mejorar o cambiar según sean los casos.

A continuación se describirán, todas las acciones, tareas, pasos, materiales y herramientas que se realizaron en esta investigación, teniendo como base la metodología de trabajo anteriormente expuesta.

4 Estudio de Caso

Es importante destacar que este estudio de caso, no solo sirve para demostrar la utilización de la propuesta, sino también es una guía o base práctica para saber aplicar esta metodología en otras investigaciones.

Dentro de la primera etapa de "Definición", se recolectó información de empresas desarrolladoras de software en Chile. Esta información se buscó a través de páginas web como búsqueda directa por Google, bajo las palabras de "Empresas desarrolladoras de software en Chile". Además se agregaron la mayoría de las empresas que se encuentran incorporadas en la página https://www.getonbrd.cl/, sitio web de anuncios laborales relacionados a la industria TI y contactos entre pares. Es relevante destacar que estas fueron las únicas fuentes que dieron resultados. Se realizaron otros tipos de contacto como sociedades, universidades, pero que no ofrecieron ningún tipo de respuesta concretas a esta investigación. De esta recolección se obtuvo un total de 90 empresas entre las que se encontraban empresas de asesoría, consultoría, diseñadoras, dedicadas a la venta de paquetes de software, sistemas de Big Data, sitios Web, plataformas de seguridad, desarrollos de videojuegos y desarrollo de software a la medida.

La segunda selección consistió en preferir solo las empresas que dentro de sus actividades económicas estaba el desarrollo de software. De las 90 empresas, 52 están dedicadas este foco comercial. Como primera aproximación, nos contactamos vía telefónica con 32 de las 52 ya que no todas tenían teléfono y algunos sitios web ya no estaban en línea. Este contacto tenía como objetivo comentar brevemente sobre nuestro proyecto y la posibilidad de mandar como segunda instancia un correo explicando con mayor profundidad el proyecto, y además adjuntando la carta de presentación del mismo. Como resultado de la tarea de Contacto, más de la mitad de las 32 respondió positivamente a nuestra petición, pero se realizaron visitas a ocho empresas, debido a factores como recursos, distancias de viaje, fechas y tiempos que se ajustaran tanto a la investigación como a las empresas a estudiar.

Es importante destacar lo complejo que es generar este tipo de contactos, ya que muchas de las empresas acusan falta de tiempo, escasez de personal que pueda atender en estos casos, fechas incompatibles entre los tiempos de investigación y disponibilidad de ellas para recibirnos y en algunos casos, no existiendo ningún tipo de respuesta.

Mientras se realizaba la tarea de contacto con las empresas, se preparaba un guion de preguntas abiertas, que conducirían el trabajo etnográfico al momento de realizar las visitas. Este guion de preguntas busca dar respuesta a las hipótesis planteadas al inicio del proyecto. Debido a que la información sería capturada a través de narraciones (respuestas a las preguntas abiertas) hechas por los propios trabajadores, estas fueron grabadas para su posterior análisis.

Para esta investigación, se contó con empresas participantes tanto en el ámbito nacional como internacional. Las empresas que respondieron a nuestra investigación en el plano nacional se encuentran en las Regiones: Metropolitana (Santiago), Valparaíso (Con-Con), Atacama (Copiapó). Las empresas a nivel internacional se encuentran en India (Calcuta), China (Hong. Kong) y España (Madrid y Barcelona).

Para la segunda fase de "Campo", se realizaron las intervenciones a las empresas participantes. Es por ello que se viajó a cada lugar donde se encuentran ubicadas estas empresas, para realizar las intervenciones y entrevistas. Entendiendo lo complejo de esta fase y bajo ese contexto, se pudo interactuar a través de las preguntas abiertas y conversaciones, con los diferentes actores o roles, que participan a la hora de desarrollar un producto de software, entre ellos; Programadores, Jefes de proyectos, Gerentes de venta, Gerentes General, etc. A su vez, se participó en reuniones de equipo, se conoció el espacio físico donde trabajan y algunas de las herramientas que utilizan a la hora de desarrollar sus proyectos.

Para la fase de "Recolección", la información (respuesta, comentario, narraciones anexos, etc.), contenida en archivos de audio, se traspasa a papel, puntualizando y clasificando dicha información en Respuestas, Problemáticas y Apreciaciones, para cada una de las empresas participantes. Una vez realizada esta primera cosecha de datos, la información es traspasada a murales colaborativos (https://www.linoit.com), lo que permite ordenar y clasificar en; Factores de Riesgo, Factores de Fracaso, Factores de Éxito, Estilo de Trabajo, Problemáticas, Apreciaciones, Datos de Empresa y además se agrega un esquema de las diferentes etapas o tareas para crear un producto de software descrito por cada una de empresas (ver Figura 2). Esta acción, es parte de la segunda tarea propuesta por la metodología de trabajo, la reconstrucción de datos.

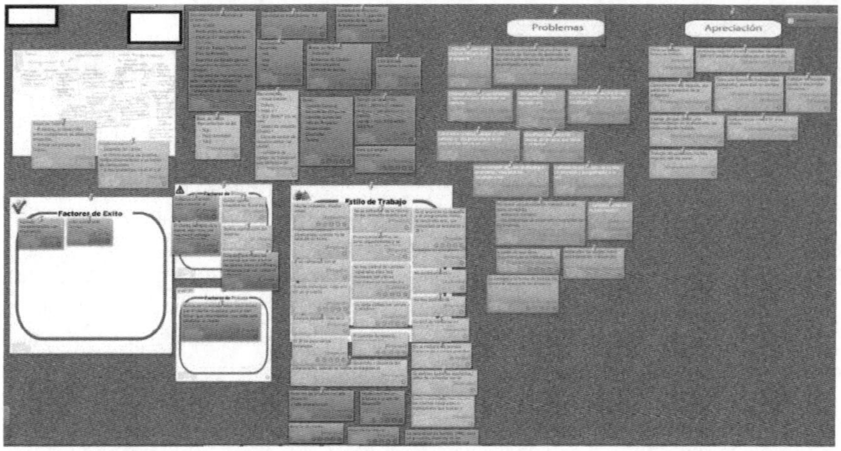

Fig. 2. Segunda re-clasificación utilizando murales colaborativos

Esta segunda clasificación viene guiado por los Elementos de análisis, que son un conjunto de conceptos clasificados (*Tag*), que ayudan a dar una respuesta más puntual y específica a las hipótesis planteas al inicio del proyecto. Estos *Tag* son agregados en los diferentes *post-it* de cada mural colaborativo, de esta manera se pueden categorizar, según estos Elementos de Análisis, como muestra la Figura 3.

Como resultado de la etapa "Recolección", se obtuvo información variada sobre cómo trabajan las empresas de desarrollo chilenas. Junto con ello, se detectaron algunas Elementos Críticos (Problemáticas, Elementos de riesgo, Factores de fracaso y Factores de riesgo).

Para la siguiente etapa de "Propuesta", se comienza a construir diferentes propuestas de mejora, a los Elementos Críticos encontrados en este estudio. Para esto, se selecciona algunos Elementos Críticos, más comunes o más destacados por las empresas participantes. Para dar respuesta a estas problemáticas, se seleccionan diferentes trabajos y artículos, que tratan estos elementos seleccionados y se exponen como posibles soluciones. Además, se comparte algunas mejoras, acciones o actividades que ya fueron implementadas por algunas empresas, sobre los elementos críticos seleccionados. Todas estas mejoras tienen que ser simples y económicas ya que están enfocadas en la realidad y contexto de la mayoría de las empresas desarrolladoras de software chilenas.

Finalmente, la etapa de "Evaluación" crea un informe que contiene no solo el estudio sobre las empresas desarrolladoras, sino además las diferentes propuestas de mejora creadas en función de los elementos críticos detectados.

Ámbito	Elementos de Análisis	Tag	Especificación del Tag
Ingeniería de Software	Herramientas (Entendiendo, que las Herramientas son para apoyar el desarrollo de un producto de software en diferentes etapas; desarrollo, requerimientos, gestión de proyecto, etc.)	**Herramientas**	Lenguaje de desarrollo
			IDE
			SCV
			BD
			Gestores de BD
			Otras Herramientas
			Diagramas
		Documentación	Documentación
	Métodos (Entendiendo que método es toda aquella etapa, tarea, actividad que conforman el proceso de producción de un producto de software)	**Metodología**	Metodologías de Desarrollo (si, no, Propias o adaptadas)
		Requisitos	Técnicas de recopilación o educción de requisitos
		Testing	Pruebas o Test
		Desarrollo	Forma de Desarrollo
		Entrega	Implementación
		Estimación	Estimación de horas de un proyecto
		Cambios	Control de cambios
	Procesos (Entendiendo, el procesos es la base para el control de la administración de un proyecto de software) (Los procesos están muy relacionados con Empereza, porque el Proceso, es la forma de cómo se trabaja y la Empresa es quien sustenta esta forma de trabajo)	**Proyecto**	Estrategias para desarrollar un proyecto
			Relación con el cliente (Reuniones, forma de comunicación)
			Equipos (Roles, Cantidad, Tipos de equipos)
			Tiempos del proyecto
			Post Morten o cierre de proyecto
	Compromiso con la calidad (Basado en las constantes mejoras y retroalimentación para el mismo objetivo)	**Calidad**	Certificaciones CMMI, ISO
			Control de calidad
			Herramientas de calidad
		Métricas	Métricas

Fig. 3. Elementos de Análisis

Este informe es enviado a todas las empresas participantes, como retribución por la participación en la investigación. A su vez, se selecciona tres de estas empresas, para consultar y recibir por parte de ellas, retrospectivas sobre esta investigación y en especial sobre las propuestas de mejora. Para esta tarea, se pone en contacto con ellas, preguntado, su parecer, si alguna de estas podrían ser implementadas, y si existe un reparo o desacuerdo frente a las propuestas.

5 Discusión

Como ya se mencionó anteriormente, existen algunos trabajos que proponen recomendaciones para poder llevar investigaciones en la ingeniera de software utilizando la etnografía como herramienta, pero en ningún caso se describen etapas, tareas, pasos y herramientas definidas para este tipo de investigación. Es por esto, que se propone esta metodología, que agrega estas recomendaciones y a su vez proporciona una serie de etapas y acciones que ayuden a soportar y guiar un proceso investigativo en la ingeniería de software utilizando la etnografía. Es importante destacar que la aplicación de esta metodología logró facilitar, ordenar y gestionar un trabajo investigativo sobre empresas desarrolladoras de software. Así también, se deben mencionar algunas dificultades. Los primeros contactos y las relaciones con empresas del ámbito TI fueron unas de las tareas más complejas de esta propuesta, acusando falta de tiempo, incompatibilidad de fechas de visitas o no respondiendo, por parte de las empresas.

Otra limitación del caso de estudio es que no fue posible realizar muestreo formal porque finalmente, en estos casos, siempre los que responden son un subconjunto de la muestra por lo que es difícil mitigar la amenaza de validez externa. En este sentido, si bien es cierto que los resultados no pueden generalizarse a la población el foco del artículo se centra más bien en la metodología y no en el caso de estudio.

6 Conclusión

Para lograr obtener el conocimiento en un proceso investigativo, es de vital importancia tener una guía o base, que trace su camino. A su vez, es importante que esta guía de trabajo esté contextualizada en base a la investigación que se va a realizar.

A pesar de que existen variadas metodologías de investigación en diferentes áreas, la escasez de propuestas que ayuden a obtener de forma empírica conocimientos sobre la Ingeniería de Software, da razones para crear y proponer una Metodología de Investigación que contenga los diferentes pasos, actividades o tareas que ayuden a obtener conocimiento, con mayor profundidad, sobre esta disciplina.

Para esto, se propuso una Metodología de Investigación que consta de 5 etapas (Definición, Campo, Recolección Propuesta y Evaluación), con tareas sugeridas, que será la guía y base para el desarrollo de trabajos de investigación cualitativa sobre ingeniera de software.

Esta Metodología, tiene un enfoque cualitativo y como técnica base para recolectar información la Etnografía. Esto permite al grupo investigador preparar la investigación y recolectar datos de una forma más cercana debido a la relación que se genera entre el grupo de estudio y los investigadores. La información que se obtiene una vez procesado los datos es más verosímil debido a la forma de obtención de la misma. Es importante destacar que aunque es una metodología que propone o sugiere tareas y herramientas a utilizar, estas pueden ser modificadas según el tipo de investigación, entendiendo que esta propuesta está enfocada a servir como base en trabajos cualitativos.

Finalmente, esta propuesta fue creada para guiar un trabajo investigativo sobre ingeniería de software. En la práctica, se logró llevar con éxito esta investigación. La utilización de esta metodología de investigación y sus diferentes herramientas ayudaron a gestionar de forma ordenada el proceso investigativo, logrando obtener información relevante y cumpliendo los objetivos del estudio.

Agradecimientos

Esta investigación es financiada por el programa de investigación de la Universidad de Atacama DIUDA 22298.

Referencias

1. Taylor, S. J. & Bogdan, R: Introduction to Qualitative Research Methods: a Guidebook and Resource. New York: John Wiley & Sons. (1998).
2. Ugalde N., Balbastre F: Investigación Cuantitativa e Investigación Cualitativa: Buscando las ventajas de las diferentes Metodologías de Investigación. (2013).
3. Balcázar, P., Gonzalez-Arratia, N., Gurrola, G., Moysen, A.: Investigación Cuantitativa. Universidad Autónoma del Estado de México, Vol 2, (2013).
4. Zapparoli, M.: Concepciones Teóricas Metodológicas Sobre Investigación. Girasol, Revista de la Escuela de Estudios Generales. 5 (2003) 191-198.
5. Nolla-Cao, N.: Etnografía: Una alternativa más en la investigación pedagógica. Revista cubana de Educación Media superior. num 11. año 2. Cuba. (1997) 107-115.
6. Kumar, M.: Ethnography a research method in software process improvements. International Journal of Advances in Computer Networks and Its Security. Vol 1 (2011) 425-429.
7. Saunders, M., Lewis, P., Thornhill, A.: Research methods for business students, Prentice Hall, Harlow (Essex) (2009).
8. Wilcox, K.: La etnografía como una metodología y su aplicación al estudio de la escuela: una visión. Haciendo la etnografía de la escuela, antropología en acción, España (1990).
9. Sharp, H., Desouza, C., Dittrich, Y.: Using ethnographic methods in software engineering research. In Proceedings of the 32nd ACM/IEEE International Conference on Software Engineering-Volume 2. ACM, 2010. p. 491-492.
10. Gonzalez, F.: Mini guía: una introducción al Design Thinking+ Bootcamp bootleg. Hasso Platner, Institute of design at Stanford. (2012).

Usability of Mobile Applications for Visually Impaired People: An Empirical Study

Efraín R. Fonseca C.[1], Diego Marcillo[1], John W. Castro[2], Ivette Ramos[1], and Priscila Rodríguez[1]

[1] Departamento de Ciencias de la Computación, Universidad de las Fuerzas Armadas ESPE, Sangolquí, Ecuador,
[2] Departamento de Ingeniería Informática y Ciencias de la Computación, Universidad de Atacama, Copiapó, Chile
{erfonseca, dmmarcillo, imramos2, pprodriguez2}@espe.edu.ec
john.castro@uda.cl

Abstract. —***Background:*** The use of mobile devices has increased significantly in recent years becoming the main means of access to communication, learning and other services. However, users with different types of disabilities are marginalized from the benefits of mobile technology. Particularly, people with visual impairment face different challenges given the complexity of its interfaces showing that the development of these applications might not considered this group of users. ***Aim:*** From this perspective, the objective of this work is to identify the usability criteria that must be incorporated within mobile applications in order to be used by people with visual disabilities. ***Method:*** Through a Systematic Mapping Study (SMS) to investigate the attributes, techniques and tools for the usability evaluation of mobile applications for the visually impaired. ***Results:*** After the study, we identified the lack of formal models for assessing the usefulness of mobile applications for visually impaired people, forcing evaluators to use traditional evaluation models and incorporating usability attributes based on their experience. ***Conclusions:*** Finally, we conclude that the poor usability of mobile applications for blind people would appear that obeys to the lack of formal usability evaluations models for this kind of applications.

Keywords: usability, mobile applications, visual impairment, usability assessment tools, systematic mapping study

1 Introducción

El uso de dispositivos móviles se ha incrementado radicalmente en los últimos años, de la mano de un sinnúmero de aplicaciones (app), a través de las cuales los usuarios pueden realizar tareas cotidianas como, por ejemplo: aprendizaje, comunicación, entretenimiento, etc. [2]. Sin embargo, los usuarios con capacidades especiales no pueden aprovechar todos estos beneficios, puesto que por su condición enfrentan retos al momento de interactuar con un dispositivo móvil; especialmente las personas con discapacidad visual [2]. Para este segmento de usuarios, el uso de dispositivos y aplicaciones móviles representa un verdadero desafío, debido a que tienen que superar diversos problemas de usabilidad y accesibilidad en términos de hardware y software [2].

En lo referente a hardware, los dispositivos móviles cuentan con diseños de tamaños reducidos, delgados y por lo general emplean una pantalla táctil como medio de interacción con el usuario [8]. Estas características reducen significativamente la posibilidad de que un usuario con discapacidad visual interactúe con un dispositivo móvil. En cuanto a software, está demostrado que no todas las aplicaciones móviles cumplen con criterios y parámetros indispensables en el marco de usabilidad móvil para este segmento de usuarios, lo que dificulta e incluso imposibilita el uso de ciertas apps por personas con esta discapacidad [4].

La usabilidad es considerada como uno de los factores más importantes para definir la calidad de un producto software [6]. Para el caso de los usuarios con discapacidad visual, la importancia de la usabilidad se acrecienta aún más. No obstante, al momento de desarrollar aplicaciones móviles, al parecer no se considera a la usabilidad como una prioridad, desde la perspectiva de este segmento de usuarios, limitando así su inclusión en la sociedad [5].

Esta situación ha puesto de manifiesto la necesidad de realizar un análisis que permita identificar los criterios para evaluar la usabilidad de las aplicaciones móviles desde la perspectiva de la discapacidad visual, en términos de: métricas, modelos y herramientas relacionadas. Por lo tanto, realizamos un Mapeo Sistemático de Literatura (SMS, de sus siglas del inglés *Systematic Mapping Study*, siguiendo las guías metodológicas propuestas por Kitchenham & Charters [9], con el fin de identificar y evaluar estudios relevantes relacionados con esta temática. Como resultado se obtuvieron 21 estudios primarios, cuya información permitió dar respuesta a las preguntas de investigación planteadas en este estudio.

Lo que resta del artículo se estructura como sigue. En la sección 2 se describen los trabajos relacionados. A continuación, en la sección 3, se especifica la metodología del SMS. En la sección 4 se presentan las respuestas y el análisis de las preguntas de investigación. En la sección 5, se discuten los resultados obtenidos y las amenazas a la validez. Finalmente, en la Sección 6 se describen las conclusiones.

2 Antecedentes

La usabilidad es considerada como un atributo de calidad del software [6]; al respecto, existen varios estudios referentes a la evaluación de la usabilidad de las aplicaciones móviles en general e incluso algunas específicas para personas con discapacidad visual. Sin embargo, estos estudios revelan la inexistencia de criterios, herramientas y métodos diseñados exclusivamente para evaluar la usabilidad, desde la perspectiva de la discapacidad visual.

Hemos encontrado estudios que evalúan la usabilidad de aplicaciones móviles para personas con discapacidad visual. Por ejemplo, en el estudio realizado por Façanha & otros [5] se emplea una evaluación inicial de usabilidad mediante la metodología de enfoque grupal, aplicando cuestionarios para descubrir, analizar, validar y mejorar requerimientos de este tipo de aplicaciones móviles; sin embargo, los autores no especifican que modificaciones realizaron a la metodología utilizada, para adaptarla a las características de los usuarios con discapacidad visual. El estudio de Leporini & otros [12] propone una inspección de usabilidad para recopilar información cualitativa de los usuarios no videntes sobre la accesibilidad y la usabilidad de los dispositivos móviles de pantalla táctil de Apple. Una vez más, en este estudio no se especifica cómo la condición de los usuarios objetivo ha condicionado la actividad realizada. Sánchez & Maureira [25] proponen una aplicación móvil para guiar a las personas ciegas en el metro subterráneo. Previo a su construcción, se realizó un estudio de usabilidad y evaluación cognitiva. Sin embargo, tampoco se precisan los detalles de cómo la condición de este segmento de usuarios influyó en la construcción del software.

Otros estudios evalúan la usabilidad de los recursos de interacción del dispositivo móvil con los elementos considerados en el diseño de la interfaz de usuario. Por ejemplo, Shaik & otros [26] han modificado un teléfono móvil, añadiéndole funcionalidades para facilitar el día a día de los usuarios impedidos visualmente. Este dispositivo emplea, entre otras cosas, retroalimentación auditiva, interfaz de usuario diseñada para minimizar la operación del usuario y su diseño considera factores tales como costo, portabilidad, aprendizaje y escalabilidad. En este estudio se realizan estudios de usabilidad a modo de retroalimentación; sin embargo, no se precisan las variantes de las técnicas utilizadas, entorno a los usuarios objetivos.

Finalmente, existen estudios en los que se hace referencia a los problemas que se enfrentan los usuarios no videntes, al interactuar con las apps móviles. Por ejemplo, Krajnc & otros [10] indican que controlar la interfaz táctil de los dispositivos móviles representa un reto para las personas con discapacidad visual, ya que al contrario de las interfaces tradicionales con botones reales y la consiguiente seguridad de ubicación fija y retroalimentación háptica, las interfaces táctiles lo desorientan y dificultan la interacción. En una pantalla táctil, el usuario con discapacidad visual tiene menos puntos de referencia y una baja respuesta [5].

En resumen, podemos afirmar que existen muy pocos elementos de juicio para poder evaluar la usabilidad de las apps móviles desde la perspectiva de los usuarios con discapacidad visual, lo cual nos motivó a realizar la presente investigación.

3 Mapeo Sistemático de Literatura

Un SMS es un método de investigación que tiene por objetivo proporcionar una visión general de un área temática particular e identificar y clasificar la literatura relacionada. Para ello, un SMS realiza una búsqueda para conocer qué temas han sido cubiertos en la literatura y dónde ha sido publicada esta literatura [18,9]. Tomando como base las guías de Petersen & otros [18] y Kitchenham & Charters [9], se plantearon las siguientes fases en la ejecución del SMS: (1) Definición de las preguntas de investigación, (2) planteamiento de la estrategia de búsqueda, (3) establecimiento del proceso de selección y, (4) extracción de datos.

3.1 Definición de las Preguntas de Investigación

Para establecer explícitamente el alcance del objetivo de la investigación es necesario definir las RQ, porque exponen de manera clara lo que se desea encontrar. Por tanto, el SMS está dirigido a responder las preguntas de investigación (RQ) [9]:

RQ1: ¿Cuáles son los elementos y actividades propuestos en el marco del desarrollo de aplicaciones móviles orientados a personas con discapacidad visual, desde la perspectiva de la usabilidad?

RQ2: ¿Qué criterios de usabilidad son pertinentes para que el desarrollo de aplicaciones móviles satisfaga los requisitos de los usuarios con discapacidad visual?

RQ3: ¿Qué características deben poseer los dispositivos móviles en términos de hardware, para facilitar la interacción con los usuarios con discapacidad visual?

RQ4: ¿Cuáles son los recursos de interacción que se emplean para el ingreso y salida de información en las aplicaciones móviles para personas con discapacidad visual?

RQ5: ¿Qué elementos deben considerarse en el diseño de la interfaz de una aplicación móvil para usuarios con discapacidad visual?

RQ6: ¿Cuáles son las herramientas, modelos y pruebas utilizadas para evaluar la usabilidad de las aplicaciones móviles para personas con discapacidad visual?

3.2 Definición de la Estrategia de Búsqueda

Para realizar el SMS es necesario definir una estrategia de búsqueda. Para este caso, se establecieron las siguientes actividades: (1) Definir los criterios de inclusión y exclusión, (2) crear el grupo de control (GC) de literatura, (3) construir la cadena de búsqueda y (4) buscar los estudios candidatos.

Previo a la búsqueda en las bases digitales es necesario realizar la **definición de los criterios de inclusión y exclusión**, que plantean las condiciones que deben satisfacer los estudios para poder ser tenidos en cuenta o no, como relevantes para la investigación. Para nuestro caso particular, definimos en consenso los siguientes criterios:

Criterios de inclusión. El artículo discute: (i) la usabilidad de aplicaciones móviles sin importar la plataforma de desarrollo de las mismas, siempre que sean orientadas a usuarios con discapacidad visual, (ii) los métodos o modelos de usabilidad utilizados para desarrollar aplicaciones móviles exclusivamente para usuarios con discapacidad visual, (iii) los resultados de prototipos/aplicaciones móviles multi-plataforma utilizados por usuarios con discapacidad visual que permiten identificar nuevos criterios de usabilidad, (iv) las dificultades a las que el usuario con discapacidad visual se enfrenta al utilizar una aplicación móvil y las posibles soluciones que pueden mejorar la usabilidad de tales aplicaciones.

Criterios de exclusión. Artículos que: (i) no hagan referencia a la usabilidad de aplicaciones móviles para usuarios con discapacidad visual, (ii) describan criterios de usabilidad de aplicaciones para personas con discapacidad visual pero que no están orientados al desarrollo móvil, (iii) discutan únicamente aspectos de hardware de dispositivos móviles y que no mencionen aspectos de usabilidad de aplicaciones móviles.

Con los criterios de inclusión y exclusión definidos, se hace posible la **creación del GC**, primordial para identificar los términos afines con el objetivo del SMS, que formarán la cadena de búsqueda. La creación del GC se realizó en dos fases. En la primera fase, por cada investigador participante en el SMS se estableció un GC preliminar. Cada investigador conformó su GC preliminar tomando como base los criterios de inclusión y exclusión y su experticia de búsqueda. Resultado de esta fase se obtuvieron 10 estudios. En la segunda fase, los estudios de los GC preliminares fueron revisados detalladamente por cada uno de los investigadores. Por último, la permanencia o no de los estudios revisados fue sometida a votación, obteniendo 8 estudios que conformaron el GC final.

En el proceso de **construcción de la cadena de búsqueda** se realiza un análisis de cada estudio del GC y se identifican y filtran términos generales que sean comunes y estén relacionados con el objetivo de la investigación. Este proceso consta de 4 fases. En la primera fase, cada uno de los investigadores busca términos afines con el objetivo de la investigación y se define una lista general de términos en consenso. En la segunda fase, por cada uno de los estudios del GC y entre estudios, se realiza un conteo de términos comunes utilizando herramientas de gestión de información documental (como Atlas.ti[1]). En la tercera fase, a través de un mapeo de los términos identificados en la fase 1, con respecto a los términos ubicados en la fase 2, se filtran y categorizan los términos. El proceso de categorización es realizado según la relevancia de los términos, es decir, los términos que: aparecen con mayor frecuencia en cada estudio y fueron identificados por la mayoría de los investigadores. En la cuarta fase se realizan iterativamente pruebas para adaptar la cadena de búsqueda a una base digital relevante (preferiblemente SCOPUS porque abarca otras bases digitales), empleando los términos identificados en la etapa anterior y los conectores lógicos OR para añadir sinónimos y AND para agregar nuevos términos. La cadena final debe ser capaz de obtener la mayoría de los estudios del GC, un número razonable de estudios, y aquellos cuyo título responda al objetivo del SMS. Finalmente, la cadena que logro satisfacer estas condiciones es:
("usability" OR "factors of usability" OR "usability issues" OR "usability model" OR "usability evaluation" OR "usability test" OR "usable" OR "usability engineering") AND ("mobile device" OR "mobile phones" OR "mobile context" OR "mobile computing" OR "accessible application" OR "software application" OR "mobile application" OR "mobile development" OR "blind navigation" OR "accessibility application") AND ("blind user" OR "blind people" OR "sighted user" OR "vision impairment" OR "blind person" OR "blind learners" OR "visually challenged" OR "blindness" OR "visually disabilities" OR "visual impaired")

A partir de la cadena de búsqueda se realizó la **búsqueda de estudios candidatos** en las bases digitales: Springer, SCOPUS y ACM. El periodo de búsqueda comprendió desde el año 2007 hasta el 2017. Para realizar la búsqueda de los estudios candidatos se consideró: (i) estudios publicados en actas de congreso, revistas internacionales y capítulos de libro, (ii) publicaciones escritas en inglés y (iii) adaptar la cadena de búsqueda a la sintaxis de cada base digital. Finalmente, teniendo en cuenta las

---

[1] www.atlasti.com

consideraciones indicadas, se obtuvieron un total de *475 estudios candidatos*, distribuidos así: 308 en Springer, 57 en SCOPUS y 110 en ACM.

3.3 Proceso de Selección de Estudios Primarios

En esta fase se aplican los criterios de inclusión y exclusión a los estudios candidatos. El proceso de selección incluye las siguientes actividades: (i) Depuración de los estudios candidatos, (ii) selección de los estudios y, (iii) selección de los estudios primarios.

La **depuración de los estudios candidatos** permitió identificar estudios duplicados, es decir estudios que habían sido recuperados más de una vez en un mismo repositorio o en dos o más repositorios a la vez. Esta depuración fue realizada por tres investigadores. Como resultado de la depuración se obtiene un listado de *430 estudios candidatos*. La **selección de estudios** consiste en aplicar los criterios de inclusión y exclusión al título, resumen y palabras claves de los *estudios candidatos*. Resultado de esta selección obtuvimos *45 estudios seleccionados* y se descartaron *385 estudios candidatos*.

Para la **selección de estudios primarios** se aplican a los estudios seleccionados los criterios de inclusión y exclusión sobre los artículos completos, por tanto, es necesario descargar los *estudios seleccionados*. Finalmente, se obtuvieron un total de *21 estudios primarios*, descartando *20 estudios seleccionados* y no fueron analizados 4 estudios porque no fue posible conseguirlos.

3.3 Extracción de Datos

Para responder a las RQ es necesario extraer la información necesaria de los estudios primarios. Este proceso consistió en una revisión completa y detallada de los *21 estudios primarios*, en el cual participaron tres investigadores. Los resultados del proceso de extracción se describen en la Sección 4.

Para permitir que el presente estudio sea replicado por otros investigadores, hemos publicado el detalle del proceso realizado en el siguiente enlace.

4 Resultados

Esta sección presenta los resultados del SMS, divididos en dos partes: (i) Generalidades de los estudios primarios y (ii) las respuestas a las RQ. En la Fig. 1 se resume la primera parte como una visión sintética de los 21 estudios primarios identificados. Esta figura consta de dos áreas. La primera (lado izquierdo), despliega dos gráficos de dispersión XY (parte superior e inferior), los cuales muestran burbujas en las intersecciones de las categorías: Tipo - año de publicación y tipo - atributos de usabilidad más utilizados. Los tipos de publicación son artículos de: revista, congreso, y capítulo de libro. La cantidad de estudios primarios que han sido clasificados en cada categoría determina el tamaño de las burbujas. En la segunda área (lado derecho) de la Fig.

1, se muestra el número de estudios primarios publicados por año. Como se observa, los estudios primarios han sido publicados en su mayoría en capítulos de libros (57%) y congresos (33%).

A continuación, se detallan las respuestas dadas a las RQ.

RQ1: ¿Cuáles son los elementos y actividades propuestos en el marco del desarrollo de aplicaciones móviles orientados a personas con discapacidad visual, desde la perspectiva de la usabilidad?

El SMS muestra que no existen marcos de desarrollo de aplicaciones móviles para personas con discapacidad visual. Sin embargo, se han recopilado pautas y recomendaciones generales (ver Tabla 1) para el desarrollo de este tipo de aplicaciones, sustentadas en la usabilidad y basadas en las vivencias y experiencias adquiridas por los autores durante el desarrollo y evaluación de sus aplicaciones.

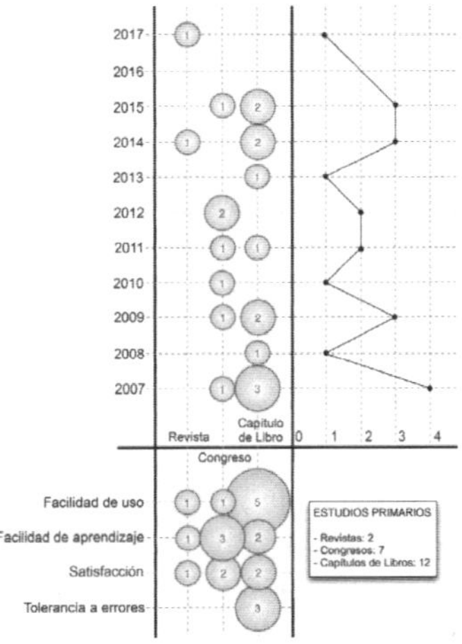

Fig. 1. Mapeo con la distribución de estudios primarios según los atributos de usabilidad más utilizados, incluyendo tipo y año de publicación

Tabla 1 Pautas y recomendaciones generales para desarrollar aplicaciones móviles para usuarios con discapacidad visual

Pautas - Recomendaciones	**Estudios**
Diseño centrado en el usuario	[21], [12], [10], [14]
Usuario no vidente participa en todas las etapas del desarrollo del aplicativo móvil	[15], [22], [23], [1]
Proceso de desarrollo iterativo	[3], [15], [8], [21], [22], [23], [16], [26] [1], [5], [10], [24], [23], [19], [13], [14]
Diseño participativo	[16], [21], [5], [19]

RQ2: ¿Qué criterios de usabilidad son pertinentes para que el desarrollo de aplicaciones móviles satisfaga los requisitos de los usuarios con discapacidad visual?
La respuesta a esta pregunta no puede ser generalizada a todas las aplicaciones móviles, debido a que al realizar un análisis sobre la usabilidad de las aplicaciones móviles se pueden emplear diversas métricas de usabilidad tanto objetivas como subjetivas. Sin embargo, estas métricas deben estar sujetas a la naturaleza de cada aplicación; ya que, un atributo no puede ser calificado con la misma importancia en todas las aplicaciones. En la Tabla 2 se muestran los atributos de usabilidad que resultaron ser los más utilizados en las evaluaciones de las aplicaciones móviles para personas con discapacidad visual.

Tabla 2. Atributos de Usabilidad según su Importancia

Métricas-Atributos	Estudios
Facilidad de aprendizaje	[7], [11], [26], [12], [19], [13]
Satisfacción	[11], [26], [1], [12], [19]
Tolerancia a errores	[7], [23], [11], [26], [12]
Calidad de sonido	[21], [22], [5]
Rendimiento	[23], [5], [19]
Interés de uso	[5], [24], [19]
Aceptación del usuario	[5], [24], [19]
Memorización	[7], [11], [26]
Eficiencia-Eficacia	[22], [11], [26]
Adaptabilidad	[21], [19]

RQ3: ¿Qué características deben poseer los dispositivos móviles en términos de hardware, para facilitar la interacción con los usuarios con discapacidad visual?
Los estudios analizados revelaron que los usuarios con discapacidad visual necesitan que el dispositivo móvil incorpore un teclado físico, puesto que podría ayudarles a reconocer la ubicación y funcionalidad de cada tecla, permitiéndoles así interactuar con mayor facilidad con el dispositivo; lamentablemente, esta característica está en desuso, y aun cuando estuviera vigente, las pantallas de estos dispositivos tendrían que ser más grandes [27]. En cuanto a las pantallas táctiles, deberían contar con límites físicos estándares y proporcionar más puntos de referencia para mejorar la interacción dispositivo móvil-usuario [5].

En el estudio realizado por Shaik & otros [26] se menciona la existencia de dispositivos de teclado braille, como alternativa para usuarios con discapacidad visual. No obstante, cuando el usuario está en movimiento la interacción con el dispositivo se ve afectada con este tipo de teclado. Por tal motivo, las características de estos dispositivos deben ser adaptadas de manera que un usuario con discapacidad visual pueda utilizarlos sin la necesidad de utilizar dispositivos adicionales [23].

RQ4: ¿Cuáles son los recursos de interacción que se emplean para el ingreso y salida de información en las aplicaciones móviles para personas con discapacidad visual?
En los estudios analizados, los autores mencionan la necesidad de que los elementos de interacción que proporcionan los dispositivos móviles deberían ser concebidos con

base en las distintas habilidades de los usuarios [3]. A modo de resumen, la Fig. 1 muestra los recursos de interacción más utilizados para el ingreso y salida de información. En esta Figura se observa que las interacciones basadas en el recurso auditivo son el principal medio de comunicación entre la aplicación móvil y el usuario con discapacidad visual.

Fig. 1. Recursos de interacción usuario - aplicación

Los estudios analizados mostraron además la necesidad de utilizar diferentes recursos de entrada y salida de información; es decir, una aplicación móvil debe tener un enfoque multimodal, de tal manera que el usuario pueda cambiar fácilmente el recurso de interacción (por ejemplo, de táctil a auditivo).

RQ5: ¿Qué elementos deben considerarse en el diseño de la interfaz de una aplicación móvil para usuarios con discapacidad visual?

Los estudios analizados identifican la necesidad de que el diseño de la interfaz de las apps móviles debería basarse en las habilidades del usuario, manteniendo en lo posible una cantidad mínima de interacción usuario-aplicación [26], ayudándose de elementos interactivos (por ejemplo, los tactons que son mensajes estructurados que pueden ser utilizados para comunicar mensajes no visuales). Además, los estudios recomiendan, por ejemplo: (i) no sobrepasar la carga cognitiva en los elementos tipo menú [25,22], (ii) simplificar la interfaz de usuario, eliminando funciones innecesarias, (iii) sustituir iconos pequeños por botones grandes de alto contraste visual para mejorar la identificación entre elementos [13].

RQ6: ¿Cuáles son las herramientas, modelos y pruebas utilizadas para evaluar la usabilidad de las aplicaciones móviles para personas con discapacidad visual?

De los estudios analizados, se puede observar que no existen herramientas ni modelos de usabilidad exclusivas para evaluar aplicaciones móviles para usuarios con discapacidad visual. Sin embargo, algunos autores han adaptado a este contexto recursos tradicionales, como: El modelo y las heurísticas de usabilidad de Nielsen [17] y los cuestionarios de usabilidad de SW, como por ejemplo MPUQ de Ryu y Smith-Jackson [20]. Este cuestionario tiene una estructura de seis factores: (1) Facilidad de aprendizaje y uso, (2) ayuda sobre el funcionamiento y resolución de problemas, (3) aspectos emocionales y capacidades multimedia, (4) comandos y carga de memoria mínima, (5) eficiencia y control, (6) tareas típicas para teléfonos móviles.

5 Discusión

El mapeo sistemático de literatura permitió identificar distintos escenarios en los que se desarrollan aplicaciones móviles y especialmente permitió determinar las pruebas de usabilidad que son aplicadas en cada caso. Sin embargo, la evaluación de la usabilidad realizada a las aplicaciones móviles para personas con discapacidad visual se lleva a cabo únicamente adaptando las técnicas de evaluación tradicionales que están orientadas a aplicaciones comunes. Esto ha causado que los problemas de desarrollo existentes, sean heredados al desarrollo de aplicaciones con fines muy particulares, que deberían ser tratadas de forma especial.

Más específicamente, se ha establecido que las técnicas de evaluación de usabilidad más utilizadas son: las encuestas, cuestionarios, entrevistas, y el recorrido cognitivo. Sin embargo, no existen modelos exclusivos para evaluar la usabilidad de app móviles para usuarios con discapacidad visual; no obstante, como se mencionó anteriormente, existen algunos modelos de usabilidad que han sido adaptados o han sido empleados como referencia para evaluación de este tipo de aplicaciones. Por ejemplo, podemos mencionar como el más utilizado al *modelo de usabilidad de Nielsen*. Varios de los autores de los estudios primarios evalúan la usabilidad basándose en su experiencia y en atributos del modelo de Nielsen tales como: aprendizaje, eficiencia, memorización, error, satisfacción y sus posibles variaciones.

Por otra parte, es importante mencionar que el mecanismo de interacción más eficiente que se ha encontrado en este estudio, entre el usuario con discapacidad visual y el dispositivo móvil es el audio; de la mano de enfoques multimodales de recursos de interacción. Sin embargo, el hardware y software desarrollados no han alcanzado un nivel adecuado, tal que la usabilidad para personas con discapacidades como la visual llegue a un nivel aceptable. Consideramos que es preciso ahondar en este tipo de investigaciones, para contribuir con la mejora de las aplicaciones móviles para personas que presentan algún tipo de discapacidad.

Es preciso mencionar que en torno al estudio realizado identificamos 3 posibles **amenazas a la validez**. En primer lugar, es probable que las RQ planteadas hayan *cubierto parcialmente* la temática de estudio, lo que intentamos mitigar definiendo un objetivo de trabajo alcanzable a través del planteamiento de varias RQ. En segundo lugar, es posible que en un SMS *se enfoque el proceso* hacia un grupo específico de estudios, lo cual evitamos conformando un *GC* y planteando en consenso una *cadena de búsqueda* con *términos de control* explícitos. Finalmente, es probable que la *calidad de evaluación* de los estudios no sea correcta debido al *desconocimiento del área* de investigación, lo cual intentamos minimizar con la inclusión de dos investigadores con experiencia en temas de usabilidad y realización de SMSs, en el equipo de trabajo.

6 Conclusiones

Este trabajo describe el estado actual del proceso de evaluación de la usabilidad de las apps móviles para personas con discapacidad visual. 21 estudios primarios referentes a esta temática fueron encontrados para dar respuesta las preguntas de investigación planteadas. El principal hallazgo de esta investigación se resume en que un diseño participativo con una muestra representativa de los usuarios objetivo, permite identificar sus necesidades y capacidades particulares, para enfocar el desarrollo de la interacción en esa perspectiva, pudiéndose obtener apps usables a la medida de las necesidades de un segmento de población particular.

Al parecer la problemática identificada, esto es la carente usabilidad de las apps móviles para segmentos de población con discapacidad visual, obedece en parte a la inexistencia de modelos formales para la evaluación de la usabilidad de este tipo de app, lo cual ha forzado a los equipos de desarrollo a utilizar modelos tradicionales de evaluación, por lo que los resultados de la evaluación de la usabilidad podrían no ser fiables. Finalmente, el diseño de la interfaz de las apps móviles para personas con discapacidad visual debe considerar un número mínimo de interacciones usuario-interfaz, tal que le permita al usuario realizar las tareas específicas para las cuales fue creada la aplicación.

Tomando en consideración los resultados obtenidos de esta investigación, como trabajos futuros nos proponemos: (i) Estructurar un modelo para la construcción de app móviles para personas con discapacidad visual, basado en la síntesis de resultados de la presente investigación, (ii) construir un prototipo de herramienta o framework de soporte para el desarrollo de apps móviles para personas con discapacidad visual y, (iii) desarrollar una app móvil a través del framework anterior, para evaluarla con usuarios reales e iterativamente ir mejorando el modelo y por ende el framework.

Agradecimientos. Este trabajo ha sido subvencionado por el proyecto de investigación denominado: "Laboratorio Industrial en Ingeniería del Software Empírica (LI2SE)" de la ESPE y además contó con la financiación del "Proyecto DIUDA 22316" de la Universidad de Atacama.

Referencias

1. de Borba Campos, M., Sánchez, J., Damasio, J., Inácio, T.: Usability Evaluation of a Mobile Navigation Application for Blind Users, pp. 117–128 (2015)
2. Chiti, S., Leporini, B.: Accessibility of android-based mobile devices: a prototype to investigate interaction with blind users. Computers Helping People with Special Needs pp. 607–614 (2012)
3. Choi, Y., Hong, K.H.: User Requirements for Camera-Based Mobile Applications on Touch Screen Devices for Blind People, pp. 48–51 (2012)
4. Discapnet, O.A.T.: Accesibilidad de aplicaciones móviles. Tech. rep., Fundación Once (August 2013)
5. Façanha, A.R., Viana, W., Pequeno, M.C., de Borba Campos, M., Sanchez, J.: Touchscreen Mobile Phones Virtual Keyboarding for People with Visual Disabilities, pp. 134–145 (2014)
6. Ferré, X., Juristo, N., Windl, H., Constantine, L.: Usability basics for software developers. Journal IEEE Software (2001)

7. Jhangiani, I., Smith-Jackson, T.: Comparison of mobile phone user interface design preferences: Perspectives from nationality and disability culture. In: International Conference on Mobile Technology. pp. 512–519 (2007)
8. Kane, S.K., Jayant, C., Wobbrock, J.O., Ladner, R.E.: Freedom to roam: A study of mobile device adoption and accessibility for people with visual and motor disabilities. In: Proceedings of the 11th International ACM SIGACCESS Conference on Computers and Accessibility. pp. 115–122 (2009)
9. Kitchenham, B., Charters, S.: Guidelines for performing systematic literature review in software engineering. Tech. rep., Keele U. & U. of Durham (July 2007)
10. Krajnc, E., Knoll, M., Feiner, J., Traar, M.: A Touch Sensitive User Interface Approach on Smartphones for Visually Impaired, pp. 585–594 (2011)
11. Kulpa, C.C., Amaral, F.G.: Evaluation of Tablet PC Application Interfaces with Low Vision Users: Focusing on Usability, pp. 273–284 (2014)
12. Leporini, B., Buzzi, M.C., Buzzi, M.: Interacting with mobile devices via voiceover: Usability and accessibility issues. In: Proceedings of the 24th Australian Computer-Human Interaction Conference. pp. 339–348 (2012)
13. Luthra, V., Ghosh, S.: Understanding, Evaluating and Analyzing Touch Screen Gestures for Visually Impaired Users in Mobile Environment, pp. 25–36 (2015)
14. Mattheiss, E., Krajnc, E.: Route Descriptions in Advance and Turn-by-Turn Instructions - Usability Evaluation of a Navigational System for Visually Impaired and Blind People in Public Transport, pp. 284–295 (2013)
15. de Mendonça Júnior, F.D., Trevisan, D.G., Tavares, T.C., Nogueira, J.L.T.: A-citizenmobile: A case study for blind users. In: 2011 International Conference for Internet Technology and Secured Transactions. pp. 713–717 (2011)
16. Mi, N., Cavuoto, L.A., Benson, K., Smith-Jackson, T., Nussbaum, M.A.: A heuristic checklist for an accessible smartphone interface design. Universal Access in the Information Society pp. 351–365 (2014)
17. Nielsen, J.: Usability Inspection Methods. John Wiley & Sons, New York, NY (1994)
18. Petersen, K., Vakkalanka, S., Kuzniarz, L.: Guidelines for conducting systematic mapping studies in software engineering: An update. Information and Software Technology 64, 1–18 (2015)
19. Rahman, A., Anam, A.I., Yeasin, M.: Emoassist: emotion enabled assistive tool to enhance dyadic conversation for the blind. Multimedia Tools and Applications pp. 7699–7730 (2017)
20. Ryu, Y.S., Smith-Jackson, T.L.: Reliability and validity of the mobile phone usability questionnaire. Usability Studies 2(1), 39–53 (Nov 2006)
21. Sáenz, M., Sánchez, J.: Indoor Position and Orientation for the Blind, pp. 236–245 (2009)
22. Sánchez, J.: Mobile Audio Navigation Interfaces for the Blind, pp. 402–411 (2009)
23. Sánchez, J., Aguayo, F.: Mobile Messenger for the Blind, pp. 369–385 (2007)
24. Sánchez, J., Aguayo, F.: AudioGene: Mobile Learning Genetics through Audio by Blind Learners, pp. 79–86 (2008)
25. Sánchez, J., Maureira, E.: Subway Mobility Assistance Tools for Blind Users, pp. 386–404 (2007)
26. Shaik, A.S., Hossain, G., Yeasin, M.: Design, development and performance evaluation of reconfigured mobile android phone for people who are blind or visually impaired. In: Conference on Design of Communication. pp. 159–166 (2010)
27. Siebra, C., Gouveia, T., Macedo, J., Correia, W., Penha, M., Silva, F., Santos, A., Anjos, M., Florentin, F.: Usability requirements for mobile accessibility. In: International Conference on Mobile and Ubiquitous Multimedia. pp. 384–389 (2015)

Experimental comparison of Microsoft's tools for using the decision tree technique

Hernán Naranjo-Ávalos, Félix Fernández-Peña, Pilar Urrutia-Urrutia

Universidad Técnica de Ambato,
Av. Los Chasquis y Río Payamino, Ambato, Ecuador
{hf.naranjo, fo.fernandez, elsapurrutia}@uta.edu.ec
http://www.uta.edu.ec

Abstract. Data mining tools are getting closer to final users, making it easier to use them without been an expert on data mining theory. Microsoft tools include decision tree as a widely used technique for supporting decision making. Nevertheless, the assessment of their actual value has not been found in the literature. This paper presents the results of a comparison between *Excel* and *Analysis Services*. Ten professionals from computer science were involved in the study. A t-student test was applied to the data resulting of a questionnaire based on the Technology Acceptance Model.

The findings confirmed that, even when *Analysis Services* is more popular among data mining experts, the usability and ease of use of Microsoft *Excel* are significantly better with a p-value of 1.1x10-2 and 6.5x10-5, respectively. Nevertheless, the results are not conclusive because they are limited to one study case. We need further studies to confirm our findings.

Keywords: decision tree, data analysis tools comparison, technology acceptance in software

1 Introducción

En la actualidad las empresas u organizaciones, independientemente de su tamaño necesitan del uso de las tecnologías de la información con el fin de alinearse a los nuevos retos mundiales. El uso de herramientas adecuadas y la explotación de estas les permite alcanzar ventaja competitiva [1].

Dentro de las técnicas de análisis de información se encuentran los "árboles de decisión", regularmente empleados en el proceso de minería de datos con el fin de estudiar los eventos que pueden presentarse a partir de una decisión asumida en cierto momento. Basados en las probabilidades permiten un análisis certero.

Desde el punto de vista empresarial, el uso de los árboles de decisión permite establecer escenarios técnicos de pronóstico para la toma de decisiones por parte de las unidades directivas dentro de las organizaciones.

Los árboles de decisión son utilizados en diferentes campos de estudio y para diferentes propósitos, de ahí la importancia de los mismos. Es por ello que dentro de su naturaleza y concepción presentan un conjunto de ventajas tales como:

- Análisis completo de toda la información, evaluando cada una de las posibles soluciones en cada una de sus ramas.
- Son fáciles de interpretar lo cual facilita la comunicación de los resultados.
- Apoya a la toma de decisiones.
- Emite un esquema cuantificable de costos de los resultados y la probabilidad que estos sucedan.
- En dependencia de la información que se posea, el árbol de decisión siempre emitirá la mejor alternativa. Esto motiva a que los datos a analizar sean lo más exactos y limpios posible.

Tomando en cuenta la importancia y aplicabilidad del uso de los árboles de decisión en el proceso de análisis de la información, dentro del mercado tecnológico existen varias herramientas que incorporan dichas funcionalidades, tales como Weka, *Analysis Services*, Rapid Miner, Orange, Keel entre otras, que debido a su importancia, se han convertido en el centro de estudio y análisis por parte de varios autores [1] [2].

Entre las herramientas de Microsoft, encontramos Microsoft *Excel*, el cual ha incorporado extensiones para la minería de datos. Por su parte, la herramienta líder de Microsoft para el análisis de información es Microsoft SQL Server *Analysis Services* el cual es un motor de datos analíticos en línea que se usa para el análisis de datos que apoyan la toma de decisiones.

Se revisaron estudios actuales con respecto a la importancia de los árboles de decisión desde diferentes ámbitos de investigación. Sin embargo, en la revisión bibliográfica llevada a cabo no se encontraron estudios donde se evalúe la utilidad de estas herramientas desde la perspectiva de usuarios no expertos en minería de datos, interesados en procesos de predicción de eventos.

El objetivo del presente trabajo es mostrar los resultados de una evaluación cuantitativa de la utilidad y facilidad de uso percibidas de *Excel* vs. *Analysis Services* para profesionales de la informática no expertos en minería de datos.

En el estudio participaron diez profesionales y se llevó a cabo una evaluación utilizando el Modelo de Aceptación de Tecnología (TAM, del inglés *Technology Acceptance Model*).

En la sección dos del presente artículo se analizan los trabajos relacionados actuales, donde se evidencia la importancia y necesidad de investigación de las técnicas y herramientas de minería de datos para el análisis de información y los beneficios de sus implementaciones. En la tercera sección se describen los materiales y métodos utilizados en el experimento llevado a cabo utilizando TAM, recalcando la importancia de TAM, los árboles de decisión y el diseño del experimento. En la sección cuatro se describen los resultados encontrados en la investigación, analizando cómo, desde la perspectiva del usuario, estas herramientas generaron expectativas de utilidad y de uso para la gestión de sus actividades. Finalmente, en la quinta sección se arriba a conclusiones y se emiten recomendaciones alcanzadas por parte del estudio y los criterios de recomendación de los autores.

2 Trabajos relacionados

Dentro del campo de la gestión del conocimiento, la minería de datos se constituye en una de las fases más importantes para el análisis de la información.

En dependencia del tratamiento y los fines de estudio, la información puede ser analizada por diferentes técnicas, las cuales han sido utilizadas con éxito en diversos contextos de aplicación. Desde el punto de vista educativo, ha evidenciado la relevancia de las técnicas de "clasificación" para mejorar el rendimiento de los estudiantes [3]. Otros estudios se centran en el análisis comparativo de los métodos de discretización sobre el rendimiento de los clasificadores. En dependencia de la selección del método se ven influenciados en gran medida el rendimiento de los métodos de clasificación [2]. Desde la perspectiva de la importancia de los árboles de decisiones, existen estudios recientes que validan la importancia y la pertinencia de esta técnica en diferentes tipos de estudios.

El estudio desarrollado por Ardiansyah, se orienta a extraer conocimiento desde redes neuronales ocultas usando Árboles de Decisión, de donde se obtiene que la inducción del árbol de decisión generalmente se desempeña mejor en resultados de extracción de conocimiento con precisión de 84.07 a 93.17 por ciento. La regla extraída puede ser utilizada para explicar el proceso de los sistemas de redes neuronales y también puede aplicarse en otros sistemas como sistemas expertos [4]. Desde el punto de vista médico, los "Arboles de Decisión" han contribuido en la detección de patrones de lesiones cutáneas en úlceras de miembros inferiores, pues muchas enfermedades de la piel se presentan de manera asintomática y con complicaciones cuando estas son detectadas de manera tardía. El aporte de los árboles de decisión en este estudio fue en el aprendizaje automático de máquina, pues con ello se obtienen enfoques más intuitivos para el análisis, dando pie a nuevos estudios [5].

Hasta la actualidad se han llevado diversos estudios donde identifican la necesidad y la importancia de las diferentes técnicas de minería de datos con el fin de aportar al análisis de la información, como por ejemplo en el estudio se enfoca en la mejor de las técnicas de predicción y clasificación con el fin de mejorar las habilidades de los estudiantes que presentan problemas previo a los exámenes semestrales finales, el cual incluye la experimentación de diferentes algoritmos en búsqueda de la solución más eficiente. Es así que para este caso el algoritmo *Multi-labeled K-Nearest Neighbour* es quien presenta la mayor exactitud de tiempo en la clasificación con respecto a otras técnicas [6].

3 Materiales y Métodos

3.1 Modelo de Aceptación Tecnológica (TAM)

El Modelo de Aceptación Tecnológica (TAM) fue desarrollado por Davis y se ha convertido en uno de los modelos más populares para predecir el uso y aceptación de tecnología y sistemas de información [7]. Según Davis, el objetivo fundamental de TAM es identificar los factores que determinan el uso de las TIC en un contexto importante de usuarios [8]. TAM sugiere que la utilidad percibida y la facilidad de uso percibida son determinantes en la intención de un individuo al momento de utilizar un sistema [9].

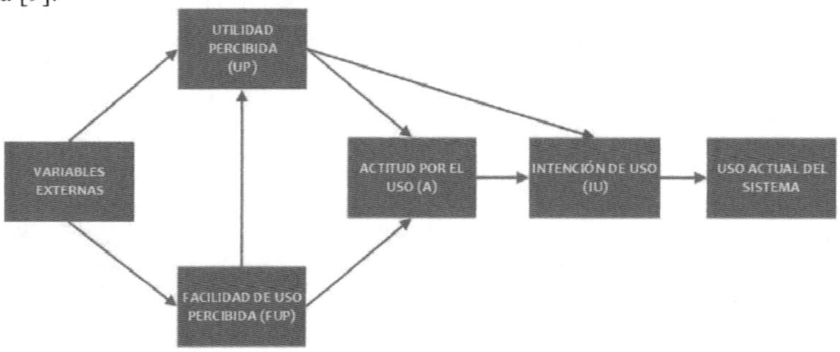

Fig. 1. Modelo de Aceptación Tecnológica [7]

3.2 Árboles de Decisión

Un árbol de decisión es un conjunto de condiciones organizadas en una estructura jerárquica, de tal manera que permite determinar la decisión final que se debe tomar siguiendo las condiciones que se cumplen desde la raíz del árbol hasta alguna de sus hojas. Los árboles de decisión se utilizan desde hace siglos, y son especialmente apropiados para expresar procedimientos médicos, legales, comerciales, estratégicos, matemáticos, lógicos, entre otros (Solarte Martínez G.R., 2009). Estos se caracterizan por la sencillez de su representación y de su forma de actuar, además de la fácil interpretación, dado que pueden ser expresados en forma de reglas de decisión. Una de las grandes ventajas de los árboles de decisión es que, en su forma más general, las opciones posibles a partir de una determinada condición son excluyentes. Esto permite analizar una situación y siguiendo el árbol de decisión apropiadamente, llegar a una sola acción o decisión a tomar. Entre los algoritmos de árboles de decisión se encuentran el ID3 (Induction of Decision Trees) y el C4.5 desarrollados por JR Quinlan. ID3 es considerado un clásico de los algoritmos de aprendizaje automático [10].

Entre las ventajas de la minería de datos con los productos de Microsoft podemos citar la integración estrecha con la plataforma de base de datos SQL Server. De esta forma, se aprovecha el desempeño, la seguridad y las características de optimización de este gestor de clase mundial.

3.3 Desarrollo del Experimento

Teniendo en cuenta la perspectiva de usuarios no expertos en minería de datos, se desarrollaron dos guías técnicas para el uso de árboles de decisión en un caso de estudio común. La primera está desarrollada en función de la herramienta *Microsoft Excel* y la segunda para la herramienta de *Analysis Services*. El caso de estudio utilizado se refiere a la predicción de posibles compradores de un artículo en específico y cómo las variables asociadas a este evento influyen en su ocurrencia con un valor probabilístico de certeza. Los contenidos de la guías constan de una descripción del caso de estudio y los objetivos que se persiguen con su definición, se describen las características de la herramienta y las funcionalidades que serán utilizadas y se fundamenta el procedimiento paso a paso, desde la carga de información, pasando por la limpieza de datos, la implementación del modelo, el entrenamiento con los datos y la predicción con los datos de análisis.

Estas guías fueron entregadas a un conjunto de diez profesionales en el área tecnológica que no habían tenido experiencia previa en el manejo de clasificación de información con árboles de decisión, los cuales bajo un compromiso técnico, procedieron a desarrollar el procedimiento definido en cada guía. La selección de profesionales no expertos en minería de datos obedece a los objetivos de esta investigación, centrada en la evaluación de la usabilidad de estas herramientas para este tipo de usuarios.

Los participantes en el experimento se dividieron en dos grupos de cinco personas cada uno. El primer grupo trabajo con la guía de *Analysis Services* y luego con la de *Excel*. El segundo grupo utilizó primero *Excel* y luego *Analysis Services*.

Una vez concluido el proceso con cada herramienta, se procedió a aplicar una encuesta, con el fin de recibir una retroalimentación desde los criterios técnicos de los encuestados basada en el TAM. El estudio se centró en dos aristas principales: la Utilidad Percibida y la Facilidad de Uso Percibida.

4 Análisis de Resultados

Una vez llevado a cabo el proceso experimental se analizaron los resultados desde las perspectivas estudiadas:

4.1 Análisis de Utilidad Percibida

A través del estudio de caso experimental llevado a cabo por parte del grupo de profesionales de TI, tanto la herramienta *Excel* como la herramienta *Analysis Services*, han sido valoradas y analizadas en dependencia de sus características y prestaciones bajo la arista de la "Utilidad Percibida". Los resultados obtenidos se muestran en la Tabla 1, de cuyos valores podemos deducir que:

- *Excel* es percibido con un mayor impacto en la gestión de análisis de información que *Analysis Services*.
- *Excel* tiene una percepción de mayor utilidad en el desempeño laboral y profesional que *Analysis Services*.
- *Analysis Services* es percibido como un producto que puede suministrar productos con mayor valor agregado que *Excel*.

- *Excel* tiene una percepción de replicar sus funcionalidades en otras situaciones e instancias que *Analysis Services*
- *Excel* se presenta con mayor interés para implementar su funcionalidad en diferentes ámbitos laborales.
- *Excel* y *Analysis Services* tienen valores similares de aplicabilidad en cuanto a la importancia de su utilización en la industria.

Tabla 1. Comparación del Valor Medio de Utilidad Percibida

UTILIDAD PERCIBIDA		
Preguntas	Excel [1-5]	Analysis Services [1-5]
¿La herramienta utilizada tendrá impacto importante en la gestión de análisis de información en su área de conocimiento?	4,4	4,1
¿Encuentra útil esta herramienta para su desempeño profesional y laboral?	4,3	3,9
¿La aplicación de este procedimiento permitirá la entrega de productos con valor agregado a su área de trabajo?	4,2	4,4
¿Cree que este procedimiento sea útil y replicable en otras áreas de trabajo?	4,5	3,7
¿Le interesaría contar ya con esta herramienta en su área de competencia laboral?	4,3	3,9
¿Cree usted que existen campos de aplicación en la industria donde se pueda implementar esta herramienta?	4,1	4

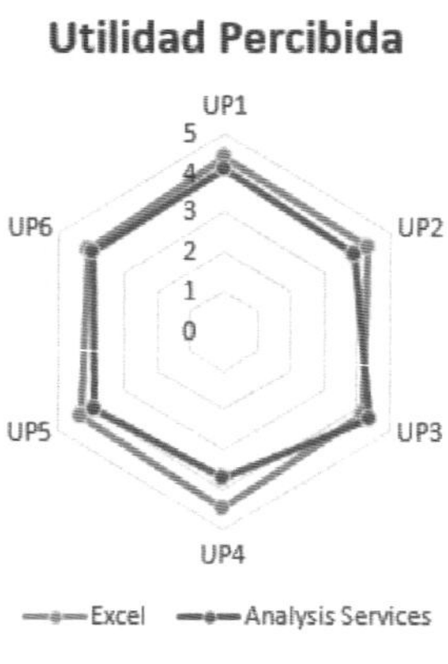

Fig. 2. Utilidad Percibida con Herramientas *Excel* y *Analysis Services*

4.1 Facilidad de Uso Percibido

Una vez realizado el experimento por el grupo de evaluación, bajo la arista de la "Facilidad de Uso Percibida" Tabla 2, se evidencia que la Herramienta *Excel* se presenta con un alto porcentaje de aceptación en comparación con la Herramienta *Analysis Services*. En base a los valores obtenidos podemos obtener los siguientes resultados:

- *Excel* es percibido con mayor facilidad de uso que la herramienta Analysis Services.
- *Excel* tiene una percepción de mostrar resultados de manera más clara y efectiva que *Analysis Services*.
- *Excel* es percibido como una herramienta que cuenta con una interface más amigable.
- *Excel* tiene una percepción de alcanzar los objetivos de análisis con menos pasos que *Analysis Services*.
- *Excel* se presenta como una herramienta más amigable e incita a investigar más de sus beneficios.
- Al momento de interpretar información existe una mejor percepción al trabajar con *Excel*.

Tabla 2. Comparación del Valor medio de Facilidad de Uso Percibida

FACILIDAD DE USO PERCIBIDA		
Preguntas	Excel [1-5]	Analysis Services [1-5]
¿Fue fácil el uso de la herramienta?	4,5	3,3
¿La herramienta mostró los datos de una manera clara y efectiva?	4,2	3,8
¿La herramienta presenta una interfaz amigable para el usuario?	4,1	3,4
¿El número de pasos para ejecutar una determinada acción es el adecuado?	3,9	3,4
¿La herramienta es lo suficientemente amigable y me motiva a investigar más beneficios de la misma?	4,1	3,6
¿La interpretación de la información es fácil y confiable?	4,1	3,7

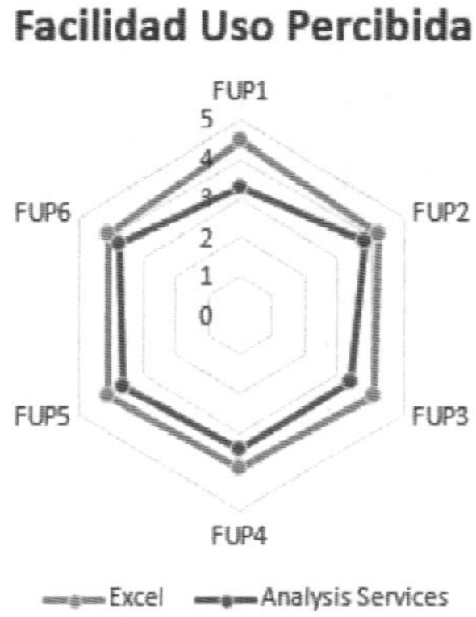

Fig. 3. Facilidad de Uso Percibido con Herramientas *Excel* y *Analysis Services*

De acuerdo a los resultados obtenidos (Figura 4 y Figura 5), se evidencia que la herramienta *Excel* supera en la "Percepción de Utilidad" y "Percepción de Facilidad de Uso" a la herramienta *Analysis Services*.

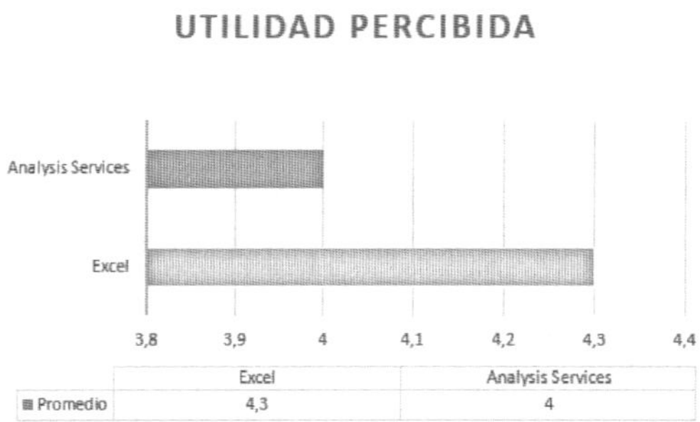

Fig. 4. Promedio de "Utilidad Percibida" de las Herramientas *Excel* y *Analysis Services*

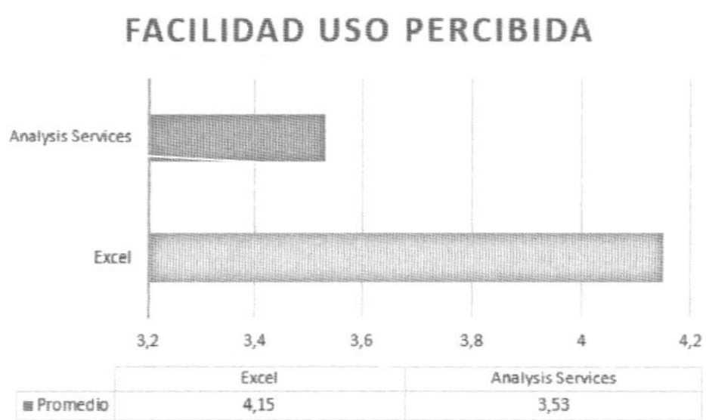

Fig. 5. Promedio de "Facilidad de Uso" de las Herramientas *Excel* y Analysis Services

El número de pasos a seguir en el proceso experimental con la herramienta *Excel* fueron de diecinueve, en comparación con los veintiuno con *Analysis Services*, lo cual es un indicador que en la herramienta *Excel* se lo puede realizar con menos pasos.

Realizando una prueba de T-Student sobre los datos utilizados se determinó que existe una diferencia significativa en cuanto a la percepción de utilidad y facilidad de uso. Esto se comprobó con un p-value de 1,17x10-2 y 6,57x10-5, respectivamente. Por su parte la prueba de Cronbach-alpha arrojó un valor de 0,92, lo cual evidencia la validez interna de los datos recogidos al aplicar la encuesta. Sin embargo, los resultados obtenidos no se consideran concluyentes.

5 Conclusiones

Ambas herramientas, Microsoft *Excel* y Microsoft *Analysis Services*, se presentan como soluciones para la gestión de clasificación de información dentro de los procesos de minería de datos. La precisión de los resultados obtenidos con una y otra herramienta es la misma y, ambas, permiten la integración con otras herramientas de procesamiento de datos de Microsoft como el gestor de bases de datos SQL Server.

Sin embargo, y a pesar de la popularidad de *Analysis Services* entre los expertos en minería de datos, hemos corroborado que Microsoft *Excel* se presenta con mejores oportunidades desde la perspectiva de usuarios no expertos en minería de datos. La utilidad y facilidad de uso percibidas resultó significativamente mayor para Microsoft *Excel* en el estudio experimental llevado a cabo.

En base a TAM se concluye que *Excel* presenta un conjunto de ventajas para la clasificación de datos utilizando árboles de decisión; entre ellas:

- Perspectiva de uso.
- Fácil interpretación de los resultados.
- Interfaz amigable para su manejo.
- Usabilidad de la herramienta.

Debido a la difusión del Microsoft Excel a nivel mundial, el impacto de las técnicas de minería de datos incluidas en esta herramienta en el análisis de información tiene un gran potencial. Los beneficios de su uso serán evidentes en la toma de decisiones. Basado en los resultados obtenidos, se recomienda su uso en el ámbito empresarial e institucional. Como trabajo futuro, se propone la validación estadística de los resultados obtenidos para un tamaño de muestra mayor y en diversos casos de estudio.

Referencias

1. Hasim, N., Haris, N.: A study of open-source data mining tools for forecasting. Proceedings of the 9th International Conference on Ubiquitous Information Management and Communication (2015).

2. Ali, Z.: Comparative Study of Discretization Methods on the Performance of Associative Classifiers. International Conference on Frontiers of Information Technology (2016) 0–5.
3. Ragab, A, Noaman, A., AL-Ghamd, A., Madbouly,A.: A Comparative Analysis of Classification Algorithms for Students College Enrollment Approval Using Data Mining. Workshop on Interaction Design in Educational Environments (2014) 106–114.
4. Ardiansyah, S.: Knowledge of Extraction from Trained Neural Network by Using Decision Tree. 2nd International Conference on Science in Information Technology (IC-SITech) (2016) 220–225.
5. Mantovani, R.: Decision Trees for the detection of skin lesion patterns in lower limbs ulcers. International Conference on Computational Science and Computational Intelligence (2016) 677–681.
6. Mayilvaganan,M., Kalpanadevi,D.: Comparison of Classification Techniques for predicting the Cognitive Skill of Students in Education Environment. International Conference on Communication and Network Technologies (ICCNT) (2014) 113–118.
7. Belanche, D., Casaló L., Flavián, C.: Integrating trust and personal values into the technology acceptance model: The case of e-government services adoption, Cuadernos de Economia y Direccion de la Empresa, Vol. 15,4, (2012) 192–204.
8. Young, L., Rivas,L., Chaparro, J.: Modelo de aceptación tecnológica (TAM): un estudio de la influencia de la cultura nacional y del perfil del usuario en el uso de las TIC. Revista Innovar, Vol. 20 (2009).
9. Park, E., Baek, S., Ohm, J., Chang, H.: Determinants of player acceptance of mobile social network games: An application of extended technology acceptance model. Telematics and Informatics, Vol. 31, 1 (2014) 3–15.
10. Aranda, Y., Sotolongo,A.: Integración de los algoritmos de minería de datos 1r, Prism E Id3 a Postgresql. Journal of Information Systems and Technology Management: JISTEM, Vol. 10, 2 (2013) 389–406.

Comprehension of Activity Diagrams for Modeling Business Processes: Initials Findings from People with Limited and not Limited Education in Computer Science

Jackeline Herrera[1,2], Omar Sánchez[1], Luis López[1], Cecilia Yánez[1], and Omar S. Gómez[3]

[1] Universidad Técnica de Ambato,
Av. Colombia y Chile, Ambato, Ecuador
{jherrera3454,os.sanchez,
llopez3490,cyanez5382}@uta.edu.ec
www.uta.edu.ec
[2] Universidad Técnica de Cotopaxi,
Av. Simón Rodríguez, Latacunga, Ecuador
jackeline.herrera@utc.edu.ec
www.utc.edu.ec
[3] Escuela Superior Politécnica de Chimborazo,
Panamericana Sur km 1 1/2, Riobamba, Ecuador
ogomez@espoch.edu.ec
www.espoch.edu.ec

Abstract. UML activity diagrams (ADs) can be extended and used in other domains such as business process modeling. Although there are some works that have studied the use of ADs in the business process modeling area, we have not found works that assess the impact of using this type of diagram among persons with different technological skills. We have developed, validated and applied a survey to 395 persons (most of them undergraduates) from different program degrees in order to assess the degree of comprehension of business processes modeled with ADs. Our findings suggest that ADs used for business process modeling are more comprehensible for persons familiarized with the Computer Science or related domains.

Keywords: comprehension, UML activity diagrams, Business process modeling, BPM

1 Introducción

Los modelos de procesos del negocio se crean para entender los mecanismos clave de un negocio ya existente, implementar mejoras, experimentar nuevos conceptos de negocio y también para identificar los elementos fundamentales [1]. Un modelo de proceso de negocio (en Inglés, Business Process Modeling o BPM) es un conjunto de actividades o tareas relacionadas, que tienen un inicio y un punto final, así como las entradas y salidas claramente definidas. BPM centra su atención en la forma en que la actividad se lleva a cabo dentro de una organización [2]. También se dice que apoya el diseño, administración, configuración, promulgación y análisis de procesos de negocio, con el propósito de alcanzar las metas de una organización [3].

Por su parte, el lenguaje de modelado unificado (en Inglés Unified Modeling Language o UML) es un lenguaje gráfico usado para especificar, visualizar, construir y documentar sistemas de información [4]. Dada la popularidad de este lenguaje, éste se ha extendido a otros dominios de aplicación tales como el modelado de procesos del negocio. Los diagramas UML tienen la capacidad de describir tanto los aspectos estructurales del negocio como las reglas que los afectan [1].

Para el diseño de modelos BPM se han creado notaciones o extendido notaciones existentes como sucede con el diagrama de actividades (DA) que forma parte del lenguaje UML [5].

Uno de los inconvenientes encontrados al modelar los procesos del negocio es la dificultad para administrarlos. A menudo, la falta de claridad en su definición así como una falta de conocimiento apropiado ocasionan una malinterpretación en la definición de modelos de BPM [6].

En la actualidad existen diferentes notaciones para BPM, sin embargo estudios reflejan que el 80% de las empresas en Latinoamérica utilizan el diagrama UML de actividad [7], lo que indica que diversas personas (con o sin dominio técnico de la Informática) en algún momento utilizarán diagramas UML de actividad para tal fin. Dada esta situación surge la motivación de conocer más sobre la facilidad de comprensión de los diagramas UML de actividad tanto en personas con conocimientos técnicos sobre informática así como en personas sin un dominio técnico.

En este trabajo reportamos la realización de un estudio cuyo objetivo es analizar si los diagramas UML de actividad pueden también ser igualmente comprensibles en personas ajenas al ámbito de la informática pero que en algún momento pueden llegar a usar este tipo de diagramas para definir modelos BPM. A través de la aplicación de un survey y un cuasi-experimento, pretendemos recabar hallazgos iniciales para conocer si este tipo de diagrama puede ser una herramienta de apoyo en la modelación de procesos de negocio para aquellas personas que no están relacionadas con roles técnicos afines al diseño o desarrollo de sistemas informáticos.

El resto del documento se estructura de la siguiente manera: En la sección 2 se presenta el trabajo relacionado; en la sección 3 describimos el método de investigación aplicado en esta investigación; en la sección 4 presentamos el análisis y los resultados obtenidos; finalmente en la sección 5 discutimos los hallazgos observados y presentamos las conclusiones.

2 Trabajo Relacionado

En un estudio realizado en [8], se señala que uno de los pasos más importantes en el desarrollo de un proceso de negocio es la fase de diseño, para lo cual se debe elegir un lenguaje o notación apropiada de acuerdo al proyecto a realizar. En los resultados presentados en [8], se revela que la representatividad con el lenguaje de modelado unificado (UML) puede favorecer el éxito del diseño de procesos empresariales.

En otro trabajo reportado en [9], se realizó una evaluación de los diagramas de actividad (DA) en UML 2.0, basado en una taxonomía de constructos genéricos y recurrentes que permiten evaluar sistemas de flujo de trabajo. Este estudio se basó en una evaluación multi-perspectiva de las capacidades expresivas de los DA [9]. Sin embargo, este enfoque es limitado porque los modelos de DA sólo capturan los patrones de control básicos definidos.

Por su parte en [10], se examinó la expresividad y la adecuación de los DA para la especificación de flujos de trabajo así como la evaluación de su capacidad para capturar una colección de patrones. En otro trabajo [11], el autor estudia pruebas basadas en modelos y DA para detectar defectos entre este tipo de diagrama UML y el diagrama de máquinas de estados. En este trabajo [11], el autor observa que los DA tienen un mayor alcance de comprensión, pero también están sujetos a un número mayor de errores que los diagramas de máquinas de estado finito, esto con respecto a la derivación de casos de prueba manuales. No obstante, los hallazgos sirven para ayudar a desarrollar directrices para la derivación manual de casos de prueba a partir de DA [11].

En el estudio reportado en [12], se llevó a cabo un experimento para evaluar dos notaciones de BPM: EPC (en Español, Cadena de Procesos Impulsada por Eventos) y DA del lenguaje UML. Esto con el fin de determinar la facilidad de comprensión al representar procesos. En este estudio se evaluaron las notaciones desde dos perspectivas: En función de un ingeniero de requisitos de software y en función del usuario final. Como resultado, se concluyó que para el ingeniero de requisitos es más comprensible el DA. Con relación al usuario final no se logró determinar cuál de las dos notaciones es más comprensible [12]. En este estudio se observa que los DA son mayormente comprensibles por personas con formación en informática, sin embrago no se establece qué ocurre con aquellas personas cuyos conocimientos en informática son limitados.

Finalmente, entre los trabajos relacionados con nuestro estudio, se encuentra el trabajo reportado en [6], en donde se realizó una comparación entre las notaciones BPMN y los DA del lenguaje UML. El análisis se enfocó en tres criterios: capacidad de ser fácilmente comprensible, adecuación de los elementos gráficos utilizados para representar los procesos reales de negocio de una organización y el mapeo de la ejecución de procesos empresariales; los resultados sugieren que existe una similitud notable entre BMPN y DA. Este estudio se centró en comparar las bondades de dos notaciones similares, manteniéndose la necesidad por conocer la comprensión de una de éstas en personas con conocimientos limitados en el área informática, es decir para personas con perfiles no técnicos.

3 Método

Una vez presentado el trabajo relacionado, en este apartado describimos el método utilizado en nuestra investigación.

Para evaluar la comprensión de los DA, empleamos dos constructos que son: la sencillez e intuitividad de los diagramas en personas relacionadas o no con el área de la informática. La pregunta de investigación planteada se define como:

RQ. ¿Es la facilidad de comprensión en DA usados en el diseño de procesos del negocio equivalente tanto en personas con un dominio técnico de la informática como en aquellas sin un dominio técnico?

La hipótesis nula (H_0) asociada a esta pregunta de investigación se define como: "*La facilidad de comprensión en DA usados en el diseño de procesos del negocio es equivalente tanto en personas con un dominio técnico de la informática como en aquellas sin un dominio técnico*".

Para responder a esta pregunta se diseñó un cuasi-experimento en donde se convocó a participar a una población de 500 estudiantes de la Universidad Técnica de Cotopaxi (UTC, Ecuador). El cuasi-experimento se llevó a cabo del 7 al 22 de febrero del 2017. La selección de los estudiantes fue aleatoria y por conveniencia (personas de la misma universidad), su participación fue voluntaria. Particularmente participaron estudiantes a partir del quinto semestre. Este criterio se aplicó con el fin de que los participantes en el estudio contaran con cierto grado de formación básica universitaria.

Para este estudio se organizaron los estudiantes en tres grupos: Grupo A, Grupo B y Grupo C. Las carreras cursadas por los estudiantes se organizaron de acuerdo a las áreas de conocimiento de la UNESCO [14]. Informática y Sistemas Computacionales corresponden al área de ciencias, sub área informática [14], ésta se consideró con un dominio técnico en informática (Grupo A). Electromecánica, Eléctrica e Industrial corresponden al área ingeniería, industria y afines [14], donde a ésta se le consideró con dominio moderado en Informática (Grupo B). A los estudiantes de Diseño Gráfico, que corresponden al área de humanidades y artes [14] se les consideró con dominio limitado en Informática (Grupo C).

Se desarrolló un instrumento (survey), el mismo que fue revisado por expertos antes de su aplicación. Posteriormente se llevó a cabo una prueba piloto para validar de manera estadística la confiabilidad del survey. Para esta validación se empleó el coeficiente alfa de Cronbach [15]. Tras dicha validación estadística se obtuvo un valor alfa de Cronbach de 0.92; lo que indicó una consistencia interna de los datos altamente satisfactoria. Una vez validado el survey en la prueba piloto, el instrumento (survey) se aplicó a los 395 estudiantes participantes, los mismos que fueron organizados en los grupos A, B y C anteriormente descritos. Para determinar la fiabilidad del survey se calculó nuevamente el alfa de Cronbach a las respuestas de los 395 estudiantes [15], cuyos resultados se muestran en la Tabla 1; donde K es el número de ítems, $\sum Vi$ es la sumatoria de cada una de las varianzas calculadas del rango de valores por columnas de las encuestas de cada ítem, y Vt es la varianza de la sumatoria de los valores obtenidos por fila de cada una de las encuestas.

En la Tabla 1 se muestra el resultado del coeficiente alfa de Cronbach de nuestro estudio, que corresponde a un valor de 0.885. El criterio comúnmente aceptado para considerar el instrumento como válido es a partir de 0.6. Dado que nuestro instrumento arrojó un valor superior a 0.6 consideramos a éste como válido.

Tabla 1. Valores obtenidos para los cálculos del alfa de Cronbach

K	34	Ítems
∑Vi	44.480	Suma de Varianzas
Vt	316.052	Varianza de los totales
Sección1	1.030	La fórmula dividida en 2 secciones, se obtiene valor absoluto para no afectar los cálculos respectivos
Seccion2	0.859	
Absoluto S2	0.859	
A	**0.885**	Resultado alfa de Cronbach

De manera complementaria, se llevó a cabo un Análisis de Componentes Principales (PCA, del Inglés Principal Component Analysis), el que evidenció que, de acuerdo a las respuestas de los encuestados en la prueba piloto, existe correlación entre las preguntas diseñadas para medir los criterios de interés (sencillez e intuitividad) por lo que también el survey diseñado se considera como un instrumento válido.

Al aplicar el análisis PCA del total de elementos se obtienen los resultados indicados en la Tabla 2. Los elementos identificados en los diagramas se etiquetaron con las letras A a I (nueve elementos por aspecto, ver Figs. 4 y 5).

Tabla 2. Correlación de variables (sencillez e intuitividad) de los 18 elementos usados en los DA con respecto al grupo A

	Media de la escala si se elimina el elemento	Varianza de la escala si se elimina el elemento	Correlación elemento-total corregida	Correlación múltiple al cuadrado	alfa de Cronbach si se elimina el elemento
A.Intuitiv	62.73	160.141	0.709	0.680	0.949
B.Intuitivo	62.66	161.835	0.697	0.672	0.949
C.Intuitivo	62.63	161.387	0.741	0.677	0.948
D.Intuitiv	62.69	160.925	0.718	0.680	0.949
E.Intuitivo	62.97	163.753	0.643	0.753	0.950
F.Intuitivo	62.97	165.228	0.608	0.755	0.950
G.Intuitiv	62.51	161.657	0.696	0.667	0.949
A.Sencillo	62.69	160.372	0.774	0.763	0.948
B.Sencillo	62.74	159.955	0.772	0.748	0.948
C.Sencillo	62.66	161.026	0.798	0.767	0.947
D.Sencillo	62.73	160.117	0.795	0.775	0.947
E.Sencillo	62.89	163.371	0.685	0.774	0.949
F.Sencillo	62.93	162.336	0.714	0.805	0.949
G.Sencillo	62.58	160.807	0.741	0.701	0.948
H.Intuitiv	62.93	164.474	0.650	0.750	0.950
I.Intuitivo	62.91	164.900	0.621	0.738	0.950
H.Sencillo	62.96	164.123	0.670	0.795	0.949
I.Sencillo	62.91	164.649	0.641	0.776	0.950

Para determinar la correlación de variables (sencillez e intuitividad) presentes en los diagramas estudiados (**Fig. 4** y **Fig. 5** del survey), se analizaron 18 elementos repartidos en las letras: A, B, C, D, E, F, G, H, e I, esto para medir el grado de sencillez e intuitividad.

En la Tabla 3 se muestra la correlación inter-elemento, donde los componentes A, B, C, D, E, F, G, H e I se juntan con el sufijo I (Intuitivo), S (Sencillo).

Tabla 3. Correlación inter-elemento, de los componentes A, B, C, D, E, F, G, H, e I

	AI	BI	CI	DI	EI	FI	GI	AS	BS	CS	DS	ES	FS	GS	HI	II	HS	IS
AI	1.0	0.7	0.7	0.6	0.5	0.4	0.7	0.6	0.5	0.5	0.5	0.4	0.4	0.5	0.4	0.3	0.4	0.3
BI	0.7	1.0	0.7	0.6	0.5	0.4	0.6	0.5	0.5	0.5	0.5	0.3	0.3	0.4	0.4	0.3	0.3	0.3
CI	0.7	0.7	1.0	0.7	0.5	0.4	0.6	0.5	0.5	0.5	0.5	0.4	0.4	0.5	0.4	0.4	0.4	0.4
DI	0.6	0.6	0.7	1.0	0.6	0.5	0.6	0.5	0.5	0.5	0.5	0.3	0.4	0.5	0.4	0.3	0.4	0.3
EI	0.5	0.5	0.5	0.6	1.0	0.8	0.5	0.3	0.4	0.4	0.4	0.4	0.5	0.3	0.4	0.4	0.3	0.3
FI	0.4	0.4	0.4	0.5	0.8	1.0	0.4	0.3	0.3	0.3	0.4	0.4	0.5	0.3	0.4	0.4	0.3	0.3
GI	0.7	0.6	0.6	0.6	0.5	0.4	1.0	0.5	0.5	0.5	0.5	0.3	0.3	0.5	0.4	0.3	0.3	0.3
AS	0.6	0.5	0.5	0.5	0.3	0.3	0.5	1.0	0.7	0.7	0.7	0.6	0.6	0.7	0.4	0.4	0.5	0.5
BS	0.5	0.5	0.5	0.5	0.4	0.3	0.5	0.7	1.0	0.8	0.7	0.6	0.6	0.6	0.4	0.4	0.5	0.4
CS	0.5	0.5	0.5	0.5	0.4	0.3	0.5	0.7	0.8	1.0	0.8	0.6	0.6	0.7	0.4	0.4	0.5	0.5
DS	0.5	0.5	0.5	0.5	0.4	0.4	0.5	0.7	0.7	0.8	1.0	0.6	0.6	0.7	0.4	0.4	0.5	0.5
ES	0.4	0.3	0.4	0.3	0.4	0.4	0.3	0.6	0.6	0.6	0.6	1.0	0.8	0.5	0.4	0.3	0.4	0.4
FS	0.4	0.3	0.4	0.4	0.5	0.5	0.3	0.6	0.6	0.6	0.6	0.8	1.0	0.6	0.4	0.4	0.4	0.5
GS	0.5	0.4	0.5	0.5	0.3	0.3	0.5	0.7	0.6	0.7	0.7	0.5	0.6	1.0	0.4	0.3	0.4	0.4
HI	0.4	0.4	0.4	0.4	0.4	0.4	0.4	0.4	0.4	0.4	0.4	0.4	0.4	0.4	1.0	0.8	0.7	0.6
II	0.3	0.3	0.4	0.3	0.4	0.4	0.3	0.4	0.4	0.4	0.4	0.3	0.4	0.3	0.8	1.0	0.6	0.7
HS	0.4	0.3	0.4	0.4	0.3	0.3	0.3	0.5	0.5	0.5	0.5	0.4	0.4	0.4	0.7	0.6	1.0	0.8
IS	0.3	0.3	0.4	0.3	0.3	0.3	0.3	0.5	0.4	0.5	0.5	0.4	0.5	0.4	0.6	0.7	0.8	1.0

A continuación en la Fig. 1 se presenta el gráfico de sedimentación del grupo A, en donde se observa que 5 de los compontes explican la mayor parte de la variabilidad, debido a que la línea comienza a ser recta después del componente 5. Los factores restantes explican una porción muy pequeña de la variabilidad y son probablemente de poca importancia.

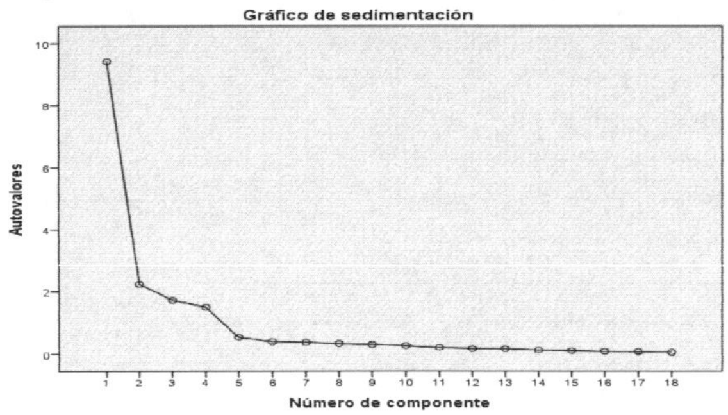

Fig. 1. Gráfico de sedimentación grupo A (carrera de Sistemas e Informática)

En la Fig. 2 se presenta el gráfico de sedimentación del grupo B, en donde se observa que 5 de los compontes explican la mayor parte de la variabilidad debido a que la línea comienza a ser recta después del componente 5.

Los factores restantes explican una porción muy pequeña de la variabilidad y son probablemente de poca importancia.

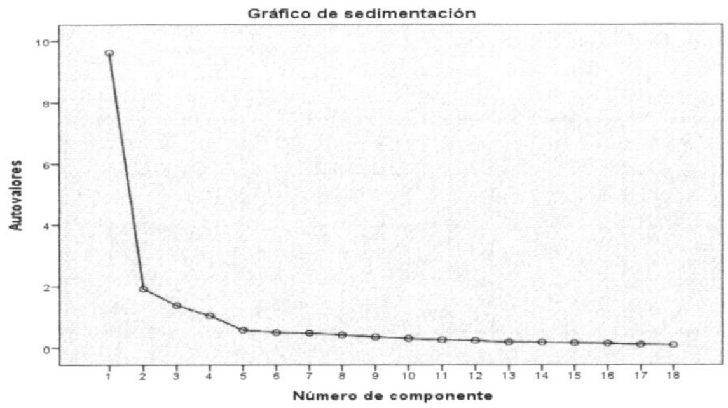

Fig. 2. Gráfico de sedimentación grupo B (carrera de Industrial, Eléctrica y Electromecánica)

En la Fig. 3 se presenta el gráfico de sedimentación del grupo C, en donde se observa que 4 de los compontes explican la mayor parte de la variabilidad debido a que la línea comienza a ser recta después del componente 4. Los factores restantes explican una porción muy pequeña de la variabilidad y son probablemente de poca importancia.

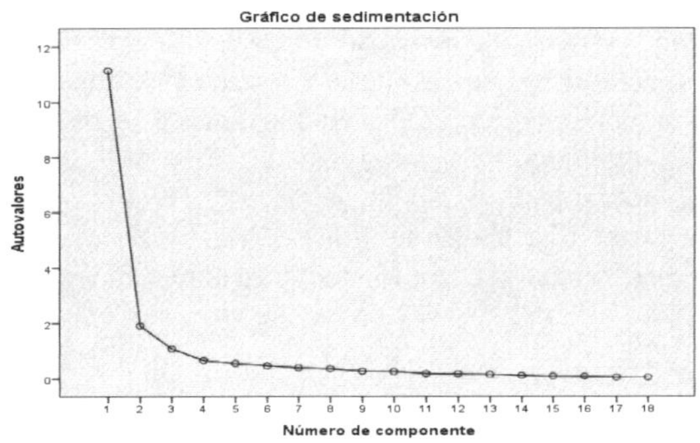

Fig. 3. Gráfico de sedimentación grupo C (encuestados que pertenecen a la carrera de Diseño Gráfico

Una vez descritos los distintos gráficos de sedimentación, en la Tabla 4 se presentan las distintas correlaciones calculadas. Donde L1, L2, L3, y L4 son los conjuntos de elementos que se correlacionan.

Tabla 4. Correlación inter elemento, de los componentes A, B, C, D, E, F, G, H, e I

Conjunto de elementos que se correlacionan	Grupo A (Informática)										Grupo B (Industrial, Eléctrica, Electromecánica)							Grupo C (Diseño Gráfico)						
L1	GI	CI	AI	BI	DI	GS	CS	AS	DS	BS	CS	DS	AS	BS	GS	ES	FS	AS	FS	GS	DS	BS	ES	CS
L2	HS	II	HI	IS							BI	AI	GI	CI	DI			DI	GI	EI	BI	AI	FI	CI
L3	ES	FS									HI	II	HS	IS				II	HI	IS	HS			
L4	EI	FI									EI	FI												

El survey desarrollado fue respondido a través de la plataforma Google Forms (éste se encuentra disponible en: https://goo.gl/h41aI2). Los estudiantes participantes accedieron al survey en línea desde los laboratorios de computación de la UTC, que fueron habilitados para tal fin. De esta manera se garantizó crear un ambiente adecuado para recoger la opinión de los encuestados. El survey se estructuró en tres secciones y estuvo compuesto por un total de 16 preguntas, divididas en las siguientes secciones:

- Información Demográfica.
- Área de formación del participante y nivel de instrucción.
- Presentación de diagramas de actividad de UML. En esta sección se presentaron dos procesos sencillos, con una explicación escrita y detallada de cada una de sus actividades y su representación gráfica en diagramas de actividad, tal como se presenta en las Fig. 4 y Fig. 5.

En la Fig. 4 se ejemplifica uno de los procesos definidos para este estudio, relacionado con cierto proceso que modela las actividades relacionas cuando alguien despierta.

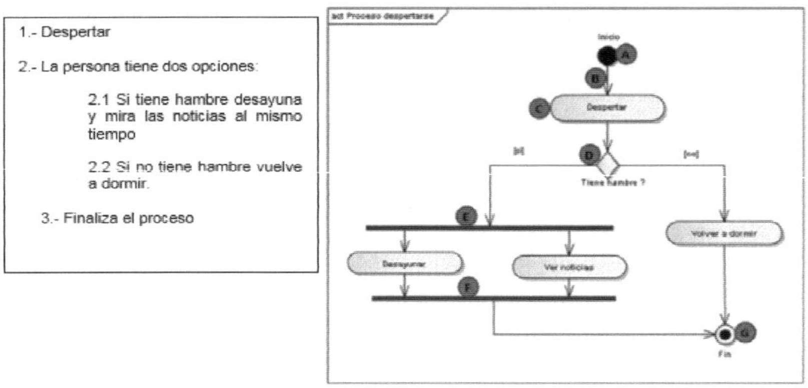

Fig. 4. Diagrama 1. Proceso despertar en la mañana

De manera similar, en la Fig. 5 se ejemplifica otro proceso definido para el estudio el cual se relaciona con un proceso para cambiar un canal de TV.

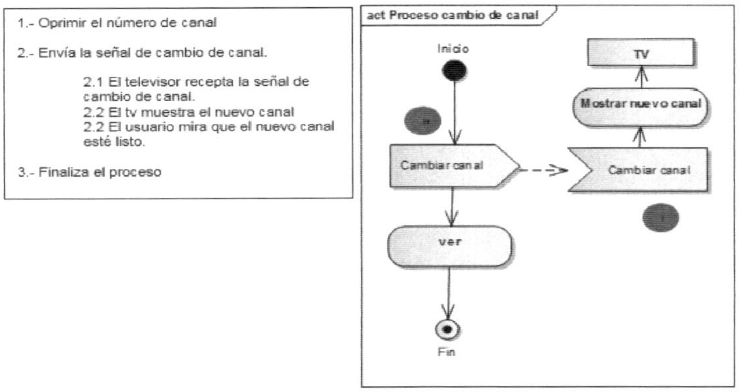

Fig. 5. Diagrama 2. Proceso Cambio de Canal en un TV. Adaptado de [13]

Con base en los diagramas anteriores se formularon varias preguntas, para conocer: qué tan intuitivos y sencillos les resultaban éstos. Las opciones de respuesta se plantearon en una escala del 1 al 5 de acuerdo a la escala Likert.

Tabla 5. Elementos A, B, C, D, E, F, G, H, I evaluados en el survey

Elemento	Gráfico	Nombre	Descripción
A		Inicio	Inicio de la actividad
B		Flujo de control	Conector que indica transición entre las acciones diagrama, imagine que un token fluye de una acción a la siguiente.
C		Acción	Acción o ejecución de una determinada actividad
D		Nodo de decisión	Bifurcación condicional, permite elegir una de dos posibilidades
E		Forknode	Divide un único flujo en flujos simultáneos, las actividades se realizan al mismo tiempo
F		Joinnode	Combina flujos simultáneos en un único flujo
G		Fin	Fin de la actividad
H	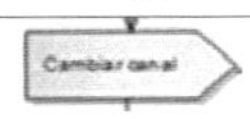	Acción que envía una señal	Acción que envía un mensaje o una señal a otra actividad.
I	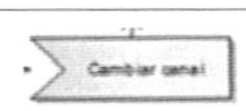	Acción que acepta una señal	Acción que recibe un mensaje o una señal antes de continuar con la siguiente acción.

En la Tabla 5 se muestran los elementos a los que hace alusión este estudio, se refieren a los componentes o figuras de los diagramas de actividad, evaluados a través del survey, estos elementos fueron etiquetados con las letras: A, B, C, D, E, F, G, H e I, encerradas en círculos azules (ver Fig.4 y Fig.5).

4 Análisis de Resultados

En el survey aplicado participaron 395 estudiantes, 287 hombres y 108 mujeres. Sus edades están en el rango entre los 19 y 42 años. Con respecto a la información demográfica se determinó que el 90% de los encuestados tienen un nivel socioeconómico medio. Respecto al área de formación: 144 son de Informática, 135 de Electromecánica, 40 de Industrial, 27 de Eléctrica y 49 de Diseño Gráfico. En relación al nivel de formación (semestre): 106 estudiantes estaban cursando el séptimo semestre, 82 el quinto semestre, 87 el octavo, 58 el sexto, 62 del último semestre o graduados.

Con respecto a los resultados del primer diagrama (despertar por la mañana, Fig 4). El 83% de los participantes respondió que en el diagrama sí se plasma lo asociado a su representación textual, mientras que el 17% respondió que no.

En la Fig. 6 se evidencian los resultados de la valoración de la intuitividad para el diagrama 1 (Fig. 4).

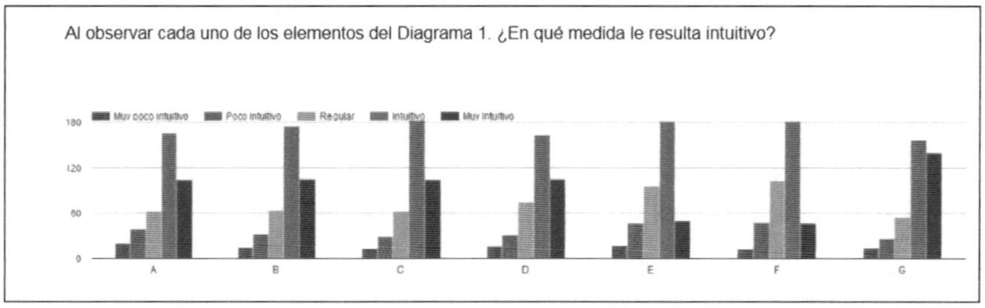

Fig. 6. Resultados con respecto a la intuitividad del diagrama 1 (Fig. 4)

En la Fig. 7 se evidencian los resultados de la valoración de la sencillez para el diagrama 1 (Fig. 4).

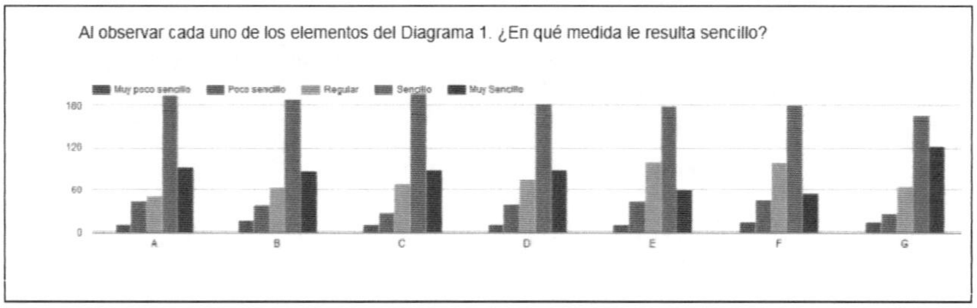

Fig. 7. Resultados con respecto a la sencillez del diagrama 1 (Fig. 4)

Con respecto a los resultados del diagrama 2 (cambio de canal, Fig. 5). El 68% de los participantes respondió que el diagrama sí corresponde con lo asociado al texto, mientras que el 32% respondió que no.

En la Fig. 8 se evidencian los resultados de la valoración de la intuitividad para el diagrama 2.

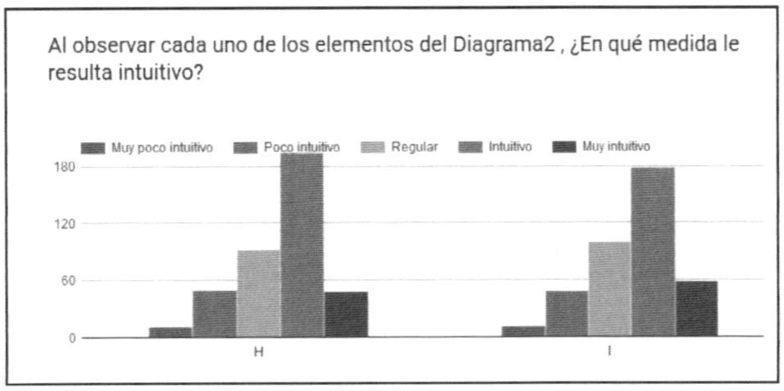

Fig. 8. Resultados con respecto a la intuitividad del diagrama 2 (Fig. 5)

En la Fig. 9 se evidencian los resultados de la valoración de la sencillez para el diagrama 2 (Fig. 5).

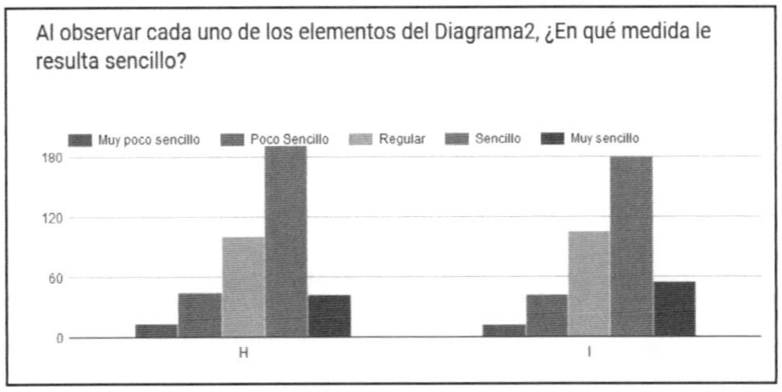

Fig. 9. Resultados con respecto a la sencillez del diagrama 2 (Fig. 5)

4.1 Análisis de la Varianza

Para contrastar la hipótesis nula previamente planteada, se empleó el análisis de la varianza (ANOVA) en donde se conformaron grupos con cierto criterio de aleatoriedad: GRUPO 1 (Con instrucción informática) Sistemas e Informática; GRUPO 2 (Sin instrucción informática – áreas afines) Industrial, Eléctrica y Electromecánica; GRUPO 3 (Sin instrucción informática) Diseño Gráfico.

En la Tabla 6 se observan los grupos homogéneos, agrupados de acuerdo al nivel de instrucción, cuya muestra para los grupos A y B fue escogida con criterio aleatorio.

Tabla 6. Conformación de grupos homogéneos

Nivel de instrucción	Grupo	Identificador	Carrera	Pob.	*n*	Participantes a considerar	Criterio
Con instrucción Informática	1	A	Sistemas e Informática	144	49	49	Aleatorio
Sin Instrucción Informática	2	B	Industrial	40	16	49	Aleatorio
			Eléctrica	27	16		Aleatorio
			Electromecánica	135	17		Aleatorio
	3	C	Diseño Gráfico	49	49	49	Todos

En la Tabla 7 se resume el análisis descriptivo de cada grupo(A, B y C), en donde se observa la sumatoria para los valores de A, B y C, los valores promedio y las varianzas. Al analizar los promedios encontramos la diferencia entre grupos, así por ejemplo: Entre A y B la diferencia es de 0.32 puntos, entre B y C de 0.5 puntos, mientras entre A y C es de 0.82 puntos.

Tabla 7. Resumen de análisis descriptivo

Grupos	*Cuenta*	*Suma*	*Promedio*	*Varianza*
Grupo A	49	197.5	4.03061224	0.3792517
Grupo B	49	182	3.71428571	0.70833333
Grupo C	49	157.5	3.21428571	0.625

En la Tabla 8 se presentan los resultados del análisis de la varianza aplicado a las mediciones recolectadas de los participantes.

Tabla 8. Análisis de Varianza, Probabilidad, Valor de P y otros

Origen de las variaciones	Suma de cuadrados	Grados de libertad	Promedio de los cuadrados	F	Probabilidad	Valor crítico para F
Entre grupos	16.60204082	2	8.30102041	14.541	1.76964E-06	3.058928
Dentro de los grupos	82.20440816	144	0.57086168			
Total	98.80644898	146				

Del análisis de varianza presentado en la Tabla 8 se deduce que el valor de F es de 14.54 y el valor de la probabilidad es 1.76964E-06; al ser menor a 0.05 de nivel de significancia, se rechaza la hipótesis nula y se valida la hipótesis alternativa: *La facilidad de comprensión de los DA para el diseño de procesos entre las personas con instrucción y sin instrucción en el área informática es diferente en al menos uno de los grupos encuestados.*

Con el fin de examinar cuáles fueron las diferencias significativas entre los tres grupos aplicamos la prueba de contrastes de Tukey [16] de acuerdo a los parámetros definidos en la Tabla 9.

Tabla 9. Parámetros definidos para aplicar la prueba por contrastes de Tukey

HSD =	0.357	Diferencia Honestamente Significativa
Multiplicador =	3.31	Multiplicador. valor de Q de alfa
Mse =	0.571	Cuadrado del error medio
n=	49	Tamaño de cada uno de los grupos. número de encuestas por grupo

Una vez determinado el HSD = 0.357 al obtener las Medias aritméticas del promedio de los Grupos de A, B y C se presenta la Tabla 10.

Tabla 10. Tabla de diferencias obtenidas entre los grupos A (Sistemas de Información), B (Industrial, Eléctrica, Electromecánica) y C (Diseño Gráfico)

	Grupo A	Grupo B	Grupo C
Grupo A		0.316	0.816
Grupo B			0.5
Grupo C			

De acuerdo a la prueba de contrastes de Tukey [16], observamos que las diferencias significativas se presentan entre los grupos A (Sistemas e Informática) y C (Diseño Gráfico); y entre los grupos B (Industrial, Eléctrica y Electromecánica) y C (Diseño Gráfico).

5 Discusión y Conclusiones

Con base a los resultados del presente estudio se responde a la pregunta de investigación antes planteada (**RQ**): *¿Es la facilidad de comprensión de DA usados en el diseño de procesos equivalente tanto en personas con un dominio técnico de la informática como en aquellas sin un dominio técnico?* En base a nuestros hallazgos, la facilidad de comprensión de los DA para el diseño de procesos entre las personas con instrucción y sin instrucción en el área informática es diferente en al menos un grupo de encuestados.

Al comparar la comprensión de los DA entre los estudiantes del Grupo A (Con dominio en Informática) con los estudiantes del Grupo B (Con dominio moderado en Informática) no observamos diferencias significativas, es decir la comprensión para estos dos grupos es equivalente, lo que demuestra que los DA son comprensibles tanto para personas con dominio en informática como para personas con dominio moderado de la misma.

Al comparar la comprensión de los DA entre los estudiantes del Grupo A (Con dominio en Informática) con los del Grupo C (Con dominio limitado en Informática)

observamos una diferencia significativa, es decir la comprensión en los diagramas para estos dos grupos no es equivalente.

Al comparar la comprensión de los DA entre los estudiantes el Grupo B (Con dominio moderado en Informática) con los del Grupo C (Con dominio limitado en Informática), también observamos una diferencia significativa, es decir la comprensión en los diagramas para estos dos grupos no es equivalente.

Para el Grupo A observamos una mayor cantidad de variables sobre las cuales la correlación de valores es fuerte. Lo intuitivo y sencillo de los diferentes elementos de los DA se evidenció más en los estudiantes informáticos que en estudiantes de otras áreas, es decir a este grupo les resultó mucho más sencillo e intuitivo los diagramas definidos.

Los elementos H e I del diagrama 2 fueron agrupados como criterio en opinión de los tres grupos (con una valoración específica que los separa del resto), por lo que lo intuitivo y sencillo de su representación gráfica se diferenció de la representación de otros elementos.

El Grupo A distinguió lo sencillo e intuitivo en los elementos de trabajo en paralelo (E y F). El Grupo B solo diferenció lo intuitivo. El Grupo C no diferenció particularmente estos elementos.

De acuerdo a los resultados obtenidos en este estudio, se recomienda el uso de diagramas de actividades para el modelado de procesos del negocio siempre y cuando las personas involucradas en esta actividad cuenten con cierto grado de conocimiento sobre el ámbito de la Informática.

Referencias

[1] Eriksson, H. E., & Penker, M.: Business Modeling with UML: Business Patterns at Work. New York, EEUU. John Wiley & Sons. (2000).

[2] Schedlbauer, M.: The Art of Business Process Modeling: The Business Analyst's Guide to Process Modeling with IJML &BPMN. CreateSpace. (2010).

[3] Souza Cardoso, E. (2013). Towards a Methodology for Goal Oriented Enterprise Management. IEEE Computer Society

[4] Booch, G., Rumbaugh, J., & Jacobson, I. (1998. First Edition October 20). The Unified Modeling Language User Guide. Publisher: Addison Wesley.

[5] Kalnins, A., & Vitolins, V.: Use of UML and Model Transformations for Workflow Process Definitions. ARXIV. (2006).

[6] Tello, E., & Carreón, J.: Approach for Semantic Business Process Management using Ontologies. (2013).

[7] GEAMBAŞU, C.: Bpmn vs. Uml Activity Diagram for business process modeling. Bucharest, Rumania. The Bucharest University of Economic Studies. (2013).

[8] Needham, M.: UML 2. 0 Superstructure. Massachusetts, OMG. (2004).

[9] Russell, N., Van der Aalst, W., & H.M,A.: On the Suitability of UML 2. 0 Activity Diagrams for Business Process Modelling. Hobart, Australia. Conferences in Research and Practice in Information Technology. Registro Oficial No. 559, pp. 279-290. (2006).

[10] Sarshar, K., & Loos, P.: Modeling the Resource Perspective of Business Processes by UML Activity Diagram and Object Petri Net. Enterprise Modeling and Computing with UML. (2007).

[11] Felderer, M. F. (2015). Manual test case derivation from UML activity diagrams and state machines: A controlled experiment. Information and Software Technology.
[12] Gross A, G.: EPC vs. UML Activity Diagram - Two Experiments Examining their Usefulness for Requirements Engineering. IEEE International Requeriments Engineering Conference. (2009).
[13]SOLVETIC. (2014). Solución a problemas informátios. Obtenido de https://www.solvetic.com/tutoriales/article/517-uml-diagramas-de-actividades-avanzado/
[14] UNESCO. (1997). Clasificación Internacional Normalizada de la Educación CINE.
[15] Cronbach, L. (1951). Coefficient alpha and the internal structure of tests. Psychometrika. 16 (3): 297–334.
[16] Tukey, J. (1949). Comparing individual means in the analysis of variance. Biometrics.

Usability evaluation mechanism with Standard ISO/IEC 9126. Case study: Tourism portals

Mayra C. Salazar-Grandes[1], Santiago P. Jácome-Guerrero[1], Alexandra Corral[1], José Luis Carrillo-Medina[1], Nancy Jacho-Guanoluisa[1], Patricio Espinel[1], Ivone Arias-Almeida[1], Juan M. Ferreira[2], Edison P. Bedón-Salazar[3]

[1] Universidad de las Fuerzas Armadas ESPE, Av. General Rumiñahui s/n, 171-5-231B Sangolquí, Ecuador
{mcsalazar,psjacome,macorral,jlcarrillo,npjacho, pgespinel,giarias}@espe.edu.ec
[2]Facultad Politécnica, Universidad Nacional de Asunción, CC 1439 San Lorenzo, Paraguay
jmferreira1978@gmail.com
[3]Universidad Técnica de Cotopaxi, Av. Simón Rodríguez, Latacunga, Ecuador
edison.bedon@utc.edu.ec

Abstract. The present research work proposes a mechanism for evaluating the usability of tourism portals, taking as reference the ISO/IEC 9126 quality model. The evaluation mechanism considers external attributes that a tourism portal associated with each selected metric should have. To evaluate each metric, techniques such as observation guide, satisfaction questionnaire and attractive interface questionnaire were used. The evaluation mechanism was used to evaluate the most representative portals of the countries with the highest number of visits per year according to OMT. This allowed us to identify the most appropriate form of compliance with usability criteria that should be taken into account in the design and implementation of a tourism portal.

Keywords: usability, ISO/IEC 9126, metrics, tourism

1 Introducción

En la actualidad la satisfacción hacia el uso de un producto software marca la diferencia al momento de elegir alguna aplicación. Por esta razón para evaluar la calidad del software se emplean ciertos modelos estándar de calidad como el modelo McCall [1], estándar ISO/IEC 9126 [2], integración del modelo de maduración de la capacidad CMMI que permitan evaluar el software desde diferentes perspectivas como funcionalidad, fiabilidad, usabilidad, eficiencia, mantenibilidad y portabilidad[3].

El momento en que una organización expresa una necesidad en materia de software, se inicia un proceso muchas veces complejo, que involucra un conjunto de actividades que deben coordinarse para satisfacer una necesidad. Tomando en cuenta lo anterior, se recomienda utilizar modelos y estándares de la industria, que proponen una serie de actividades y procesos a ser aplicados en el desarrollo de software, para obtener productos de calidad competitivos en el mercado. El diseño de software sin tomar en cuenta criterios establecidos por los modelos de calidad acarrea la obtención de productos de baja calidad.

Con la finalidad de determinar los criterios de usabilidad que se deben considerar en el diseño de un portal de turismo, el presente artículo describe el mecanismo utilizado para su identificación, en base a la evaluación del cumplimiento de las métricas de la característica de usabilidad del estándar ISO/IEC 9126 y del modelo en uso, aplicado a portales de turismo de los países más visitados del mundo. Cada métrica debe ser analizada por técnicas que permitan cuantificar su cumplimiento. Según Jakob Nielsen [4], la usabilidad contiene dos componentes principales, uno enfocado a la funcionalidad del sistema (*evaluada por expertos*) y el otro a como los usuarios pueden usar dicha funcionalidad (*evaluada por usuarios finales*). Los factores principales que deben considerarse en la usabilidad son facilidad de aprendizaje, efectividad de uso y satisfacción de los usuarios al realizar tareas en el producto. Para evaluar la usabilidad existen varios tipos de técnicas [5]:

Inspección: Es una técnica utilizada por usuarios expertos en usabilidad para analizar aspectos de la interfaz del sistema relacionados con la usabilidad y la accesibilidad las cuales son: heurística, recorrido cognitivo, recorrido de usabilidad plural, inspección de estándares.

Indagación: Es la interacción de los usuarios finales con el producto software. Esta técnica le permite al evaluador observar cómo se comporta el usuario frente al producto así como también recabar las experiencias u observaciones del usuario, se clasifica en: observación de campo, grupo de discusión dirigido, entrevistas, cuestionarios y grabaciones del uso

Test: Esta técnica consiste en que los usuarios trabajen en tareas definidas dentro del sistema, los resultados obtenidos son utilizados por los evaluadores para ver como la interfaz brinda soporte a las tareas, se clasifica en: pensando en alta voz, interacción constructiva, método conducido, medición del rendimiento, ordenamiento de tarjetas.

En este trabajo, se ha seleccionado los tipos de técnicas de indagación (observación de campo, cuestionarios) y test (método conducido y medición del rendimiento) debido a que se está analizando portales que se encuentran en ejecución lo que ha permitido evaluar el uso de los portales desde el punto de vista del usuario final.

El artículo se organiza de la siguiente manera. La sección 2 describe trabajos relacionados. La sección 3 presenta modelos de calidad del software. La sección 4 describe el análisis y selección de métricas de la característica de usabilidad y del modelo de uso del estándar. La sección 5 considera a los portales de turismo para determinar los criterios de usabilidad. La sección 6 evalúa, analiza la información obtenida y define criterios de usabilidad a tomar en cuenta en el diseño de un portal de turismo. Finalmente la sección 7 termina con las conclusiones y líneas de trabajo futuro.

2 Trabajos Relacionados

El objetivo del presente trabajo es analizar la característica de usabilidad y el modelo de uso del estándar ISO/IEC 9126, con la finalidad de presentar los aspectos más relevantes a tomar en cuenta al diseñar un portal de turismo, a continuación se describe algunos trabajos relacionados:

Perurena y Moraguez en [6] analizan las diferentes técnicas utilizadas para evaluar la usabilidad y presentan un caso práctico de un sistema de evaluación basado en heurística, llamado SIRIUS, que integra un conjunto de elementos que lo distinguen de otras propuestas, como elementos claves para desarrollar sistemas interactivos usables.

Guedez, Gómez y Numa en [7] desarrollan un sistema de información geográfico con el propósito de mejorar las deficiencias del levantamiento cartográfico, la evaluación de la calidad del sistema de información geográfico se lleva a cabo mediante el criterio de expertos y las normas ISO/IEC 9126 demostrándose así que el mismo cumple con los atributos de confiabilidad, usabilidad, eficiencia, mantenibilidad, portabilidad y uso.

Muñoz y Vianello en [8] propone un modelo cognitivo-emocional de análisis de usabilidad basado en heurísticas, dicho modelo se aplica a los portales web de dieciocho bibliotecas universitarias.

3 Modelos de calidad del software

Al desarrollar productos y servicios de software es recomendable hacer uso de algún modelo de calidad, para garantizar su adecuado uso y funcionamiento. La calidad en el software puede abordarse desde dos ámbitos: la calidad del producto y la calidad del proceso. En cada una de los ámbitos se han definido una gran variedad de estándares.

La calidad del producto y del proceso son complementarias no se deben analizar de forma aislada, la calidad en el proceso de desarrollo garantizará un producto de calidad [9]. En la Figura 1, se muestran los modelos de calidad más representativos.

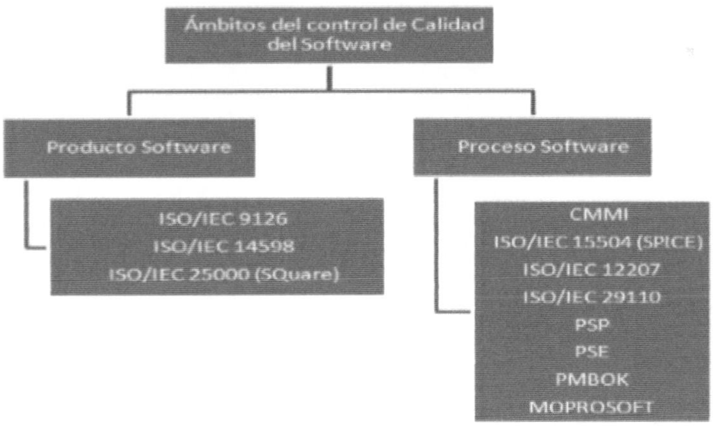

Fig. 1. Ámbitos de calidad del software [10]

3.1 Estándar ISO/IEC 9126

Este estándar fue publicado en 1992. En sus inicios contenía una descripción de calidad del software y tenía seis características (funcionalidad, fiabilidad, usabilidad, eficiencia, mantenibilidad y portabilidad). Lo que el estándar no mencionaba era las métricas ni el método de medición a ser utilizado. Por lo que el modelo, es dividido en cuatro normas: Estructura del Modelo de Calidad (9126-1), Métricas Externas (9126-2), Métricas Internas (9126-3), y Métricas de Calidad en Uso (9126-4) [11].

Modelo de Calidad (9126-1)

El modelo de calidad hace referencia a las especificaciones de las características de la calidad del producto software. El modelo de calidad se encuentra definido en dos partes: Calidad interna y calidad externa, y Calidad en uso [12].

Calidad interna y calidad externa: La calidad interna y externa, define 6 características, una de ellas es la usabilidad. Cada característica se encuentra dividida en sub-características.

- ***Característica de Usabilidad:*** Es la capacidad del producto software de ser: comprendido, aprendido, usado y atractivo para el usuario, cuando se utiliza en condiciones específicas, el estándar define las siguientes sub-características
- ***Capacidad para ser entendido:*** Corresponde al esfuerzo del usuario de entender si el software es adecuado y cómo se puede utilizar para las tareas y condiciones de uso particulares.
- ***Capacidad para ser aprendido:*** Se refiere al esfuerzo del usuario en aprender a usar una aplicación.
- ***Capacidad para ser operado:*** Se evalúa la operación y control del usuario frente a una aplicación.
- ***Capacidad de ser atractivo:*** Capacidad del producto de software de ser atractivo para el usuario.
- ***Cumplimiento de la usabilidad*:** Capacidad del producto de software en adherirse a normas, convenciones y regulaciones relacionadas con la usabilidad.

Calidad en uso: La calidad en uso se divide en cuatro características, que son: efectividad, productividad, seguridad y satisfacción. Estas no se subdividen en sub-características.

Métricas externas (9126-2)

Define las métricas externas para las seis características del modelo de calidad. Pueden ser utilizadas cuando el software está siendo ejecutado en un ambiente de operación o de pruebas. El investigador puede hacer uso de las métricas que más se ajusten a las características del producto software a ser evaluado, así como también podrá modificar o utilizar otras métricas que no estén definidas en el estándar, siempre y cuando se justifique la relación que exista con el estándar [13].

Métricas internas (9126-3)

Establece las métricas internas para las seis características del modelo de calidad. Son aplicadas a los productos intermedios generados en el proceso de desarrollo del software, por esta razón no son tomadas en cuenta en la presente investigación. [13].

Métricas en uso (9126-4)

Estas métricas tienen una relación directa con el comportamiento de los usuarios frente al uso del producto software [13]. Especifica las métricas en uso que permite evaluar lo fácil o difícil que fue para el usuario alcanzar metas específicas con efectividad, productividad, seguridad y satisfacción en un contexto de uso específico.

4 Análisis y selección de métricas

Las métricas de la característica de usabilidad escogidas para el estudio fueron las más relevantes y que guardan relación con los requerimientos de los expertos de la línea de negocio (operadores de turismo). Para escoger las características del modelo de calidad en uso se tomó como referencia el estudio realizado en [14], en el cual se construyen cuatro redes bayesianas que permiten relacionar las características de *calidad externa* con las características de *calidad de uso*, mediante un análisis pormenorizado de las definiciones de las características y su influencia sobre cada una de ellas. Se utiliza este estudio porque una red bayesiana provee una forma compacta de representar el conocimiento y métodos flexibles de razonamiento. En la Figura 2, se muestra que la característica de *usabilidad* se encuentra dentro del nodo de *efectividad* y *satisfacción* (características del modelo de *calidad de uso*). Lo cual señala, la relación e influencia que existe entre éstas.

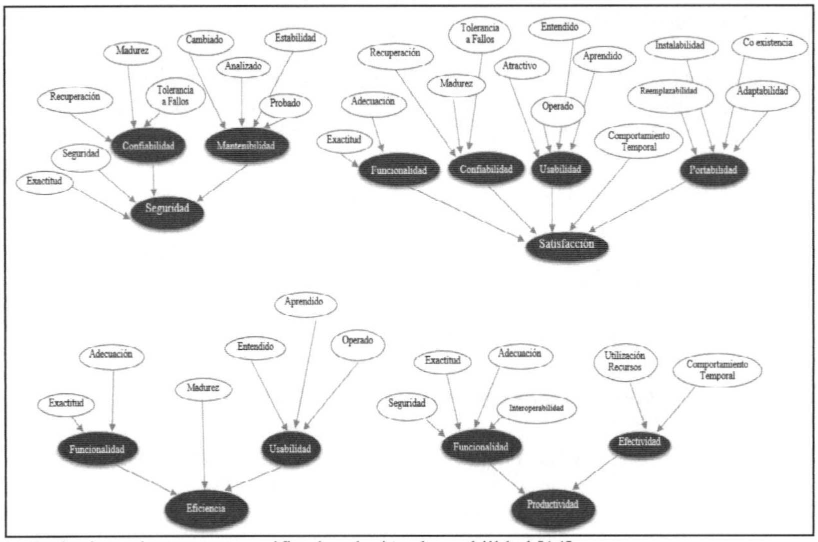

Fig. 2. Redes bayesianas que especifica la relación de usabilidad [14]

En la Tabla 1 se detalla las métricas de la característica de usabilidad utilizadas para la presente investigación.

Tabla 1. Métricas de la característica de usabilidad

Sub-características	Métricas
Capacidad para ser entendido	Demostración de accesibilidad
	Entendimiento de entrada y salida
Capacidad para ser aprendido	Aprendizaje al realizar una tarea
	Ayuda frecuente
Capacidad para ser administrado	Consistencia operacional en uso
	Corrección de error
Capacidad de ser atractivo	Interacción atractiva

La Tabla 2 define las características y métricas del modelo de calidad en uso para el estudio realizado.

Tabla 2. Métricas del modelo de calidad en uso

Características	Métricas
Efectividad	Finalización de tareas
Satisfacción	Cuestionario de satisfacción

En las normas ISO/IEC 9126-2 (modelo de calidad externa en el que define la característica de usabilidad) e ISO/IEC 9126-4 (modelo de calidad en uso) el estándar define por cada métrica, los siguientes aspectos: propósito, método de aplicación, fórmulas, interpretación del valor medido, tipo de escala, entrada para la medición y audiencia; que el investigador debe tomar en cuenta al utilizar la métrica.

5 Caso de estudio: Portales web de turismo

De acuerdo a la Organización Mundial del Turismo (OMT), durante décadas el turismo ha experimentado un continuo crecimiento y una profunda diversificación hasta convertirse en uno de los sectores económicos que crece con mayor rapidez en el mundo [15]. La influencia de las TIC's en el sector turístico (portales de turismo) ha permitido difundir masivamente la información. La OMT periódicamente difunde una revista llamada Barómetro OMT del Turismo Mundial en la que presenta una visión concisa del turismo a nivel mundial, tendencias y estadísticas por año [16]. Según la revista los países mejor posicionados en ingreso de turistas son Francia, Estados Unidos y España. Por esta razón, se ha seleccionado un portal de turismo de cada uno de estos países, procurando que dichos portales sean los más completos en cuanto a funcionalidad y servicios turísticos, para evaluarlos con las métricas seleccionadas.

Los portales considerados para la investigación fueron de Francia (www.france-voyage.com), de Estados Unidos (www.discoveramerica.com) y de España (www.spain.com)

6 Evaluación y análisis de resultados

En esta sección se presenta las técnicas de evaluación utilizadas para medir la usabilidad de los portales de turismo seleccionados, el análisis de los datos y un conjunto de criterios de usabilidad que se deberían tomar en cuenta en el diseño e implementación de un portal de turismo.

6.1 Técnicas de evaluación de usabilidad

Como se señaló anteriormente, la usabilidad puede ser evaluada desde diferentes enfoques, la *evaluación experta* y la *evaluación de usuarios*. La primera es recomendable cuando se está desarrollando un sitio web, ya que nos permitirá detectar fallos en fases iniciales lo que ahorrará tiempo y dinero. En cambio es aconsejable la evaluación de usuario cuando el sitio web se encuentra en ejecución aunque tampoco se descarta la evaluación por parte de expertos [17]. Las técnicas utilizadas para evaluar las métricas de usabilidad del estándar ISO/IEC 9126 seleccionadas para el caso de estudio son: *guía de observación*, *cuestionario de interfaz atractiva* y un *cuestionario de satisfacción dirigido a usuarios finales.*

Guía de observación: Se consideró diez (10) tareas que el usuario debe realizar en cada portal [18]. Por cada una de las tareas se formuló preguntas elaboradas por los investigadores acorde a la naturaleza de la métrica, así como también se registró el comportamiento del usuario al realizar la tarea encomendada. Cada tarea está relacionada a una métrica, por lo que los valores obtenidos de cada tarea corresponde a lo que indica la norma ISO/IEC 9126-2 del estándar [13].

Para obtener el valor de cada métrica de la muestra obtenida por cada portal, se calculó el promedio y la desviación estándar de los valores obtenidos.

Cuestionario interfaz atractiva: Se elaboró catorce (14) preguntas cerradas planteadas por los investigadores, las respuestas eran cualitativitas (alta, media y baja) [18].

Por esta razón se transforma a valores numéricos para que se pueda interpretar y analizar de mejor manera la información obtenida. Al realizar esta transformación se obtiene que el valor más alto del cuestionario es de cuarenta y dos (42) puntos.

Para calcular el valor de cada métrica de la muestra obtenida por cada portal, se calculó el promedio de los valores obtenidos.

Cuestionario de satisfacción: Se utiliza el cuestionario System Usability Sacale (SUS) que fue desarrollado por Digital Equipment Corporation [19]. El cuestionario tiene 10 preguntas, para su calificación hace uso de la escala de Likert. El cuestionario SUS ha sido utilizado para el estudio de diferentes productos de software tales como: aplicaciones de escritorio, páginas web, sistemas de respuestas de voz, productos de consumo, etc. El cuestionario considera tres criterios de usabilidad, como son: efectividad, eficiencia y satisfacción.

Para obtener el valor de cada métrica de la muestra obtenida por cada portal, se calculó el promedio de los valores obtenidos.

6.2 Selección de la muestra

La muestra utilizada para el caso de estudio fue de treinta (30) usuarios, distribuidos en tres (3) grupos de diez (10) usuarios para cada portal a ser evaluado. El ISO/IEC 9126-1 indica que se puede tomar una muestra de al menos ocho (8) usuarios para considerar que los resultados obtenidos en la investigación sean confiables [12].

Para seleccionar la muestra se tomó en consideración los siguientes aspectos: usuarios que utilicen el internet como herramienta de búsqueda de información, usuarios que han utilizado portales de turismo para planificar viajes ya sea por placer o trabajo y usuarios que no han utilizado portales de turismo.

6.3 Atributos externos para evaluar las métricas seleccionadas

En la Tabla 3 se detalla los atributos, técnicas y fórmulas que se aplicó para evaluar las métricas seleccionadas para la investigación.

Tabla 3. Atributos externos

Métricas	Atributos	Técnicas	Fórmula
Demostración de accesibilidad	Mapa del sitio, Reporte de circuitos turísticos, Reporte de actividades que el turista puede realizar.	Guía de Observación	X=A / B A= número de tareas realizadas con éxito B= número de tareas disponibles
Entendimiento de entrada y salida	Formularios	Guía de Observación	X=A / B A= número de campos ingresados con éxito en el formulario B= número de campos del formulario
Facilidad de aprendizaje al realizar una tarea	Video de un lugar turístico	Guía de Observación	Promedio del tiempo de tres intentos para aprender a ser una tarea
Ayuda frecuente	Tutoriales, Búsqueda, Ayuda en línea	Guía de Observación	Número de veces que necesito de la ayuda para realizar una tarea
Consistencia Operacional en uso	Búsqueda, Información de un lugar turístico, Información de servicios turísticos	Guía de Observación	X=1-A/B A= número de inconsistencias al realizar las tareas B= número de tareas Y= N/OUT N= número de inconsistencias al realizar las tareas OUT= suma del tiempo (segundos) en realizar las tareas
Finalización de la Tarea	Búsqueda, Información de un lugar turístico, Información de servicios turísticos	Guía de Observación	X=A/B A= numero de tareas finalizadas B= número total de tareas
Corrección de errores	Búsqueda de un hotel	Guía de Observación	T= Tc- Ts Tc= tiempo en completar la corrección del error Ts= tiempo en iniciar la corrección del error
Interacción atractiva	Interfaz del sitio web	Cuestionario Interfaz Atractiva	Sumatoria de los valores numéricos
Cuestionario de satisfacción	Satisfacción total del sitio web	Cuestionario de Satisfacción	Escala de Likert

6.4 Análisis de resultados

La Tabla 4, presenta los valores de la aplicación de las técnicas (guía de observación, cuestionario de interfaz atractiva y cuestionario de satisfacción) para cada métrica y portal analizado.

Tabla 4. Valores obtenidos

Métrica	Tipo de medición	Portales de turismo		
País		EE UU	ESPAÑA	FRANCIA
Demostración de accesibilidad	Cantidad	0.67	0.93	1
Entrada y salida comprensible	Cantidad	0.94	0.98	0.98
Facilidad de aprendizaje para realizar una tarea en uso	Tiempo	00:06:08	00:05:27	00:03:52
Ayuda frecuente	Cantidad	0.5	1	0.3
Consistencia Operacional en uso	Cantidad Tiempo (Min)	0.90 0.09	0.93 0.039	1 0
Finalización de la tarea	Cantidad	0.9	0.93	1
Corrección de errores	Tiempo	00:01:56	00:00:36	00:01:13
Interacción Atractiva	Puntos	31.6	34.11	39.2
Cuestionario de Satisfacción	Puntos	47.0 No Aceptable	70.0 Marginal	100 Aceptable

- Para la métrica *demostración de accesibilidad*, el estándar indica que cuanto más se acerca a uno (1), es mejor. El portal de Francia con uno (1) cumple con lo estipulado en el estándar.
- Para la métrica *entrada y salida comprensible*, el estándar señala que cuanto más se acerca a uno (1) es mejor. Los portales que cumplen son Francia y España con 0.98 cada uno.
- Para la métrica *facilidad de aprendizaje* para realizar una tarea en uso, el estándar ISO/IEC 9126 indica que el más corto es el mejor. El portal de Francia con 3 minutos y 52 segundos es el más corto.
- Para la métrica *ayuda frecuente*, el estándar indica que el más cercano a cero (0) es el mejor. El portal de Francia con 0.3 cumple con lo que indica el estándar.
- Para la métrica *consistencia operacional* en uso, el estándar indica que es consistente cuanto más se acerca a uno (1) y en el tiempo de funcionamiento el más pequeño y cercano a cero (0) es el mejor. El portal de Francia obtiene uno (1) en consistencia operacional y cero (0) en tiempo de funcionamiento cumpliendo con lo que indica el estándar.
- Para la métrica *finalización de la tarea* el estándar señala que mientras más cerca al uno (1) es mejor. El portal de Francia con uno (1) cumple con el requerimiento del estándar.
- Para la métrica *corrección de errores*, el estándar revela que el tiempo más corto es el mejor. El portal de España con 36 segundos cumple con lo que indica el estándar.
- Para la métrica *interacción atractiva* el estándar menciona que dependerá del método de puntaje utilizado en el cuestionario, para el presente trabajo de investigación se consideró que el puntaje más cercano a 42 puntos es el mejor. El portal de Francia con 39.2 tiene mayor puntaje frente al resto.
- Para la métrica *cuestionario de satisfacción*, el estándar menciona que dependerá del método de puntaje utilizado en el cuestionario, en la presente investigación se

ha utilizado el cuestionario System Usability Sacale(SUS). El portal de Francia es el mejor punteado, alcanzando 89.5 puntos.

Se puede concluir que el portal de Francia obtuvo mejores resultados en 7 de 9 métricas (demostración de accesibilidad, facilidad de aprendizaje para realizar una tarea en uso, ayuda frecuente, consistencia operacional en uso, finalización de la tarea, interacción atractiva, cuestionario de satisfacción), mientras que el portal de España obtiene mejor puntaje en la métrica corrección de errores y en la métrica entrada y salida comprensible iguala en puntaje al portal de Francia.

6.5 Criterios de usabilidad identificados

La evaluación a los portales de turismo señalados, así como también información recabada a expertos de la línea de negocio (operadores de turismo) ha permitido establecer los siguientes criterios que deben ser tomados en cuenta en el diseño e implementación de un portal de turismo.

1. ***Visión del sitio:*** El portal dispondrá de un mapa (estructura del portal web) que le permita al usuario tener una visión general del portal con la finalidad de facilitar la navegación.
2. ***Circuitos turísticos:*** El portal debe contener información de circuitos turísticos, que son un conjunto de diversos destinos que se unen en forma articulada y programada, contemplan recursos naturales y culturales, así como también un conjunto de servicios ofrecidos al turista.
3. ***Actividades de un lugar turístico:*** Información de actividades como paseos, acontecimientos, actividades de ocio, etc.
4. ***Entrada y salida de información comprensible:*** La información que solicite el portal al llenar un formulario debe ser de fácil ingreso.
5. ***Ayuda y documentación:*** El portal permitirá acceder de forma fácil a tutoriales, ayuda en línea y opciones de búsqueda para realizar tareas, la información debe ser concreta y no demasiada extensa.
6. ***Control del usuario:*** El portal le permitirá al usuario deshacer opciones seleccionadas al realizar una tarea sin que tenga que cancelar el proceso para volverlo a ejecutar.
7. ***Interfaz atractiva:*** El portal debe ser accedido desde cualquier navegador, el color, estilo y tipo de letra deben mantenerse en todo el portal, la información presentada debe ser actual, precisa y relevante, enlaces operativos y funcionales, la galería de imágenes debe contener fotos de alta resolución, los videos deben tener una correcta audición y visualización, el usuario debe saber dónde se encuentra dentro del portal, apariencia agradable y sencilla
8. ***Flexibilidad y eficiencia en el uso:*** Para realizar una tarea el usuario puede hacerlo de diferentes maneras ya sea utilizando las opciones del menú o mediante un mapa del lugar turístico. Por ejemplo, si ponemos el mapa de la provincia de Pichincha-Ecuador con sus cantones al dar click en uno de ellos se visualizará las parroquias urbanas y rurales, al escoger una parroquia, el portal presentará fotos,

videos y un mapa geo-referencial en donde se encuentra detallado los sitios turísticos, paseos, actividades de ocio, restaurantes y hoteles.

9. ***Recuperación de errores:*** Los mensajes de error deben tener un lenguaje claro y simple, presentando de forma precisa el problema y posibles soluciones.
10. ***Satisfacción en el uso del portal:*** Grado de cumplimiento y satisfacción al usar el portal de turismo.

7 Conclusiones y trabajos futuros

En la presente investigación se analizó la característica de usabilidad y el modelo de uso del estándar ISO/IEC 9126, con la finalidad de proponer un mecanismo de evaluación de usabilidad para portales de turismo. Lo que permitió identificar la forma más adecuada de cumplimiento de los siguientes criterios de usabilidad: visión del sitio, circuitos turísticos, actividades de un lugar turístico, entrada y salida de información comprensible, ayuda y documentación, control del usuario, interfaz atractiva, flexibilidad y eficiencia en el uso, recuperación de errores y satisfacción en el uso del portal. Criterios que deberían ser tomados en cuenta en el diseño e implementación de un portal de turismo.

Resultado de la investigación se presenta un cuadro comparativo de los valores obtenidos por cada métrica y portal analizado, así como también un conjunto de criterios a tomar en cuenta al momento de diseñar e implementar un portal de turismo.

Como trabajos futuros se plantea establecer criterios de usabilidad de portales web en otros ámbitos como educativo, comercial, gubernamental. Para lo cual se podrían utilizar otros modelos de calidad.

Referencias

1. Cervera, *El modelo de McCall como aplicación de la calidad a la revisión del software de gestión empresarial.* Dpto. organización de Empresas Núñez moraleda, bernardo M, depto lenguajes y sistemas informáticos, universidad Cádiz, 2000.
2. Estayno, M.G., et al. *Modelos y Métricas para evaluar Calidad de Software.* in *XI Workshop de Investigadores en Ciencias de la Computación.* 2009.
3. Navarro, J.M. and J. Garzás, *Experiencia en la implantación de CMMI-DEV v1. 2 en una micropyme con metodologías ágiles y software libre.* Revistas española de innovación, calidad e ingeniería del software, 2010. 6(1): p. 6-15.
4. Nielsen, J., *Usability engineering*1994: Elsevier.
5. Torrente, M.d.C.S., D.D.J.M.C. Lovelle, and D.D.A.B.M. Prieto, *SIRIUS: Sistema de Evaluación de la Usabilidad Web Orientado al Usuario y basado en la Determinación de Tareas Críticas*, 2011, Ph. D. Universidad de Oviedo, España.
6. Perurena Cancio, L. and M. Moráguez Bergues, *Usabilidad de los sitios Web, los métodos y las técnicas para la evaluación.* Revista Cubana de Información en Ciencias de la Salud, 2013. 24(2): p. 176-194.
7. Guedez, F., A. Gómez, and M. Numa, *DISEÑO DE UN SISTEMA DE INFORMACIÓN GEOGRAFICO PARA LAS MICROAREAS.* Universidad&Ciencia, 2017. 3(1).

8. Muñoz-Egido, D. and M.V. Osti, *Evaluación de usabilidad de los portales web de las bibliotecas universitarias españolas a partir de un modelo heurístico cognitivo-emocional.* Revista española de Documentación Científica, 2017. **40**(1): p. 165.
9. Kan, S.H., *Metrics and models in software quality engineering*2002: Addison-Wesley Longman Publishing Co., Inc.
10. Jácome, S., *Propuesta de un modelo de evaluación y mejora de los procesos de ingeniería en el desarrollo de software para la empresa Icono Sistemas*, 2012, LATACUNGA/ESPE/2012.
11. Jung, H.-W., S.-G. Kim, and C.-S. Chung, *Measuring software product quality: A survey of ISO/IEC 9126.* IEEE software, 2004. 21(5): p. 88-92.
12. Carvallo, J.P. and X. Franch. *Extending the ISO/IEC 9126-1 quality model with non-technical factors for COTS components selection.* in *Proceedings of the 2006 international workshop on Software quality*. 2006. ACM.
13. Bhatti, S.N., *Why quality?: ISO 9126 software quality metrics (Functionality) support by UML suite.* ACM SIGSOFT Software Engineering Notes, 2005. **30**(2): p. 1-5.
14. Muñoz, C.C., M.G.P. Velthuis, and M.Á.M. de la Rubia, *Calidad del producto y proceso software*2010: Editorial Ra-Ma.
15. del Turismo, D.M., A.D.L.L.Y. DESIGNACiÓN, and D.L.P. ANFITRIONES, *Organización Mundial del Turismo.* 2011.
16. Intelligence, W.T.O.M. and P. Section, *UNWTO world tourism barometer*. Vol. 5. 2007: World Tourism Organization.
17. Obeso, M.E.A., J.M.C. Lovelle, and A.B.M. Prieto, *Metodología de medición y evaluación de la usabilidad en sitios web educativos*2005: Universidad de Oviedo.
18. Salazar Grandes, M.C., *Diseño e implementación de una plataforma Web Open Source para E-Turismo en la oficina de Gestión y Promoción Turística de Cotopaxi*, 2015, Universidad de las Fuerzas Armadas ESPE. Vicerrectorado de Investigación, Innovación y Transferencia de Tecnología.
19. https://measuringu.com/10-things-sus/.

Conceptions of the students around object-oriented design: A case study

Pamela Flores[1], Nelson Medinilla[2]

[1] Departamento de Informática y Ciencias de la Computación, Escuela Politécnica Nacional, Quito, Ecuador.
[2] Departamento de Lenguajes y Sistemas Informáticos e Ingeniería de Software, Universidad Politécnica de Madrid, Madrid, España
pamela.flores@epn.edu.ec
nelson@fi.upm.es

Abstract. Software design has had several perspectives in terms of approaches, one of them is the object-oriented approach, that is currently used in both industry and academia. However, until now this approach shows difficulties at the moment of implement an efficient software development. This study was conducted in the world of academia in order to clarify the foundations of software design, which the students have, through of a qualitative case study in the Software Engineering subject. As a result, we have found some misunderstandings related with concepts like inheritance, object, software design and the overvaluation of the coding respect to designing.

Keywords: object-oriented design, conceptions of students, qualitative case study

1 Introduction

Object-oriented design is today one of the most used approaches in the industry and one of the mandatory topics taught in academia. However, several studies reveal that there are difficulties when designing under this approach [2, 4, 15, 16]. Many of the difficulties lie in the lack of understanding of essential elements of object-oriented software design such as Abstraction, Inheritance, Object, Class, Encapsulation, etc. [1]. Others reveal that the lack of differentiation between prior approaches such as the structured approach may be negatively influencing students [2].

The aim of this research is to know the ideas that the students have about designing with objects before they started a module corresponding to this topic.

The following research question guides our study: *What do software design students understand about concepts around object-oriented design*?

The paper is organized as follows, Section 2 describes some related work, Section 3 show the methodology, Section 4 presents the qualitative research and Section 5 presents a discussion of the work, and finally Section 6 presents the conclusions and future work.

2 Related Work

The main objective of this study is to know the initial perception of the students around different concepts of object-oriented approach (OO). However, other authors have gone in search of fundamental concepts in OO. One of them is the one made by Debora Armstrong [1], who argues that the difficulty of learning OO can be rooted in the lack of understanding of concepts such as inheritance, object, classes, encapsulation, method, etc. These concepts were extracted through an exhaustive literary review.

In [11], the authors focus on what concepts are presented to first-year students, who are learning object-oriented programming; the study analyzes the assignments of the students, field notes, observations, audio and video recordings. Sanders et al. [13], studies the technical programs in which a group of students enrolls; this qualitative study aims to identify concepts and misconceptions in object-oriented programming.

Sally at. Al [6], identifies possible threshold concepts through interviews, focus groups and workshops with students, tutors and academics. The merit of this work is to use a qualitative approach, but in a very broad scope such as engineering. Finally, a research was done by the authors of this research where it focuses mainly on the understanding of the Information Hiding Principle [2], whose contribution is both conceptual and methodological.

The contribution of this study focuses on to know what kind of ideas have the students regarding object-oriented design before and during an instruction.

3 Methodology

Learning is a complex phenomenon difficult to study. In order to discover the understanding of the students around software design concepts in the students, we have applied a qualitative approach.

In order to apply this methodology, we have chosen the qualitative case study, since it is characterized by descriptions and intensive analyzes of a single object of social research, for example a classroom [8, 14].

For this qualitative case study, two techniques were used: the survey and interview. Qualitative data were quantified, not in order to generalize, but rather with the idea of visualizing the results. The interview, allowed to know in detail the understanding of the students and these data were treated in a qualitative way.

4 Qualitative research

This section will describe the context of the case study, the stages by which it was formed and a description of how the analysis of the data obtained was developed.

4.1 Context

The subject chosen for this case study was Software Engineering, belonging to the sixth semester of the Degree of Informatics Engineering. This subject contains 4 modules, which were given by different professors throughout the semester. This study was carried out on the third module called "Software Design".

Most students are in a range from 21-25. All the students were of different nationalities. For the majority of students, it was the first time that they had studied this subject and they have not taken courses related to software design. Everyone knows at least one programming language.

The initial number of students was 18, who answered an initial survey and exposed to participate in voluntary way in the study and also collaborated with a personal interview.

4.2 Qualitative case study

In a qualitative analysis, the researcher attempts to capture data on the perceptions of local actors "from within" through processes of deep understanding, leaving aside their preconceptions. The investigator is the main "mechanism" of measurement in the qualitative type study [3]. Below, we show the process of analysis of the data extrac-ted from the students.

- Data analysis.

The objective of this study was to know the initial ideas of the concepts related to object-oriented design. For getting this goal, an initial survey was conducted, the same that was answered by the 18 students who attended the first day of class. The survey consisted of 9 questions. After digitizing the answers, they were transcribed. Subsequently, parts of the answer that were removed from the question were eliminated, to finally refine it in simpler sentences. One color was assigned for each similar or rela-ted response, and different colors for different responses. Similar colors were grouped, to obtain the number of people who responded in a similar way and how many did not. In this way we obtained the categories that are shown below with each question.

- Survey

An initial survey of 10 questions was carried out that aimed to know in general terms the ideas and knowledge about object-oriented design. The survey was conducted in the second week of the module. Later in the final weeks, an interview was made to the participants, who voluntarily signed up in the last question of the survey. The objective of the interview was to research in depth the origins of the phenomenon observed in the survey and throughout the module. The relevance of the responses has been sorted from largest and smallest.

Analysis of survey by question

Question 1. What do you think a software object serves? The most relevant answers were "Cover a need" and "Solve a problem", followed by "Create easy software" and "Provide functionalities".

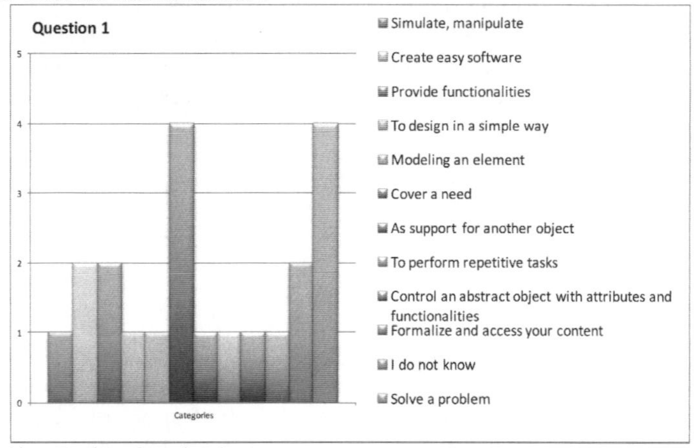

Fig. 1. Chart Design, Question 1

Question 2. On what occasions or why would you create a software object? The most relevant answers were "Because it is easier and intuitive" followed by "Create programs with functions and applications".

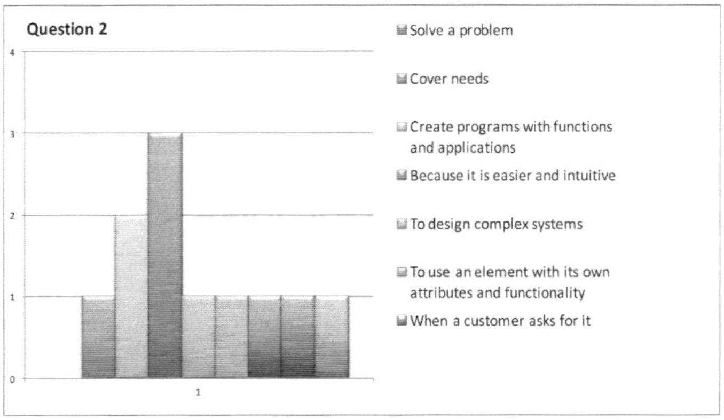

Fig. 2. Chart Design, Question 2

Question 3. For you, what is the difference between real objects and software objects? "The most relevant answer was "Real object is tangible and software object is abstract".

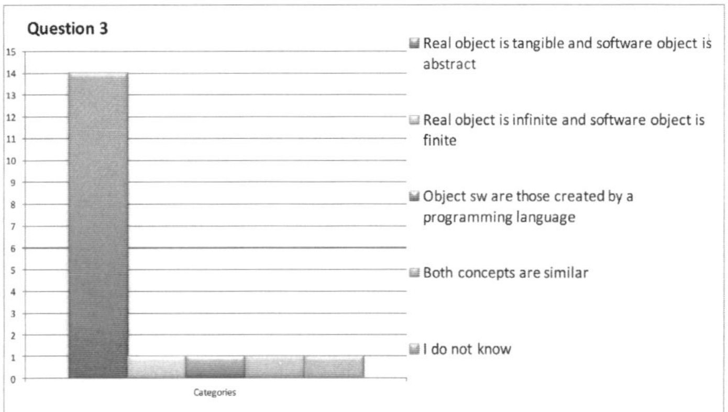

Fig. 3. Chart Design, Question 3

Question 4. What does it mean for you to design software systems? The most relevant answers were "To troubleshoot issues" and "It is the structure with the characterristics and functionalities of the system".

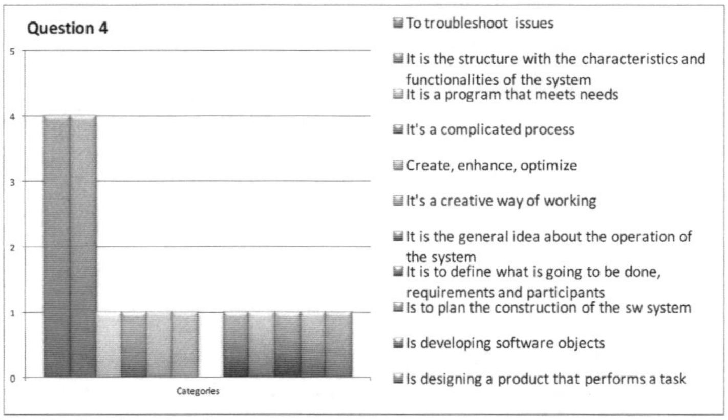

Fig. 4. Chart Design, Question 4

Question 5. Could you mention some methodology for designing software systems? The most relevant answers were "Waterfall" and "Spiral", followed by "Object oriented design" and "Structured design".

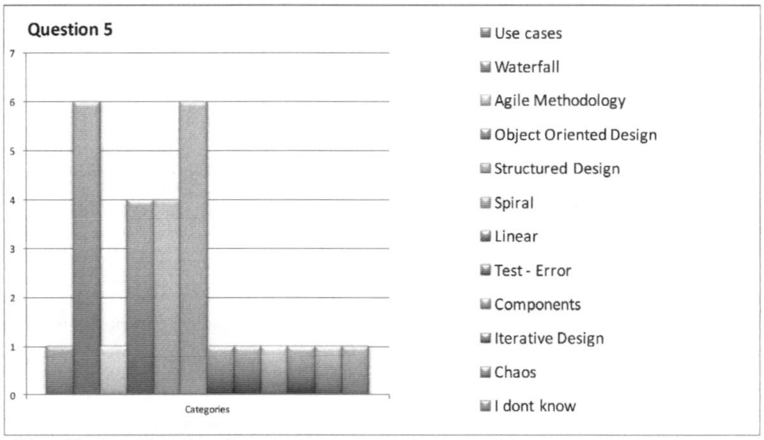

Fig. 5. Chart Design, Question 5

Question 6. What is the difficulty that you find when designing software systems? The most relevant answers were "Meet and understand the requirements" and "Where and how to start".

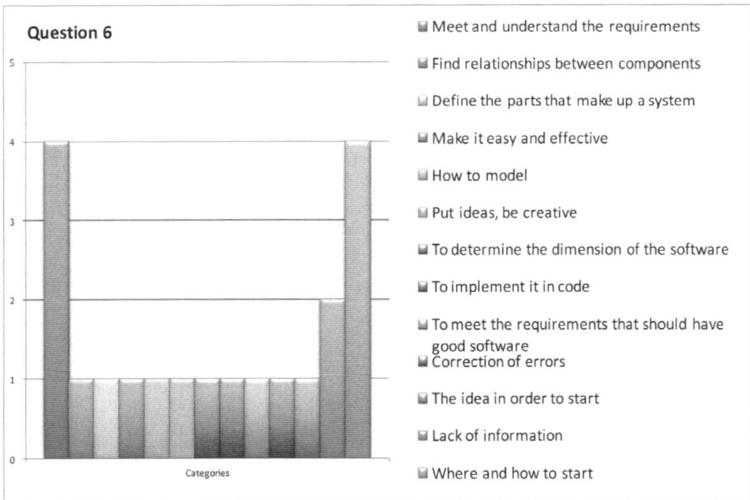

Fig. 6. Chart Design, Question 6

Question 7. Do you think that to code a system it is necessary to have a previous design? The most relevant answers were "Yes, because it is necessary to have a basic or previous design", followed by "Depending on the complexity or size of the system" and "Yes, because it facilitates further implementation".

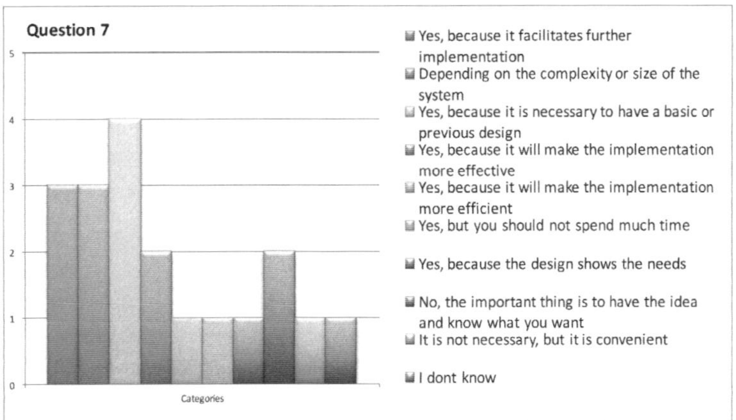

Fig. 7. Chart Design, Question 7

Question 8. According to your criteria, could you design a software system without knowing how to program? The most relevant answers were "Yes, because one thing is to design and another is to program" followed by" Yes, provided that certain parameters or requirements are known".

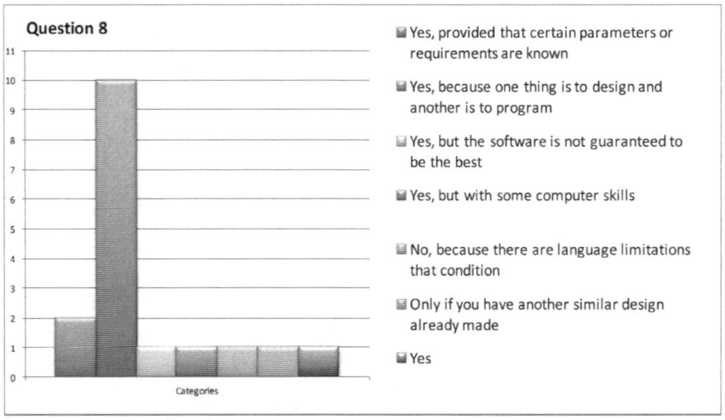

Fig. 8. Chart Design, Question 8

Question 9. From your point of view how can you tell if a design is good or bad? Relevant responses were "It is good, if it meets the requirements and expectations proposed by the client," followed by "It is good if it is efficient and effective".

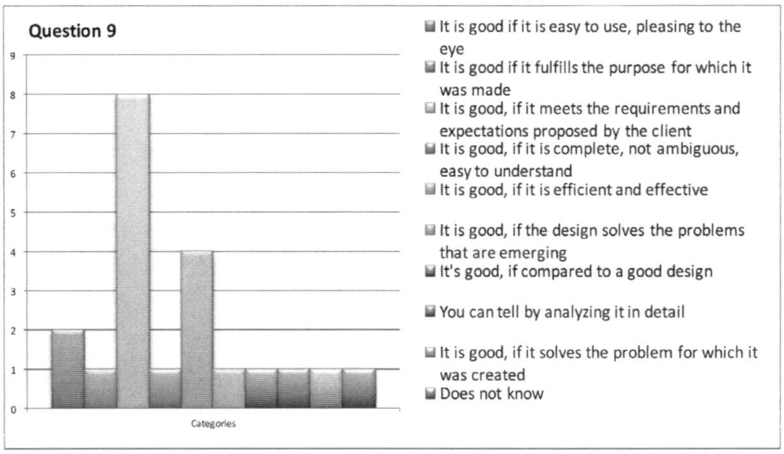

Fig. 9. Chart Design, Question 9

– Interview

The interview was conducted with open question. The main questions were focused on talking about the object-oriented design, objects, difficulties in the concepts and also, about the understanding around the Information Hiding Principle [9], because the professor put a particular emphasis on that. And finally, the student was asked which strategy helped him the most in learning.

Analysis of interview

The interview is another technique of a qualitative research, which had as objective to know the perceptions of the students around the subject. We have extracted the most relevant responses of the interview within of four categories, which show below:

Related with Inheritance

- Inheritance is the way to convey properties or common sense to a series of related objects. Way to simplify the code, to regroup under the same flag.
- To introduce ambiguity
- When a child object of the father, obtains everything that the father
- Creation of dependence

Related with objects

- Software objects to represent both real and abstract objects.

Related with software design

- To design trying that they were adaptable and simple, all according to its criteria.
- The concepts related to software design are adaptability and modularity.
- To try to throw in small things in problems easier to tackle or small modules, although that also does in structured approach.
- One of the most difficult concepts was the Information Hiding Principle since it was not known when to use it.
- The concepts related with designing would be modularity and ambiguity.
- The concepts that come to his mind are related with the structure, classes and their relationships. The most difficult area to assimilate is patterns.
- The idea that the scheduling is more important than knowing how to design.
- To conceiving the code is a way of designing. If the code is good, then the design is good.
- The importance of minimizing the dependencies between the parts. There is a little confusion with the Information Hiding Principle.
- To know how many objects to create or not to create.
- The most difficult thing is to define the parts of which he will be composed and thinks that depending on the complexity of the system, a prior design is more or less necessary.
- The concepts of modularization are understood
- The idea of the importance of being able to see different ways of solving a problem and to see possible solutions through design.
- Difficulty in understanding the concepts of pass messages between different objects and how to make it more reusable.

Related with learning and teaching

- The student would like to see the professor develop a complex model correctly. Designing the models on the board seems interesting as you learn from others.
- The activity more productive is the fact of drawing the designs to the board and commenting on them all. Correcting another partner is not so good because you are not sure if it corrects itself well.
- The student believes that the best strategy to learn is to show examples made by the professor, or see the designs made by his peers on the board.
- The way he learns is by looking at examples of software design.
- The strategy that works best is to analyze on the board the designs of colleagues. Correcting another partner is not so good because he is not sure if it is correct.

5 Discussion

For the elaboration of the qualitative study, the previous pilot studies were taken into in account, for example videos, analysis of tasks and observations. We have taken this experience and material in order to elaborate the initial survey. Among the most difficult concepts to define are Uncertainty and to implement the Information Hiding Principle. On the other hand, a learning strategy that has greater acceptance within students, is when they show their designs on the board and is criticized by all, included the professor.

As an activity that was not more welcome was correcting the work of other students or being corrected by other students, does not give confidence because they do not believe they have the best criteria that the professor in order to correct or to be corrected.

Finally, the Information Hiding Principle was not assimilated as a design criteria and it was difficult for the students could visualize the Principle at the moment of designing software and their meaning. Finally, the Information Hiding Principle was not assimilated as a design criteria and it was difficult for the students could visualize the Principle at the moment of designing software and additionally their meaning was not clear for them. This is comparable with author of the Principle, who said in 2002: "The Principle is easy to understand, and difficult to implement" [10].

Within the study, some misunderstandings were mentioned:

- In question number 8: In your opinion, can you design a software system without knowing how to program? Most students were agree that both things are separate and can be done independently but when asked in question 6 : "What is the difficulty you encounter when designing a system?, the students mention the difficulty in coding and the code errors that arise. This shows us a certain contradiction with question number 8, since it can be evidenced, because of the students directly associate codification with design, although they think they are different things. We think that this result could be related with the structured approach, where the analysis and design are very clearly separated [7].

- Also, in question 8, there are ideas from some students that the fact of designing must begin with a very clear idea, and for this reason it is necessary to thinking very well, it must from the first instance be known the magnitude of what is going to be done, being totally the opposite because many times Software Design gets it based on approximations.
- Some students answer the question related to software objects and real objects. The response most accepted was that both are the same. This thought could come from of the idea around that the software objects must be a reflection of real objects, which is not necessarily true [10, 12].
- Many students think that creating objects is easier and more intuitive, and makes work easier. But really designing software with objects is often more complex and you need to invest more time and thought to design under this approach.
- It can be seen under question 6, that most students think that the requirements must be very clear and well defined from the beginning, since this depends on the rest of the steps, this is not easy to conceive because the requirements are almost never well-defined explicitly and are appearing throughout the design and during the time. For this reason, there are many methodologies that are being successful, such as Agile Methodology, which is more flexible in terms of requirements and other processes [5].
- Finally, it is good to mention that this study was conducted previously to a formal empirical research. This study permitted to conceive a long term research; this can be seen in [19].

6 Conclusions and future work

The research question conducted for this study was: "*What do software design students understand about concepts around object-oriented design*?" and it was answered through a qualitative case study.

Many students start the module with ideas like that the object-oriented design is not as important as coding. Some students ignore basic principles of design such as the Information Hiding Principle and concepts such as object, inheritance, ambiguity, etc.

In a future work, it will be important to take into in account the influence over the students around paradigms studied before, like structured approach.

From this qualitative case study, we can appreciate that the software design has been underestimated in previous subjects during its instruction, although finished the module, the understanding was better and the students took more value of making a previous design.

Our results are encouraging and should be validated in a long-term study. These findings are promising and should be explored with another technique like model mental or cognitive studies. In a future work, it will be important to take into in account the influence over the students around previous approaches.

References

1. D. Armstrong. The quarks of object-oriented development. Communications of the ACM, 49(2):123–128, 2006.
2. P. Flores, N. Medinilla, and S. Pamplona. What do software design students? understand about information hiding? A qualitative case study. In Proceedings of the 14th Koli Calling International Conference on Computing Education Research, Koli Calling '14, pages 61–70, New York, NY, USA, 2014. ACM.
3. M. Huberman and M. Miles. The qualitative researcher's companion. Sage, 2002.
4. L. Kaczmarczyk, E. Petrick, P. East, and G. Herman. Identifying student misconceptions of programming. In Proceedings of the 41st ACM Technical Symposium on Computer Science Education, SIGCSE '10, pages 107–111. ACM, 2010.
5. J. Lpez-Martnez, R. Jurez-Ramrez, C. Huertas, S. Jimnez, and C. Guerra-Garca. Problems in the adoption of agile-scrum methodologies: A systematic literature review. In 2016 4th International Conference in Software Engineering Research and Innovation (CONISOFT), pages 141–148, April 2016.
6. S. A. Male and C. A. Baillie. Engineering threshold concepts. In Proceedings of SEFI Annual Conference, Lisbon, 2011.
7. N. Medinilla. Elementos para el anlisis de mtodos de ingeniera del software segn su complejidad de incertidumbre. PhD thesis, Boadilla del Monte, Madrid, Spain, 2008.
8. S. Merriam. Qualitative Research and Case Study Applications in Education. Re- vised and Expanded from" Case Study Research in Education. ERIC, 1998.
9. D. Parnas. On the criteria to be used in decomposing systems into modules.
10. Commun. ACM, 15(12):1053–1058, Dec. 1972.
11. D. Parnas. The secret history of information hiding. In Software pioneers, pages 398–409. Springer, 2002.
12. N. Ragonis and M. Ben-Ari. A long-term investigation of the comprehension of oop concepts by novices. 2005.
13. M. B. Rosson and S. Alpert. The cognitive consequences of object-oriented design.
14. Hum. -Comput. Interact., 5(4):345–379, Dec 1990.
15. K. Sanders and L. Thomas. Checklists for grading object-oriented cs1 programs: concepts and misconceptions. In ACM SIGCSE Bulletin, volume 39, pages 166– 170. ACM, 2007.
16. J. Seidel. Qualitative data analysis. 1998.
17. T. Sirkia¨ and J. Sorva. Exploring programming misconceptions: an analysis of student mistakes in visual program simulation exercises. In Proceedings of the 12th Koli Calling International Conference on Computing Education Research, pages 19–28. ACM, 2012.
18. S. Xinogalos. Object-oriented design and programming: An investigation of novice es’ conceptions on objects and classes. Trans. Comput. Educ., 15(3):13:1–13:21, July 2015.
19. Pamela Flores, Nelson Medinilla, and Sonia Pamplona. 2016. Persistent Ideas in a Software Design Course: A Qualitative Case Study. International Journal of Engineering Education 32, 2 (2016), 937–947.

Influence of Using Specialized Software In The Automotive Industry To Boost Internal Combustion Engines

Germán Erazo[1], Alexandra Corral[1], Leonidas Quiroz[1], Luis Mena[1], José Quiroz[1], Danilo Zambrano[1], and Darwin Semanate[1]

[1] Universidad de las Fuerzas Armadas ESPE, Departamento de Ciencias de la Energía y Mecánica, Latacunga, Ecuador
wgerazo@espe.edu.ec, macorral@espe.edu.ec, laquiroz@espe.edu.ec, lamena@espe.edu.ec, jlquiroz@espe.edu.ec, vdzambrano@espe.edu.ec, dasemanate@espe.edu.ec.
http://www.espe.edu.ec

Abstract. The application of specialized software in the automotive industry is becoming more extensive, through computational programs applied in the systems of electronic control of vehicle are obtained improvements in the mechanical systems. With the use of dedicated software implemented in the computer that controls the internal combustion engine, the parameters of mechanical performance such as power and torque are raised, pollution is reduced. Cartographies, three-dimensional maps of the injection and switched on system of the manufacturer's base program are obtained and analyzed, modifying sectors of relevance, the experimentation and laboratory tests in standard and repowered conditions are performed, that ratify the feasibility to obtain improvements in the performance of the motor of internal combustion through modifications by software without having developed modifications of mechanical type.

Keywords: automotive industry, internal combustion engines, software

1 Introducción

La ingeniería del software influye de manera directa en las aplicaciones de la ingeniería automotriz optimizando el desempeño de los sistemas electrónicos y mecánicos del automóvil a través de la programación y reprogramación de su sistema informático a través del uso de software específico y dedicado.

La investigación trata sobre la modificación y calibración del software que se utiliza en las unidades de control electrónica para obtener la variación de los parámetros de desempeño del motor de combustión interna sin realizar modificaciones de tipo mecánico.

La programación y calibración de los parámetros que recibe como información la unidad de control electrónico es esencial en el proceso de desarrollo de los motores de combustión interna [1],[2] para obtener el ajuste de emisiones adecuado cuando se modifica el tiempo de inyección y encendido. La automatización y la calibración basada en modelos computacionales ha generado una solución importante en el desempeño del motor, ya que se reduce al máximo el uso de prototipos o bancos de pruebas[3],[4]. Estos requisitos excluyen en la mayoría de los casos el modelado físico se prefieren los métodos de aproximación matemática, para describir el comportamiento del motor o del vehículo [5].

Las funciones mecánicas son optimizadas con funciones de software considerados patrones de innovación potencial en la industria automotriz de nuevos productos ya que son diversos y ampliamente difundidos en los sistemas de vehículos [6], van desde software de control de bajo nivel hasta sistemas avanzados de asistencia al conductor, de información y mantenimiento. Son altamente interactivos y distribuidos a lo largo de varias unidades de control electrónico conectadas en red, más del 80% de las innovaciones en la industria del automóvil se realizan mediante software intensivo.

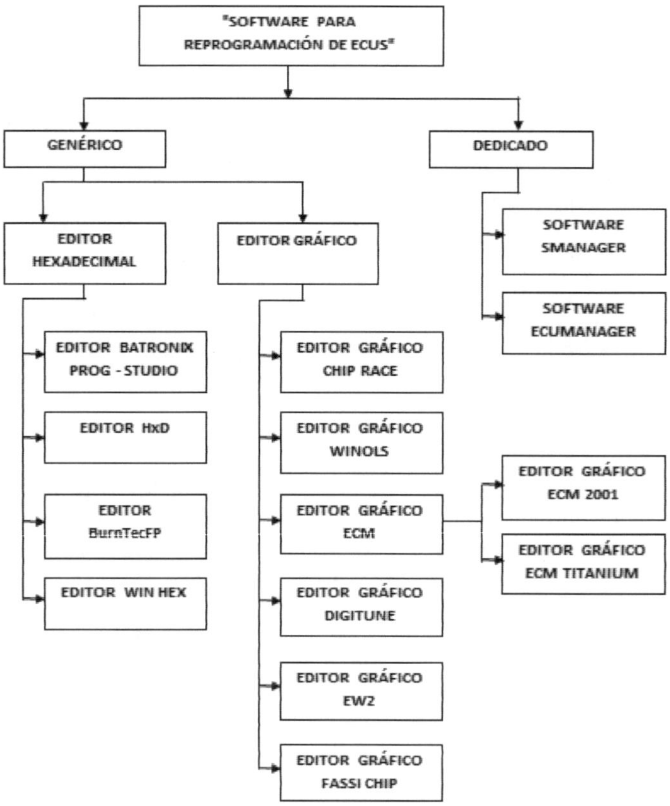

Fig. 1. Clasificación del software utilizado en la industria automotriz

La industria automotriz asocia una variedad de tipos de software como se presenta en la Fig. 1, se utilizan para programar y reprogramar diferentes memorias que se implementan en las unidades de control o computadoras automotrices. El software genérico se emplea en diversos tipos de memorias utiliza editores hexadecimales o gráficos, entre tanto el software dedicado es específicos para un sector de marcas de memorias y vehículos [7].

La unidad de control electrónica o ECU automotriz dispone de memorias de almacenamiento y procesamiento de datos de las variables que influyen en el motor de combustión interna. La memoria RAM es de tipo volátil, la información se elimina al perder su energía. La memoria ROM es donde se almacena el software de operación del sistema esta no es volátil, la memoria PROM, EPROM son programables, disponen de información referente a parámetros de corte de combustible, temperatura de arranque en frío y parámetros de diseño del vehículo.

La información que se dispone en las memorias, son utilizados por el microprocesador para determinar las condiciones de operación y estado de funcionamiento de actuadores. Este proceso se realiza a elevada velocidad, inalcanzable de interpretar por el ser humano. Esto significa que para cada conjunto de datos recibidos de los distintos sensores la ECU analiza la mejor alternativa para ese instante [8]. Por lo tanto se tiene como datos validos las direcciones en las memorias, que serán de mayor a menor cantidad dependiendo de su capacidad como se expresa en la Tabla 1

Tabla 1. Capacidad de memoria, tamaño en bytes y posición

Capacidad de las memorias (Kb)	Tamaño (Bytes)	Posiciones hexadecimales
256	32768	0000 - 7FFF
512	65536	0000 – FFFF
1024	131072	0000 - 1FFFF
2048	262144	0000 - 3FFFF
4096	524288	0000 - 7FFFF
8192	1048576	0000 – FFFFF

2 Metodología Para La Reprogramación De La Unidad De Control Electrónico.

[9] Los mapas de inyección de combustible y avance al encendido del motor de combustión interna se refieren a tablas numéricas de valores y cartografías que generan gráficos en tres dimensiones en los ejes de (x,y,z). Las cartografías son introducidas en la unidad de control por el fabricante en función de las lecturas de las variables para determinar el mapa más lógico de acuerdo a la potencia y torque requeridos.

[13]Con esas consideraciones se selecciona los métodos y técnicas que combinados con el uso de los diferentes recursos tecnológicos permitieron recopilar la información de relevancia de la influencia del uso del software en la industria automotriz.

El método inductivo y deductivo orientan de modo significativo el desarrollo de la reprogramación de la unidad de control electrónico que utiliza una memoria programable, generando resultados finales combinados con la experimentación y observación de acuerdo a la modificación del software del fabricante implementada en la misma que permitió verificar los la elevación de los valores potencia y torque con el uso del equipo dinamométrico [12].

A través del método analítico se definió las variaciones que se presentaron en los parámetros característicos del motor de combustión interna y emisiones que se produjeron tanto al trabajar con la cartografía y mapa tridimensional del fabricante como con la personalizada las mismas que se sintetizaron en la modificación del sistema de inyección y avance al encendido a través del software SManager, generando información para ser utilizada en calibraciones futuras de la unidad de control electrónico por medio de la reprogramación, se analizó y revisó cada uno por separado, para obtener resultados finales .

Utilizando equipos de medición y pruebas como el dinamómetro de rodillos, analizador de gases previamente calibrados se realizó la experimentación para validar la confiabilidad de la modificación del software sin haber realizado cambios de tipo mecánico centrándose en la comparación de los resultados finales, cartografías y mapas tridimensionales.

3 Reprogramación Del Control De La Inyección Y Encendido.

3.1 Cartografía y mapeo tridimensional del fabricante

La aplicación del software en la reprogramación de computadoras automotrices es notable tanto en el ámbito comercial como en el deportivo es una alternativa válida que mejorar el desempeño de los motores de combustión interna. Para iniciar la reprogramación de la unidad de control electrónica, mecánicamente el motor de combustión no debe tener ningún tipo de falla, se accede a la lectura de la memoria flash para modificar sus asignaciones de memoria con el criterio científico para posteriormente realizar pruebas de tipo dinámico [9]. Utilizando el software SManager el sistema es enlazado a través del puerto USB Fig. 2 con lo que se asegura la conexión adecuada para el procesamiento y carga de la información.

Fig. 2. Enlace de software y hardware por USB

Los mapas cartográficos de inyección y avance al encendido se basan en asignaciones de memoria agrupados en cuadriculas que representan la carga y velocidad que se aplica al motor de combustión interna, que se modifican de acuerdo a los requerimientos, en esta investigación se realiza la lectura de la cartografía de fábrica Fig. 3 y se generan dos reprogramaciones personalizadas para analizar el desempeño del motor de combustión interna y sus emisiones [15].

Col	1	2	3	4	5	6	7	8	9	10
mBar	886	714	600	485	370	256	141	84	26	30
500	18,50	18,50	18,50	18,50	13,00	8,00	3,25	0,00	-2,00	-3,00
600	18,50	18,50	18,50	18,50	13,00	8,00	3,25	0,00	-2,00	-3,00
700	18,50	18,50	18,50	18,50	13,00	8,00	3,25	0,00	-2,00	-3,00
800	18,50	18,50	18,50	18,50	13,00	8,00	3,25	0,00	-2,00	-3,00
1000	23,75	23,75	23,75	21,25	16,50	12,00	6,00	3,00	0,00	-1,00
1300	28,00	28,00	28,00	25,25	21,50	16,25	11,25	8,00	5,50	4,50
1500	30,25	30,25	30,25	28,00	24,50	19,00	12,50	9,50	7,50	7,00
1700	32,75	32,75	32,75	30,50	27,25	21,00	15,75	11,50	9,75	8,50
2000	34,50	34,50	34,50	32,25	29,25	25,00	19,50	14,75	11,50	9,50
2200	36,75	36,75	36,75	33,75	30,75	28,00	21,50	17,00	13,25	12,25
2600	40,50	40,50	40,50	37,25	34,50	31,50	25,00	21,25	16,75	15,25
2900	43,25	43,25	43,25	40,75	37,50	34,50	28,00	23,00	18,00	16,00
3000	44,00	44,00	44,00	41,75	38,50	35,50	29,75	24,75	19,75	17,25
3400	44,00	44,00	44,00	42,00	40,00	38,00	32,50	29,50	26,00	26,00
4000	44,00	44,00	44,00	42,00	40,00	38,00	34,00	31,50	28,25	28,25
4450	44,00	44,00	44,00	42,00	40,00	38,00	34,00	31,50	28,25	28,25
5000	44,75	44,75	44,75	42,75	40,75	38,75	35,00	32,75	29,25	29,25
6000	44,75	44,75	44,75	42,75	40,75	38,75	36,00	33,50	30,25	30,25
7000	44,75	44,75	44,75	42,75	40,75	38,75	36,00	33,50	30,25	30,25
8000	44,75	44,75	44,75	42,75	40,75	38,75	36,00	33,50	30,25	30,25

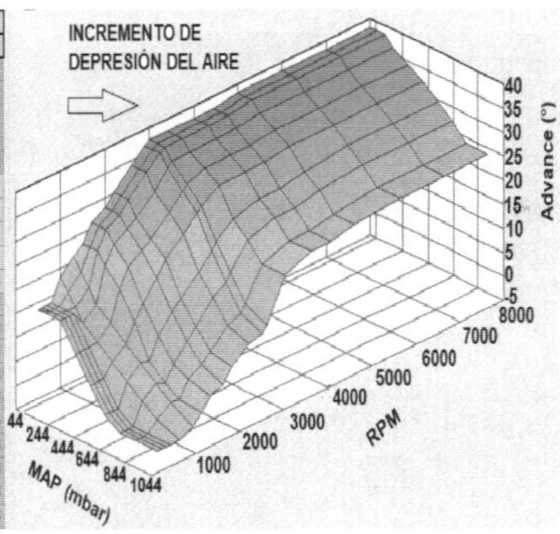

Fig. 3. Cartografía y mapa tridimensional de encendido base

3.2 Cartografia De Inyección Y Encendido Reprogramado Por Software

Los valores de funcionamiento del sistema encendido generan la cartografía y mapas tridimensionales [11] como en la Fig. 4 que representan los grados de adelanto al salto de chispa considerando el número de revoluciones, el número de grados de avance incrementa. El software identifica los valores de porciones de combustible sobre el valor límite máximo de carga en función de la depresión del aire y el número de revoluciones del motor de combustión interna.

Col	1	2	3	4	5	6	7	8	9	10
mBar	886	714	600	485	370	256	141	84	26	30
500	4	89	144	273	320	389	450	503	550	603
600	4	89	153	278	336	396	465	518	561	615
700	4	89	153	285	336	412	483	523	572	624
800	4	96	159	293	338	410	483	523	572	627
1000	4	98	165	255	315	378	450	485	531	576
1300	8	104	165	272	336	392	453	488	539	591
1500	4	99	159	263	336	378	453	488	539	591
1700	14	110	171	264	341	412	483	495	550	594
2000	16	104	162	257	322	412	483	503	558	603
2200	17	105	159	255	326	412	473	503	556	594
2600	18	113	171	273	336	419	473	520	569	606
2900	20	107	168	270	336	401	493	550	619	669
3000	20	105	165	270	338	410	495	553	619	675
3400	20	101	159	263	336	412	483	533	594	630
4000	20	110	186	288	364	428	510	550	605	651
4450	34	135	209	311	392	468	553	598	641	681
5000	54	159	244	348	429	513	593	638	671	708
6000	53	157	233	339	415	495	583	615	657	690
7000	51	155	232	339	413	493	580	613	657	690
8000	52	155	234	341	413	493	583	615	657	690

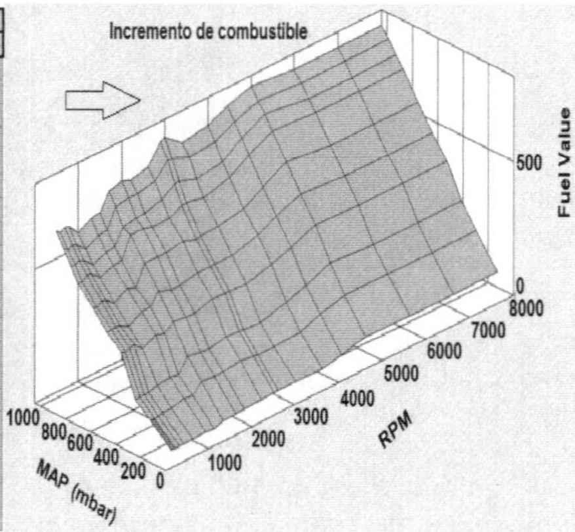

Fig. 4. Cartografía y mapa tridimensional de inyección

Las modificaciones personalizadas en los mapas de inyección y encendido están en 1500 rpm hasta 3400 rpm se muestran en la Fig. 5 que es donde se produce el torque y potencia esperado.

Col	1	2	3	4	5	6	7	8	9	10
mBar	886	714	600	485	370	256	141	84	26	30
500	18,50	18,50	18,50	18,50	13,00	8,00	3,25	0,00	-2,00	-3,00
600	18,50	18,50	18,50	18,50	13,00	8,00	3,25	0,00	-2,00	-3,00
700	18,50	18,50	18,50	18,50	13,00	8,00	3,25	0,00	-2,00	-3,00
800	18,50	18,50	18,50	18,50	13,00	8,00	3,25	0,00	-2,00	-3,00
1000	23,75	23,75	23,75	21,25	16,50	12,00	6,00	3,00	0,00	-1,00
1300	28,00	28,00	28,00	25,25	20,58	15,92	11,25	8,00	5,50	4,50
1500	30,25	30,25	30,25	32,00	26,83	21,67	16,50	9,50	7,50	7,00
1700	32,75	32,75	32,75	34,50	31,25	25,00	19,75	11,50	9,75	8,50
2000	34,50	34,50	34,50	36,25	33,25	29,00	23,50	14,75	11,50	9,50
2200	36,75	36,75	36,75	37,75	34,75	32,00	25,50	17,00	13,25	12,25
2600	40,50	40,50	40,50	41,25	38,50	35,50	29,00	21,25	16,75	15,25
2900	43,25	43,25	43,25	44,75	41,50	38,50	32,00	23,00	18,00	16,00
3000	44,00	44,00	44,00	45,75	42,50	39,50	33,75	24,75	19,75	17,25
3400	44,00	44,00	44,00	46,00	42,83	39,67	36,50	29,50	26,00	26,00
4000	44,00	44,00	44,00	42,00	39,33	36,67	34,00	31,50	28,25	28,25
4450	44,00	44,00	44,00	42,00	40,00	38,00	34,00	31,50	28,25	28,25
5000	44,75	44,75	44,75	42,75	40,75	38,75	35,00	32,75	29,25	29,25
6000	44,75	44,75	44,75	42,75	40,75	38,75	36,00	33,50	30,25	30,25
7000	44,75	44,75	44,75	42,75	40,75	38,75	36,00	33,50	30,25	30,25
8000	44,75	44,75	44,75	42,75	40,75	38,75	36,00	33,50	30,25	30,25

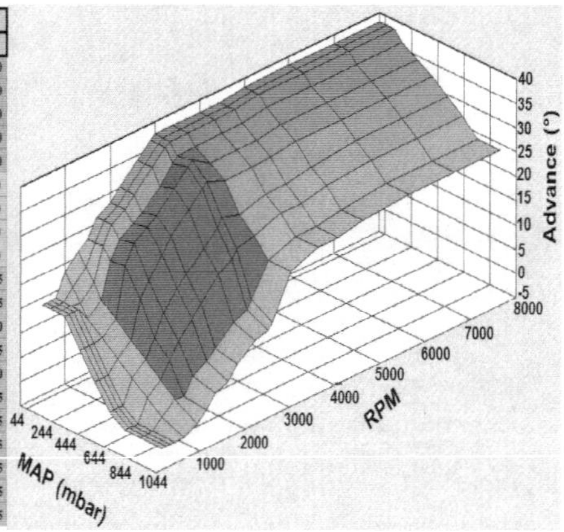

Fig. 5. Cartografía y mapa tridimensional encendido I reprogramación

Con el software SManager se modifica los grados de avance al encendido dependiendo de la necesidad del usuario, para la aplicación este sector del mapa se incrementó 4° en el encendido y en un 5% de inyección de combustible con lo que se mejora la combustión y se eleva el torque y potencia. La cartografía y el mapa tridimensional del primer ajuste de software en la ecu está en la Fig. 6 que corresponde a la inyección de combustible ajustada en función a la depresión generada por el motor de combustión interna cuando su velocidad aumenta.

Col	1	2	3	4	5	6	7	8	9	10
mBar	886	714	600	485	370	256	141	84	26	30
500	4	89	144	273	320	389	450	503	550	603
600	4	89	153	278	336	396	465	518	561	615
700	4	89	153	285	336	412	483	523	572	624
800	4	96	159	293	338	410	483	523	572	627
1000	4	98	165	255	315	378	450	485	531	576
1300	8	104	165	272	326	380	434	488	539	591
1500	4	99	159	276	335	394	453	512	539	591
1700	14	110	171	277	358	432	507	520	550	594
2000	16	104	162	269	338	432	507	528	558	603
2200	17	105	157	268	342	432	496	528	556	594
2600	18	113	171	287	353	439	496	546	596	606
2900	20	107	168	284	353	421	517	578	619	669
3000	20	105	165	284	355	430	520	580	619	675
3400	20	101	159	276	347	417	488	559	594	630
4000	20	110	186	288	354	419	485	550	605	651
4450	34	135	209	311	392	468	553	598	641	681
5000	54	159	244	348	429	513	593	638	671	708
6000	53	157	233	339	415	495	583	615	657	690
7000	51	155	232	339	413	493	580	613	657	690
8000	52	155	234	341	413	493	583	615	657	690

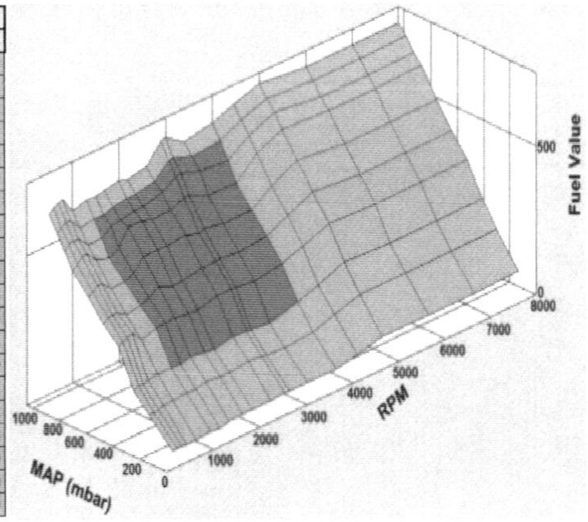

Fig. 6 Cartografía y mapa tridimensional de inyección I reprogramación"

Existe el incremento de combustible cuando se produce el adelanto o retraso al encendido caso contrario se pierde eficiencia al no existir una mezcla correcta de aire – combustible, por lo que se espera combustionar más cantidad de mezcla para producir un mayor índice de potencia y torque en el motor [15]. Para la segunda experimentación de la reprogramación, Fig. 7 se incrementa 3° de avance al encendido, para elevar el torque a velocidades de 800 rpm a 1300 rpm, cuando se eleva en 2° se observa la modificación del sector y la mejora el desempeño mecánico

Col	1	2	3	4	5	6	7	8	9	10
mBar	886	714	600	485	370	256	141	84	26	30
500	18,50	18,50	18,50	18,50	13,00	8,00	3,25	0,00	-2,00	-3,00
600	18,50	18,50	18,50	18,50	13,00	8,00	3,25	0,00	-2,00	-3,00
700	18,50	18,50	18,50	14,80	11,10	7,40	3,70	0,00	-2,00	-3,00
800	18,50	18,50	21,50	17,80	14,10	10,40	6,70	3,00	-2,00	-3,00
1000	23,75	23,75	26,75	24,25	19,50	15,00	9,00	6,00	0,00	-1,00
1300	28,00	28,00	31,00	28,25	24,50	19,25	14,25	11,00	5,50	4,50
1500	30,25	30,25	34,25	32,00	28,50	23,00	16,50	13,50	7,50	7,00
1700	32,75	32,75	36,75	34,50	31,25	25,00	19,75	15,50	9,75	8,50
2000	34,50	34,50	38,50	36,25	33,25	29,00	23,50	18,75	11,50	9,50
2200	36,75	36,75	40,75	37,75	34,75	32,00	25,50	21,00	13,25	12,25
2600	40,50	40,50	44,50	41,25	38,50	35,50	29,00	25,25	16,75	15,25
2900	43,25	43,25	47,25	44,75	41,50	38,50	32,00	27,00	18,00	16,00
3000	44,00	44,00	48,00	45,75	42,50	39,50	33,75	28,75	19,75	17,25
3400	44,00	44,00	46,00	44,00	40,00	40,00	34,50	31,50	26,00	26,00
4000	44,00	44,00	46,00	44,00	40,00	40,00	36,00	33,50	28,25	28,25
4450	44,00	44,00	46,00	44,00	40,00	40,00	36,00	33,50	28,25	28,25
5000	44,75	44,75	46,75	44,75	40,75	40,75	37,00	34,75	29,25	29,25
6000	44,75	44,75	46,75	44,75	40,75	40,75	38,00	35,50	30,25	30,25
7000	44,75	44,75	46,75	44,75	40,75	40,75	38,00	35,50	30,25	30,25
8000	44,75	44,75	46,75	44,75	40,75	40,75	38,00	35,50	30,25	30,25

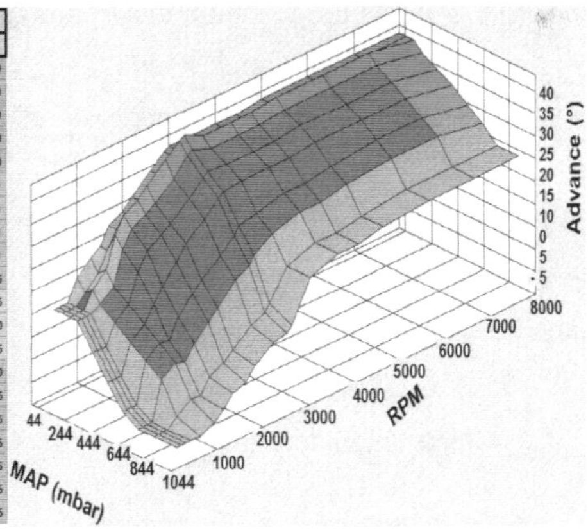

Fig. 7. Cartografía y mapa tridimensional avance al encendido II reprogramación

En el mapa de inyección se incrementó el 5% de inyección de combustible en la columna (3 - 8), desde 1000 rpm a 3000 rpm y un incremento de 10% desde 3400 rpm a 7000 rpm, en el mapa tridimensional de potencia final obtenida en la Fig. 8.

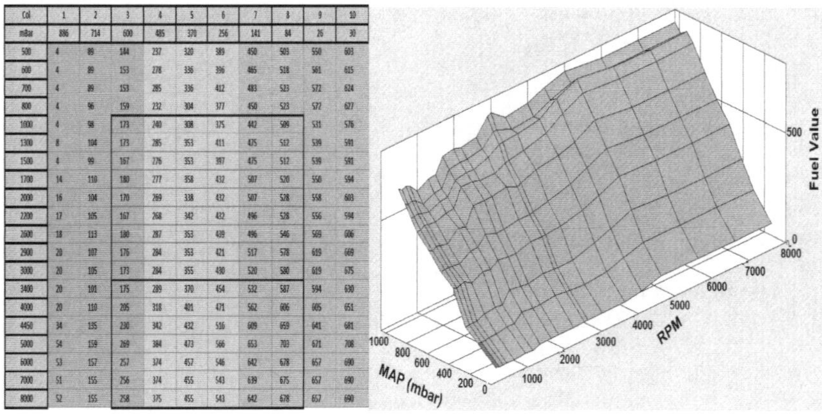

Fig. 8. Cartografía y mapa tridimensional de inyección II reprogramación

3.3 Análisis De Resultados

Para verificar como influyó el uso de software en las reprogramaciones y modificaciones aplicados en la unidad de control electrónica del motor de combustión interna se desarrollan las pruebas de torque, potencia y emisiones con el uso de equipos especializados, los resultados se presentan en la Tabla 2 en donde se registran los valores máximos de potencia cuando se produce en la más alta velocidad que el motor de combustión interna puede alcanzar al aplicarle carga.

Tabla 2. Parámetros de Torque y Potencia con modificación del software

Condición de prueba	Torque [ft-lb]	Potencia [HP]
Mapa base o de fábrica	57,8	67,05
I reprogramación	63	70,05
II reprogramación	65,5	72,00
Incremento I programación	5,2	3,00
Incremento porcentual I programación	9%	4%
Incremento II programación	7,7	4,95
Incremento porcentual II programación	13%	7%

Los valores obtenidos en la investigación permiten determinar el porcentaje de incremento de potencia y torque que se han obtenido mediante las reprogramaciones realizadas tomando como referencia el mapa base o de fábrica en relación a los personalizados como se observa en la Fig. 9.

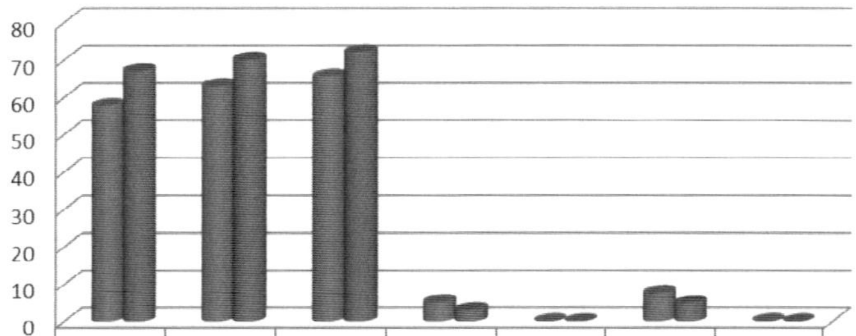

	Mapa base o de fábrica	I reprogramación	II reprogramación	Incremento I programación	Incremento porcentual I programación	Incremento II programación	Incremento porcentual II programación
■ Torque [ft-lb]	57,8	63	65,5	5,2	9%	7,7	13%
■ Potencia [HP]	67,05	70,05	72,00	3,00	4%	4,95	7%

Fig. 9. Influencia del software en la potencia y torque en el motor de combustión interna

3.4 Prueba de análisis de gases

El motor de combustión interna se sometió a pruebas de análisis de gases para determinar la cantidad de CO_2, CO, O_2 y ppm HC, generando un registro de mediciones con la programación base y con las reprogramaciones I y II. [11]Los valores de CO (monóxido de carbono) relacionan el estado de la eficiencia volumétrica, cantidad de masa de aire, cantidad de combustible y chispa.

Tabla 3. Registro de emisiones con el uso de software especificado en I y II reprogramación

Condición de prueba	CO [%]	CO_2 [%]	ppmHC	O_2 [%]
Norma INEN	2	8	200	10
I reprogramación	1,2	10	180	11
II reprogramación	0,8	12,00	140	12

Los valores de CO2 (dióxido de carbono); presentan el estado en que se encuentran los componentes mecánicos del motor los cuales intervienen directamente en la eficiencia volumétrica en el cilindro como: filtro de aire, bujías, inyectores [11], [13]. Los valores de O2 (oxígeno); relacionan directamente la cantidad de oxigeno que se encuentra en las emisiones de gases de escape. Los valores de ppm HC indican la cantidad de hidrocarburos no combustionados en el interior de la cámara de combustión y están representados como ppm [14].

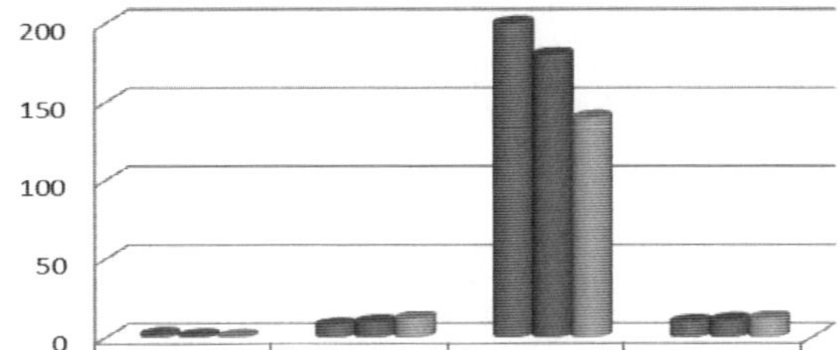

	CO [%]	CO2 [%]	ppmHC	O2 [%]
Norma INEN	2	8	200	10
I reprogramación	1,2	10	180	11
II reprogramación	0,8	12,00	140	12

Fig. 10. Influencia del uso del software en las emisiones del m.c.i.

4. Conclusiones

El uso de software dedicado contribuye de manera notable a optimizar el desempeño del motor de combustión interna sin realizar modificaciones de tipo mecánico.

Se comprobó la viabilidad de la modificación del software de fábrica en unidades de control electrónico de uso automotriz por software personalizado de acuerdo a las necesidades y requerimientos del usuario.

La utilización del software especializado reduce la utilización de modelos y prototipos de pruebas de verificación de optimización de procesos en la industria automotriz.

Se observa un incremento entre el 9% y 13% de torque , de 4% al 7% en la potencia y la reducción de emisiones del motor de combustión interna cuando se hacen modificaciones usando software dedicado a la industria automotriz sin alterar componentes de tipo mecánico.

Referencias

1. Petersen, S. Vakkalanka, L. Kuzniarz, Guidelines for conducting systematic mapping studies in software engineering: An update, Information and Software Technology 64 (2015) 1–18.T.
2. López, J., Vidarte, "Estudio y modificación de la gestión electrónica del motor e implantación del sistema eléctrico del prototipo MotoStudent," 2014.
3. Paternoster, N., Giardino, C., Unterkalmsteiner, M., Gorschek, T., Abra-hamsson P., Software development in startup companies: A systematic map1405 ping study, Information and Software Technology 56 (10) (2014) 1200–1218.
4. Martínez. S., Fernández, C., Ayala, X. Franch, E., Nakagawa, Y. A survey on the benefits and drawbacks of autosar, in: Proceedings of the First International Workshop on Automotive Software Architecture, ACM, 2015, pp. 19–26.

5. Rodriguez, P., Haghighatkhah, A., Lwakatare, L., Teppola, S., Continuous deployment of software intensive products and services: A systematic mapping study, Journal of Systems and Software 123 (2017) 263–291.
6. Haghighatkhah, A., Banijamali, A., Pakanen, O., Oivo, M., and Kuvaja, P., "Automotive software engineering: A systematic mapping study," *Journal of Systems and Software,* vol. 128, pp. 25-55, 2017.
7. Aleti, A. designing automotive embedded systems with adaptive genetic algorithms, Automated Software Engineering 22 (2) (2015) 199–240.
8. Sagñay, T. , Iván, N. and Altamirano E., "Diseño de un Sistema de Mantenimiento Preventivo y Correctivo con el Uso de Interfaces Gráficas con Software," 2013.
9. Kianifar, R., Campean, F. , Wood, A., "Application of permutation genetic algorithm for sequential model building–model validation design of experiments," *Soft Computing,* vol. 20, pp. 3023-3044, 2016.
10. Tocci, R., Widmer,. Moss, G., *Sistemas digitales: principios y aplicaciones*: Pearson Education, 2014.
11. Semanate, D., Erazo, G., "Reprogramación de la unidad de control electrónica del vehículo honda civic si, para mejorar los parámetros característicos del motor de combustión interna serie D16A9," Universidad de las Fuerzas Armadas ESPE Extensión Latacunga. Carrera de Ingeniería Automotriz., 2016.
12. Echavarría, J., "El método analítico como método naturall," *Nómadas,* vol. 25, pp. 327-353, 2010.
13 Quimbita, G., Erazo G., "Análisis del control de emisiones de gases de combustión del motor gasolina Toyota serie 2TR cuando se generan DTC´ S en el sistema de control electrónico de combustible," Universidad de las Fuerzas Armadas ESPE Extensión Latacunga. Carrera de Ingeniería Automotriz., 2016
14. Grasreiner, S., Neumann, J., Wensing, M., & Hasse, C. (2017). Model-based virtual engine calibration with the help of phenomenological methods for spark-ignited engines. Applied Thermal Engineering, 121, 190-199 .
15. Turkson, R. F., Yan, F., Ali, M. K. A., & Hu, J. (2016). Artificial neural network applications in the calibration of spark-ignition engines: An overview. Engineering Science and Technology, an International Journal, 19(3), 1346-1359.

The vision of aspects to improve problem solving skills: A case study

Carlos E. Anchundia[1], Efraín R. Fonseca C.[2], Pamela Flores[1], Marco A. Bolaños[1], and Gabriela J. Farinango[1]

[1] Facultad de Ingeniería de Sistemas, Escuela Politécnica Nacional, Quito, Ecuador
{carlos.anchundia, pamela.flores}@epn.edu.ec
alejandro.bolanos@outlook.es, gabriela.farinango@hotmail.com
[2] Departamento de Ciencias de la Computación, Universidad de las Fuerzas Armadas ESPE, Sangolquí, Ecuador
erfonseca@espe.edu.ec

Abstract. Software industry requires proficient personnel to solve problems. Keeping in mind, third level education centers apply several mechanisms based on the perspective of programming paradigms, such as object-oriented. This work is focused on analyzing the influence of an abstraction paradigm known as Aspect, on the level of student's knowledge and problem solving skills. A case study method research has been applied on the context of the Proprietary Environments Applications subject, on 20 students of the System Faculty of the National Polytechnic School of Ecuador. This process has been supported by and qualitative analysis tool known as ATLAS.ti, and also by Bloom's taxonomical pyramid of knowledge levels. It was observed that an improvement of knowledge levels on problem solving skills, based on the abstraction of aspects, can be achieved. It seems that a collateral characteristic of aspects is related to students' abstraction, their understanding and solving problem skills.

Keywords: case study, empirical software engineering, object oriented programming, aspect oriented programming.

1 Introducción

Dado que el software ha llegado a ser un elemento presente en muchos aspectos del quehacer diario, las formas de construirlo adecuadamente es un tópico importante en la Ingeniería de Software (IS). Para esto, los ingenieros o profesionales de la industria de software requieren poseer tanto conocimientos técnicos, como capacidades que les permita construir una aplicación de forma eficiente [1], [2]. En este contexto, los conocimientos técnicos hacen referencia al uso de herramientas de configuración de sistemas, inspección de código y de diseño; mientras que, las capacidades aluden a las habilidades de comprensión de la complejidad del proceso de ingeniería, el entendimiento de un problema y sus relaciones causa-efecto, y las competencias de comunicación. Sin embargo, en este ámbito, los desarrolladores novatos o recién graduados puede presentar un déficit en sus capacidades o conocimientos [3]. Tal como cita el estudio de Radermacher et al. [4], existe una serie de deficiencias que presentan alumnos recién graduados, entre las que se encuentra la capacidad para la "resolución de problemas".

Ante esto, las universidades son responsables de impartir y mejorar la capacidad de análisis y comprensión de problemas, con el propósito de que los futuros desarrolladores puedan descomponerlos y presentar una solución informática a través de la abstracción. Según la Real Academia de la Lengua (RAE) [5], la abstracción es el "acto de separar por medio de una operación intelectual un rasgo o una cualidad de algo para analizarlos aisladamente o considerarlos en su pura esencia o noción". Según Kramer [2] una adecuada abstracción permite producir código claro y elegante; pudiendo ser un principio fundamental de la ingeniería de software para lidiar con la complejidad, ya que permite la identificación de aspectos críticos requeridos en un sistema, así como aquellos que son irrelevantes. Este entendimiento de abstracción puede ser alcanzado a través de la comprensión y aplicación adecuada de paradigmas de programación, como por ejemplo la Programación Orientada a Objetos (POO) o la Programación Orientada a Aspectos (POA).

En este ámbito, pese a que la POO es ampliamente impartida por centros de estudios de tercer nivel; la problemática entorno a la resolución de problemas parecería persistir aún. Con esto en consideración, y basados en las observaciones de Kramer [2], creemos pertinente abordar a profundidad el paradigma orientada a aspectos, como medio para mejorar las capacidades de comprensión y resolución de problemas. Consideramos que POA podría ser apropiado, ya que basa su filosofía de análisis en conceptos de objetos [6], [7], lo cual podría reducir el tiempo de entrenamiento para incorporar nuevos conceptos de separación de código. Además, existen implementaciones en muchos lenguajes de programación que incorporan los conceptos y sintaxis para soportar la programación orientada a aspectos.

Con este fin, se ha considerado realizar un estudio de caso en los estudiantes de una asignatura dictada en la Facultad de Sistemas de la Escuela Politécnica Nacional del Ecuador. Este estudio permitirá analizar el nivel de conocimiento y capacidades para la resolución de problemas bajo la perspectiva de abstracción POA. El proceso de desarrollo del caso se encuentra dividido siguiendo las recomendaciones de Runenson y Höst [8] de la siguiente manera: En la Sección 2 se describirán estudios relacionados al mejoramiento de las capacidades de resolución de problemas; en la Sección 3 se detallará como se ha preparado diseño del estudio de caso; en la Sección 4 se presentarán los resultados y hallazgos; y finalmente se describen las conclusiones y trabajo futuro.

2 Trabajos relacionados

Con respecto al mejoramiento de las capacidades de resolución de problemas, como punto clave en la Ingeniería de Software, existen diversas propuestas. Por ejemplo, Hwang et al. [9] propone el aprendizaje basado en juegos. Esta propuesta sostiene que aplicar juegos para el aprendizaje permite completar logros e incrementa la motivación hacia aspectos científicos, resolución de problemas y aceptación tecnológica. En su estudio se utilizó el esquema de trabajo en pares como mecanismo para evaluar y mejorar el desempeño en las evaluaciones. Otro tipo de enfoque se centra en el aprendizaje basado en problemas (Problem Based Learning - PBL) que consiste en la aplicación de principios para resolver problemas reales en un entorno de monitorización constante. Por ejemplo, Santos y Soares [10] sostienen que la aplicación de esta metodología de aprendizaje incentiva la participación de los estudiantes para practicar y desarrollar habilidades; permitiendo que se superen debilidades y que se maximicen las fortalezas a través de la guía de los instructores y del trabajo en equipo. Los proponentes de estos enfoques critican el proceso tradicional de evaluación basado en cuestionarios. Como sugiere Lishinski et al. [11] los cuestionarios sirven primordialmente para la valoración de comprensión de contenido, pero no son apropiados para la evaluación de habilidades de programación de nivel superior, que requieren mediciones de pensamiento y procesos para resolución de problemas.

En adición a los esquemas propuestos anteriormente, la capacidad de resolución de problemas puede ser analizada a través de la abstracción. Por ejemplo, Kramer [2] sostiene que la generalización es un tipo de análisis que permite la interpretación de un programa en un dominio real mapeado a un dominio que capture la semántica de proceso computacional. Este proceso de pensamiento abstracto no solo tiene aplicaciones en la Ingeniería de Software sino también en otras áreas donde la creatividad juega un papel importante en la creación de productos, como lo es el arte y las matemáticas. De esta manera, la capacidad de abstracción puede ser inducida a través de modelos formales y apropiados para diseño e implementación, como los presentados por los diversos paradigmas de programación. El mismo autor denota que el proceso de pensamiento abstracto requiere condiciones especiales de entrenamiento en adolescentes y adultos.

Debido a la importancia de contar con desarrolladores calificados [3], evaluar alternativas en pro de la mejora de las capacidades de resolución de problemas, en los estudiantes de las carreras de Ingeniería de Software, es necesario. Por lo tanto, el abordaje más profundo del paradigma de abstracción POA podría ayudar a mejorar habilidades de pensamiento de alto nivel; que incluyen el pensamiento crítico, capacidades de síntesis, y resolución de problemas [1].

3 Diseño del estudio de caso

Para poder analizar el efecto de la enseñanza de POA para mejorar las capacidades de resolución de problemas y los cambios frente a POO, se ha seleccionado la técnica de investigación, el estudio de caso.

3.1 Preguntas de investigación

Consecuentemente, para poder determinar si la propuesta presentada aporta al proceso de formación de profesionales, consideramos las siguientes preguntas de investigación:

P1: ¿Cómo influye el aprendizaje de POA en la capacidad de resolver problemas?

P2: ¿Qué aspecto de desarrollo de software es mayormente sustentado por el aprendizaje de POA?

3.2 Selección de caso y sujetos

De acuerdo al propósito de la investigación, analizar el nivel de conocimiento y capacidades para la resolución de problemas bajo una perspectiva nueva de abstracción, se aplicó un estudio de caso de tipo interpretativo. El estudio de caso de tipo interpretativo permitió entender el fenómeno a través de la interpretación de los participantes dentro del contexto elegido; que en este caso fue, la interpretación de la asimilación y efecto del aprendizaje de POA en los estudiantes.

Para la selección de la unidad de análisis se consideró a los estudiantes de la asignatura de Aplicaciones en Ambientes Propietarios, del ciclo 2016-A de la Facultad de Ingeniería de Sistemas de la Escuela Politécnica Nacional. Esta asignatura se la imparte a mitad de la carrera (quinto nivel) y se enfoca en el desarrollo de software con la utilización de herramientas propietarias, como C\#. De acuerdo al currículo de la carrera y a los objetivos de aprendizaje, los alumnos a este nivel cuentan con experiencia y bases necesarias en temas como programación básica, diseño, programación estructurada y orientada a objetos, lenguajes de programación, y nociones de diagramación.

3.3 Procedimiento de recolección de datos

Debido a la naturaleza cuantitativa del análisis, se diseñaron instrumentos para recabar datos (ver Tabla 1). Los instrumentos fueron aplicados a lo largo de cinco sesiones que incluyeron componentes teóricos y prácticos, en las que se contó además con el equipamiento y software necesario para instruir sobre POA y para ejecutar prácticas de laboratorio.

Tabla 1. Instrumentos diseñados para recolección de datos

Recurso	Tipo	Descripción
A	Encuesta	Determina los antecedentes académicos de los participantes
B	Evaluación	Determina el nivel de conocimientos inicial para la resolución de un problema
C	Evaluación	Determina el nivel de conocimientos sobre desarrollo
D	Práctica de laboratorio	Verifica la efectividad de lo aprendido
E	Práctica de laboratorio	Verifica la efectividad de lo aprendido
F	Evaluación	Determina el nivel de conocimientos final para la resolución de un problema

Para la recolección de datos, se definieron tres fases: Preparación, Entrenamiento, y Recolección. En la fase de preparación se planificó la instalación de herramientas informáticas, se estableció la locación para realizar las prácticas, y se elaboraron los instrumentos a utilizarse durante el desarrollo de los ejercicios. En la fase de entrenamiento se ejecutó la planificación de cinco sesiones, aplicando los instrumentos. Finalmente, para la fase de recolección, se digitalizó los instrumentos y se cargaron en la herramienta de análisis de datos, convirtiéndose en recursos de análisis.

3.4 Procedimiento de análisis

El procedimiento utilizado para el análisis incluyó cuatro fases [12]: Recolección de datos cualitativos, Identificación de citas, Codificación de citas y Agrupación de códigos. Con el objetivo de soportar estas actividades, se propuso utilizar una herramienta informática para el análisis cualitativo llamada ATLAS.ti [13], a la cual nos referiremos simplemente como Atlas de aquí en adelante. Atlas permite clasificar los recursos y generar etiquetas denominadas códigos, los cuales pueden ser ordenadas y agrupadas para poder extraer los datos cualitativos. Estos códigos se generan a partir de un proceso de descubrimiento de características. Finalmente, para la agrupación y categorización de estas etiquetas se crearon familias basada en la pirámide de la taxonomía de Bloom. En la Fig. 1 se muestra una parte de la pantalla de trabajo en donde se puede observar: (1) el recurso digitalizado, (2) la cita remarcada, y (3) los códigos asociados.

En este procedimiento, se consideraron principalmente los recursos B, E y F (Tabla 1). Los códigos se generaron de acuerdo a la identificación de elementos o novedades descubiertas en los recursos, tal como se muestra en la plantilla de la Fig. 2. Este proceso de codificación es un proceso iterativo de refinamiento, agrupación o separación de los mismos. La agrupación de códigos se la realizó a través de la creación de familias basadas en las habilidades de Pensamiento de Orden inferior (LOTS, por sus siglas en inglés) de la taxonomía de Bloom: Memorización, Comprensión y Aplicación. En esta etapa se utilizó los verbos correspondientes a cada nivel de la taxonomía. Finalmente, para comprender el fenómeno se utilizó redes semánticas

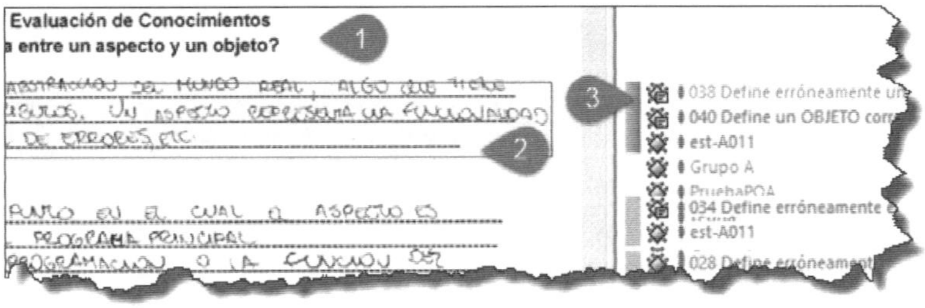

Fig. 1. Captura de pantalla de una cita identifica (*izquierda*) y sus códigos asociados (*derecha*)

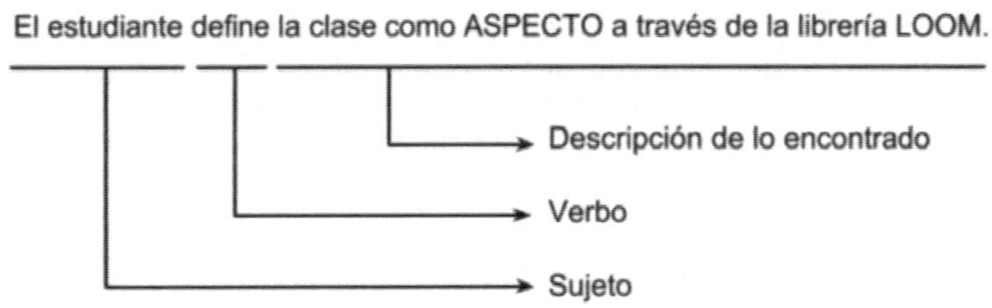

Fig. 2. Plantilla de codificación de citas

extraídas de la misma aplicación Atlas.

3.5 Procedimiento de validación

Como parte de la validación del proceso se considerarán las siguientes estrategias para reducir las amenazas internas y externas a la validez [14], [15]:

- Se han considerado estudiantes de quinto nivel que poseen conocimientos de programación. Creemos que los estudiantes a este nivel poseen los conceptos básicos para poder desarrollar soluciones a problemas en un lenguaje de programación.
- La asignatura que se ha tomado, no se enfoca en enseñar técnicas de programación.
- En el quinto nivel, no se dictan otras asignaturas que se enfoquen en técnicas o lenguajes de programación adicionales a las aprendidas anteriormente. Se considera que otras asignaturas no influenciarán los resultados de las intervenciones.
- Se ha propuesto el incentivo en notas por la participación y resultados de aprendizaje.
- Se ha establecido una línea base para la comparación al final del tratamiento.
- Se han definido varios instrumentos o recursos de evaluación como parte del diseño de estudio de caso.

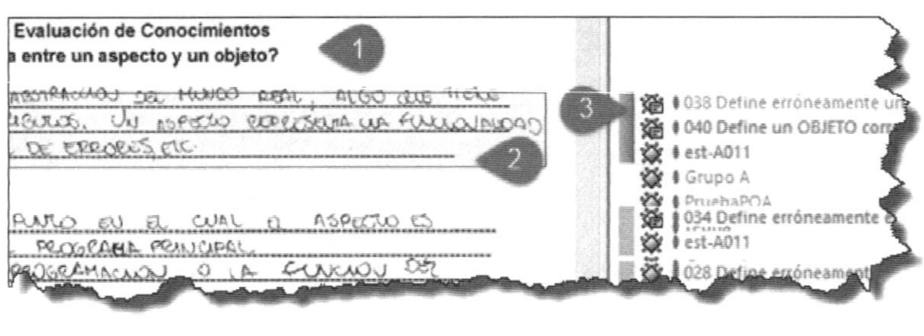

Fig. 1. Captura de pantalla de una cita identifica (*izquierda*) y sus códigos asociados (*derecha*)

4 Resultados

Después de haber depurado los códigos, se obtuvo un total de 93 códigos que hacen referencia a novedades o características descubiertas en los recursos analizados. A más de estos códigos, se crearon códigos adicionales para discriminar entre los diferentes estudiantes y tipos de prueba que intervinieron en el proceso. La intersección de ambos tipos de códigos permitió la determinación de la frecuencia en que un código aparece en el proceso, así también analizar la correlación entre diferentes códigos.

Por otro lado, para la agrupación de los códigos, se crearon familias que reflejen indicadores basados en las habilidades de Pensamiento de Orden inferior (LOTS, por sus siglas en inglés) de la taxonomía de Bloom, como se menciona en la Sección 3.4. En la Tabla 2 se muestra la clasificación de los códigos de acuerdo a los verbos que contenían. Como resultado, la cantidad de códigos tomados en cuenta se redujeron a 29 debido a que en la taxonomía no se consideran aquellos verbos que demuestran alguna carencia o factor negativo en la aplicación del conocimiento, sino que únicamente se toman en consideración los logros de un objetivo de aprendizaje en particular. Adicionalmente se han generado familias de documentos en los que se consolidan los instrumentos de cada estudiante agrupados en los recursos B, E y F con un total de 62 documentos, distribuidos en 26, 14 y 22 documentos por recurso respectivamente.

Tabla 2. Familias de códigos y verbos asociados

Familia	Verbos
01 Memorizar: El estudiante memoriza o recuerda conceptos y hechos sin comprenderlos necesariamente	Anotar, citar, dar a, conocer, decir, definir, describir, duplicar, encontrar, enumerar, examinar, identificar, listar, memorizar, mostrar, narrar(relatar), nombrar, ordenar, organizar, perfilar, presentar, reconocer, recordar, relacionar, rememorar, repetir, reproducir, reunir, rotular, tabular
02 Comprender: El estudiante comprende e interpreta la información aprendida en el transcurso de la capacitación sobre POA	Asociar, cambiar, clarificar, clasificar, construir, contrastar, convertir, decodificar, defender, describir, diferenciar, discriminar, discutir, distinguir, estimar, explicar, expresar, extender, generalizar, identificar, ilustrar, indicar, inferir, informar, interpretar, localizar, parafrasear, predecir, reconocer, reescribir, re-formular, revisar, seleccionar, solucionar, traducir
03 Aplicar: El estudiante aplica los conocimientos aprendidos para implementar un código válido que permita resolver el problema solicitado	Aplicar, evaluar, calcular, cambiar, seleccionar, completar, computar, construir, demostrar, desarrollar, descubrir, dramatizar, emplear, examinar, experimentar, encontrar, ilustrar, interpretar, manipular, modificar, operar, organizar, practicar, predecir, preparar, producir, relatar, programar, seleccionar, mostrar, esbozar, solucionar, transferir, utilizar

Una vez codificada y agrupada la información, se procedió a generar redes semánticas por cada estudiante para extraer las características de la evolución del aprendizaje. La red semántica se caracteriza por presentar: (1) el estudiante, (2) los códigos relacionados, (3) los indicadores o familias según la taxonomía y (4) los diferentes recursos clasificados por color; tal como se muestra una de las redes generadas para el estudiante A006 en la Fig. 3. La red de esta figura fue extraída siguiendo el siguiente proceso: Se inició especificando el código del estudiante a analizar. Como paso siguiente se importan los códigos que se relacionan a ese estudiante. Después, se ordenaron los códigos con fines estéticos y de comprensión. Para lograr comprender el proceso se asignaron colores a los diferentes códigos de acuerdo al recurso en el que fueron encontrados. Finalmente, se obtuvieron la red semántica que produce una tabla que recopila toda la información, cuyo extracto se muestra en la Tabla 3.

Fig. 3. Red semántica del estudiante A006

Finalmente, a modo de resumen se obtuvieron los niveles de conocimiento que han demostrado todos los estudiantes durante el proceso. Cabe recalcar que, al momento de asignar los niveles, se tomó en consideración el mayor de los niveles conforme a lo que sugiere Bloom.

Tabla 3. Familias de códigos y verbos asociados

Estudiante	Recurso B	Recurso E	Recurso F
Est-A006	El estudiante COMPRENDE e interpreta el enunciado del problema debido a que identifica las clases necesarias para la resolución del problema	El estudiante prefiere utilizar los conceptos de POO y los APLICA al resolver el problema pese a que se solicitó hacerlo con POA	El estudiante APLICA conocimientos de los elementos de POA aprendidos en clase, su implementación cumple con el objetivo solicitado

4.2 Evaluación de la validez

Los procedimientos establecidos en la Sección 3.5 fueron ejecutados para asegurar la validez del análisis de resultados. Sin embargo, durante la ejecución existieron estudiantes (A003, A008, A013, A014, B006 y B007) que no participaron en todas las sesiones establecidas, y que por lo tanto no pudieron generar los recursos necesarios mininos para su evaluación. En este caso los estudiantes que no pudieron ser evaluados con al menos dos de los tres recursos, como se había planificado, fueron excluidos.

4.2 Evaluación de la validez

P1: ¿Cómo influye el aprendizaje de POA en la capacidad de resolver problemas? Para responder esta pregunta se utilizaron instrumentos que permitieron comparar un estado inicial y el estado final del proceso. En este caso los recursos B y F representan inicio y fin del proceso mientras que el recurso E permite verificar el proceso intermedio. El estado inicial en el Recurso B permite observar que un gran porcentaje de estudiantes alcanzan un nivel máximo de comprensión. En este aspecto los estudiantes fueron capaces de responder de forma acertada a preguntas teóricas sobre la POO, así mismo como la capacidad de poder interpretar formas de resolución de problemas a través de técnicas de POO; sin embargo, no fueron capaces de poder generar una solución funcional y concreta utilizando este lenguaje de programación. Esto ubica sus capacidades de abstracción y resolución en un nivel 2 de comprensión. En contraste, en el recurso E, se obtiene que los alumnos son capaces de resolver problemas utilizando la abstracción del paradigma POA. Este avance se puede obser-

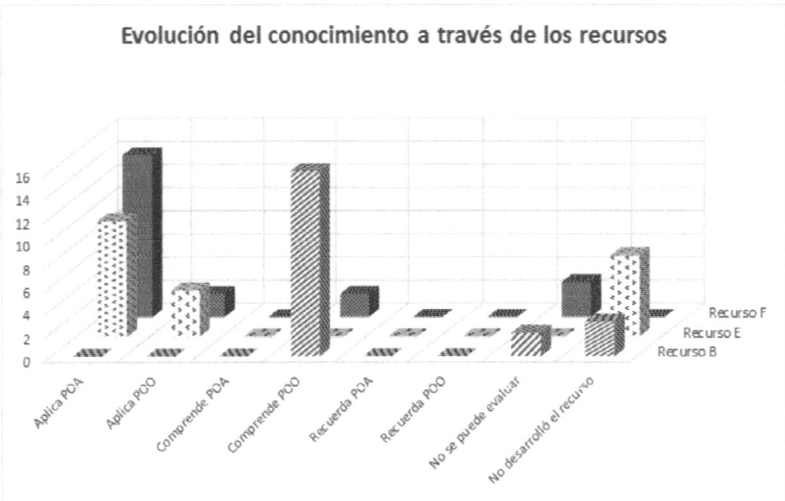

Fig. 4. Resultados del análisis

var también en el recurso F, en donde se obtiene un resultado similar. Cabe mencionar que en el recurso F, no se evaluó la aplicación estrategias o sintaxis utilizados para POO o POA, sino al contrario, se evaluó la capacidad de análisis aplicado. En el recurso E se planteó una pregunta sobre la aplicación de POA frente a POO, en la cual se demostró que los estudiantes pudieron resolver un problema utilizando POA, mientras que ellos pensaban estar utilizando POO. Muy posiblemente POA, al incorporar mejoras en el tipo de abstracción, no se diferencia en gran manera de POO; sin embargo, su capacidad de abstracción se mejoró al punto de poder separar adecuadamente los componentes del sistema. Estos resultados pueden observase en la Fig. 4.

P2: ¿Qué aspecto de desarrollo de software es mayormente sustentado por el aprendizaje de POA? En este ámbito, se pudo observar una mejora considerable en la separación de requisitos funcionales y no funcionales. De manera directa o indirecta los estudiantes pudieron comprender de mejor los conceptos de objeto y aspecto dentro de un sistema software. Esto se demostró a través de la correlación entre los códigos ¨037 Define un ASPECTO correctamente, lo representa como la parte no funcional de un sistema" y los códigos "040 Define un OBJETO correctamente, conoce que es lo que representa un objeto del mundo real en el código" y "042 Define erróneamente un OBJETO debido a que piensa que el objeto sirve para divide datos.". Esto significa que pese a la interpretación correcta o no, a través de POA los estudiantes pueden separar o abstraer de mejor manera la solución para un problema.

5 Conclusiones y trabajo futuro

En este trabajo, se condujo un estudio de caso de tipo interpretativo para analizar el proceso de resolución de problemas a partir del aprendizaje de la Programación Orientada a Aspectos en el contexto de estudiantes de quinto nivel de la Facultad de Sistemas de la Escuela Politécnica Nacional. Dentro de los hallazgos se ha observado el posible beneficio que tiene el aprendizaje de un mecanismo diferente de abstracción para la resolución de problemas al momento de comprender y diseñar una solución de software. Más allá de los posibles usos o aplicaciones reales que puedan desarrollarse bajo el paradigma de aspectos, su aplicación puede aportar a los estudiantes de una visión diferente para abstraer elementos importantes y relevantes sobre un problema a solventar.

Se aplicaron diferentes estrategias para minimizar las amenazas a la validez de los resultados; sin embargo, existieron condiciones que dificultaron en cierto grado el proceso planteado en el caso de estudio. Por ejemplo, se esperaba un mayor porcentaje de estudiantes que tuvieran un nivel de aplicación en el recurso B. En otro caso, los estudiantes no se familiarizaban con el uso del entorno gráfico de la herramienta de desarrollo, complicando el proceso de inducción. Sin embargo, la participación de los estudiantes y profesores colaboradores permitieron ejecutar y solventar estos contratiempos. En este apartado, el uso de la interfaz gráfica no fue considerada inicialmente como parte del proceso de entrenamiento, por lo que se optó por reemplazar los ejercicios en modo consola y así no depender del grado de familiaridad con los controles y entornos gráficos por parte de los sujetos ya que no forma parte del alcance, pero podría ser considerado en futuros trabajos.

Esta investigación puede ser considerada como el inicio de futuros análisis que se encaminen en evaluar y mejorar el proceso de aprendizaje de estudiantes de Ingeniería de Software. Hemos podido observar una mejora en las capacidades de los estudiantes; sin embargo, es necesario continuar con un proceso de replicación o mejora del estudio tomando en consideración las dificultades mencionadas con el propósito de extraer resultados concluyentes. Las futuras investigaciones pueden ampliar la unidad de análisis; es decir, incluir a más participantes, y mejorar los instrumentos de evaluación. Debido a que esta investigación trató un estudio de caso, la aplicación de métodos cuantitativos como la experimentación podrán ser propuestos para la corroboración y generalización de los hallazgos encontrados.

Referencias

1. Y. Liguo, Overcoming Challenges in Softwre Engineering Education: Delivering Non-Technical Knowledge and Skills, 2014.
2. J. Kramer, "Is abstraction the key to computing?" vol. 50, no. 4, 2007.
3. ACM, Software Engineering 2014 Curriculum Guidelines for Undergraduate Degre Programs in Software Enginnering, 2015.
4. A. Radermacher, G. Walia, and D. Knudson, "Investigating the skill gap between graduating students and industry expectations," 2014.
5. R. A. Española. (10/04/2017) Abstraer. [Online]. Available: http://dle.rae.es/?id=0CxZRfR
6. S. Almonacid Arismendi, Rodrigo; Hernández Venegas, Programación Orientada a Aspectos, 2008.
7. A. Alonso, M. C. Gastaldo, and M. Santamaría, Programación Orientada a Aspectos - POA, 2008.
8. P. Runeson and M. Höst, "Guidelines for conducting and reporting case study research in software engineering," vol. 14, no. 2, pp. 13-164, 2009.
9. G.-J. Hwang, C.-M. Hung, and N.-S. Chen, "Improving learning achievements, motivations and problem-solving skills through a peer assessment-based game development approach," 2013.
10. S. dos Santos and F. Soares, "Authentic assessment in software engineering education based on pbl principles: A case study in the telecom market," 2013.
11. A. Lishinske, A. Yadav, R. Enbody, and J. Good, "The inuence of problem solving abilities on students? performance on different assessment tasks in cs1," 2016.
12. P. Flores, N. Medinilla, and S. Pamplona, "What do software design students understand about information hiding? a qualitative case study," 2014.
13. S. Friese, "Atlas.ti guía rápida," 2012.
14. C. Wohlin, P. Runeson, M. Höst, M. Ohlsson, B. Regnell, and A. Wesslén, Experimentation in Software Engineering. Springer Heidelberg, 2012.
15. M. Genero, J. A. Cruz-Lemus, and M. Piattini, Métodos de investigación en ingeniería del software. Ra-ma, 2014.

Software Engineering Reproducible Research: A Proposal For Analyzing The Effectiveness Of Test Driven Development

Geovanny Raura[1], Efraín R. Fonseca C.[1], Tatiana Gualotuña[1], and Celia R. Mejía C.[2]

[1]Departamento de Ciencias de la Computación
[2]Departamento de Ciencias Humanas y Sociales
Universidad de las Fuerzas Armadas ESPE, Sangolquí, Ecuador.
{jgraura,erfonseca,tmgualotunia,crmejia}@espe.edu.ec

Abstract. — *Background*: Several technological proposals have been developed to help the researcher in carrying out experimental replications with the highest degree of similarity. Those proposals have been performed mainly for: definition, execution, analysis and report of experiments; but lately, the reproducible research paradigm is considered. **Aim**: Define a platform to study the effectiveness of Test Driven Development (TDD) technique, under the principles of reproducible research in a context setup. **Method**: We defined a conceptual and process model to study different aspects regarding the application of TDD technique, followed by the construction of a support prototype platform as validation, from the perspective of the reproducible research, based in a specific family of experiments. **Results**: A first approximation of a technological platform was developed which covers: design, data collection, data measurement an analysis of results. **Conclusions**: Support tools for the experimental process based on reproducible research are needed, in such a way that gives the elements required for both, facilitate the reproducibility of families of experiments in different contexts and obtain comparable data by other researchers.

Keywords: reproducible research, test driven Development, TDD, experimental software engineering

1 Introducción

El desarrollo de la ciencia se ha fundamentado principalmente en el grado de reproducibilidad de los resultados de investigación [27]. La Investigación Reproducible (IR) se caracteriza por proporcionar un entorno detallado de ejecución de estudios empíricos y que contenga datos, códigos y procedimientos; justamente para facilitar la reproducción de los resultados y validar los hallazgos de otros investigadores [25].

Se han realizado varios estudios sobre investigación reproducible en diferentes disciplinas [11], [31], [30], los cuales muestran que en estas áreas es común el uso de este paradigma; de hecho, incluso existen normas para impulsar la reproducibilidad como es en el caso de la ISO5725-2 [32].

La adopción del método científico en las ciencias de la computación ha crecido en los últimos tiempos. Los investigadores cada vez más reconocen a la computación como una rama independiente y metodológica de la ciencia [10]. No obstante, aún no son numerosos los estudios que consideran a la reproducibilidad como un aspecto básico en las ciencias computacionales [12].

En lo que concierne a la ingeniería de software empírica, la IR es aún más escasa. Hemos ubicado únicamente un par de estudios que se encuentran en sus etapas iniciales, como es el caso del realizado por de Oliveira & otros [22] y el de Dit & otros [9] que están orientados a la investigación en técnicas de pruebas y mantenimiento de software; lo cual nos lleva a preguntarnos ¿Cómo ampliar el uso de la reproducibilidad en Ingeniería de Software Empírica al nivel de otras disciplinas?

En este trabajo proponemos una plataforma experimental enfocada en medir la calidad externa y la productividad de los desarrolladores, utilizando diferentes estrategias de programación. La plataforma está orientada a dar soporte a los estudios sobre TDD [3] en comparación con otras aproximaciones al desarrollo de software.

La razón que ha motivado el desarrollo de esta plataforma, radica en que a pesar de contar con la realización de múltiples investigaciones sobre la aplicación de TDD en ambientes académicos e industriales, los resultados obtenidos no han permitido llegar a conclusiones definitivas, como lo muestran diferentes trabajos de síntesis publicados [21], [20], [6], [18]. De acuerdo a los autores de estas publicaciones, las causas son entre otras: la falta de estudios especialmente en la industria, la presencia de ciertos defectos metodológicos por la carencia de variables respuesta homogéneas y la falta de contrastación entre experimentos realizados en la industria y la academia.

Creemos que una plataforma de investigación reproducible permitirá a los investigadores homogeneizar diferentes aspectos analizados para medir la efectividad de los desarrolladores utilizando TDD, dentro de una familia específica de experimentos, en las mismas condiciones que el experimento original y con el objeto de que sus resultados sean comparables.

El artículo está estructurado como sigue. En la Sección 2, se presentan los trabajos relacionados con la temática de investigación. En la Sección 3, se detalla el experimento que sirvió como base para la definición del modelo conceptual de la propuesta. En la Sección 4 se presenta la plataforma tecnológica. Finalmente en la Sección 5 se exponen las conclusiones y trabajo futuro.

2 Antecedentes y Trabajos Relacionados

Luego de una revisión inicial de literatura hemos identificado varios estudios referentes a la IR en las ciencias computacionales, de los cuales destacan el estudio de Stodden & Miguez [28] en el que reportan el desarrollo de un conjunto de recomendaciones relativas al almacenamiento, control de versiones, y la publicación de datos; tendientes a la investigación reproducible. Aún más representativo es el estudio de Burnett & Thompson [29] en el que sugieren que los estudios de reproducibilidad se los puede categorizar desde tres puntos de vista: 1) apoyo al análisis estructurado mediante scripts, 2) apoyo a la investigación de cómputo intensivo y, 3) difusión de los objetos de investigación. Consideramos a este estudio como base para analizar los trabajos relacionados con la temática de investigación.

1. Apoyo al análisis estructurado mediante scripts
   Los científicos en diferentes disciplinas utilizan scripts como un medio de análisis de datos y estudios empíricos reproducibles, para lo cual se basan en lenguajes de propósito general como Python, Perl y R. Para LeVenque [17] en su estudio presenta la adecuación del software Clawpack con Python, detallando el uso de herramientas que ayudan a la IR en problemas hiperbólicos. Leish en cambio [16] propone el concepto de programación de scripts orientados a la creación de documentos estadísticos reproducibles, sugiere que los sripts sean documentados para que puedan ser fácilmente entendidos por terceros y permitir la aplicación de la IR.
2. Apoyo a la investigación de cómputo intensivo
   Para apoyar a la investigación donde hay exigencias de cómputo masivo, es necesario proponer arquitecturas de software basadas en tecnologías modernas, de esta forma poder crear entornos informáticos reproducibles y fácilmente escalables para ejecutar, gestionar y recoger los resultados de los experimentos. Los workflow son los más utilizados, se encadenan y se aplican los pasos sucesivos de un experimento, para permitir que otros científicos puedan reproducir la investigación, con el fin de validar los resultados encontrados [8], [26]. En el workflow también se detallan las actividades, herramientas, técnicas y estrategias utilizadas, es decir que el protocolo de investigación este explícito y accesible [24]. Es importante realizar un análisis de requerimientos de reproducibilidad para lograr un diseño robusto que describa en detalle al workflow y permitan reproducir el trabajo científico [23], [19, [33].
3. Difusión objetos de investigación
   Los objetos de investigación permiten agregar datos y métodos para facilitar la reproducibilidad de los hallazgos científicos [2]. La difusión de los objetos de investigación proporciona acceso a código ejecutable y otros recursos necesarios para la replicación de una investigación [5]. Los datos y experimentos científicos requieren ser interactivos, reproducibles y dinámicos, por lo que se necesita un marco de colaboración de las tecnologías semánticas que ayuden a mantener la uniformidad de los datos y faciliten su difusión [4].

En IS el panorama es muy diferente, dado que son escasos los aportes basados en IR. Por ejemplo: González-Barahona & Robles [14] definen los elementos que deben ser considerados para caracterizar la reproducibilidad en estudios empíricos de ingeniería de software, proponiendo un enfoque sistémico que recomienda el conjunto de datos, metodología y herramientas a utilizar. En la investigación de Cleland-Huang & otros [7] realizaron algunas acciones tendientes a resolver el problema de reproducibilidad de los experimentos, como es la creación de diferentes infraestructuras y buenas prácticas de trazabilidad. Para de Oliveira & otros [22] proponen una base para la evaluación de técnicas de pruebas de software que proporciona a los investigadores una herramienta que permite la ejecución automática y análisis de experimentos que apoyan a la IR. En el estudio de Dit & otros, en este mismo tema [9] desarrollan una biblioteca de experimentos y componentes resultantes del mapeo de varias técnicas y enfoques de mantenimiento de software, proponiéndolo como una solución que permite que los estudios sean reproducibles.

En lo que respecta a la evaluación de la calidad y productividad de los programadores utilizando técnicas de desarrollo basadas en pruebas (como por ejemplo TDD), hemos encontrado una vasta cantidad de investigaciones, especialmente en la familia de experimentos [1] sobre TDD de N. Juristo [15] y su equipo. No obstante, no se ha encontrado reportes de esta temática referidos a la investigación reproducible, lo cual motivó nuestro trabajo.

3 Experimento base para el desarrollo de la plataforma

En este apartado describimos de forma resumida el experimento base a partir del cual desarrollamos una herramienta tecnológica que permite la reproducibilidad de experimentos sobre la efectividad en el uso de la estrategia de desarrollo basado en pruebas (TDD de las siglas del inglés Test-Driven Development) en comparación con otras técnicas de desarrollo. La principal meta fue lograr que las replicaciones de este experimento sean del tipo literal [13].

Es preciso mencionar que este experimento fue seleccionado como base de este trabajo, ya que representa la base de distintas series de replicaciones que le permitieron definir a N. Juristo y su equipo una familia de experimentos sobre esta temática. La bondad de una familia de experimentos, es permitir la generalización de resultados experimentales, ya que es común que el tamaño de las muestras en cada instancia experimental es limitado [1].

El experimento base tiene un diseño factorial de medidas repetidas con dos Factores: La aproximación al desarrollo (*programming approach*) y el nivel de descripción de la tarea experimental (*slicing*). Los niveles utilizados para el factor (*programming approach*), son: Iteractive Test Last Development (ITLD), Test Driven Development (TDD) y la estrategia de desarrollo que el programador conoce (Generalmente: Test Last development (TLD), pero no necesariamente). Esta estrategia ha sido denominada "Your Way" (YW).

Hemos considerado en nuestra propuesta las mismas variables de estudio que las definidas en el experimento original. Esto es: La calidad externa en el código (QLTY), la productividad de los programadores (PROD) y la cantidad de trabajo realizado (TUS), donde:

QLTY representa la calidad externa medida en términos de la conformidad de los requerimientos desarrollados por los sujetos mediante test de aceptación, y se define como:

$$QLTY = \frac{\sum_{i=1}^{\#tus} QLTY_i}{\#TUS} \quad (1)$$

Donde $QLTY_i$ es la calidad de la historia de usuario i-ésima implementada por el sujeto. $QLTY_i$ se define como:

$$QLTY_i = \frac{\#Assert_i\,(Pass)}{\#Assert_i\,(All)} \tag{2}$$

Mientras que #TUS es la cantidad de trabajo realizado. Se contabiliza si por lo menos una aserción ha sido superada con éxito en un caso de prueba, y se define como:

$$\boldsymbol{QLTY} = \sum_{i=1}^{\#tus} \#Assert_i\,(Pass) \geq 0 \rightarrow True \tag{3}$$

En ambos casos, $\#Assert_i$ (Pass) representa el número de aserciones de jUnit (ya que el experimento se realizó utilizando el lenguaje de programación Java) correctamente ejecutados en la historia de usuario i-ésima.

PROD representa la cantidad de trabajo realizada por los sujetos de manera satisfactoria, y se define como:

$$PROD = \frac{\#Assert\,(Pass)}{\#Assert\,(All)} \tag{4}$$

Adicionalmente, el experimento original contempla la ejecución de tres tareas experimentales aplicando ITL y TDD. Estos problemas fueron: **MarsRover API** (MR)**, Bowling Scorekeeper** (BSK) **y Spread Sheet** (SS)**.** MR, BSK y SS son programas comúnmente utilizados en la comunidad de desarrollo ágil. Estos programas se caracterizan por tener una complejidad similar en términos de número de historias de usuario, tiempo estimado de resolución y nivel de dificultad en su implementación.

Las tareas experimentales fueron realizadas utilizando el lenguaje de programación Java, jUnit como framework de pruebas y como plataforma de desarrollo se utilizó el IDE Eclipse. En todos los casos se entregaron a los sujetos una estructura o esqueleto básico de código, con el propósito de que el sujeto se enfoque en la resolución del problema y en la escritura de las pruebas que considere necesarias. Para replicar con la mayor similitud el experimento original, tanto las tareas experimentales así como los casos de prueba utilizados para mediar las variables respuesta, fueron obtenidos de los experimentadores originales e incorporados en la herramienta propuesta. De igual manera, utilizamos Eclipse y Java como herramienta y lenguaje de desarrollo.

Algunos estudios experimentales sobre la efectividad de TDD, reportan haber utilizado encuestas demográficas aplicadas ya sea al inicio y/o al concluir las tareas experimentales. Estas encuestas buscan complementar los análisis con otras variables de contexto, como son las características personales de los programadores (por ejemplo: la experiencia, el conocimiento del dominio, motivación, entre otros). También advertimos que en general los estudios no publican los cuestionarios demográficos aplicados, limitándose a la presentación y análisis de sus resultados. Durante la construcción de nuestra herramienta, tuvimos acceso a las encuestas realizadas por los experimentadores originales, con lo cual, este aspecto clave para la reproducibilidad, también fue considerado dentro del diseño conceptual que se presenta en la Sección 4.1.

4 Propuesta

Esta iniciativa surge como parte de las experiencias obtenidas a lo largo de una serie de replicaciones experimentales referentes a la medición de la efectividad de TDD en contextos académicos e industriales, realizadas por los investigadores de la Universidad de las Fuerzas Armadas ESPE de Ecuador y de la Universidad Politécnica de Madrid de España, como parte de diferentes proyectos institucionales.

A medida que las replicaciones se fueron ejecutando, se advirtió la necesidad de contar con una plataforma que permita, entre otros aspectos, automatizar el proceso de medición, la toma de datos, el registro de participantes, la aleatorización de tareas experimentales, la planificación del experimento y el diseño experimental. Por otro lado, se precisó que además de servir para los objetivos propios de la investigación, la plataforma sirva para que otros investigadores puedan ejecutar experimentos, compartir y reproducir sus hallazgos, de acuerdo a los lineamientos de la investigación reproducible [22].

Es preciso aclarar que se consideró la posibilidad de realizar cambios en el diseño experimental dependiendo de las características particulares de cada contexto de estudio. También se definieron los mecanismos para la toma de datos, realización de mediciones, análisis de información y presentación de resultados.

4.1 Modelo conceptual de la plataforma propuesta

La figura, presenta un diagrama conceptual que expone de manera general los componentes que contiene la plataforma de experimentación. El diagrama se ajusta a la propuesta de [22] para experimentos relacionados con pruebas de software, ya que es de nuestro interés comparar los cambios introducidos respecto a una iniciativa similar.

De manera análoga a la propuesta de [22], la plataforma desarrollada está conformada por componentes que cubren las distintas etapas de ejecución de un experimento. Los mismos artefactos y librerías pueden ser reutilizados en la replicación, pudiendo introducir cambios si fuese necesario. Por otra parte, se podrá a definir un único diseño experimental en varios estudios, para posibilitar la realización de trabajos de síntesis como el meta-análisis y con ello generalizar los resultados sin introducir mayores amenazas a la validez.

A partir de los datos obtenidos para las variables respuesta, los scripts de R, sirven para definir mecanismos de análisis estadístico o para comparar diferentes estudios. Por ejemplo: para realizar pruebas de hipótesis, determinar los p-valores, aplicar modelos de regresión, análisis de diseños factoriales completos, intra sujetos o inter sujetos, etc.

Si bien nuestra propuesta, puede ser comparable con [22] en cuanto al diseño conceptual, sin embargo los objetivos experimentales difieren por completo. Esto se debe a que nuestras variables de estudio se encuentran orientadas a establecer la efectividad de la técnica TDD en términos de la calidad y productividad de los desarrolladores, en tanto que en [22], se consideran variables tendientes a analizar la efectividad en la realización de pruebas de software. (Por ejemplo):

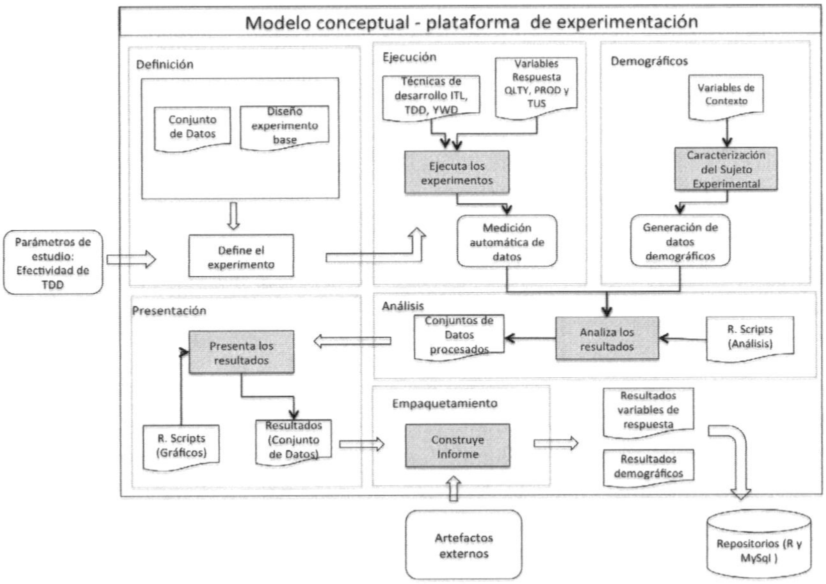

Fig. 1. Diagrama Conceptual

Se utiliza como métrica de respuesta, el porcentaje promedio en la detección de defectos (APFD).

4.2 Características del prototipo desarrollado

El modelo conceptual descrito en la Sección 4.1 permitió desarrollar un prototipo funcional de la plataforma que brinda la opción de configurar múltiples experimentos sobre la efectividad de TDD, reutilizando los distintos componentes descritos en la sección anterior.

La plataforma contiene una interfaz de usuario web desarrollada con el gestor de contenidos Drupal y sirve principalmente para la autenticación de usuarios para el acceso a la realización de los experimentos, y la presentación de resultados en línea. Para la definición y obtención de datos demográficos se utilizó el gestor de cuestionarios LimeSurvey con el cual se implementaron dos cuestionarios: el primero con preguntas orientadas a recabar datos que son requeridos previo a la ejecución del experimento (por ejemplo: nivel de educación de los sujetos, experiencia en programación, uso de herramientas de pruebas, experiencia en lenguaje Java y jUnit, entre otros) y el segundo con preguntas para obtener información una vez concluido el proceso experimental (por ejemplo: la percepción sobre el grado de dificultad de la tarea, número de historias de usuario desarrolladas a criterio del programador, entre otros).

El componente central que sirve para la ejecución del experimento fue desarrollado tomando como base la plataforma Ulteo OVD. Este es un aplicativo open source que permite gestionar máquinas virtuales sobre plataformas Windows y Linux. Sobre esta plataforma se desarrolló un componente para que el investigador pueda definir un experimento (fechas de inicio y finalización, tipo de diseño experimental, número de sujetos permitidos, etc.) y combinar los factores y niveles que va a utilizar de acuerdo a lo determinado en el experimento original (por ejemplo, al definir un experimento donde se analice la técnica TDD en comparación con la técnica ITL, utilizando los niveles *sliced* y no *sliced* para la descripción de la tarea experimental, y utilizar los esqueletos de los programas MR y BSK que deberán ser implementados por los sujetos).

El prototipo desarrollado, permite instanciar máquinas virtuales en ambiente Linux, las mismas que tienen preinstalado el IDE de desarrollo Eclipse con los esqueletos de las tareas en lenguaje Java, y además contienen la herramienta Adobe Reader para visualizar la descripción de la tarea en formato pdf.

La medición de las variables respuesta QLTY, PROD y TUS, son realizadas con un plugin hecho en Java que se ejecuta automáticamente una vez que el usuario concluye la tarea experimental. El plugin ejecuta los casos de prueba definidos en el experimento, y contabiliza el número de aserciones pasadas, no pasadas, número de errores y los porcentajes obtenidos en las variables respuesta. Finalmente genera un informe detallado de las mediciones en formato texto y por otro lado muestra de forma gráfica los principales resultados obtenidos como se muestra en la figura. Esta información es almacenada en una base de datos MySql en conjunto con el código desarrollado por el sujeto.

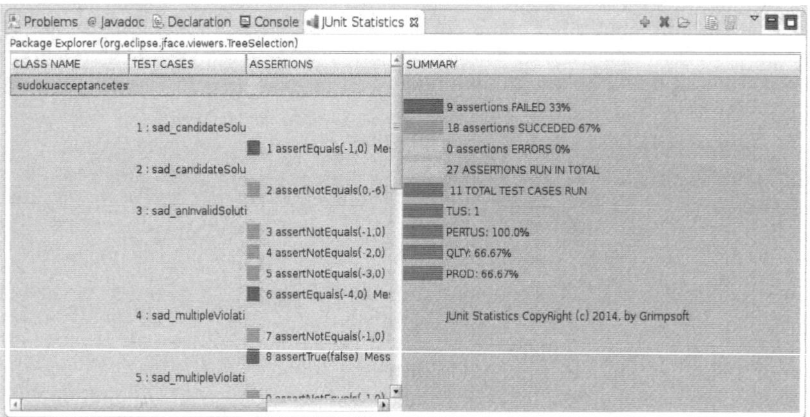

Fig. 2. Plugin de medición

Para la presentación de resultados, se ha tomado como base Latex y la herramienta de análisis estadístico R, con el complemento Sweave - Knir, que permiten generar documentos en formato pdf, conteniendo plots estadísticos provenientes de los análisis obtenidos en las diferentes replicaciones.

4.3 Proceso de ejecución del experimento

El proceso de ejecución del experimento que soporta la plataforma propuesta se resume en la Figura 3.

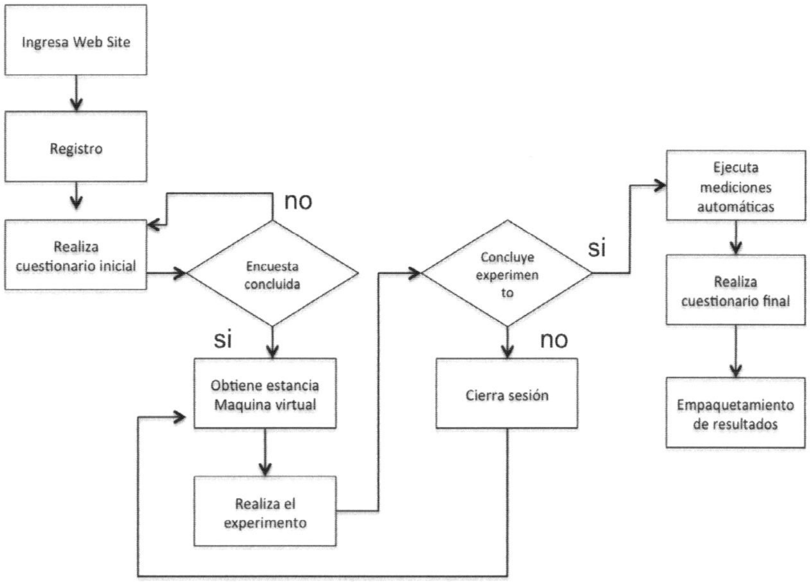

Fig. 3. Proceso de ejecución

El proceso inicia con el registro del usuario que lo realiza mediante la interfaz web. Posteriormente la plataforma habilita el acceso para la realización de la encuesta previa. Si la encuesta es concluida, se obtiene una instancia a una máquina virtual y se genera aleatorización de las asignaciones del sujeto a las tareas de forma automática propendiendo a tener grupos balanceados en las diferentes combinaciones para un diseño factorial completo o de medidas repetidas, de acuerdo a cómo se haya diseñado el experimento.

El usuario tiene la posibilidad de concluir el experimento, o de cerrar la sesión y continuar en otro momento. Si decide cerrar la sesión, la plataforma guarda en un log el estado actual de la ejecución del experimento, así cuando se reanude la sesión, se levante otra instancia de la máquina virtual sin perder el trabajo realizado.

Finalmente, si el usuario decide que ha concluido el experimento, se ejecutan automáticamente las mediciones de las variables respuesta, se solicita la realización de una encuesta final y se empaquetan los resultados.

5 Conclusiones

Este trabajo describe una propuesta tecnológica para la reproducibilidad de experimentos sobre la efectividad de TDD en comparación con otras aproximaciones al desarrollo.

La literatura muestra pocos estudios que proponen alternativas para realizar investigación reproducible en ingeniería de software empírica, aun cuando en otras disciplinas ha tenido una constante evolución.

La propuesta se basa en la aplicación de diferentes herramientas que pretenden cubrir el ciclo de experimentación, desde la definición del experimento en cuanto a sus factores, niveles y diseño, hasta la publicación de sus resultados estadísticos.

El principal aporte de la propuesta radica en el hecho de que la ejecución del experimento, la toma de datos crudos y la medición de las variables respuesta se realiza de forma automática en procura de replicaciones de tipo literal. Consecuentemente, se disminuyen los errores de medición que podrían causarse especialmente por fatiga o cansancio del experimentador al realizar estas tareas de forma manual.

Se propone para trabajos futuros la validación de la operatividad de la plataforma con la participación de investigadores interesados en la temática de estudio.

Referencias

1. Basili, V.R., Shull, F., Lanubile, F.: Building knowledge through families of experiments. IEEE Transactions on Software Engineering 25(4), 456-473 (July/August 1999)
2. Bechhofer, S., De Roure, D., Gamble, M., Goble, C., Buchan, I.: Research objects: Towards exchange and reuse of digital knowledge. The Future of the Web for Collaborative Science 10 (2010)
3. Beck, K.: Test-driven development: by example. Addison-Wesley Professional (2003)
4. Belhajjame, K., Zhao, J., Garijo, D., Gamble, M., Hettne, K., Palma, R., Mina, E., Corcho, O., Gómez-Pérez, J.M., Bechhofer, S., et al.: Using a suite of ontologies for preserving workflow-centric research objects. Web Semantics: Science, Services and Agents on the World Wide Web 32, 16-42 (2015)
5. Carvalho, L.A., Belhajjame, K., Medeiros, C.B.: Converting scripts into reproducible workflow research objects. In: e-Science (e-Science), 2016 IEEE 12th International Conference on. pp. 71-80. IEEE (2016)
6. Causevic, A., Sundmark, D., Punnekkat, S.: Factors limiting industrial adoption of test driven development: A systematic review. In: Software Testing, Verification and Validation (ICST), 2011 IEEE Fourth International Conference on. pp. 337-346. IEEE (2011)
7. Cleland-Huang, J., Czauderna, A., Dekhtyar, A., Gotel, O., Hayes, J.H., Keenan, E., Leach, G., Maletic, J., Poshyvanyk, D., Shin, Y., et al.: Grand challenges, benchmarks, and tracelab: developing infrastructure for the software traceability research community. In: Proceedings of the 6th international workshop on traceability in emerging forms of software engineering. pp. 17-23. ACM (2011)
8. Davison, A.: Automated capture of experiment context for easier reproducibility in computational research. Computing in Science & Engineering 14(4), 48-56 (2012)

9. Dit, B., Moritz, E., Vasquez, M.L., Poshyvanyk, D.: Supporting and accelerating reproducible research in software maintenance using tracelab component library. In: ICSM. pp. 330-339 (2013)
10. Donoho, D.L., Maleki, A., Rahman, I.U., Shahram, M., Stodden, V.: Reproducible research in computational harmonic analysis. Computing in Science & Engineering 11(1) (2009)
11. Errington, T.M., Iorns, E., Gunn, W., Tan, F.E., Lomax, J., Nosek, B.A.: An open investigation of the reproducibility of cancer biology research. Elife 3, e04333 (2014)
12. Fomel, S.: Reproducible research as a community effort: Lessons from the madagascar project. Computing in Science & Engineering 17(1), 20-26 (2015)
13. Gómez, O., Juristo, N., Vegas, S.: Replications types in experimental disciplines. In: Proceedings of the 2010 ACM-IEEE International Symposium on Empirical Software Engineering and Measurement. pp. 1-10. No. 3, Bolzano-Bozen, Italy (2010)
14. González-Barahona, J.M., Robles, G.: On the reproducibility of empirical software engineering studies based on data retrieved from development repositories. Empirical Software Engineering 17(1-2), 75-89 (2012)
15. Juristo, N., Others: A test-driven development experiment at ericsson, unpublished
16. Leisch, F.: Sweave: Dynamic generation of statistical reports using literate data analysis. In: Compstat. pp. 575-580. Springer (2002)
17. LeVeque, R.J.: Python tools for reproducible research on hyperbolic problems. Computing in Science & Engineering 11(1), 19-27 (2009)
18. Mäkinen, S., Münch, J.: Effects of test-driven development: A comparative analysis of empirical studies. In: International Conference on Software Quality. pp. 155-169. Springer (2014)
19. Mesirov, J.P.: Accessible reproducible research. Science 327(5964), 415-416 (2010)
20. Munir, H., Moayyed, M.: Systematic literature review and controlled pilot experimental evaluation of test driven development (tdd) vs. test-last development (tld) (2012)
21. Munir, H., Moayyed, M., Petersen, K.: Considering rigor and relevance when evaluating test driven development: A systematic review. Information and Software Technology 56(4), 375-394 (2014)
22. De Oliveira Neto, F.G., Torkar, R., Machado, P.D.: An initiative to improve reproducibility and empirical evaluation of software testing techniques. In: Proceedings of the 37th International Conference on Software Engineering-Volume 2. pp. 575-578. IEEE Press (2015)
23. Peng, R.D.: Reproducible research in computational science. Science 334(6060), 1226-1227 (2011)
24. Piccolo, S.R., Frampton, M.B.: Tools and techniques for computational reproducibility. GigaScience 5(1), 30 (2016)
25. Rodríguez-Pascual, M., Rubio-Montero, A.J., Mayo-Garc a, R., Kanellopoulos, C., Prnjat, O., Darriba, D., Posada, D.: A fault tolerant workflow for reproducible research. In: Information and Computer Technology (GOCICT), 2014 Annual Global Online Conference on. pp. 70-75. IEEE (2014)
26. Santana-Pérez, I., Perez-Hernandez, M.S.: Towards reproducibility in scientific workflows: An infrastructure-based approach. Scientific Programming 2015 (2015)
27. Sinha, R., Sudhish, P.S.: A principled approach to reproducible research: a comparative review towards scientific integrity in computational research. In: Ethics in Engineering, Science and Technology (ETHICS), 2016 IEEE International Symposium on. pp. 1{9. IEEE (2016)

28. Stodden, V., Miguez, S.: Best practices for computational science: Software infrastructure and environments for reproducible and extensible research (2013)
29. Thompson, P.A., Burnett, A.: Reproducible research. CORE Issues in Professional and Research Ethics 1(6) (2012)
30. Topalidou, M., Leblois, A., Boraud, T., Rougier, N.P.: A long journey into reproducible computational neuroscience (2014)
31. Verdejo, D.G., Kinnings, S., Xie, L., Xie, L., Zhang, Y., Bourne, P.E., Gil, Y.: Quantifying reproducibility in computational biology: The case of the tuberculosis drugome (2013)
32. Waltemath, D., Henkel, R., Winter, F., Wolkenhauer, O.: Reproducibility of model-based results in systems biology. In: Systems Biology, pp. 301-320. Springer (2013
33. Woodman, S., Hiden, H., Watson, P., Missier, P.: Achieving reproducibility by combining provenance with service and workflow versioning. In: Proceedings of the 6th workshop on Workflows in support of large-scale science. pp. 127-136. ACM (2011)

Computer System for Monitoring and Control of UAVs

Wilson Medina-Pazmiño[1], Anibal Jara-Olmedo[1],
Jessica S. Ortiz[2] and Christian P. Carvajal[2]

[1] CIDFAE Centro de Investigación y desarrollo de la Fuerza Aérea Ecuatoriana
[2] Universidad de las fuerzas armadas ESPE, Sangolquí, Ecuador
{wilsonmedina81,chriss2592}@hotmail.com
lenin.jara@cidfae.gob.ec,jsortiz4@espe.edu.ec

Abstract. This article presents the development of a system for monitoring and controlling an Unmanned Aerial Vehicle (UAV) in real time. It was developing a computer application that will be installed on a server inside the ground control station (GCS). The information generated in the aircraft is concentered and transmitted by a control device that is on board the UAV through a DataLink wireless communications system specific to UAV. The parameters of the physical variables and events generated in the UAV are showed to the system operator and stored in a database engine for post flight analysis of the UAVs...

Key words: UAV, Database, HMI, Monitoring, Control

1 Introducción

Los UAV (Unmanned Aerial Vehicles) son sistemas que han evolucionado en el tiempo. Inicialmente eran plataformas aéreas teleoperadas que no alcanzaban grandes distancias de operación y carecían de un sistema de monitoreo que indique el estado de la aeronave en tiempo real [1]. Actualmente los UAV llevan a bordo equipos y sistemas que ejecutan sofisticados algoritmos de control [2], [3] que permiten a los UAV volar de forma autónoma y segura, emplean sistemas de DataLink generalmente bidireccionales [4] i.e. que sirven para transmitir información en tiempo real desde la aeronave (UAV) hasta la GCS (Estación de Control en Tierra) y viceversa [5]. Los sensores electro-ópticos a bordo del UAV son parte de la carga útil, que permiten realizar aplicaciones de i) control, ii) vigilancia, iii) reconocimiento de zonas en lugares estratégicos, entre otros [6]. Los UAV en el campo civil y militar son relevantes ya que se pueden emplear en i) reconocimiento de zonas de riesgo, ii) filmografía, iii) vigilancia de fronteras [1], [5], iv) identificación de zonas de contaminación por derrame de hidrocarburos [8] [7], entre otras; son aplicaciones en las que los UAV han mostrado sus ventajas y crecimiento tecnológico.

Los UAV tienen sistemas de instrumentación [9] que permiten valorar el estado de los componentes de la aeronave. Los sistemas que van a bordo de un UAV necesitan ser monitoreados y controlados desde puntos remotos ubicados a decenas de kilómetros, los UAV se complementan con las aplicaciones informáticas que se encuentran ejecutándose en la GCS, la cual cuenta con sistemas de monitoreo denominados HMI, mostrando así la información necesaria de la aeronave no tripulada.

Las HMI (Human Machine Interface) son aplicaciones informáticas que permiten monitorear y controlar equipos y sistemas que van a bordo del UAV, la información transmitida del UAV a la GCS Fig. 1 permiten al operador realizar tareas de monitoreo y control de la aeronave en tiempo real. Estos sistemas no tripulados llevan a bordo sofisticados computadores que establecen comunicación entre la estación en tierra y el UAV, este enlace permite el intercambio de información mediante el sistema de comunicaciones denominado DataLink [4]. Los computadores a bordo del UAV realizan tareas complementarias como: i) administración de datos, ii) ejecutar algoritmos complejos de navegación, iii) liberar carga útil, iv) administrar parámetros de emergencia [10], entre otras; adicional la información obtenida en la GCS proveniente del UAV puede ser almacenada en un motor de base de datos para un análisis post-vuelo del comportamiento y eficiencia del UAV.

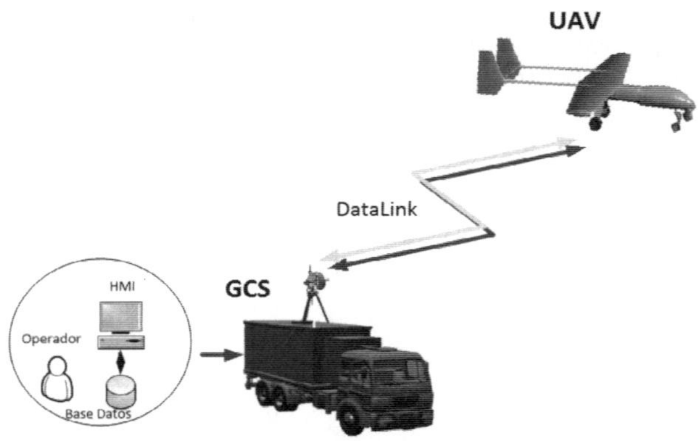

Fig. 1. Estructura de un Sistema Aéreo no Tripulado UAS

Actualmente a nivel comercial existen múltiples alternativas de sistemas HMI para monitoreo y control de UAVs. Algunas aplicaciones disponibles en el mercado de tipo COTS (Commercial off-the-shelf) [11], [12] como: *i)* Horizont de MicroPilot, *ii)* BlighterView HMI 2 [13], *iii)* IData tool [14], entre otras que permiten supervisar y controlar aeronaves UAV en tiempo real. A nivel de investigación el Establecimiento de Desarrollo Aeronáutico de la India [15] y la Universidad de Belgrado [16] detallan los requerimientos y características que debe tener un HMI para realizar tareas de control y monitoreo de un UAV. La propuesta del presente trabajo es desarrollar una aplicación informática para realizar estas tareas de tres aeronaves (UAV) diferentes. El sistema tiene la capacidad de conectarse a la aeronave correspondiente y obtener la información requerida por el operador del sistema UAV. El HMI debe poder almacenar la información que se genera durante una misión en un motor de base de datos para poder realizar análisis comparativos de eficiencia de los UAV después de cada vuelo.

Este trabajo consta de 5 Secciones incluida la introducción: En la Sección 2, se describe la arquitectura del sistema de monitoreo y control para UAV's. En la Sección 3 se detalla el funcionamiento y desarrollo del sistema de monitoreo y control de los UAV's. En la Sección 4 se analizan los resultados obtenidos de las pruebas. Finalmente en la Sección 5 las conclusiones y trabajos futuros son presentados.

2 Sistema de Monitoreo y Control del UAV

La arquitectura de un sistema de monitoreo y control para UAV Fig. 2, cuenta con la capacidad de escoger la aeronave disponible para ejecutar las tareas de i) vigilancia ii) control iii) y reconocimiento. La aplicación puede almacenar información en un motor de base de datos; que permite satisfacer los requerimientos del CID-FAE logrando monitorear cualquier aeronave mediante el uso de un solo sistema instalado en la estación de mando y control en tierra EMCT.

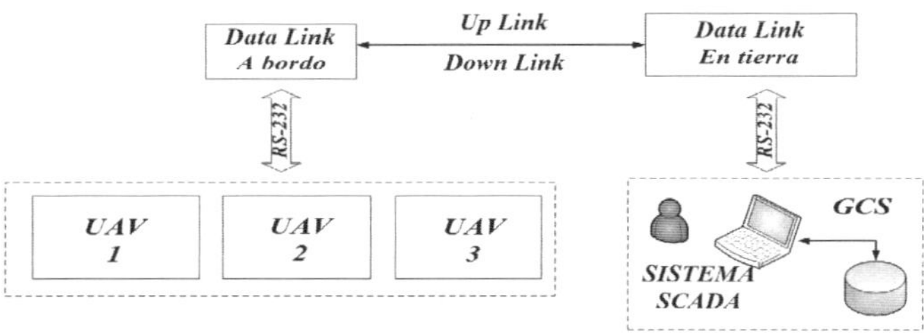

Fig. 2. Arquitectura del sistema aéreo no tripulado UAS

Las pruebas del software de monitoreo y control se lo realizará sobre las plataformas aéreas construidas en el Ecuador por el CID-FAE. Las aeronaves UAV es diseñadas para realizar trabajos como: i) detección, ii) observación, iii) control iv) y reconocimiento de zonas distantes. Las misiones realizadas por la aeronave UAV son efectuadas a decenas de kilómetros de distancia, donde el sistema de monitoreo y control obtendrá información e indicará el estado de los sub sistemas dentro de la aeronave tales como: i) energía, ii) instrumentación (sistema de propulsión), iii) apuntador de antenas, iv) sensor electro-óptico, entre otros a bordo del UAV.

2.1 Algoritmo del sistema de control a bordo del UAV.

En el UAV-1 se encuentra instalado un dispositivo que concentra la información que se produce en la aeronave Fig. 3, el dispositivo de control transmite la información obtenida de i)sensores análogos, ii)sensores digitales entre otros equipos que están dentro del UAV. La información es transmitida al sistema de monitoreo y control que se encuentra en la GCS mediante un sistema de comunicaciones inalámbrico (Data-Link) propio de los UAV [4].

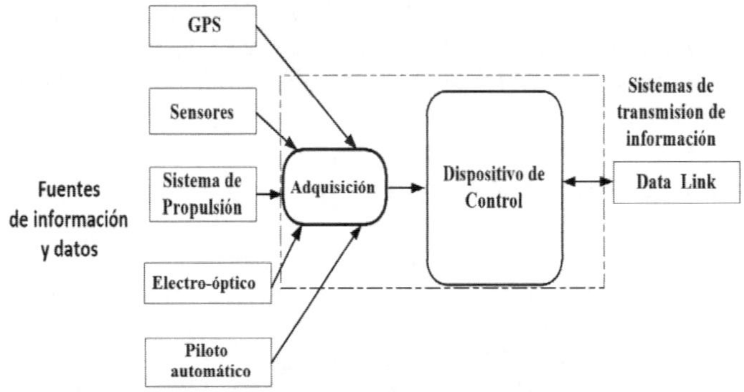

Fig. 3. Diagrama de bloques del sistema de control a bordo del UAV

El dispositivo de control a bordo del UAV está desarrollado bajo la arquitectura maestro esclavo o también conocido comunicación punto–punto a través del estándar de comunicación RS-232 [17]. El dispositivo de control responde a las peticiones realizadas por el HMI instalado en la GCS. La aplicación de monitoreo y control instalada en la GCS está configurada como maestro de comunicaciones. El esquema de funcionamiento lógico Fig.4 para el sistema a bordo del UAV-1 está en la capacidad de ejecutar múltiples acciones de forma simultánea esto garantiza las respuestas oportunas a las peticiones de la GCS.

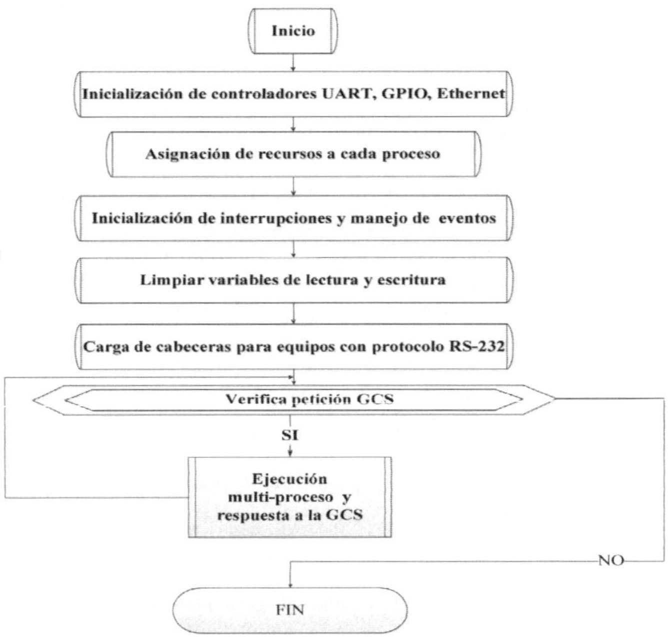

Fig. 4. Algoritmo de funcionamiento del computador principal

La GCS establece comunicación con el sistema de control a bordo del UAV mediante el sistema Data Link. El sistema de control a bordo del UAV se encuentra en modo escucha es decir espera las instrucciones que desde la GCS se generan para responder las solicitudes requeridas por el operador del UAV.

3. Funcionamiento y Desarrollo del Sistema de Monitoreo

3.1. Estructura de la trama de comunicaciones

Se detalla la trama de comunicaciones [18] existente entre el sistema de monitoreo y control de la GCS y el dispositivo de control que va a bordo del UAV, para poder generalizar la aplicación de software de la GCS se desarrolló una trama de comunicaciones dedicada de longitud variable Tabla 1.

Tabla 1. Estructura de la trama de comunicaciones entre el UAV y la GCS

3 Bytes	1Byte	2 Bytes	N Bytes	2 Bytes
Inicio de trama	Función	Dirección de escritura	Datos variables	Control de Errores CRCH-CRCL

La trama de comunicación desarrollada se detalla en cinco partes, las cuales son muy esenciales, para lograr establecer una comunicación estable y estandarizada para el UAV, cada campo de la trama cumple con una función específica tales como: *i)* el inicio de trama [19] que contiene tres registros que indican el inicio de una petición de datos y el modelo de UAV que se va a monitorear y controlar, *ii)* bloque función [20], el cual contiene funciones de lectura y de escritura de datos análogos, y digitales que se generan en la aeronave, *iii)* la dirección de escritura o lectura internamente en el sistema de control, a bordo del UAV-1 se disponen de 0x03E8 direcciones de memoria que pueden ser leídas o escritas, *iv)* los datos variables que escribirán o leerán (N) registros por petición, la longitud de la trama es variable *i.e.* el número de Bytes depende de cada variable en cada petición y por último *v)* el bloque para detectar errores en las comunicaciones, se emplea el algoritmo de control de redundancia cíclica CRC16 [21] para determinar si la trama contiene errores.

El desarrollo del HMI se basa en las características y criterios de un sistema SCADA [22]. Los HMI's implementados en el servidor de la GCS son interactivos con el usuario. El HMI proporciona las herramientas necesarias para que el operador de UAV realice tareas de monitoreo y control de forma eficiente sobre los UAV.

El uso del software Laboratorio Virtual (LabView) permite realizar las actividades de supervisión control y adquisición de datos de las aeronaves construidas en el CIDFAE. En la GCS se encuentra instalada una aplicación multiuso. La aplicación permite escoger entre tres plataformas aéreas a monitorear.

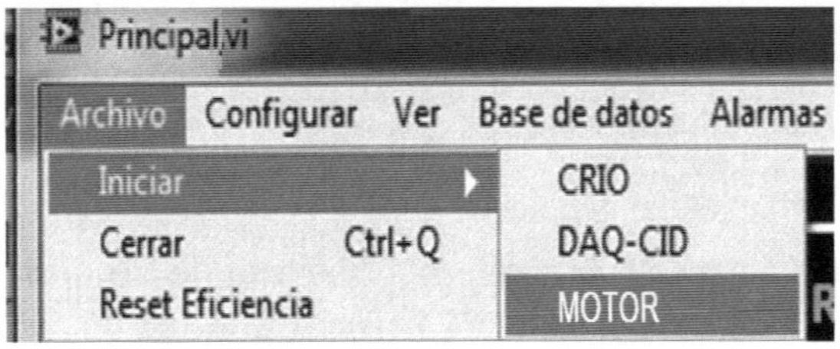

Fig. 5. Barra de menú principal del sistema de supervisión y control del UAV

Mediante el uso de la barra de menú Fig. 5 ubicada en la parte superior de la aplicación informática se podrá seleccionar la plataforma aérea que el sistema supervise y controle. El HMI cuenta con tres posibilidades de software de monitoreo y control que se pueden ejecutar Fig. 6. El diseño y la presentación de las aplicaciones son parecidas en color, forma y ubicación de los componentes y sistemas a ser monitoreados y controlados.

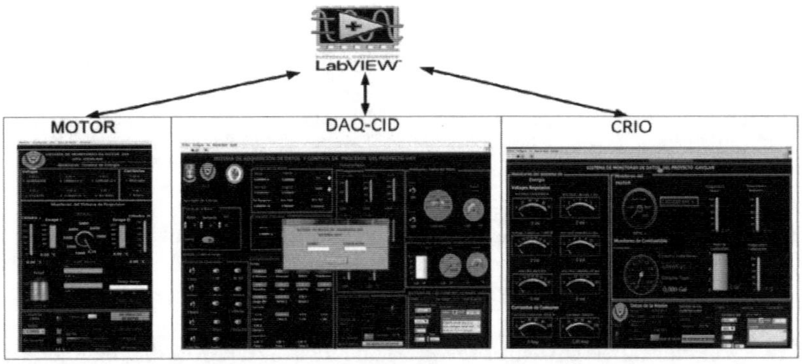

Fig. 6. HMI's de las plataformas aéreas del CIDFAE

El sistema puede monitorear y controlar tres aeronaves diferentes. A nivel de operador, las aplicaciones son conocidas como Motor, DAQ-CID y CRIO. La clasificación de las aplicaciones se las realizó por el sistema de control y adquisición de datos que se encuentra a bordo del UAV-1 y el sistema de propulsión de la aeronave.

La aplicación Motor en la parte superior muestra la información del sistema de energía, voltajes y corrientes, generados en el UAV-1. En la parte central la aplicación muestra información del sistema de propulsión. Las señales del sistema de propulsión que se monitorean son: la temperatura de los cilindros, la temperatura de los tubos de escape, las RPM del motor, se controla el porcentaje de aceleración del motor, se mide el nivel del tanque de combustible. En la parte inferior se visualiza la calidad de señal del sistema de comunicaciones. La calidad de señal del sistema de comunicaciones permite determinar en qué momento se ha perdido comunicación entre la GCS y el UAV-1.

En la aplicación DAQ-CID a más de monitorear las variables del sistema de *i)* energía, *ii)* de propulsión y *iii)* de comunicaciones puede controlar el sistema de apuntamiento de antenas; el sistema de apuntamiento consiste en realizar un seguimiento de posición a la aeronave mediante coordenadas GPS.

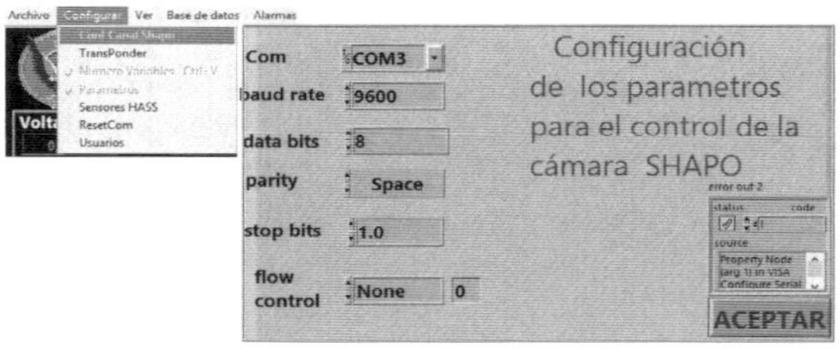

Fig. 7. HMI de configuración del sensor electro-óptico que va a bordo del UAV

La aplicación CRIO muestra variables del sistema de energía y del sistema de comunicaciones. Esta aplicación CRIO difiere de las otras aplicaciones en las variables que adquiere del sistema de propulsión; mide y registra con énfasis la eficiencia del sistema de propulsión. Las variables como el consumo de combustible, la temperatura del combustible y la temperatura del aceite del motor son incrementadas en esta aplicación. A demás la aplicación CRIO incorpora el control y configuración de un sensor electro-óptico Fig.7, la aplicación del sensor electro-óptico esta anexa al HMI principal.

4 Resultados

Las pruebas realizadas con el UAV-1 se observaron en la GCS Fig.8, los datos obtenidos del UAV fueron visualizados y almacenados, en tiempo real. El almacenamiento de los datos se los realizó mediante la aplicación del concepto de histéresis con porcentaje +/- 1%. La histéresis se refiere a tener cambios significativos en las variables a guardar. Debido que la información obtenida del UAV es en tiempo real hay variables que pueden permanecer invariantes durante períodos largos de tiempo que sin aplicar el valor de histéresis se podrían guardar datos repetitivos produciendo saturación a la base de datos.

Fig. 8. Pruebas realizadas dentro de la GCS, con la aeronave UAV-1

Las variables monitoreadas en tiempo real Fig. 9 de los distintos sistemas a bordo del UAV se almacenan en la base de datos, para acceder a ellos se lo hace desde la interfaz desarrollada Fig. 6 a través de la barra de menú. Los datos son almacenados por áreas (Energía, Apuntamiento de antenas, Instrumentación (sistema de propulsión)).

Fig. 9. Visualización de las variables del sistema de propulsión del UAV en tiempo real

5 Conclusiones

La obtención de información del UAV a través del canal de comunicación del sistema Data Link propio del UAS se realizó en tiempo real. El operador puede supervisar y controlar la capacidad que el sistema tiene de compartir información entre los distintos sistema que van a bordo de la aeronave pudiendo tomar decisiones acertadas sobre la operación del sistema. La aplicación instalada en el servidor de la GCS registra todos los datos y eventos ocurridos durante las misiones del UAV. Con la aplicación del concepto de histéresis se ha podido optimizar recursos físicos espacio de disco en la base de datos.

Como trabajo futuro se propone realizar la publicación de los datos mediante un web server con la finalidad de tener monitoreo en cualquier parte del mundo a través de internet.

Agradecimiento

Este trabajo se desarrolló en el Centro de Investigación y Desarrollo de la FAE buscando el aporte a la investigación, desarrollo e innovación de tecnología en el Ecuador.

Referencias

1 Samad, A.M. Kamarulzaman, N.; Hamdani, M.A.; Mastor, T.A.; Hashim, K.A. (2013). The potential of Un manned Aerial Vehicle (UAV) for civilian and mapping application, System Engineering and Technology (ICSET), 2013 IEEE 3rd International Conference on. 313-318. Doi 10.1109/ICSEngT.2013.6650191

2 David, V., Octavio, G., David, B., & Victor, E. (2015). Analysis, Design, and Implementation of an Autopilot for Unmanned Aircraft - UAV's Based on Fuzzy Logic. 2015 Asia-Pacific Conference On Computer Aided System Engineering. http://dx.doi.org/10.1109/apcase.2015.42

3 Roy, T., Pervej, M., Tumpa, F., Paul, L., & Sarkar, M. (2016). Robust nonlinear adaptive backstepping controller design for unmanned autonomous vehicles. 2016 International Workshop On Computational Intelligence (IWCI). http://dx.doi.org/10.1109/iwci.2016.7860328

4 Medina-Pazmino, W., Jara-Olmedo, A., & Valencia-Redrovan, D. (2016). Analysis and determination of minimum requirements for a data link communication system for unmanned aerial vehicles- UAV's. 2016 IEEE Ecuador Technical Chapters Meeting (ETCM). http://dx.doi.org/10.1109/etcm.2016.7750816

5 Bhaskaranand, M., & Gibson, J. (2015). Global Motion Assisted Low Complexity Video Encoding for UAV Applications. IEEE Journal Of Selected Topics In Signal Processing, 9(1), 139-150. http://dx.doi.org/10.1109/jstsp.2014.2345563

6 Ryan, J., & Cummings, M. (2016). A Systems Analysis of the Introduction of Unmanned Aircraft Into Aircraft Carrier Operations. IEEE Transactions On Human-Machine Systems, 46(2), 209-220. http://dx.doi.org/10.1109/thms.2014.2376355

7 Obanawa, H. (2015). Quantitative measurement of the topographic change at overhanging sea cliff with small UAV survey system. 2015 IEEE International Geoscience And Remote Sensing Symposium (IGARSS). http://dx.doi.org/10.1109/igarss.2015.7326874

8 Lyu, Y., Pan, Q., Zhang, Y., Zhao, C., Zhu, H., Tang, T., & Liu, L. (2015). Simultaneously multi-UAV mapping and control with visual servoing. 2015 International Conference On Unmanned Aircraft Systems (ICUAS). http://dx.doi.org/10.1109/icuas.2015.7152283

9 Malpica, D., Aparicio, M., Palomino, A., Felix, O., Vergara, S., & Vargas, A. (2009). Construction, modeling and instrumentation of a mini-unmanned aircraft in delta (Δ) configuration. 2009 6Th International Conference On Electrical Engineering, Computing Science And Automatic Control (CCE). http://dx.doi.org/10.1109/iceee.2009.5393345

10 COM Express vs. PC/104 for Small UAV Systems - COTS Journal. (2017). Archive.cotsjournalonline.com. Retrieved 6 March 2017, Disponible en: http://archive.cotsjournalonline.com/articles/view/101656. Última Vista 01-05-2017

11 Vigder, M., & Kark, A. Maintaining COTS-Based Systems: Start with the Design. Fifth International Conference On Commercial-Off-The-Shelf (COTS)-Based Software Systems (ICCBSS'05). http://dx.doi.org/10.1109/iccbss.2006.19

12 Iai.co.il. Israel Aerospace Industries. Advanced Ground Control Station Disponible en: http://www.iai.co.il/2013/36946-37386-en/BusinessAreas_UnmannedAirSystems.aspx. Última Vista 23-05-2017

13 Blighter. BlighterView HMI 2 - Envitia MapLink Pro based display and control software for Blighter radars and slew-to-cue CCD cameras & thermal image", Blight-

er.com. Disponible en: http://www.blighter.com/products/blighterview-hmi-2.html. Última Vista 23-04-2017.

14 IData Tool Suite | HMI Designer Tool |ENSCO Avionics Embedded Software Display Product", Ensco.com, 2016. [Online]. Available: http://www.ensco.com/avionics/idata. Última Vista 27-05-2017

15 G. Natarajan, "Ground control stations for unmanned air vehicles (Review Paper)", Defence Science Journal, vol. 51, no. 3, pp. 229-237, 2001. http://dx.doi.org/10.14429/dsj.51.2234.

16 M. Jovanović, D. Starčević and Z. Jovanović, "Reusable Design of Data Visualization Software Architecture for Unmanned Aerial Vehicles", Journal of Aerospace Information Systems, vol. 11, no. 6, pp. 359-371, 2014

17 Taylor, J., & Hoole, J. (2016). Robust protocol for sending synchronisation pulse and RS-232 communication over single low quality twisted pair cable. 2016 IEEE International Conference On Industrial Technology (ICIT). http://dx.doi.org/10.1109/icit.2016.7474832

18 DRAFT AMMENDMENT TO IEEE STD 802.3-2005 "Media access control frame structure", 2005. Disponible en: http://www.ieee802.org/3/as/public/0503/3d0_1_CMP.pdf. Última Vista 23-04-2017

19 American National Standard for Telecommunications "Generic Framing Procedure", 2001 Diponible en: http://www.ieee802.org/17/documents/presentations/may2001/gfp.pdf. Última Vista 23-03-2017

20 Thomas H. Morris, Bryan A. Jones, Rayford B. Vaughn, Yoginder S. Dandass, "Deterministic Intrusion Detection Rules for MODBUS Protocols", 2014 47th Hawaii International Conference on System Sciences, vol. 00, no. , pp. 1773-1781, 2013, doi:10.1109/HICSS.2013.174

21 Chuang, Y., Yang, J., & Lin, S. (2015). Analysis of using chained computing CRC-16 mechanism for wireless sensor mesh networks. 2015 International Symposium On Consumer Electronics (ISCE). http://dx.doi.org/10.1109/isce.2015.7177795. Sajid, A., Abbas, H., & Saleem, K. (2016). Cloud-Assisted IoT-Based SCADA Systems Security: A Review of the State of the Art and Future Challenges. IEEE Access, 4, 1375-1384. http://dx.doi.org/10.1109/

Expert System for the Control of Physiological Signals of Aircraft Pilots: A Systematic Mapping Study.

Milton Escobar-Sánchez[1], José Luis Carrillo-Medina[1], Patricio Espinel[1], Katya Torres-Vásquez[1], Joseph Alay-Chimborazo[2]
[1]Universidad de las Fuerzas Armadas ESPE, Av. General Rumiñahui s/n, 171-5-231B Sangolquí, Ecuador.
{meesacobar1, jlcarrillo, gpespenel, kmtorres}@espe.edu.ec
[2]Universidad de las Américas, Av. José Queri, 170137 Quito, Ecuador
jalay@udlanet.ec

Abstract: Artificial intelligence through of expert systems allow taking decisions in different domains of the science such as physics, medicine, agriculture, electronic, informatic and others. The expert systems are based in the knowledge acquisition of an human specialists. In the area of the aviation these systems allow to develop control systems that facilitate their operability. This research shows a systematic mapping on expert systems used for the analysis and control of physiological signals of the aircraft pilot for know their state health (vital signs) and so prevent possible accident in simulations and missions of flight. The results obtained, shows that exist much works on the control of failures of aircraft or control air traffic or the develop of devices mechanics or electronics as support of pilot, with an 85% of the paper found. Therefore, only the 15% of papers are approaches at the object of study, this result indicate the lack of studies in this area, being one open area of research.

Keywords: artificial intelligence, expert systems, systematic mapping

1 Introducción

En las últimas décadas se ha producido un notable desarrollo en el área de la inteligencia artificial. En el caso particular, los sistemas expertos permiten realizar tareas que involucran la toma de decisiones mediante la abstracción del conocimiento de un experto humano [1]. Para satisfacer necesidades en diferentes dominios como: la medicina, agricultura, industria, finanzas, entre otros. En la mayoría de estos dominios se dispone de resultados que muestran su uso, lo que ha permitido mejorar su productividad, eficiencia, reducir costos, entre otros [2].

En el campo de la aviación se han desarrollado sistemas de control de instrumentos de vuelo. El hecho de volar una aeronave requiere de un preciso control de todos los sistemas, tanto los de la aeronave como los fisiológicos de los pilotos. Estos se enfrentan a varios factores estresantes, como son: amenaza de la seguridad, incremento de la ansiedad, el decolaje, el aterrizaje y una gama de factores ambientales que afectan directamente su desempeño [3]. Por lo que, se exige un perfecto desempeño de los sistemas de comunicación de la aeronave. Las alteraciones fisiológicas del ser humano cuando es sometido a los efectos de cambio de altura, aceleraciones, desaceleraciones, variación de la presión atmosférica y en general a todos los cambios en los diferentes ambientes aeronáuticos dan la posibilidad "según medicina de aviación", de que se puedan presentar accidentes aéreos, debido a la falta de dispositivos encargados de supervisar el comportamiento fisiológico humano de los pilotos en sus diferentes tareas, que conllevan a fallas humanas por reacciones tardías en los procedimientos operacionales[4].

En este trabajo se presenta un estudio de mapeo sistemático (EMS)[1], realizado con la finalidad de mapear el campo de los sistemas expertos que controlan las señales fisiológicas de los pilotos. Los resultados que se obtuvieron a partir del análisis de un grupo de artículos seleccionados nos permitieron evidenciar la problemática, la solución y los aportes en esta temática.

El artículo está estructurado de la siguiente manera: En la sección 2, se describe la pregunta de investigación y la metodología propuesta. En la sección 3, se detalla el proceso de planificación y ejecución. Los resultados son detallados en la sección 4. En la sección 5 se discuten aspectos relevantes de los artículos localizados y seleccionados. Las situaciones que amenazan la validez de esta investigación son presentadas en la sección 6. Finalmente, en la sección 7 se dan las conclusiones de la investigación.

2 Pregunta de Investigación y Metodología

Dirigimos el alcance de esta investigación sobre artículos relacionados a sistemas expertos para el control de señales fisiológicas hasta marzo de 2017. La pregunta de investigación que se planteó en esta investigación es la siguiente: RIQ1 ¿Que Investigaciones Existen sobre Sistemas Expertos para el Control de Señales Fisiológicas de Pilotos de Aviones?

La RIQ1 que se plantea en esta investigación, busca localizar los artículos donde se identifique indicios de la aplicación de sistemas expertos en el control de las señales fisiológicas de pilotos. Se realiza un MSL (Systematic Mapping Study, SMS en inglés) cubriendo las actividades de planificación y ejecución para identificar la cantidad y tipo de publicaciones disponibles sobre esta temática. Según [6], los pasos para llevar a cabo un mapeo sistemático son: la definición de la pregunta de investigación, la búsqueda de artículos relacionados, el análisis de resultados, la selección de artículos, el keywording del resumen y la extracción y mapeo de los datos. En cada uno de estos pasos se producen ciertos resultados y al final del proceso se tiene el mapa de los artículos relacionados sobre la temática. Además, la ejecución de estos pasos requiere el uso de recursos humanos, materiales, técnicos etc. Los recursos utilizados para la búsqueda de artículos incluyen un conjunto de reglas, actividades, elementos e instrumentos, que formalizan y dan soporte a las actividades de:

---

1 EMS es un método de investigación basado en la evidencia, que proporciona una visión general de un área de investigación, e identifica la cantidad, el tipo de investigación y los resultados disponibles dentro de ella [5].

1. Selección de fuentes de artículos.
2. Definición de la cadena de búsqueda.
3. Definición de los criterios de inclusión y exclusión.
4. Preselección de artículos.
5. Selección de artículos.
6. Extracción de datos de los artículos.

Para la selección de fuentes de artículos establecemos un conjunto de reglas para garantizar la calidad y cantidad de los artículos. Las reglas que consideramos son: definición de criterios de selección de fuentes y motores de búsqueda. En la actividad de definición de cadenas de búsqueda, se estructuraran las cadenas de búsqueda utilizadas para responder a la pregunta de investigación. Como lo propone [7], la cadena de búsqueda se construye a partir de la pregunta de investigación planteada con la estrategia PICOC y para refinar la pregunta de investigación se aplica las estrategia propuesta por [8]. Para la definición de los criterios de inclusión y exclusión se establecen previamente un conjunto de criterios utilizados durante la actividad de ejecución de la búsqueda para la preselección y selección de artículos. En la actividad de preselección de artículos se procede a la lectura de algunas secciones del artículo, a fin de identificar en el texto términos utilizados en la cadena de búsqueda. En la actividad de selección de artículos se hace una lectura completa del artículo, donde se establece la aplicación de los términos de la cadena de búsqueda. Además para la extracción de datos de los artículos, se crea un instrumento que permite recolectar la información relacionada con la temática.

3 Planificación y Ejecución del Mapeo Sistemático de la Literatura

La localización de artículos se realiza aplicando las tareas de planificación y ejecución que se describen a continuación:

En la planificación se formaliza el soporte de las actividades de organizar, ejecutar y entregar resultados de la búsqueda de artículos. Para la selección de fuentes de artículos se estableció como reglas:

a) Criterios de selección de las fuentes:
   • Artículos originados en fuentes fiables como revistas, revistas científicas, conferencias internacionales y capítulos de libros.
b) Idioma:
   • Artículos escritos en el idioma inglés.
c) Motores de Búsqueda:
   • Artículos buscados en ACM, Scopus y IEEE.

En la actividad definición de la cadena de búsqueda se establece la cadena que se usa para responder la pregunta de investigación, fundamentándose en la estrategia PICOC: Population, Intervention, Comparison, Output, Contexto [7]. Quedando la pregunta de investigación planteada de la siguiente forma:

- Población: Sistema Expertos.
- Intervención: Control.
- Comparación: No Aplicable.
- Salida: No Aplicable.
- Contexto1: Vuelo
- Contexto2: Piloto

Definidos los términos según PICOC, población, intervención y el contexto, se procedió a definir la estructura de la cadena. Utilizamos el término Sistemas Expertos para la población y sus correspondientes sinónimos de acuerdo con [9]. Para la intervención se incluyeron varios términos relacionados con la palabra control: monitoring en [10, 11] y diagnosis en [12]. Para el contexto lo hemos dividido en dos; el contexto1esta relacionado con el término flight [13], determinándose palabras relacionadas con: aviation en [14], air forcé en [15] y aircraft en [16]. El contexto 2 está relacionado con el término pilot en [4]. En la Tabla 1 se detallan los sinónimos relacionados con los términos de la pregunta de investigación.

Tabla 1. Sinónimos y términos relacionados de búsqueda de artículos PICOC

PICOC	Término	Sinónimo/Término relacionado
Población	Expert System	Intelligent systems, Knowledge engineering, Intelligent techniques, Biomedical engineering.
Intervención	Control	Monitoring, Diagnosis, Data monitoring.
Contexto 1	Flight	Aviation, Air Force, Aircraft
Contexto 2	Pilot	Pilot

Al momento de crear la cadena se establecieron cuatro subcadenas de búsqueda, utilizando operadores lógicos entre los componentes de PICOC para relacionar los términos y sus sinónimos correspondientes.

La Tabla 2 muestra las actividades y los insumos de la planificación para la ejecución de la búsqueda de los artículos relacionados con el objeto de estudio. Detallándose las actividades planteadas en la sección 2.

De la pregunta de investigación planteada se determinan los criterios de inclusión y exclusión, dichos criterios se utilizan en la ejecución de la búsqueda de preselección y selección de los artículos.

Tabla 2. Actividades e insumos de planificación

No.	Actividad	Insumos de Planificación
1	Seleccionar Fuentes para la Búsqueda de Artículos	Fuentes: Revistas, capítulos de libros, artículos de revistas. Idioma: Inglés. Motores de Búsqueda: Scopus, IEEE y ACM.
2	Definición de los criterios de inclusión y exclusión.	¿Que investigaciones existen sobre Sistemas Expertos para el Control de Señales Fisiológicas de Pilotos de Aviones?
3	Preselección de artículos.	Criterios de inclusión: Evidencia del uso de los términos de la cadena de búsqueda en el contenido del artículo. Criterio de exclusión: No se evidencia el uso de los términos de la cadena de búsqueda en el contenido del artículo
4	Selección de artículos.	Criterios de inclusión: Evidencia de la aplicación de Sistemas Expertos para el Control de Señales Fisiológicas de Pilotos de Aviones. Criterios de exclusión: No se evidencia de la aplicación de Sistemas Expertos para el Control de Señales Fisiológicas de Pilotos de Aviones.
5	Dentición de la cadena de búsqueda.	Cadena_Resultamte = ("Expert system" OR "Intelligent systems" OR "Knowledge engineering" OR "Intelligent techniques" OR "Biomedical Engineering") AND ("control" OR "monitoring" OR "diagnosis" OR "data monitoring") AND ("Aviation" OR "Flight" OR "Air force" OR "Aircraft") AND ("Pilot").
6	Extracción de datos	Información básica de los artículos seleccionados.

En la actividad de preselección de artículos, los criterios de inclusión permiten incorporar artículos en los que se evidencie el uso de términos de la cadena de búsqueda en las secciones como: título del trabajo, resumen y palabras claves. Por lo contrario los criterios de exclusión permiten descartar los artículos en los que se utilizan los términos de la cadena de búsqueda, pero que no corresponden al contexto de Sistemas Expertos para el Control de Señales Fisiológicas de Pilotos de Aviones. Esta actividad genera una lista que contiene los estudios primarios de la búsqueda.

Durante la actividad de selección de artículos se toman los criterios de inclusión para incorporar los artículos en los que se evidencie actividades sobre la temática de sistemas expertos para el soporte a especialistas en medicina de aviación. En cambio, se aplican los criterios de exclusión para descartar los artículos en los que no se detallen el soporte con sistemas expertos, para ello se realiza una lectura completa del artículo. Esta actividad genera una lista que contiene los estudios seleccionados, posteriormente se realiza la extracción de datos, registrando la información básica de los artículos seleccionados como: Título del artículo, Año de publicación y autores.

4 Ejecución

En esta actividad del mapeo sistemático se lleva a cabo las tareas planificadas, para buscar artículos relacionados con la temática planteada, se inicia ingresando la cadena (Cadena_Resultante) en las bases digitales Scopus, IEEE y ACM. La Tabla 3 muestra los resultados de la ejecución de la Cadena_Resultante, filtrándose los resultados a través del título, abstract y keywords correspondientes, obteniéndose 146 artículos en Scopus, 59 artículos en IEEE y 72 artículos en ACM, logrando acceso a 54, 57 y 9 respectivamente. Se aplican los criterios de inclusión y exclusión determinados para la preselección de artículos, obteniéndose 7 artículos de Scopus, 5 de IEEE y ninguno de ACM. Cabe destacar que la columna precisión en la Tabla 3 es la relación porcentual entre el número de artículos preseleccionados versus el número de artículos localizados.

Tabla 3. Artículos localizados, preseleccionados y precisión en relación a la cadena de búsqueda Cadena_Resultante

Motor	Artículos Localizados	Artículos Preseleccionados		Precisión
Scopus	54	7	[SCOPUS1CAD[34]], [SCOPUS1CAD[39]], [SCOPUS1CAD[57]], [SCOPUS1CAD[90]], [SCOPUS1CAD[109]], [SCOPUS1CAD[140]], [SCOPUS1CAD[146]].	12,96 %
IEEE	57	5	[IEEE1CAD[31]], [IEEE1CAD[44]], [IEEE1CAD[46]], [IEEE1CAD[48]], [IEEE1CAD[51]].	8,77 %
ACM	09	0	[Ninguno]	00,00 %
Total	120	12		

Una vez realizado el análisis de los artículos preseleccionados se encontró como términos relacionados, a señales fisiológicos, las palabras “health” y “medicine”. Siendo estas una parte primordial de la pregunta de investigación planteada en esta investigación. Por tal razón se realizó una segunda iteración, generándose una nueva cadena de búsqueda (Cadena_Resultante_Dos) donde se incluye dichos términos.

A continuación se muestra la nueva cadena de búsqueda:

Cadena_Resultamte_Dos = ("Expert system" OR "Intelligent systems" OR "Knowledge engineering" OR "Intelligent techniques" OR "Biomedical Engineering") AND ("control" OR "monitoring" OR "diagnosis" OR "data monitoring") AND ("Aviation" OR "Flight" OR "Air force" OR "Aircraft") AND ("Pilot") AND ("health" OR "medicine").

Siguiendo los pasos previos a la ejecución de la de la Cadena_Resultante, realizamos la búsqueda con la Cadena_Resultamte_Dos en los mismos motores de búsqueda (Scopus, IEEE y ACM), obteniéndose 19 artículos en Scopus, 10 artículos en IEEE y 2 artículos en ACM. Luego de aplicar los criterios de inclusión y exclusión, se obtienen 2 artículos en Scopus, 5 en IEEE y 1 en ACM, como se muestra en la tabla 4.

Tabla 4. Artículos localizados, preseleccionados y precisión en relación a la cadena de búsqueda Cadena_Resultante_Dos

Motor	Artículos Localizados	Artículos Preseleccionados		Precisión
Scopus	19	2	[SCOPUS2CAD[7]], [SCOPUS2CAD[9]].	10,52 %
IEEE	10	5	[IEEE2CAD[4]], [IEEE2CAD[6]], [IEEE2CAD[7]], [IEEE2CAD[8]], [IEEE2CAD[9]].	50 %
ACM	2	1	[ACM2CAD[1]].	50 %
Total	**31**	**08**		

En general de los artículos encontrados se excluyeron aquellos que no evidencian en su contenido la aplicación del Sistema Experto para el Control de Señales Fisiológicas de Pilotos de Aviones, sino que están enfocados en dar soporte a los pilotos en el diagnóstico de la aeronave y del manejo del tráfico aéreo por parte de controladores de vuelo, o a su vez dar un soporte al piloto mediante sensores electrónicos o mecánicos.

El total de artículos excluidos en la primera cadena (Cadena_Resultante) son 117 de los 120 localizados, por no cumplir alguno de los criterios establecidos. Por lo que, 3 artículos cumplen con el propósito de la investigación. El total de artículos excluidos en la segunda cadena (Cadena_Resultante_Dos) son 30 de los 31 encontrados. Por lo tanto, un solo artículo cumple con el objeto de estudio. El artículo encontrado en la segunda cadena de búsqueda es uno de los tres artículos seleccionados en la primera cadena de búsqueda. Cabe notar que los términos agregados a la primera cadena (forman la segunda cadena de búsqueda) limitaron aún más el número de artículos encontrados. Dos artículos escogidos en la primera cadena no se encontraron: Estos artículos, por su contenido, son de mucha importancia para nuestra investigación. Los datos de los tres artículos seleccionados se detallan en la Tabla 5

Tabla 5. Datos de los artículos seleccionados

Título del Artículo	Año de Publicación	Autores
Comparison between artificial neural network and multilinear regression models in an evaluation of cognitive workload in a flight simulator.	16 September 2008	Manne Hannulaa, Kerttu Huttunenb, Jukka Koskeloc, Tomi Laitinenc, Tuomo Leinob.
An expert system for generation of anti –G control schedule for jet fighter pilots.	2002	T.W.Yeow,V.Askari,Z. Lu, A. Kapps, W. Fraser, A.A. Goldenberg.
Non-Invasive Sensing Systems for Acceleration – Induced Physiologic Changes. 2	March 1991	William B. Albery and Robert E. Van Patten. Harry G, Amstrong Aerospace Medical Reserch Laboratory, Wright Laboratory, Patterson AFB.

5 Análisis de Resultados

RIQ1: ¿Qué investigaciones existen sobre Sistemas Expertos para el Control de Señales Fisiológicas de Pilotos de Aviones? Como se muestra en la tabla 5 se seleccionaron 3 artículos, donde se evidenció el uso de sistemas expertos para el control de Señales Fisiológicas de Pilotos de Aviones. Específicamente los estudios encontrados fueron: [SCOPUS1CAD[34]], [SCOPUS1CAD[57]], [SCOPUS1CAD[90]] y [SCOPUS2CAD[9]] los investigadores combinan conocimiento experto y datos fisiológicos de los pilotos.

6 Discusión

Desde el mapeo sistemático de la literatura que llevamos a cabo, concluimos que la búsqueda sobre estudios relacionados a desarrollo de Sistemas Expertos para el Control de Señales Fisiológicas de Pilotos de Aviones permitió: 1) Localizar y analizar pocos artículos, a pesar de que el diseño, implementación e implantación de sistemas expertos se han incrementado en los últimos años y, 2) Eliminar otros trabajos por no cumplir con los criterios de exclusión definidos.

El porcentaje de trabajos excluidos es alto, como se puede ver en la tabla 5, y esto se debe a que en la preselección de artículos se buscó excluir artículos en donde la aplicabilidad de sistemas expertos o señales fisiológicas no corresponde al objeto de estudio. A continuación detallamos los artículos localizados:

En [SCOPUS1CAD[34] se evalúa la carga de trabajo cognitivo que induce el estrés psicofisiológico (PPS) de pilotos de combate, durante la simulación de complejos combates, para lo cual se propone una red neuronal artificial y la medición de la frecuencia cardiaca, basándose en modelos de regresión multilínea. En

[SCOPUS1CAD[57]] se diseñó e implementó un sistema experto que controle el traje de fuerzas de aceleración G y la presión de la máscara de los pilotos de aviones caza a reacción, a través de la combinación de conocimiento experto, datos antropométricos y fisiológicos de los pilotos. Finalmente, [SCOPUS1CAD[90]] o [SCOPUS2CAD[9]] detalla un sistema en desarrollo, realizado por la Fuerza Aérea para la detección y recuperación de la pérdida de conciencia de un piloto, centrándose en un conjunto de métricas fisiológicas.

De los resultados obtenidos, podemos indicar que existen muchos trabajos sobre sistemas de control de fallas en aeronaves, sistemas de control de tráfico aéreo y/o desarrollo de dispositivos mecánicos o electrónicos que dan soporte a pilotos. Teniendo un 85% de los artículos encontrados. Un 15% de artículos tienen relación con el objeto de estudio, es decir, el uso de sistemas expertos para el control de señales fisiológicas de pilotos de aviones. Estos resultados señalan, la poca existencia de trabajos realizados sobre esta área de estudio.

7 Amenazas a la Validez

La principal amenaza es la utilización de las palabras claves, términos y sinónimos que empleamos para la construcción de las cadenas de búsqueda, debido a que se puede sesgar la búsqueda del tema a investigar, por lo cual fue necesario la orientación de expertos en inteligencia artificial, médicos especialistas en aviación de la Fuerza Aérea Ecuatoriana. Adicionalmente, el factor humano al momento de aplicar los criterios de inclusión y exclusión para la preselección y selección de artículos es una amenaza, debido a la subjetividad en los criterios, razón por la cual se realizaron chequeos individuales y cruzados entre el investigador y los expertos, llegando a una lista única de artículos.

8 Conclusiones

Se ha realizado un estudio de mapeo sistemático que permite identificar la cantidad y tipo de publicaciones disponibles sobre sistemas expertos para el control de señales fisiológicas de pilotos de aviones. Se obtuvieron tres artículos sobre la temática propuesta, tomando en consideración la pregunta de investigación. Utilizamos la estrategia PICOC, los sinónimos propuestos por los expertos correspondientes, los criterios de inclusión y exclusión para las actividades de preselección y selección de artículos. Se puede concluir la escasa existencia de artículos sobre la temática. El análisis de los artículos encontrados en su mayoría están relacionados a estudios que controlan el fallo de la aeronave, controlan el tráfico aéreo o desarrollan dispositivos electrónicos o mecánicos como soporte al piloto. Los sistemas expertos para el control de señales fisiológicas de pilotos de aviones, es un ámbito aún no explotado, y por medio de este artículo pretendemos brindar información de interés para así investigar la aplicabilidad de los sistemas expertos en el campo de la aviación.

Referencias

1. Díez, R. P., Gómez, A. G., & de Abajo Martínez, N. (2001). Introducción a la inteligencia artificial: sistemas expertos, redes neuronales artificiales y computación evolutiva. Universidad de Oviedo.
2. Srihari, K., & Muthukrishnan, R. (1991). An expert system methodology for aircraft-gate assignment. Computers & Industrial Engineering, 21(1-4), 101-105.
3. Edson, B. P., Duvan, C. Y., & Leonardo, R. L. (2007). Sistema de monitoreo de cardiaco para pilotos de combate en pleno vuelo. In IV Latin American Congress on Biomedical Engineering 2007, Bioengineering Solutions for Latin America Health (pp. 417-420). Springer Berlin Heidelberg.
4. Méndez Veloza, J. A., & Rentería Rentería, A. (2007). Diseño e implementación de un instrumento de monitoreo de señales fisiológicas y alarma para pilotos de aeronaves no presurizadas. https://link.springer.com/chapter/10.1007/978-3-540-74471-9_96
5. Petersen, K., Feldt, R., Mujtaba, S., & Mattsson, M. (2008, June). Systematic Mapping Studies in Software Engineering. In EASE (Vol. 8, pp. 68-77).
6. Petersen, K., Feldt, R., Mujtaba, S., & Mattsson, M. (2008). Systematic mapping studies in software engineering. 12th International Conference on Evaluation and Assessment in Software Engineering, 17 1.
7. Beecham, S., Baddoo, N., Hall, T., Robinson, H., & Sharp, H. (2006). Protocol for a systematic literature review of motivation in software engineering. University of Hertfordshire.
8. Petticrew, M., & Roberts, H. (2008). Systematic reviews in the social sciences: A practical guide Wiley-Blackwell.
9. Müller-Karger, C., Wong, S., & La Cruz, A. (Eds.). (2007). IV Latin American Congress on Biomedical Engineering 2007, Bioengineering Solutions for Latin America Health, September 24th-28th, 2007, Margarita Island, Venezuela: IV Congreso Latinoamericano de Ingeniería Biomédica, CLAIB 2007 Soluciones de Bioingeniería para la salud en Latina, 24 al 28 Septiembre de 2007, Isla de Margarita, Venezuela (Vol. 18). Springer Science & Business Media.
10. Fox, J. (1993). On the soundness and safety of expert systems. Artificial Intelligence in Medicine, 5(2), 159-179.
11. Hermanis, A., Cacurs, R., Nesenbergs, K., Greitans, M., Syundyukov, E., & Selavo, L. (2016, February). Demo: Wearable Sensor System for Human Biomechanics Monitoring. In EWSN (pp. 247-248).
12. Kuncheva, L. (1993). Two-level classification schemes in medical diagnostics. International journal of bio-medical computing, 32(3), 197-210.
13. Bass, E., Gainer, C., Katz, A., Mclnerny, S., & Merritt, W. T. (1999). In-Flight Advisor, Phase 1 (No. DOT/FAA/AR-99/67). ALABAMA UNIV TUSCALOOSA DEPT OF AEROSPACE ENGINEERING AND MECHANICS.
14. Bapst, G. W., Butcher, S. C., Clifford, R. S., & Jordan, R. L. (2001). Portable maintenance aids (No. LMI-LG005T2). LOGISTICS MANAGEMENT INST MCLEAN VA.
15. Greenhill, S., Venkatesh, S., Pearce, A., & Ly, T. C. (2002). Representations and processes in decision modelling (No. DSTO-GD-0318). DEFENCE SCIENCE AND TECHNOLOGY ORGANISATION VICTORIA (AUSTRALIA) AERONAUTICAL AND MARITIME RESEARCH LAB.
16. Board, M. S., on Engineering, C., & National Research Council. (1984). Applications of robotics and artificial intelligence to reduce risk and improve effectiveness: A study for the United States Army. Robotics and Computer-Integrated Manufacturing, 1(2), 191-222.

Control of a Robotic Arm LYNX AL5D Using Electromyography Through Technology MYO ARMBAND

Oscar Arteaga, Diego Camacho, Erick Mera, Alvaro Velasco, Ismael Medina, Luis Mena, María I. Erazo, Richard Toasa and Juan Vela
Universidad de las Fuerzas Armadas ESPE Sangolquí, Ecuador
{obarteaga, docamacho, epmera1, apvelasco, iamedina, mierazo, lemena, rptoasa, jcvela1}@espe.edu.ec

Abstract. The control of manipulators has represented a constant development in the operation of autonomous systems that cover a wide field in the robotics. This article details the design and implementation of a closed loop controller aimed at the control of a robotic arm using the electrical signals generated by the forearm muscles from body reconnaissance, which are processed through MYO ARMBAND technology that is in charge to redirect the information by means of wireless communication to the robotic arm to allow its movement. This control is focused on the manipulation of objects found in environments hostile to men.

Keywords: electromyography, manipulators, MYO arm band, hand gesture recognition

1 Introducción

La búsqueda del hombre de crear herramientas y sistemas que hagan de sus labores menos tediosas y agotadoras, ha implicado que la robótica se desarrolle a tal punto de evolucionar al lado del hombre haciendo de su vida cada vez más sencilla y amigable. Existen muchas circunstancias en las cuales no es conveniente emplear personas para la realización de algunas labores debido al alto riesgo a que ellos se exponen [1]; por esta razón se han desarrollado diversas herramientas o equipos que permiten reemplazar al hombre al realizar estas operaciones a distancia. Dentro de estos equipos se encentran los manipuladores operados a distancia [2]. Los robots operados a distancia brindan una gran utilidad y se operan en diversos campos. Este tipo de manejo supone una ventaja desde el punto de vista de la protección y seguridad del usuario, ya que, en caso de realizar trabajos en ambientes inseguros, inestables o con sustancias potencialmente peligrosas, como químicos, no se arriesga su integridad física. [3][4].

Las posibilidades de aplicación y el rendimiento diagnóstico de la electromiografía han evolucionado paralelamente al conocimiento de las propiedades de la energía eléctrica y al desarrollo de la tecnología eléctrica y electrónica [5]. El desarrollo posterior de la tecnología digital ha permitido disponer de sistemas controlados por microprocesadores cada vez más fiables y potentes para captar, representar, almacenar, analizar y clasificar las señales mioeléctricas. Es esperable que el avance de las nuevas tecnologías de la información y la comunicación pueda conducir en un futuro próximo a la aplicación de desarrollos de inteligencia artificial que faciliten la clasificación automática de señales, así como sistemas expertos de apoyo al diagnóstico electromiográfico. [5,6].

El MYO se construye alrededor de ocho sensores EMG (electromiografía) que representan la actividad muscular junto con una unidad de medición inercial de tres ejes cada uno para acelerómetro, giroscopio y magnetómetro [7,8], lo que significa que se obtiene una detección de gesto del antebrazo junto con una detección de movimiento relativo (como en oposición a la posición absoluta) además de convertir los gestos de los músculos del antebrazo de un usuario en actividades eléctricas y puede reconocer 20 gestos distintos, algunos tan sutiles como el toque de un dedo [9,10]. Por lo tanto, es ineludible el reconocimiento y estudio del manejo y funcionalidad del MYO ARMBAND, de esta manera se podrá aprovechar toda la potencialidad de dicha tecnología e implementar su comunicación y control adecuadamente.

Es así que el presente documento muestra el proceso de desarrollo al diseño de un control en lazo cerrado para un brazo robótico que pueda realizar un trabajo continuo y sistemático, además de que permite realizar labores sin una completa intervención del operador asegurando la integridad física del mismo. El mencionado brazo robótico es controlado por sensores superficiales implantados en tecnología MYO, el mismo que toma datos de señales electromiográficas, dado que a través de los músculos del antebrazo se generan biopotenciales, estos serán controlados por el mencionado sistema de control [9], en el cual dependiendo de la diferencia de potencial que circule por el músculo va a activar indistintamente los 6 servomotores que controlan el brazo robótico a emplearse.

Este artículo tiene 6 secciones incluyendo la introducción, en la sección 2 se presenta el problema u objetivo referente a electromiografía, la sección 3 muestra los sensores electromiográficas unificados en un dispositivo conocido como MYO Armband. A continuación, en la sección 4 se aprecia el desarrollo del control del brazo robótico mediante el dispositivo MYO Armband mediante movimientos del brazo humano. En la sección 5 se presenta el funcionamiento del brazo robótico mediante el efecto de las señales electromiográficas bajo las condiciones establecidas, en la sección 6 se observa los resultados obtenidos al aplica el control del brazo robótico mediante las señales electromiográficas y finalmente la sección 7 muestra las conclusiones.

2 Presentación del Problema

El presente documento nos brinda el desarrollo y diseño de un control en lazo cerrado para un brazo robótico, dada la problemática a ser situado en ambientes hostiles al ser humano, además de palpar en su óptimo funcionamiento un trabajo continuo, sistemático y acceder a realizar cualquier tipo de labor sin la intervención de alguna persona, para de esta manera garantizar tanto el trabajo a realizarse como la seguridad integra de los operarios.

La manipulación del brazo robótico con señales eléctricas generadas por los músculos, se puede realizar mediante electrodos de área pequeña (aguja) [11], que son insertados dentro del músculo; o electrodos de área grande, que son aplicados a la piel que cubre al músculo, los primeros son los más comunes en la neurología clínica, son utilizados en el estudio de las unidades motrices, lo segundo explora la actividad eléctrica de una masa muscular mayor, estudio conocido como electromiografía superficial (Electromiografía global). [12,13,14]

La técnica que utiliza la pulsera es superficial, midiendo las señales eléctricas que genera el antebrazo al realizar distintos movimientos con los dedos y la muñeca, son procesadas por el MYO ARMBAND y enviadas mediante BLUETOOTH a la PC, en la cual son interpretadas por la interfaz de MYODUINO, la cual nos permite enlazar la tarjeta Arduino con los gestos producidos por el dispositivo MYO.

La necesidad de vincular la tarjeta Arduino y las señales provenientes de la pulsera electromiográfica recaen directamente sobre la problemática de investigación que se presenta en este artículo, ya que para controlar los servomotores del brazo robótico se vuelve necesaria la generación de una señal PWM. Todo lo anteriormente citado en cuanto al control de servomotores, es lo que se debe generar en el entorno IDE de programación de Arduino con la finalidad de controlar todos los grados de libertad que posee el brazo robótico utilizando las señales provenientes del MYO.

3 MYO Armband

MYO es un dispositivo que utiliza una técnica conocida como electromiografía, este pequeño brazalete es capaz de leer las señales eléctricas de los músculos de su antebrazo, asignarlos a los gestos realizados con la mano, y controlar otros dispositivos con esos gestos. [15]

Es evidente el cambio radical en la forma en que los comandos de gestos suelen ser registrados. La mayoría de los sistemas de control de gestos, como el Kinect de Microsoft, todavía detectan movimientos con cámaras, que pueden ser lanzados fuera por las malas condiciones de iluminación, la distancia y las obstrucciones simples. Este dispositivo adquiere la información directamente de los músculos del brazo en lugar de una cámara, además de evitar todos estos problemas y también funciona con dispositivos que no cuentan con una cámara. [16]

Para leer la actividad muscular en el antebrazo, MYO envuelve en ocho bloques diferentes, cada una de las cuales contiene un sensor de EMG de grado médico. El brazalete también utiliza un giroscopio de tres ejes, acelerómetro de tres ejes, y magnetómetro de tres ejes para detectar el movimiento en cualquier dirección como se observa en la Fig. 1.

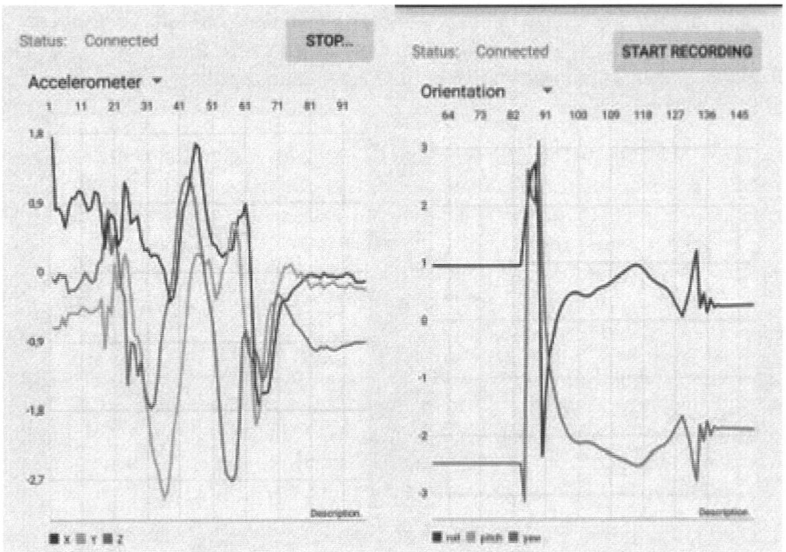

Fig. 1 Medición y control: Giroscopio, Acelerómetro y Magnetómetro

Las lecturas de actividad muscular y el movimiento son manejados por un procesador Cortex M4 ARM a bordo, que se comunica con sus dispositivos a través de Bluetooth. Para los dispositivos que no cuentan con la funcionalidad Bluetooth incorporada, MYO ARMBAND también viene con un adaptador Bluetooth que se conecta a cualquier puerto USB. [17]

4 Desarrollo de la Interfaz con Arduino

La interfaz de conexión de Arduino y la pulsera MYO se realiza mediante la aplicación MYODUINO, este programa realiza la conexión con el puerto COM al que se encuentre conectada la Arduino.

Para llevar a cabo el proceso es necesario la librería MyoController, que se encuentra disponible en internet. Al importar la librería al entorno de programación de Arduino como se muestra en la Fig. 2, una vez cargada la librería a Arduino es seleccionada el ejemplo MyoController y cargado el programa a la tarjeta como se muestra en la Fig. 3.

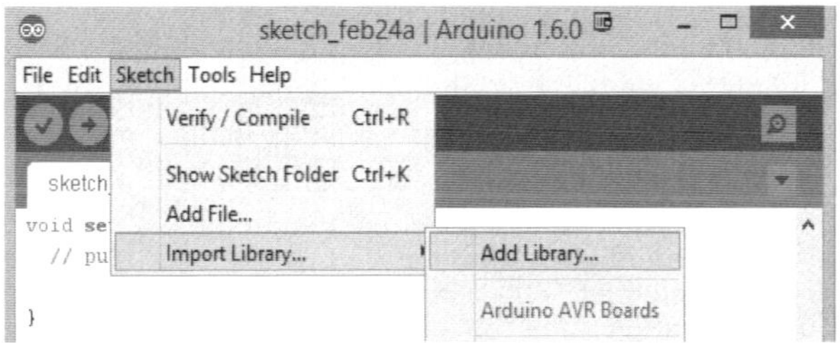

Fig. 2 Importar la librería a Arduino

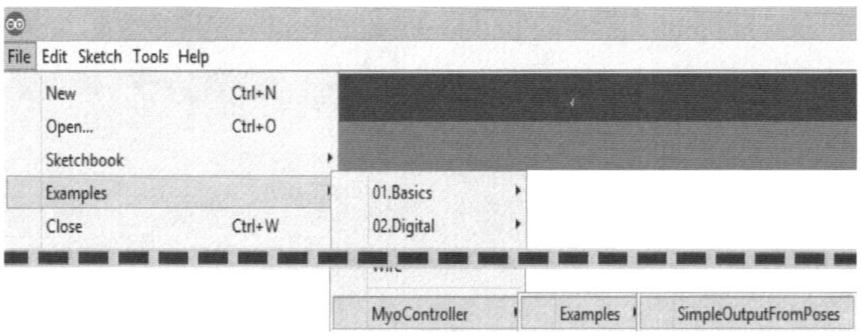

Fig. 3 MyoController

Ese código de ejemplo establece una base para desarrollar el algoritmo, el cual será capaz de controlar en ambas direcciones los servos que controlan los movimientos del brazo robótico.

Algoritmo de control de gestos

Para desarrollar el código pertinente se utiliza del ejemplo de la librería MyoController las siguientes líneas, las cuales definen los gestos capaces de reconocer la librería.

```
#define FIST_PIN 1 //Puño
#define FINGERSSPREAD_PIN 2 //Mano Abierta
#define WAVEIN_PIN 3 // Movimiento hacia adentro
#define WAVEOUT_PIN 4 //Movimiento hacia afuera
#define DOUBLETAP_PIN 5 //Doble Toque
```

Una vez definidos los gestos que serán utilizados se crea un diagrama de flujo como se ve en la Fig. 4.

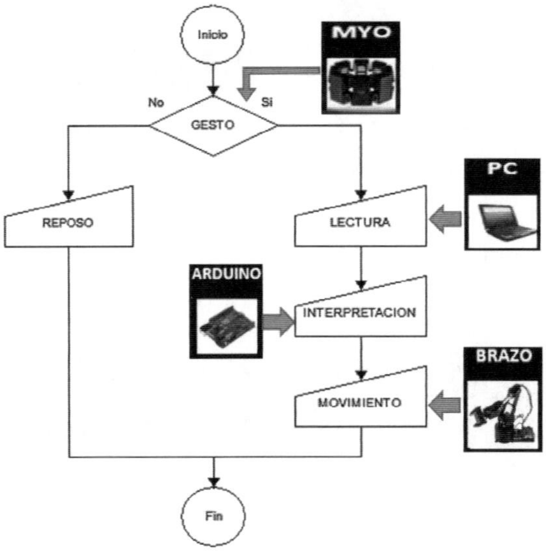

Fig. 4 Diagrama de Flujo

El diagrama de flujo muestra que al realiza uno de los movimientos o gestos determinados, este será recibido por un computador, inmediatamente será interpretado por Arduino y enviará una señal a los servos que controlan el movimiento del Brazo Robótico como se indica en la Fig. 4, caso contrario el sistema permanecerá en reposo.

Para poder manipular el Brazo Robótico se considera que sus 6 seis grados de libertad se mueven por efecto de servo motores, es decir, se necesita también hacer uso de la librería para servos de Arduino con la cual se envia señales a los mismos para que se giren en ambas direcciones controlando así la posición del Brazo Robótico. El código que permite controlar el giro de un servomotor mediante las señales recibidas de MYO ARMBAND se indican a continuación:

```
case fist: //Caso Puño
     digitalWrite(FIST_PIN,HIGH); //Envia una señal HIGH (alta)
      rightleft.write(servo_val + 1); //Incrementa en un grado la
   posición
     delay(35); //Espera un periodo de 35ms
     servo_val = rightleft.read(); //Lee la posición del servo
     Serial.println("Right HIGH"); //
   break; //Fin del caso
```

Este código hace referencia al caso FIST (puño), mientras nuestra mano se encuentre cerrada Arduino está recibiendo una señal alta, la cual está incrementando la posición del servo correspondiente en un grado cada 35ms en sentido horario y leyendo la posición del mismo pudiendo así controlar la posición del eje del Brazo Robótico.

Cabe recalcar que el servo se mueve un grado cada 35ms, es decir, es capaz de dar un giro de 180 grados en un periodo de 6,3 segundos, de tal forma que el movimiento se realiza lentamente permitiendo una mayor precisión a la hora de manipular objetos, si el tiempo de espera fuera menor el movimiento que realiza el brazo robótico seria brusco y dificultoso para manipular objetos.

5 Movimientos del Brazo LYNX AL5D con el Myo Armband

La programación desarrollada permite al usuario mover 2 servos en dos direcciones diferentes al mismo tiempo con los movimientos hacia adentro o hacia afuera de la muñeca y abriendo la mano o haciendo puño, para cambiar a otros dos servos se debe realizar el quinto movimiento programado de DOUBLE TAP, es decir, dar un doble clic con el dedo medio y el pulgar.

Al cambiar de servos nuevamente se habilita los 4 movimientos mencionados anteriormente para mover otros dos servos en ambas direcciones. Es necesario citar que para mantener un movimiento continuo del brazo robótico en una dirección se debe mantener la posición de la muñeca o el puño, hasta llegar al punto deseado, la Fig. 6 nos indica lo siguiente:

Al realizar un gesto, el cual es interpretado por el brazalete y enviado inalámbricamente por Bluetooth al computador, este es interpretado por MYODUINO quien se encarga de enlazar la señal entre MYO ARMBAND y Arduino que envía un pulso al servo correspondiente permitiendo el control de la posición del Brazo Robótico en todos sus grados de libertad.

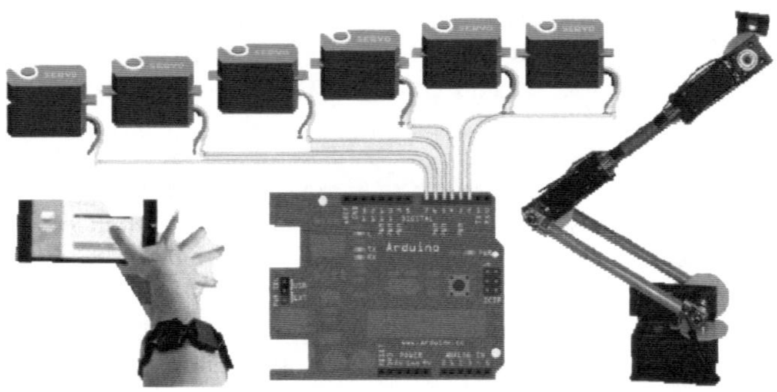

Fig. 5 Funcionamiento

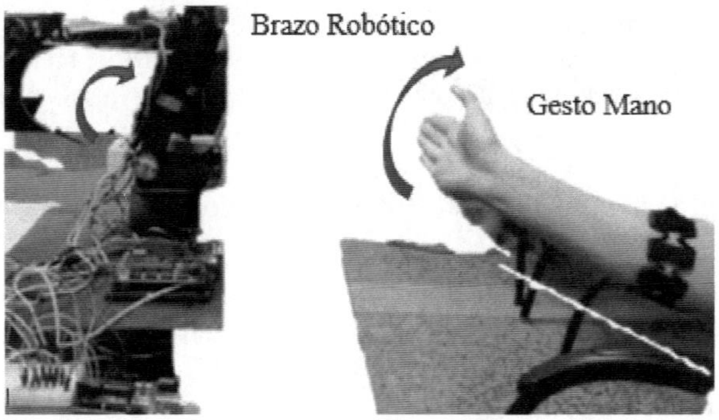

Fig. 6 Manipulación del Brazo Robótico mediante MYO ARMBAND

6 Resultados

Es evidente que la tecnología MYO permite el control parcial del brazo robótico, logrando la manipulación de los 6 servos, habilitando el control de 2 servos en dos direcciones diferentes al mismo tiempo.

El movimiento de los servos consta de un grado cada 35ms, lo que permite un control adecuado al momento de manipular algún tipo de objeto, ya que si este valor se incrementa su manipulación genera un error muy considerable, caso contrario si el valor temporal se reduce, permite una manipulación muy brusca.

Los movimientos del brazo se limitan dado que las pruebas realizadas en el control del mismo, se determinó que la interfaz MYOduino únicamente permite reconocer 4 movimientos o gestos musculares del brazo portador, por lo cual se obtiene un control parcial del brazo robótico

Dentro de la manipulación del brazo robótico se contó con 3 casos de movimientos, donde el caso primero se refiere al movimiento conjunto de la base y el denominado antebrazo del robot, segundo caso se manipuló brazo y muñeca del manipulador y finalmente un tercer caso para el movimiento giratorio y apertura del gripper del mismo, cabe recalcar que dichos estados se intercalarán de uno a otro al obedecer el cambio de estado de la designación conocida como DOUBLE TAP.

Dentro del funcionamiento se pudo establecer la limitación de distancia máxima del control a 10 m, dado que el tipo de comunicación que emplea el dispositivo MYO ARMBAND es de tipo Bluetooth, el cual trabaja en un rango de banda ISM 2.4 GHz lo que nos permite un intercambio de datos seguros ya que el dispositivo realiza automáticamente una petición de reenvió de datos al existir alguna interferencia como un gesto muscular mal interpretado o mal ejecutado.

7 Conclusiones

Al emplear la interfaz MYOduino automáticamente esta genera designaciones establecidas para cada gesto muscular generado, de las cuales posteriormente se puede hacer uso ya en programación abierta.

Es evidente que la tecnología MYO ARMBAND brinda una manera muy práctica de manipulación a distancia mediante señales eléctricas receptadas de los músculos del brazo portador, permitiendo así un movimiento determinado y un control eficiente.

Es ineludible realzar que para el funcionamiento óptimo y funcional del brazo robótico se disponga de una alimentación externa y adecuado a la alimentación de los servomotores para garantizar mejor estabilidad y control del mismo.

La tecnología electromiagráfica puede ser aplicada en muchos campos de la industria donde existen lugares donde se necesite operar máquinas a una cierta distancia por seguridad a los operarios.

Al desarrollar el proyecto se determinó que el mismo tiene una gran utilidad en el campo de las prótesis humanas, ya que la rapidez de respuesta hacia algún cambio de gesto muscular permite el control total de un mecanismo replicando el movimiento de un brazo humano "brazo robótico".

Para que el dispositivo MYO pueda interpretar el mando muscular correcto es necesario que el movimiento muscular del usuario sea ejecutado en su totalidad.

Referencias

1. Cárdenas, M. M., Barrios, P. P., Moreno, K. M. G., Arismendy, J. F. S., & Ávila, M. C. O.:Diseño y Construcción del Prototipo de un Brazo Robótico con Tres Grados de Libertad, como Objeto de Estudio. Ingeniare, (18), 87-94.. (2016)
2. J. Villamizar, R. Padilla y G. Cabrera.: "Brazo robotico controlado por electromiografia,". Colombia, pp. 2-3, (2012)
3. H. Everet.: "Sensor for Mobile Robots – Theory and Aplication," A. K Peters Ltd. Wellesley, Massachussets. (2014)
4. J. Jones.: "Mobile Robots, Inspiration to Implementation," A. K. Peters Ltd. Wellesley, Massachussets. (2012)
5. Gila, L., Malanda, A., Rodríguez Carreño, I., Rodríguez Falces, J., & Navallas, J.: Métodos de procesamiento y análisis de señales electromiográficas. In Anales del Sistema Sanitario de Navarra, Vol. 32, pp. 27-43. (2009)
6. Buitrago Salazar, G. D., & Ramos Sandoval, O.: LInterfaz de control teleoperado para dos manipuladores industriales usando un marcador visual humano. Ingeniería Electrónica, Automática y Comunicaciones, 37(2), 28-38.(2016)
7. Kumpel del Castillo, H. D., & Scatton Lóndero, A.: Entorno de realidad virtual controlado en tiempo real por señales motoras para la rehabilitación del miembro superior en pacientes con daño cerebral. (2016)

8. R. Nuwer.: "Armband añade un tic de control por gestos". New Scientist, pp 29 . (2013)
9. G. Gardner.: "Sistema muscular. Anatomia,". Ed interamericana. Mexico, pp. 20-43, (2012)
10. E. Moller.: "Clinical Electromyography in Dentistry." Int Dent J. pp. 250-66. (2013)
11. M. B. I. Reaz, M. S. Hussain, F. Mohd-Yasin.: "Techniques of EMG Signal Analysis: Detection, Processing, Classification andApplications", Biological Procedures Online, vol. 8, issue 1, pp. 11–35, (2013)
12. Villa-Hernández, J., Ponce, M. A., & Cano, G. V.: Prototipo de silla de ruedas inteligente controlada por electromiograma. Boletín Científico INVESTIGIUM de la Escuela Superior de Tizayuca, 2(4). (2017)
13. Hewitt, J. The MYO Gesture-Control Armband Sense Your Muscle's Movements, ExtremeTech (online magazine), (2013)
14. J: Garrido.: "Cool Tech: Thalmic Labs Myo Gesture Control Armband", pp 2-5, (2014)
15. Kerber, F., Lessel, P., & Krüger, A.:Same-side Hand Interactions with Arm-placed Devices Using EMG. In Proceedings of the 33rd Annual ACM Conference Extended Abstracts on Human Factors in Computing Systems (pp. 1367-1372). ACM. (2015)
16. Polsley, S.: An analysis of electromyography as an input method for resilient and affordable systems: human-computer interfacing using the body's electrical activity. (2014)
17. Nuttall, G. A., Abenstein, J. P., Stubbs, J. R., Santrach, P., Ereth, M. H., Johnson, P. M., ... & Oliver, W. C.: Computerized Bar Code–Based Blood Identification Systems and ar-Miss Transfusion Episodes and Transfusion Errors. In Mayo Clinic Proceedings (Vol. 88, No. 4, pp. 354-359). Elsevier (2013).

Embedded Human Machine Interface for Flow Control System

Edwin Pruna, Pablo J. Salazar, Marcelo Silva S. and Carlos Bustamante D.

Universidad de las Fuerzas Armadas ESPE, Sangolquí-Ecuador

{eppruna, pjsalazar1, mjsilva1, cibustamante}@espe.edu.ec

Abstract. This paper presents the development of an intuitive and effective embedded Human Machine Interface (HMI) based in the ISA 101 standard that is responsible for monitoring the dynamic flow rate, this interface contains user levels, alarms and process trends, essential interfaces in the automatic control of processes. In order to get reliable results, performance tests are made on the automatic flow control under different parameters, simultaneously the interaction between the user and the process is verified in real time with the different screens developed along the entire test.

Keywords: industrial process, human machine interface, flow control , touch screen

1 Introducción

Varios procesos industriales en la actualidad son utilizados en la formación de profesionales [1] así como en las empresas o fábricas, donde los procesos implementados necesitan ser automáticos y supervisados por medio de un software específico, ya sea éste creado por el fabricante de un equipo o por un tercero. La principal ventaja de utilizar un sistema embebido es que no se necesita tener un sistema adicional, como un computador, conectado de forma permanente a los equipos para poder acceder sus prestaciones, en este caso la pantalla tacto sensible contiene toda la programación dentro de un software que se encarga de controlar los procesos de caudal en tiempo real [2].

El funcionamiento de una planta o de un proceso en sí, depende directamente de todos los elementos que lo componen (transmisor, controlador, elemento de control final, interfaz de visualización o HMI) y del estado en que se encuentren [3], por esta razón es importante verificar que trabajen de forma correcta y dentro de los parámetros que requiere dicho proceso; los elementos mencionados deben tener estándares de conexión, así como de programación para lograr la funcionalidad requerida [4]. El elemento de control final trabaja conjuntamente con el transmisor ya que su acción depende de la señal que éste envíe al controlador, por lo tanto, es necesario desarrollar un algoritmo óptimo y preciso para que las acciones realizadas en el proceso cumplan con las especificaciones necesarias [5].

El HMI (Human Machine Interface) implementado en este trabajo se desarrolla bajo la norma ISA101; básicamente el estándar pretende ser una guía de elaboración para los HMI a nivel mundial y de esta forma asegurar su efectividad y eficiencia durante la aplicación práctica a lo largo de su vida útil ya que son sistemas que funcionan generalmente las 24 horas del día durante todo el año; de esta forma el usuario podrá responder adecuadamente al software, garantizando un mayor rendimiento y calidad de los procesos de una planta [6].

Existen diferentes proyectos científicos relacionados con el control de procesos a través de HMI's. En [7] se puede ver un ejemplo en donde se realiza el control y monitoreo en el ámbito de la agricultura hidropónica, se establecen alarmas y niveles de usuario, tanto de control como monitorización, así como propiedades que afectan directamente a los elementos físicos que integran dicho trabajo [8]. También existen módulos didácticos implementados para diferentes procesos y no solamente para control de caudal, esto valida que el desarrollo de sistemas embebidos es altamente necesario tanto en la industria así como para la formación de profesionales [9].

En el presente trabajo se ha desarrollado un HMI intuitivo y eficiente capaz de supervisar el proceso de caudal aplicando algoritmos de control que mediante el panel tacto sensible pueden ser configurados cambiando los parámetros de sintonización del controlador y estableciendo los valores de caudal según como se requiera en la planta. Cada uno de los temas mencionados en la introducción de este artículo serán explicados de manera detallada en las secciones posteriores.

2 Descripción del Proceso de Caudal

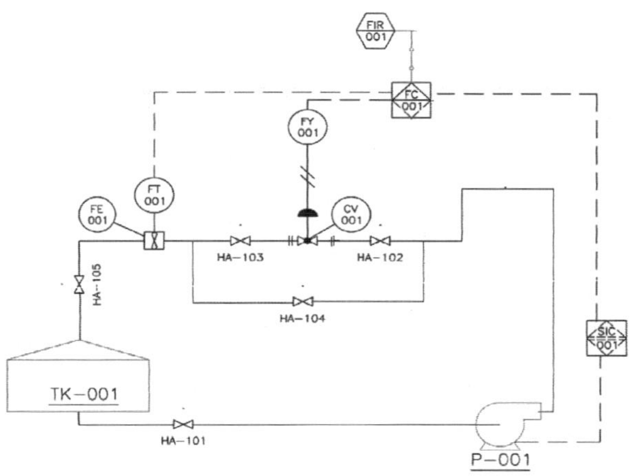

Fig. 1. Diagrama P&ID del proceso de caudal

El sistema de control de caudal, representado en la Fig. 1., consta esencialmente de una bomba centrífuga (P-001), que impulsa el fluido almacenado en un tanque (TK-001), el cual es realimentado por la tubería en la que se sitúa la instrumentación con la que se realiza el control del proceso. El proceso contiene válvulas manuales, representadas en el diagrama como HA-101 y HA-105, que permiten generar carga al sistema para evaluar los controles ante perturbaciones [5].

La medición de la variable flujo es efectuada por medio de un transmisor industrial, representado como FT-001, situado en la tubería del proceso cuyo elemento primario es un sensor de rueda de paletas, que se representa en el diagrama como FE-001, el mismo que envía una señal estándar de 4 a 20 mA de corriente continua al controlador lógico programable.

El controlador, dispuesto en el diagrama como FC-001, se encuentra situado en el panel frontal con acceso directo al operador, realiza las funciones de adquisición de datos, así como el control de la variable mediante la implementación de algoritmos P, PI, PID, según la respuesta que se requiera, el autómata programable envía señales eléctricas hacia los elementos de control final.

La válvula, simbolizada en el diagrama como CV-001, controla el desplazamiento del vástago del actuador y es ejecutado por medio del conversor corriente a presión, que se simboliza como FY-001 en el diagrama, el cual convierte una señal estándar de instrumentación de corriente, que proviene del controlador, a una señal neumática compatible con el actuador de la válvula de control.

La velocidad del motor que se encuentra implícito en la bomba centrífuga es regulada por medio de la acción del variador de frecuencia (SC-001), por ende, el caudal impulsado por la bomba varía según la señal de voltaje enviada desde el controlador hacia el variador de frecuencia.

El monitoreo y visualización (Supervisión) del proceso es efectuado por la pantalla sensible al tacto que se conecta al autómata programable mediante enlace Profinet.

3 Acción Del Controlador

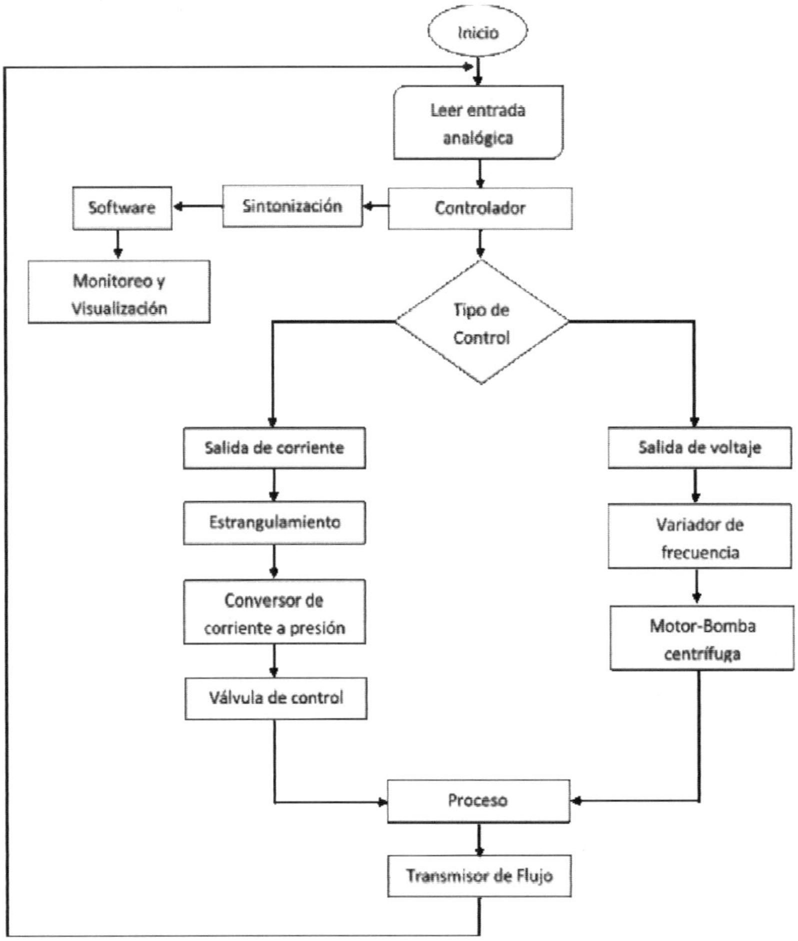

Fig. 2. Diagrama de flujo del controlador

El diagrama de flujo representado en la Fig. 2. detalla la forma de operación del controlador, en este caso el PLC Simatic S7-1200, el cual realiza acciones de adquisición de datos y control; la programación de este dispositivo se realiza mediante el lenguaje de programación KOP o diagrama de escaleras, por ser el más utilizado y por su facilidad de programación. [12]

El controlador inicia con la lectura de datos de la variable dinámica caudal, el mismo que mediante el algoritmo de control correspondiente envía datos al elemento de control final que el operador desee efectuar, sea este por válvula de control o variador de frecuencia para la regulación de caudal que circula por la tubería desde y hacia un tanque reservorio, de tal manera que permite al operador interactuar con el proceso mediante el HMI implementado en la pantalla tacto sensible de forma interactiva e intuitiva en tiempo real.

4 Diseño y Desarrollo de la Interfaz de visualización

El desarrollo de las pantallas se realiza en el software Wincc V12 de TIA Portal, el mismo que permite la programación de la TOUCH PANEL KTP 600 de Siemens, mediante el cual se realiza la programación por medio del uso de pantallas, las cuales se desarrollan de acuerdo a la necesidad del usuario mediante objetos básicos como líneas, rectángulos, círculos, campos de texto, visor de gráficos; también se destaca el uso de elementos como campos de entrada y salida, botones e interruptores, asi como controles entre los que se utilizan los visores de avisos, curvas, usuarios y recetas. Las pantallas programadas muestran la variable del proceso, la cual es de tipo flotante para mayor precisión, vinculada al autómata programable en tiempo real, asimismo permite el uso de las variables del controlador para graficar tendencias y hacer uso de las mismas para el manejo de alarmas, el diagrama de flujo de la Fig. 3. presenta las operaciones que permite la interfaz desarrollada desde la ejecución de niveles de usuario, dando jerarquía a las opciones de uso dependiendo del operador, visualización del proceso hasta las acciones de control del caudal, lo que otorga al usuario un ambiente de trabajo afable y con facilidad de uso.

La interfaz desarrollada se encuentra acorde a la normativa ISA 101 [10], referido a las interfaces humano máquina para sistemas de automatización de procesos. El uso de esta norma proporciona una orientación para el diseño, construcción y mantenimiento de las interfaces con el fin de resultar en un control con mayor eficiencia y eficacia del proceso, tanto en situaciones normales como en situaciones inesperadas. La normativa ISA 101 presenta características y lineamientos coadyuvantes en lo que se refiere al diseño de interfaces como son [11]:

- El contenido de la interfaz debe contener todo tipo tareas y actividades requeridas por el operador.
- Las técnicas de interacción con el usuario, así como el estado del sistema, deben ser consistentes y claras
- Los símbolos y el estado del proceso requieren ser representados en una manera simple, significativa y consistente.
- El diseño de la interfaz debe ser destinado para el conocimiento de la situación actual del proceso en respaldo del usuario
- Se debe evitar la falta de claridad de la interfaz debido a la simplicidad en el diseño gráfico.

Además, la norma sugiere que los colores de las pantallas de la interfaz deberían ser distinguibles unos de otros, asimismo, la prominencia de los colores usados en la pantalla, deben reflejar la importancia de la información que se presenta. El color debe ser usado para enfatizar la información clave como lo son alarmas y situaciones inesperadas.

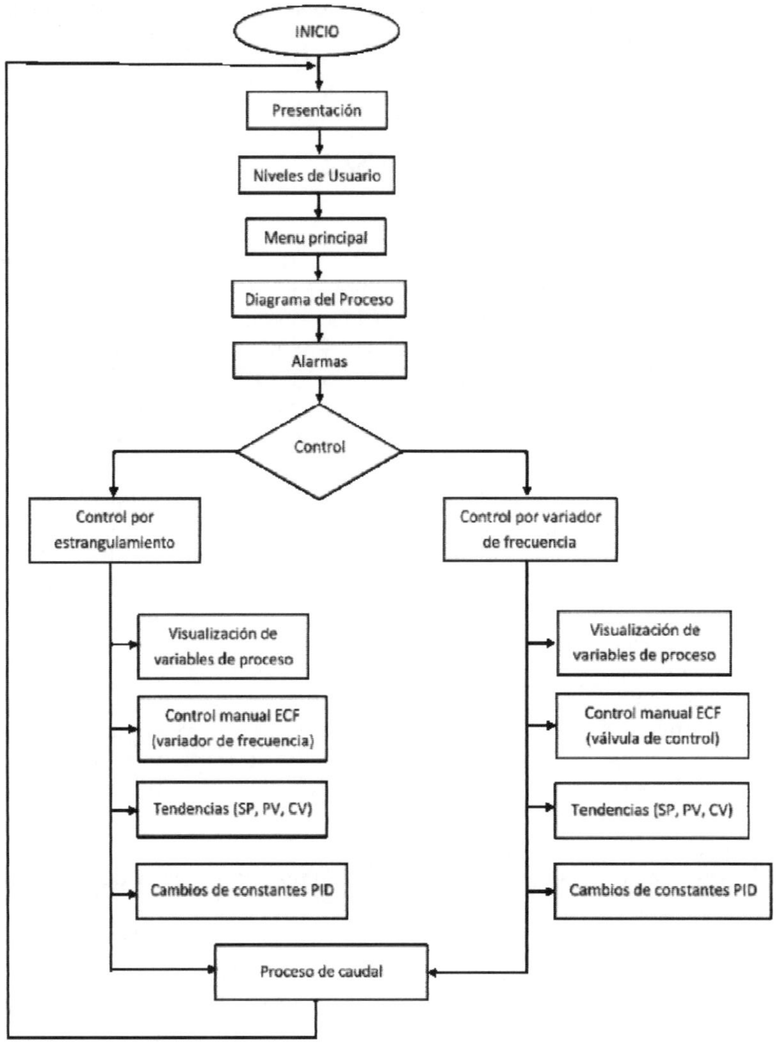

Fig. 3. Diagrama de flujo del HMI

5 Pruebas y Resultados Experimentales

En esta sección se demuestra la implementación de la interfaz diseñada. En la Fig. 4 se presenta el menú principal, donde destacan las opciones que el operador puede realizar conjuntamente con la pantalla tacto sensible.

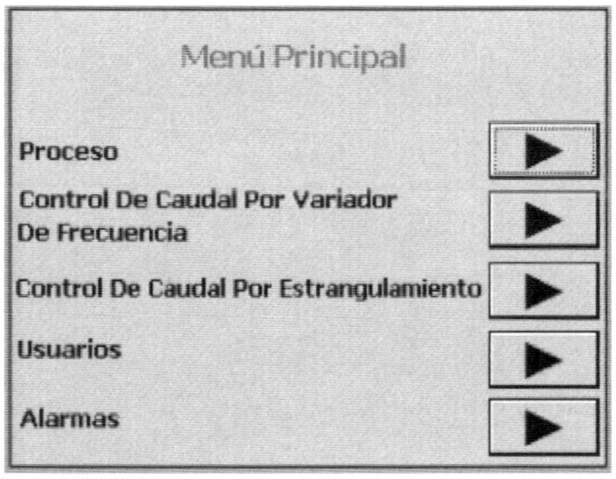

Fig. 4. Menú principal del HMI

Las interfaces humano máquina a nivel industrial requieren de un establecimiento de jerarquía a nivel de usuarios, como se muestra en la Fig. 5., que brinda accesos particulares al usuario debido al grado de responsabilidad así como conocimiento que puede poseer. Los niveles de usuario declarados en esta interfaz son:

- Administrador, posee todos los privilegios y control total del HMI, así como la capacidad de crear nuevos usuarios.
- Operador, es capaz de realizar las operaciones del administrador, con la excepción de crear nuevos usuarios y modificar los parámetros PID.
- Supervisor, realiza las acciones de monitoreo del proceso, así como la visualización de tendencias.

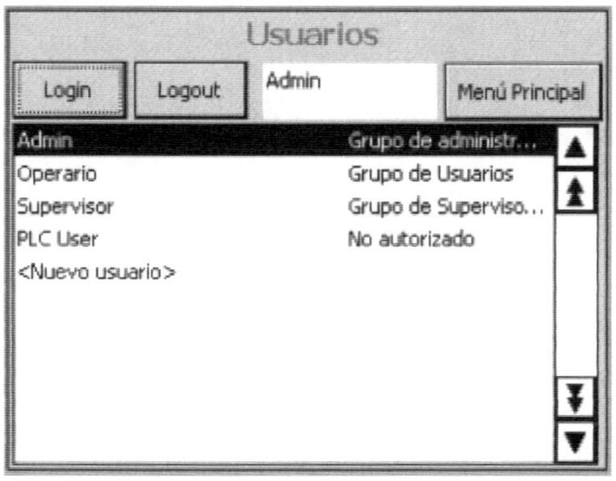

Fig. 5. Menú principal del HMI

El proceso de caudal de la Fig. 6a., se visualiza en el HMI junto con los valores de la variable dinámica caudal, variador de frecuencia y conversor de corriente a presión (I/P) en tiempo real; asi como las conexiones de las tuberías, en la Fig. 6b., presenta una animacion de parpadeo cuando existe el paso del fluido desde y hacia el tanque reservorio.

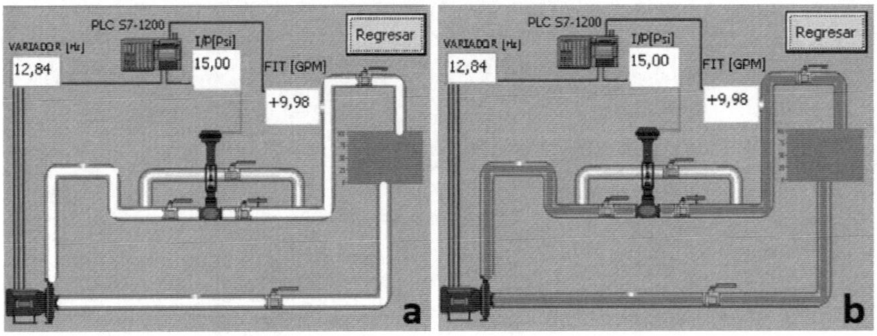

Fig. 6. Diagrama del proceso

El controlador PID requiere de sintonización, para ello se determinan las constantes kp, ti y td en este caso obtenidas por el método de tanteo, las cuales deben ser establecidas previamente al funcionamiento de la planta para obtener una respuesta adecuada de acuerdo a las necesidades del proceso. En la Fig. 7a. se presenta el método de control de caudal por variador de frecuencia en donde el usuario debe realizar el control manual del elemento de control final (válvula de control) y del setpoint deseado. En la Fig. 7b. se muestra las tendencias del proceso con las variables actuales tanto del SP, PV y CV.

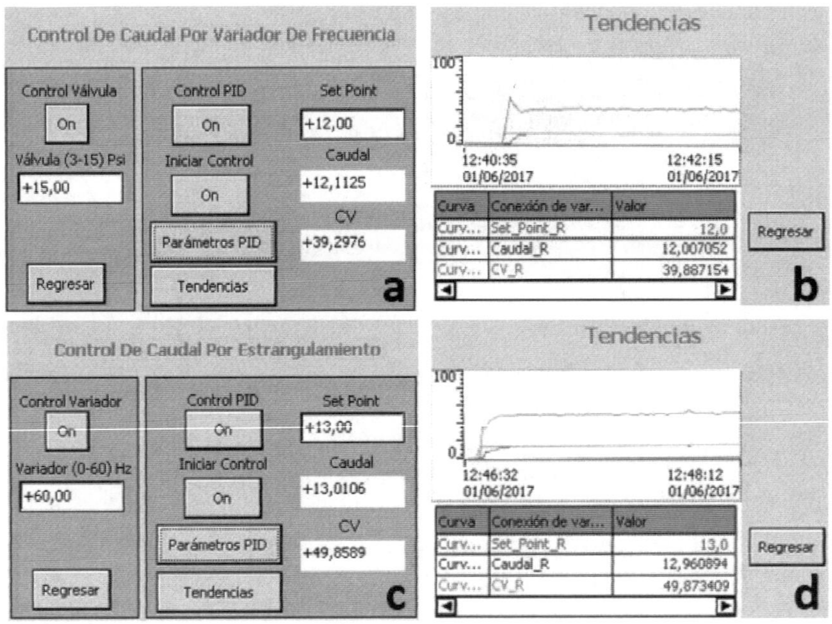

Fig. 7. Métodos de control de caudal implementados

En el método de control de caudal por estrangulamiento se debe ejecutar el control mediante el variador de frecuencia para que la bomba impulse el fluido para llegar y mantener al valor deseado de setpoint como se muestra en la Fig. 7c. y 7d.

El HMI consta de una pantalla con el registro de alarmas, las cuales se almacenan en una base de datos en la memoria del PLC, como se muestra en la Fig. 8a., asi como pantallas provisionales que se despliegan cuando la variable del proceso se encuentra en estado de alarma, además de contar con la capacidad de realizar el reconocimiento de las alarmas presentes.

Las Alarmas configuradas para el proceso son: High y Low cuando el valor de la variable del proceso excede o se encuentra por debajo de un valor de caudal previamente establecido respectivamente, como se indica en la Fig. 8b.

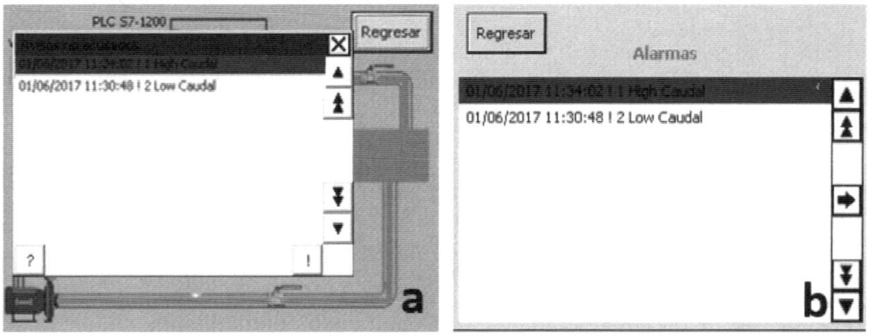

Fig. 8. Alarmas del proceso

6 Conclusiones

La interfaz desarrollada es capaz de realizar el control del caudal por dos métodos diferentes como son por válvula de control y variador de frecuencia en un mismo proceso, teniendo en consideración que cada uno de los elementos de control final trabaja independientemente uno del otro.

Al encontrarse la interfaz embebida en el proceso, suprime la necesidad de la utilización de ordenadores, registradores o algún otro dispositivo externo de visualización o control del proceso.

La implementación de la normativa ISA 101 asegura que el proceso sea manejado de forma eficiente e intuitiva por los diferentes usuarios, lo cual garantiza la calidad del manejo del proceso, al tener en consideración los limites cognitivos y sensoriales del factor humano.

Referencias

1. Pruna, E., Andaluz, V. H., Proaño, L. E., Carvajal, C. P., Escobar, I., & Pilatásig, M.: Construction and analysis of PID, fuzzy and predictive controllers in flow system. In Automatica ICA-ACCA (2016), IEEE International Conference 1-7
2. Pruna, E., Calvopiña, J., Serna, E., Escobar, I., Freire, W., & Chang, O.: Implementación de una herramienta didáctica para el diagnóstico de válvulas de control. In Biennial Congress of Argentina ARGENCON (2016) IEEE 1-6
3. Quian, H., Heng, Q., Sun, J.: Designing Industrial Batching System Based on Touch Panel And PLC. The Ninth International Conference on Electronic Measurement & Instruments. ICEMI (2009), Beijing China 281–284
4. Nicolae, M., Lucaci, L., & Moise, I. Embedding Android devices in automation systems. In Design and Technology in Electronic Packaging (SIITME), 2013 IEEE 19th International Symposium for (pp. 215-218). IEEE.
5. Pruna, E., Chang, O., Jiménez, D., Pérez, A., Ávila, G., Escobar, I., Gordon, A.: Building a training module for modern control. In Electrical, Electronics Engineering, Information and Communication Technologies CHILECON (2015) CHILEAN Conference, Chile 369-373
6. Ikuma, L. H., Harvey, C., Taylor, C. F., & Handal, C.: A guide for assessing control room operator performance using speed and accuracy, perceived workload, situation awareness, and eye tracking. Journal of loss prevention in the process industries (2014), 32, 454-465
7. Andaluz, V. H., Tovar, A. Y., Bedón, K. D., Ortiz, J. S., & Pruna, E.: Automatic control of drip irrigation on hydroponic agriculture: Daniela tomato production. In Automatica ICA-ACCA (2016), IEEE International Conference 1-6
8. Pruna, E., Bayas, F., Cocha, H., Escobar, I., Gordon, A., & Constante, P.: Implementation of a simulator of industrial processes. In Automatica ICA-ACCA (2016), IEEE International Conference 1-6
9. Bustamante, M., Moreno, G., Pelaez, A., & Madrigal, C. Design and implementation of an automation didactic module focused to machine vision and programmable logic control. In Engineering Mechatronics and Automation (CIIMA), 2014 III International Congress of (pp. 1-5). IEEE.
10. International Society of Automation, "ISA101, Human-Machine Interfaces - ISA," 2015. [Online]. Available: https://www.isa.org/isa101/. [Accessed: 01-Apr-2017].
11. Zapata, G., Salazar, A., Moreno, D., & García, R.: Supervision of a distributed energy resources generation system using IEC and ISA standards. In Robotics and Automation (CCRA) 2016, IEEE Colombian Conference 1-6
12. G. Bayrak, P. J. Murr, S. Ulewicz and B. Vogel-Heuser.: Comparison of a transformed Matlab/Simulink model into the programming language CFC on different IEC 61131-3 PLC environments, Proceedings of 2012 IEEE 17th International Conference on Emerging Technologies & Factory Automation (ETFA 2012), Krakow, 2012, 1-8

Voice and Movement Alerts Integration in a Blind Navigation System and Service

Luis Yanchatuña[1], Geovanni Brito[1], Carlos Gordón [1], Vicente Morales [1]

[1] Facultad de Ingeniería en Sistemas, Electrónica e Industrial. Universidad Técnica de Ambato, 180150 Ambato, Ecuador
luisk.yop@gmail.com; {geovannidbrito, cd.gordon, jvmorales99}@uta.edu.ec

Abstract. We report the successful design and implementation of an obstacle detection device within the mobility pathway of visually impaired students in the library of blind people located within the general library of the Technical University of Ambato. This project addresses the creation of two modules, a master and a slave, which together forms a body area network and through ultrasonic sensors acquire information from nearby obstacles and immediately inform the user through voice and motion alerts. The master module is located at the front and it is responsible for detecting obstacles at the top and playing voice alerts. The slave module is located in the middle of the user to detect medium and inferior obstacles, which provides movement alerts. In addition, the user can access an audio guide by pressing a button on the slave module in order to move from the library door to the blinds section.
Keywords: blind navigation system, alerts system, software, hardware

1 Introduction

According to the World Health Organization (WHO), an estimated 285 million people worldwide are visually impaired, of whom 39 million are blind and 246 million are visually impaired [1]. Among them, 5.9 million live in Africa, 3.2 million in the United States and 2 million in Europe. In Germany, there are 150 thousand people with total blindness and 500 thousand people with visual impairment [2] and 5 million blind people live in China [3]. In the same way, In Ecuador according to the National Council for Equality of Disabilities in its last national registry of disabilities carried out in September 2014, there are 46435 visually impaired people, of whom 1154 are in the province of Tungurahua and 806 are in the city of Ambato [4]. Also, considering to the information acquired in the Office of Student Welfare and University Assistance at the Technical University of Ambato, there are only two students with visual impairment to date. Besides, It is important to mention that loss of vision is accompanied by a loss of independence so blind people are unable to take advantage of navigation, social interactivity and communication due to the lack of mobility according to travel safely, comfortably and independently by the environment" [5]. Actually, technological advances make it easier for people with disabilities to acquire, develop and improve their cognitive, perceptual and functional abilities, contributing to improve their quality of life. [6] With the enormous development of technology since 1890, new solutions have pursued the development of new electronic devices for mobility assistance (DEAM) [7].

The DEAMs represent intelligent devices that aim to overcome human limitations, perceive the environment and represent the blind people through touch, vibration, speech or acoustic signals [8]. Taking into account a chronological development, the first DEAM, known as Neiszewski's Electroftalm, was developed in 1897 by Starkiewicz and Kuliszewsky. Through this device, the user was able to distinguish between light and dark [9]. In 1912, Nye and Bliss developed a new device, D'Albe's Exploring Optophone. This device follows a technology analogous to the previous one, turning light into sounds [10]. The principle of operation of these devices lies in the use of a sound player that emits a sound when the light intensity decreases. Most, DEAM devices are classified according to the system for acquiring the information in the environment. Thus, several groups of DEAM are distinguished: ultrasound, sensors or lasers, global positioning and artificial vision Systems [11].

Besides, the most prominent ultrasound-based devices are the Lindsay Russell Pathsound [12], the Mowat Sonar Sensor [13] and the Sonicguide [14]. The Lindsay Russel Pathsound is an obstacle detection device that informs the user of the presence by acoustic sounds and tactile system. The device has three types of sound that represent three different distances in two zones: the area within the hazard and the area out of danger. The maximum detected distance is 6 feet. Despite of its objectives, the device has not become commercial, since its design is very bulky [12]. The Mowat Sonar Sensor has a sound output and a touch. The device emits a conical and elliptical ultrasound of 15° of width and 30° of high, covering an area equivalent to the human form. Its distance range is 1 to 4 meters [13]. Then we have the Sonicguide, also known as Binaural Sonar Electronic Travel Aid. The device is implemented in glasses and has as output a stereo system. The Sonicguide emits a conical sonic signal that ranges from 45° to the left to 45° to the right with a range up to four meters away from the user's central line of vision. According to the variation of the tone, the user is able to perceive and recognize the distances [14].

Taking into account, the sensors or laser devices, the most prominent are the Laser Cane, Talking Light, Pilot Light, SONA, Easy Walker [15]. Among navigation devices based on Global Positioning Systems (GPS) are the MoBIC [16], the GPS Braille Note [17], the TORMES, the Loadstone GPS, and the Personal Guidance System (PGS) [18]. Among the devices based on stereovision, we find the Navigation Assistance for Visually Impaired (NAVI), which is a device for detecting obstacles both static and slow moving [19]. Another interesting device is the System for Wearable Audio Navigation (SWAN), which also allows the detection of obstacles [20]. As a result, we are able to appreciate a wide range of devises used to assist blind people with their respective strengths and weaknesses.

The present work aims to present an innovative device, which provides voice and movement alerts to assist in the mobility of visually impaired people within the Library of blind people in the Technical University of Ambato. This device detects obstacles in the mobility path and immediately alerts the user by pre-recorded voice alerts in a memory and different movement alerts. With this device the visually impaired user will obtain more information of the medium preventing possible accidents. Also, the device includes an audio guide implemented specifically to direct the user from the library door to the blinds section.

2 Methodology

The following steps were analyzed for the design and implementation of the obstacle detection device for visually impaired students of the Technical University of Ambato:

2.1 Requirement Analysis

The library of blind people of the Technical University of Ambato is located in a section of the General Library, so it does not have different characteristics that identify it as unique for blind people and there are no different materials and tools to help to prevent possible accidents within its route of mobility within it.

The main requirements for the implementation of this project have been identified based on a study of the characteristics of obstacles in the mobility path within the library and based on the needs established through an interview with 50 blind students about their main problems of their mobility in their daily life.

Then, the following requirements have been identified:

- ✓ Feasibility of using the prototype
- ✓ Portability
- ✓ Short and medium range of obstacle detection
- ✓ Reliability of use for the user
- ✓ Understanding alerts
- ✓ Affordable prototype cost

2.2 Obstacle Analysis

In order to solve the problem, the obstacle analysis was carried out in the environment of the library of blind people, which is depicted in Fig. 1(a) and Fig. 1(b). So, 8 tables and 28 bookshelves were the main obstacles identified within the environment in Fig. 1(a) and Fig. 1(b), respectively. Then, we chose the main features of them, which are the high, long, wide and the spacing among them. For the tables, we have 80 cm high, 1 m long, 1 m wide and 1 m spacing. In the same way, for the bookshelves we have 2 m high, 2 m long, 50 cm wide and 1 m spacing. Also, the distribution of the tables and bookshelves in the library of blind people is shown in Fig. 1(c).

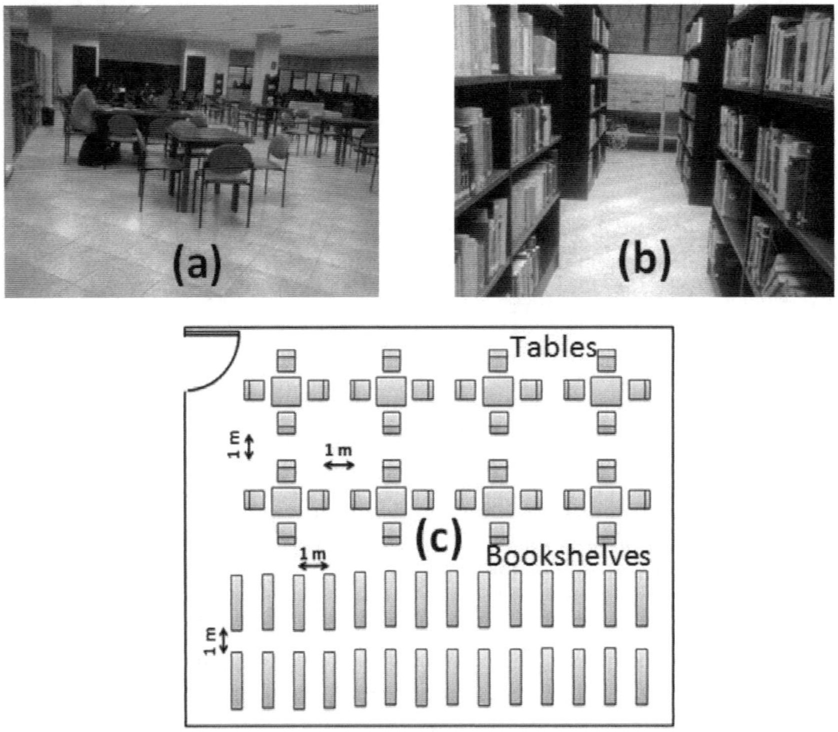

Fig. 1. Library of blind people. (a) Tables, (b) Bookshelves, and (c) Distribution of tables and bookshelves

2.3 Hardware Selection

There are several types of hardware that have been developed with the advancement of technology, but based on the requirements set forth above, free hardware has been selected because of the freedoms. It was also established to use small hardware for the implementation of a prototype that provides greater comfort of portability to the user.

Control Board

Within the Arduino platform, we find a variety of cards of different characteristics, sizes and prices. Due to the advanced characteristics of the Arduino Pro Mini, it is considered the most optimum. In addition, the price that is the most economical, it also has identical characteristics to the other cards but with a much smaller size and weight.

Sensor

The HY-SRF05 and HC-SR04 ultrasonic sensors are the most efficient, since they have a detection range of 0.02m to 4.5m, an excellent resolution of 3mm, a low cost that is very important for this project and also it is compatible with Arduino.

Communication Modules

It has been selected to use two Bluetooth modules HC-05, since it can be configured as master or slave, it has a range of 10m length, and 8gr weight. In addition, its price is cheaper than the Bluetooth module HC-06.

Audio Module

The audio decoder that adapts to the needs of the present project and it is compatible with the platform Arduino, is the Audio Decoder Module WTV020-SD, because it uses a maximum micro-sd card of 1 Gb in which you can record alert messages which are easily reproduced with the help of the control card.

2.4 Software Selection

The software used for programming is based on the previously selected hardware, as it has its own language based on the high-level programming language processing. So, Arduino IDE has been selected, the Integrated Development Environment of Arduino free hardware.

For the design of the printed circuit board, Eagle software was used for the feasibility of creating new component libraries which are used in this prototype. Eagle is software for electrical and electronic circuit design.

2.5 Block Diagram of the device

The block diagram of the device is composed of two elements, they are the Master Module and the Slave Module.

Master Module

When the master module is switched on, it reproduces a greeting message and instructions for its use. It is responsible for censoring obstacles by means of an ultrasonic sensor at the top of the user, subsequently the information is obtained on the control card, which, depending on its programming, generates alerts with prerecorded voice. In addition, it receives information, which is sent from the slave module through a wireless link and based on its programming, it also generates voice alerts or a guide for the user, so that the user acquires more information about their environment which facilitates their mobility. The block diagram of the master module is shown in Fig. 1.

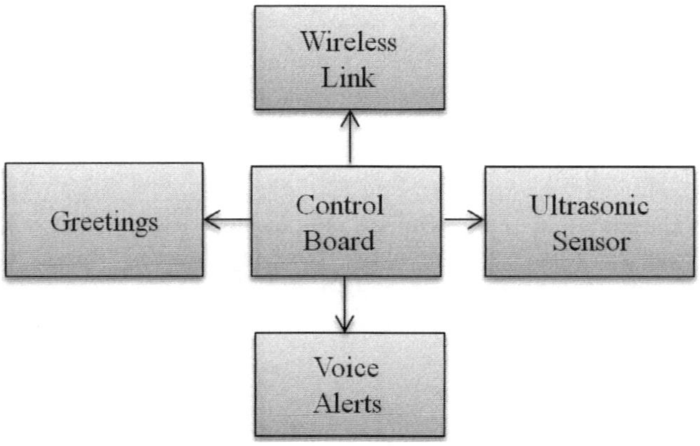

Fig. 2. Block Diagram – Master Module

Slave Module

The slave module is responsible for censoring obstacles by means of an ultrasonic sensor in the middle and lower part of the user. Then, the information is obtained on the control card which, depending on its programming, generates movement alerts. Also, pressing the button 2 via the wireless link reproduces a user guide in the master module or pressing the button 1 via the wireless link changes the movement alerts by voice alerts reproduced by the master module. The block diagram of the slave module is depicted in Fig. 2.

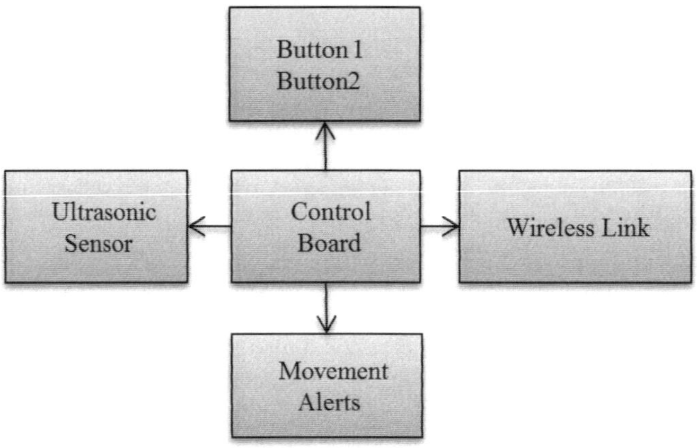

Fig. 3. Block Diagram – Slave Module

2.6 Programming Algorithm

In the Arduino Pro Mini card, both the master module and the slave module, sends a 10ms high pulse on the pin 11 to the Trig pin of the ultrasonic sensor, which emits a wave of audible sound for humans, if the wave bounces in some near obstacle the pin 12 of the Arduino is in charge of reading the time in high of the Echo pin of the sensor and by means of a small equation the distance of said obstacle is obtained.

$$\text{Distance} = (0.017 * \text{time in high Echo pin}). \quad (1)$$

0.017 is a constant

Master module

In the master module, a welcome message is displayed with the operating instructions. In addition, if data received via the Bluetooth wireless link of the character type in the variable "c" is received, the received data is received and voice alerts of medium and inferior obstacles or a user guide are issued. Otherwise, if no data is received, depending on the distance obtained, high-pitched voice alerts are displayed on the front.

Slave Module

And without pressing button 1 or button 2, depending on the distance, 3 motion alerts are played to inform the user of any medium and lower obstacles.

The slave module consists of two buttons: the 1 button to change vibration alerts for voice alerts and the button 2 to initiate a user routing guidance to the blinders section.

When button 1 is pressed, a wireless connection is established between the two modules via bluetooth and depending on the distance data 3 is sent to the master module by the character variable "c".

If the button 2 is pressed after turning on the module, it sends a data via the wireless link to start the user guide. And without pressing button 1 or button 2, depending on the distance, 3 motion alerts are played to inform the user of any medium and lower obstacles.

2.7 Implementation

For the implementation of the two modules, the following steps were performed:

1. Printed circuit and plastic box designs.
2. Soldier of the elements.
3. Implemented design in the plastic box.
4. Final assembly.

The printed circuit and the plastic box designs are sketched in Fig. 4(a) and Fig. 4(b), respectively. In the same way, the picture of the 3D printer while printing the plastic box is shown in Fig. 4(c) and the implemented design in the plastic box is depicted in Fig. 4(d). Also, Fig. 4(e) and Fig. 4(f) sketch the photographs of the final assembly of the Master and Slave modules, respectively.

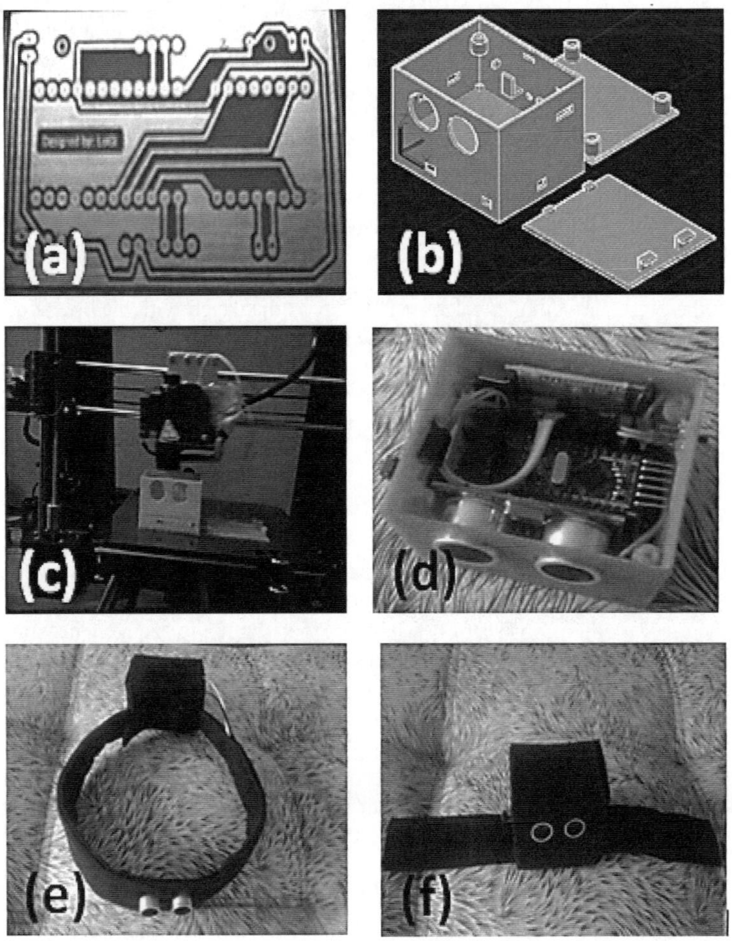

Fig. 4. (a) Printed circuit design, (b) Plastic box design, (c) 3D printer, (d) Implemented design,(e) and (f) Final assembly of the Master and Slave modules, respectively

2.8 Device features

This device implemented in this project has the following characteristics, sketched in Table 1:

Table 1. Main Device Features

Features	Device
Component	• 2 cards Arduino Pro Mini • 2 sensors HY-SRF05 • Audio decoder module • 2 bluetooth HC05 • Micro motor out of phase • Electronic elements
Biasing	5V-65 mA
Detection range	2 cm a 4 meters.
Alert range	2 cm a 150 cm.
Operation Frequency	16 kHz.
Model	Adaptable to different users
Weight	200 grams
Communicarion Speed	9600 Bauds.

2.9 User Interface

The user interface allows setting the voice and motion alerts of any blind person due to the fact that the device lets to set the specifications for the required person. As a result, the welcome message with the instructions and the voice alerts are very clear delivering detailed information of the distance of obstacles to the user. Also, the movement alerts that were configured of three different types provide detailed information that after the user adapts, it is easy to understand them.

3 Results

The tests were carried out with the help of a blind student of the Faculty of Human Sciences and Education with the name of Santiago Gutiérrez, 26 years old. Voice and motion alerts were configured to user specifications to improve device understanding and operation.

By analyzing the results obtained based on the tests performed and the user's opinions. We are able to infer that the device is comfortable, light and easy to use, because the welcome message with the instructions and the voice alerts are very clear delivering detailed information. In addition, the audio guide to direct the student from the door to the blinds section allows blind people to depend less on another person.

There are many devices and applications developed for people with visual disabilities, but some of the most efficient devices only detect obstacles at the top and others only at the bottom of the user that also have high prices. But, with the use of the device developed in this project, the user obtains information through voice alerts and alerts of movement of objects high, medium and low, which allows the user to feel safer to move avoiding possible accidents in their route of mobility. Besides, the study was carried out only in the General Library of the Technical University of Ambato which allowed to include a welcome message with the information of the space and to add a guide in audio especially for its displacement towards the section of blinders. As a result, the user is more independent and can be developed more easily within the library. Fig. 5(a) and Fig. 5(b) show the test of the device in different places within the library of blind people.

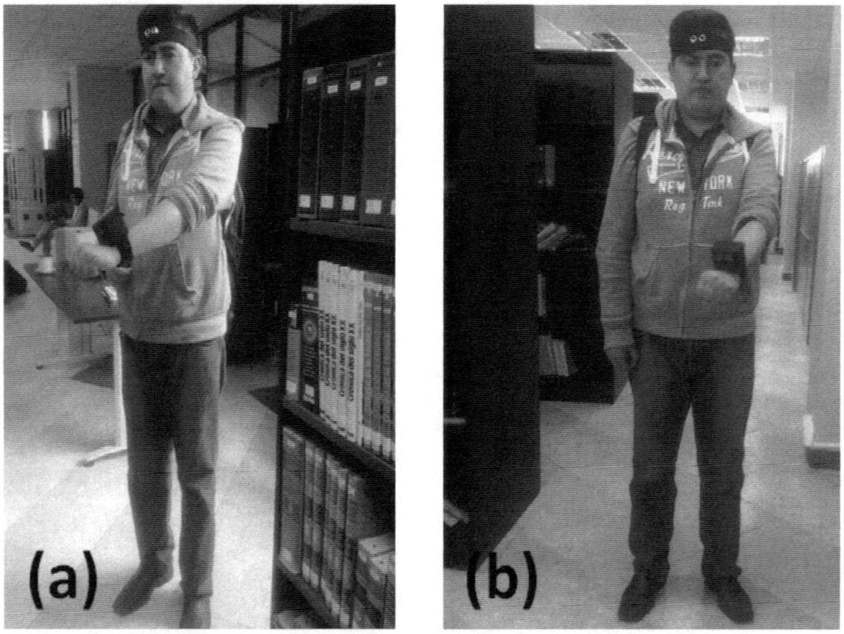

Fig. 5. Test the device in different places within the library of blind people.
(a) Between the bookshelves and tables. (b) Between the bookshelves and the wall

4 Conclusions

The existing obstacles in the library of blind people, located inside the general library of the Technical University of Ambato in the campus Huachi, present a danger for the visually impaired person when moving within it, because some obstacles such as: bookshelves and tables are not easily detected by the use of the white stick normally used by visually impaired persons and can cause blows or shocks in the upper and middle part of the person.

With the advancement of technology today, there are different types of proximity sensors such as: inductive, capacitive, reflex, ultrasonic and optical. These sensors are used to measure distances and detect obstacles, but the most efficient for this project are the ultrasonic ones to have a wide range of detection and to detect objects in movement, these characteristics allow detecting different obstacles in the route of mobility of the user obtaining greater Reliability when using the developed prototype.

The use of free hardware and software like Arduino and IDE, has many advantages because of its freedoms that it offers. Allowing the developer to program and use these products without having to pay a license or higher costs, which allowed obtaining this device at an affordable cost. Actually, it is important to mention that the device has an accessible price of less than \$ 150 which means that anybody who needs the device can obtain it.

The HY-SRF05 ultrasonic sensors used in this project deliver excellent results allowing you to detect obstacles in your mobility route. But, a drawback is its coverage angle <15 °, which causes obstacles outside this range not to be detected unless the user directs the sensors to them.

The information obtained by the visually impaired user through the voice and movement alerts provided by this prototype helps to move more easily and safely inside the library, avoiding problems and dangers of shocks or blows against different obstacles.

5 Recommendations

To avoid problems in the mobility of visually impaired people within the general library, there should be a specific route without dangerous obstacles to avoid any type of accidents. At the moment of selecting the sensors, they should be chosen who have higher detection range and greater coverage angle because these characteristics allow better results in this project. This prototype should have a price accessible to the user so it is recommended to use free hardware and software, in this way, it reduces the costs for the freedoms they offer. To solve the problem of sensor coverage, in this prototype there is the possibility of using sensors in the network and expand its detection angle. It is recommended that you configure voice and motion alerts together with the user to meet your needs and tailor it specifically to your deficiencies.

References

1. World Health Organization (WHO), Visual impairment and blindness, March 2014. [on line]. Available: http://www.who.int/mediacentre/factsheets/fs282/es/.
2. DBSV (German Federation of Blind and Partially Sighted). February 2017. [on line]. Available: http:// www. dbsv.org/infothek/zahlen-und-fakten/

3. ChinaDis. February 2017. [on line]. Available:http://disabilitychina.org/admin/ upLoadPic/ 2009326152139974.pdf
4. CONADIS, National Council for Equality of Disabilities, 2017. [on line]. Available: http://www.consejodiscapacidades.gob.ec/wp- content/uploads/downloads/ 2014/ 11/registro _nacional _discapacidades.pdf.
5. Starkiewicz, W., Kuliszewsky, T.: Active energy radiating system: the 80-channel Electroftalm. Proceedings Int. Congress of Technology and blindness. Vol. 1. (1963) 157-166.
6. Toro, S.: Visual deficiency: psycho-evolutionary and educational aspects. Coords. Málaga: Aljibe (1994).
7. Nye, P. W., Bliss, J. C.: Sensory aids for the blind: A difficult problem with lessons for the future. Proceedings of the IEEE. Vol. 12. (1970). 1878-1898.
8. Capp, M., Picton, P. D.: The opophone: An electronic blind aid. Engineering Science and Journal Education. Vol. 3. (2000) 13-20.
9. Dakopoulos ,D., Bourbakis, N.G.: Wearable Obstacle Avoidance Electronic Travel Aids for Blind: A Survey. IEEE Transactions on Systems, Man, and Cybernetics, Vol. 40. (2010). 25-35.
10. Dunai, L., Peris Fajarnes, G., Praderas, S., Defez B.: Electronic travel aid systems for visually impaired people. IV International Congress of Design, Research Networks and Technology, conference of DRT4ALL 2011, Madrid, España (2011).
11. Quintiàn, P., Calvo, H., Fontenla, R.: Application of a low cost commercial robot in object tracking task, Dyna (2012).
12. Mann, R. W.: Aids for the Mobility of the Blind-An argument in favor of a computer-based environment device device, interactive system, simulation. Conference on the Evaluation of Mobility Assistance for the Blind, National Academy of Engineering (1970).
13. Morrissette, D. C, Goddrich, G. L., Henesey, J. J.: A follow-up and study of Mowat sensor applications, frequency of use, and reliability of maintenance Impairment Blidness. Journal of Visual Impairment and Blindness, Vol. 75. (1981) 244–247.
14. Kuc, R.: Electronic binaural sonar travel aids provides vibrotile signals of interest, reflector movement and surface texture classification. IEEE Transactions on Biomedical Engineering, Vol. 49. (2002).
15. Ando, B.: Electronic sensor systems for the visually impaired. IEEE Instrumentation and Measurement Magazine, Vol 6, (2003) 62-67.
16. H. Petrie, V. Johnson, T. Strothotte, Journal of Visual Disability. Vol. 15-2, pp. 63, 1997. Petrie, H., Johnson, V., Strothotte, T., Michel, A. R., Reichert, L., Schalt. MoBIC, A.: An Aid to Increase the Independent Mobility of Blind Travellers. British Journal of Visual Impairment, Vol. 15. (1997) 63–66.
17. Loomis, J.: Digital Map and Navigation System for the Visually Impaired. Personal Communication. University of California, Santa Barbara, (1985).
18. Loomis, J. M., Golledge, R.G., Golledge, Klatzky, R. L.: GPS-Based Navigation Systems for the Blind. Basics of Laptops and Augmented Reality. Mahwah, (2001).
19. Lawrence, N. J., Marston, J. R.: Assisting wayfinding in visually impaired travellers. Applied Spatial Cognition: From Research to Cognitive Technology. Mahwah, (2007).
20. Sainarayanan, G., Nagarajan, R., Yaacob, S.: Diffuse image processing scheme for autonomous blind human navigation, (2007).

Fuzzy-Logic Control to Avoids Obstacles of Mobile Robot Using Matrix Language Software

Oscar Arteaga, María I. Erazo, Pablo Miranda, David Escorza, Hector C. Teran, Jakelyn Romero, Diego Camacho, Erick Mera and Alvaro Velasco
Universidad de las Fuerzas Armadas ESPE, Sangolquí, Ecuador
{obarteaga, mierazo, pdmiranda, jdescorza, hcteran, jxromero, docamacho, epmera, apvelasco}@espe.edu.ec

Abstract. In this paper could see the implementation of an intelligent control, specifically a fuzzy control on a mobile robot that avoid obstacles; the algorithm to develop will run on a system with multiple inputs and multiple outputs using fuzzy logic techniques previously collected. Also, in this work will include simulations on programming environment MATLAB of membership functions chosen for the control described in conjunction with the various rules of inference, also will be reflected the mobile robot avoiding the obstacles.

Keywords: fuzzy, rules of inference, mobile robot

1 Introducción

La robótica se ha centrado en gran medida en sistemas de interior y exterior, los cuales poseen una variedad de aplicaciones de servicio: industriales, médicas y domésticas [1]. Los robots móviles que han sido diseñados para ambientes exteriores están típicamente limitados a ambientes estructurados específicos, pero para que un sistema robótico sea eficaz y generalmente aplicable, debe apoyar una amplia variedad de tareas cooperativas, ejecutar estas tareas de manera eficiente y ser capaz de operar en entornos desconocidos o no estructurados [2] para lo cual será necesario un control adecuado que permita llevar a cabo dichas funciones.

Hoy en día, la lógica difusa ha ganado mucho espacio teniendo una mayor aplicabilidad en sistemas en los que el controlador es una parte esencial del mismo, es así que debido a la versatilidad y sencillez que brinda la formulación tanto de reglas de inferencia, como de funciones de membresía, se puede operar de mejor manera al sistema con el fin de conseguir la estabilidad para un desempeño mucho más desarrollado [3,4,5,6], puede ser utilizado en cualquier sistema robotizado debido a sus funciones y su alta eficiencia para aplicaciones en las que el controlador deba tomar decisiones automáticamente en base a parámetros establecidos. [7]

La literatura de robots móviles contiene numerosos ejemplos de enfoques que tratan de resolver problemas de comportamiento, los cuales son responsables de producir ciertas acciones (típicamente acciones de movimiento y percepción), dirigidas a lograr o mantener un objetivo particular, como mantenerse alejado de los obstáculos [8,9], es así como se presentan distintos trabajos como el Diseño del Sistema de Evitación de Obstáculos para Robots Móviles con Sistemas de Lógica Fuzzy donde se diseña un sistema de lógica difusa y se propone un algoritmo de evitación de obstáculos para una planificación de trayectos en un entorno desconocido para el robot móvil [10].

En el presente trabajo, se obtiene un algoritmo de programación para el control de un robot móvil evita obstáculos, utilizando el software MATLAB que permite el análisis difuso y presenta una amigable interfaz en la que se puede implementar todas las posibles funciones de membresía que abarquen el sistema a través de programación gráfica; sin embargo, se debe tener claro cómo se realiza el proceso de difusificación hasta la desdifusificación de una o varias variables de entrada [11], además genera una gran aplicabilidad para androides que en situaciones de catástrofes naturales pueden auxiliar en la búsqueda de sobrevivientes.

Este artículo tiene 5 Secciones incluyendo la Introducción. En la Sección 2 se presenta las bases de estudio del control lógico difuso para el robot móvil evita obstáculos. A continuación, en la Sección 3 se diseña un sistema de control lógico difuso con alto rendimiento para un robot móvil utilizando software de lenguaje matricial, seguido en la Sección 4 se muestra las simulaciones del control en el software MATLAB y finalmente se presentan las Conclusiones en la Sección 5.

2 Bases de estudio

La lógica difusa (fuzzy logic) está definida como un sistema matemático que modela funciones no lineales y convierte unas "entradas" en "salidas", acorde con los planteamientos lógicos que usa el rozamiento aproximado. Se fundamenta en los denominados conjuntos borrosos y un sistema de inferencia difuso basado en reglas de la forma "IF…, THEN…", donde los valores lingüísticos de la premisa y el consecuente están definidos por conjuntos borrosos, es así como las reglas siempre convierten un conjunto impreciso en otro. Esta nueva manera de representar el conocimiento digital, en la forma de normas lingüísticas, ha logrado reducir el número de reglas requeridas para cubrir un determinado universo de conocimiento y al mismo tiempo, se ha logrado producir en estos sistemas una respuesta más estable. [12]

La lógica difusa se aplica en procesos de mediana complejidad, aunque también en aquellos que son complicados, siempre y cuando no exista un modelo de solución simple o un modelo matemático preciso. De la misma manera se puede aplicar cuando ciertas partes de un sistema a controlar son desconocidas y no pueden medirse de forma confiable y cuando el ajuste de una variable puede producir la inestabilidad de otras. No es recomendable utilizar la lógica difusa cuando algún modelo matemático ya soluciona eficientemente el problema, cuando los problemas son lineales o cuando no tienen solución. [13]

Cuando se habla de la metodología que se empleara en la realización del presente proyecto se pueden diferenciar que se aceptan números como entradas, después se traslada estos términos numéricos a términos lingüísticos (como Lento, Medio y Rápido), llamado disfusificación. Las reglas después asignan los términos lingüísticos de entrada a salidas similares. Finalmente, los términos lingüísticos de salida son trasladados a términos numéricos, conocido como desdifusificación. [14]

El tipo de control seleccionado, emplea una serie de funciones de membresía en las cuales basa su comportamiento; la recomendación general para este tipo de funciones promueve la utilización de un número impar de las mismas, lo cual inevitablemente exigirá que una de las funciones se sitúe exactamente en la mitad de todo el control, siendo ésta la función cuando el sistema está estable; es decir, simplemente debe mantenerse en dicho estado. Cada función tiene su rango de actuación, no obstante, se pueden producir cruces entre las funciones permitiendo el cambio de estado mucho más rápido, llegando a ser aparentemente un tanto predictivo, estas funciones pueden ser variadas, sin embargo, para este tipo de control se utilizaron formas muy comunes como trapecios (extremos) y triángulos entre ellos. La idea es conseguir una respuesta muy semejante a una lineal para producir una estabilidad mucho mejor en menor tiempo. Cabe resaltar que, la forma que tiene cada función de membresía repercute directamente en la gráfica de comportamiento general que tiene el sistema, por lo tanto, se debe tomar muy en cuenta la gráfica de respuesta a medida que se va probando el control.

Otro de los factores que resalta su participación, indudablemente es la definición de las variables de entrada y salida. Para este caso, se toma en cuenta el tipo de variación que se proporcionaba a los sensores óptico y ultrasónico cada vez que el robot móvil se aproxime a obstáculos. Con dicha consideración se definen las entradas como aquellas señales que son enviadas por el sensor, mientras que las salidas se definen como las señales que deben ser enviadas a los motores del robot para que corrija su velocidad. Si se habla de señales que van a ser destinadas hacia los motores, entonces se entiende que los motores deben ser elegidos previamente, para proporcionar un movimiento acorde a la variación que sufra el prototipo; además que sean capaces de actuar con la magnitud de las señales eléctricas que son emitidas por el control. Este es un indicador de la importancia que tiene la selección de la relación que deben poseer los motores en cuanto a su velocidad y torque.

3 Diseño

La etapa de diseño del algoritmo para el control de un robot móvil tipo uniciclo evita obstáculos está basado en el diagrama de bloques de un sistema difuso, el cual se esquematiza en la Fig.1; en la etapa de fuzzificación se procede a la toma de los valores entregados por los sensores ópticos y ultrasónico, para traducirlas en tres funciones de membresía identificadas cada una con sus respectivas etiquetas.

Fig. 1. Diagrama de bloques de un controlador difuso

Debido a las características limitadas de la representación digital de señales, se usa únicamente las funciones de pertenencia trapezoidal y triangular.

3.1 Selección de Entradas y Salidas

Por medio del análisis teniendo en cuenta diferentes tipos de obstáculos se considera tres tipos de sensores, en los cuales dos de dichos sensores de tipo óptico serán colocados en los extremos de la parte delantera del carro, mientras que el tercer sensor ultrasónico se ubicara en la parte media del frente.

Una vez especificado la posición de los sensores se tiene tres entradas y dos salidas borrosas. La Entrada 1 corresponde al sensor SD, la Entrada 2 corresponde al sensor SC y la Entrada 3 corresponde al sensor SI. Las salidas son dos y corresponden a los motores tanto derecho como izquierdo MD y MI respectivamente.

3.2 Diseño de los conjuntos de entradas y salidas borrosas

La Entrada 1, con información del sensor SD tiene cinco subconjuntos, dos trapezoidales y tres triangulares, Muy Cerca (MC), Muy Lejos (ML), Cerca(C), Normal(N), Lejos(L), respectivamente. La Entrada 2, con información del sensor SC tiene la misma configuración y distribución de la Entrada 1, lo mismo sucede con la Entrada 3, como se muestra en la Fig.2.

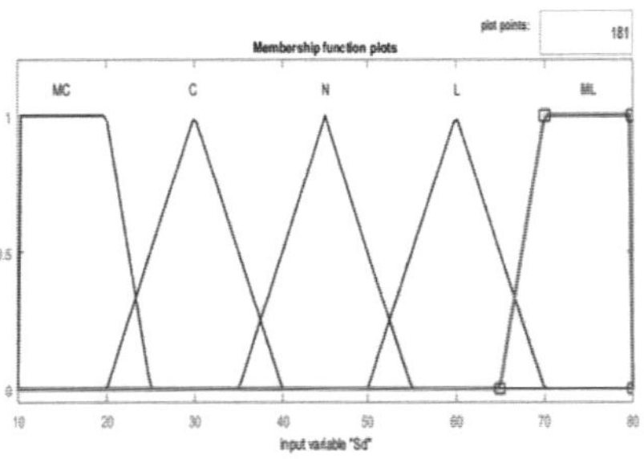

a) Entrada 1, sensor derecho SD

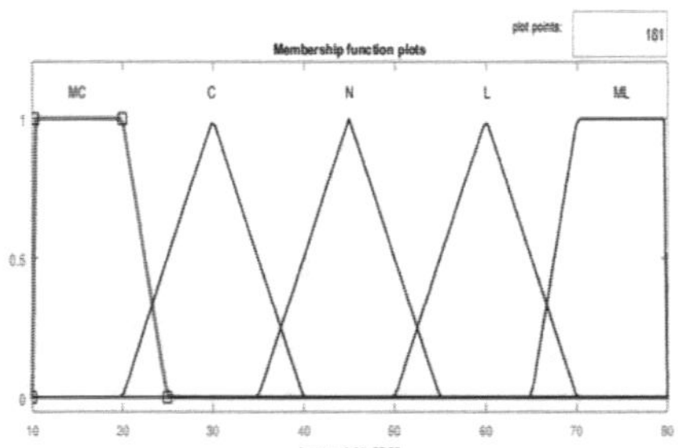

b) Entrada 2, sensor central SC

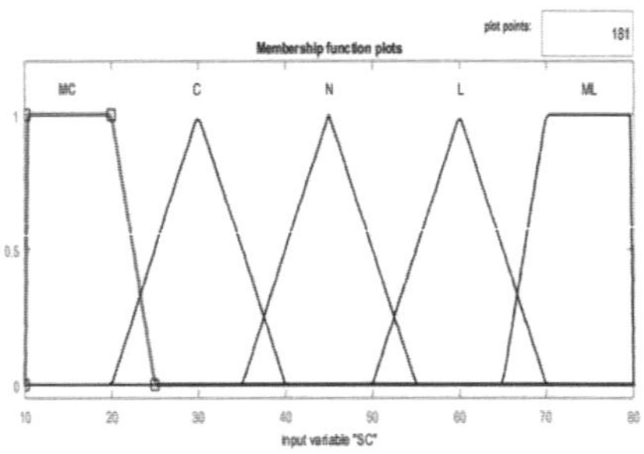

c) Entrada 3, sensor izquierdo SI

Fig. 2. Conjuntos borrosos de las entradas

El conjunto borroso de salida 1 correspondiente al Motor derecho (Md) posee dos subconjuntos trapezoidales Muy Lento (ML) y Muy Rápido (MR), tres subconjuntos triangulares Lento (L), Normal(N) y Rápido(R). La salida del Motor izquierdo posee la misma configuración de salida anterior, como se muestra en la Fig.3.

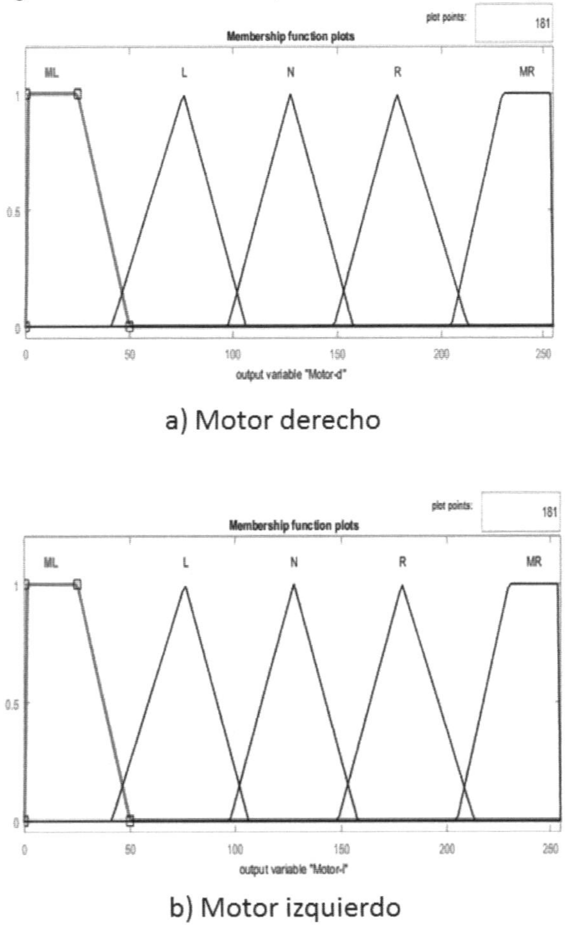

Fig. 3. Conjuntos borrosos de las salidas

3.3 Diseño del conjunto de reglas del control.

Para la etapa correspondiente a las reglas de inferencia se ha establecido reglas suficientes para obtener el control requerido; tomando en cuenta que se tiene tres variables de entrada y dos variables de salida, las mismas que se detallan en la Tabla 1.

Tabla 1. FAM (Fuzzy Asociative Memory) del robot móvil evita obstáculos

		SI										SC										SD									
		MC		C		N		L		ML		MC		C		N		L		ML		MC		C		N		L		ML	
SI	MC											ML	MR	L	MR	N	R	N	R	N	R	ML	MR	L	MR	N	R	N	R	N	R
	C											ML	MR	L	R	N	R	N	R	N	R	ML	MR	L	R	N	R	N	R	N	R
	N											ML	MR	L	R	N	N	N	N	N	N	ML	MR	L	R	N	N	N	N	N	N
	L											ML	MR	L	R	N	N	N	N	N	N	ML	MR	L	R	N	N	N	N	N	N
	ML											ML	MR	L	R	N	N	N	N	N	N	ML	MR	L	R	N	N	N	N	N	N
SC	MC	ML	MR	ML	MR	ML	MR	ML	MR	ML	MR											MR	ML	MR	ML	MR	ML	MR	ML	MR	ML
	C	L	MR	L	R	L	R	L	R	L	R											MR	L	R	L	R	L	R	L	R	L
	N	N	R	N	R	N	N	N	N	N	N											R	N	R	N	N	N	N	N	N	N
	L	N	R	N	R	N	N	N	N	N	N											R	N	R	N	N	N	N	N	N	N
	ML	N	R	N	R	N	N	N	N	N	N											R	N	R	N	N	N	N	N	N	N
SD	MC	ML	MR	ML	MR	ML	MR	ML	MR	ML	MR	MR	ML	MR	L	R	N	R	N	R	N										
	C	L	MR	L	R	L	R	L	R	L	R	MR	ML	R	L	R	N	R	N	R	N										
	N	N	R	N	R	N	N	N	N	N	N	MR	ML	R	L	N	N	N	N	N	N										
	L	N	R	N	R	N	N	N	N	N	N	MR	ML	R	L	N	N	N	N	N	N										
	ML	N	R	N	R	N	N	N	N	N	N	MR	ML	R	L	N	N	N	N	N	N										

4 Simulaciones

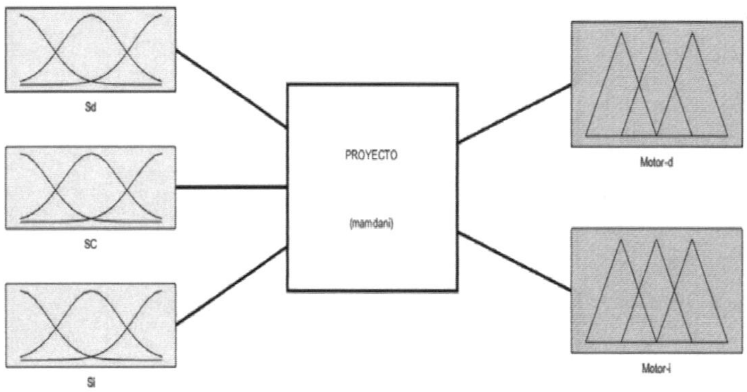

Fig. 4. Esquema del sistema de control difuso ingresado a MATLAB

Una de las principales ventajas de la utilización del fuzzy designer es la visualización del comportamiento del sistema mediante gráficas de la relación obtenida entre las entradas y salidas con la ayuda de las reglas implementadas para el control, véase la Fig. 4.

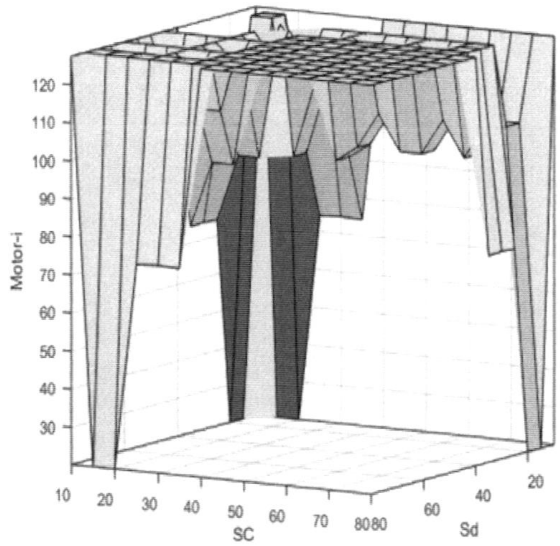

Fig. 5. Superficie de relación entre las entradas y la salida motor izquierdo

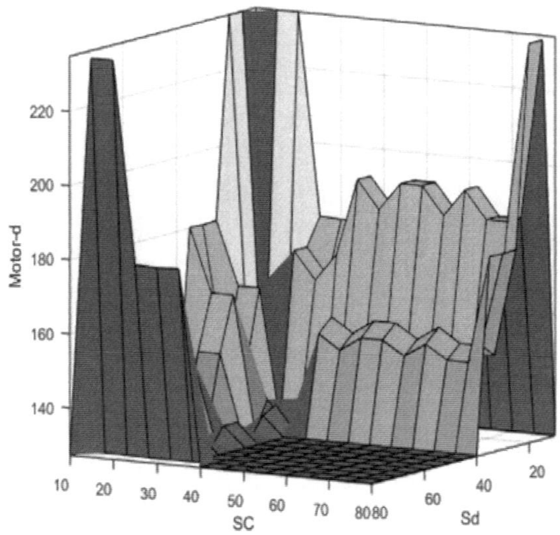

Fig. 6. Superficie de relación entre las entradas y la salida motor derecho

Para simular el sistema se utilizó la herramienta de Simulink en el entorno de MATHLAB, como se puede ver en la Fig. 7 se presenta el diagrama para efectuar dicha simulación.

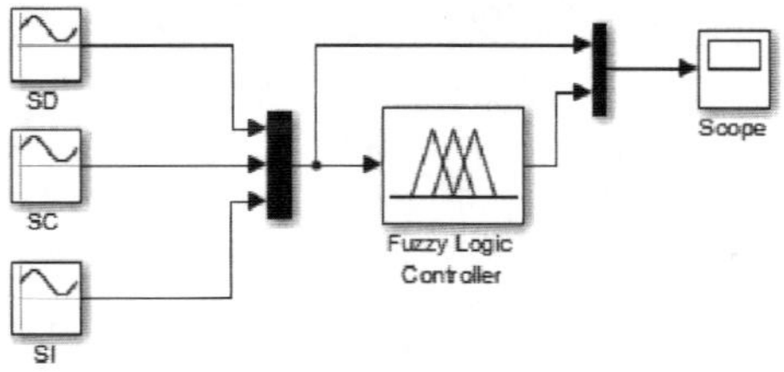

Fig. 7. Diagrama Simulink

Como se puede ver ingresan tres señales sinusoidales las cuales emularan en lo posible a los sensores de posición tanto ópticos como ultrasónicos SD, SI y SC respectivamente, dichas señales se unen y entran al controlador lógico difuso como entradas parecidas a las de la vida real, se posee un graficador donde se puede comprobar si el controlador es óptimo.

En la Fig. 8 se muestra las señales tanto de entrada como las de salida del controlador, en donde se puede ver las relaciones de los sensores con las respuestas del controlador, por ejemplo, si el sensor izquierdo SI se encuentra muy cerca MC, el sensor central está cerca C entonces nuestras salidas serán muy rápido MR y lento L, para el motor izquierdo y el motor derecho respectivamente, es así como se dan las respuestas de nuestro controlador.

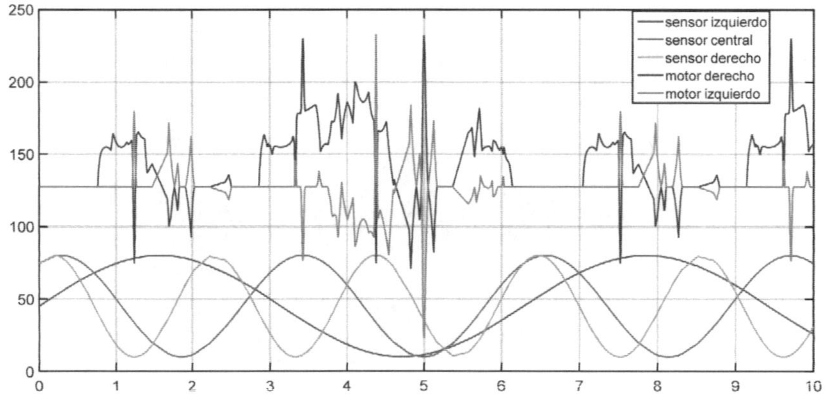

Fig. 8. Método para la desdifusificación

Se realizó la simulación en proteus del circuito a implementarse en el robot móvil evita obstáculos para un correcto funcionamiento como se indica en la Fig. 9.

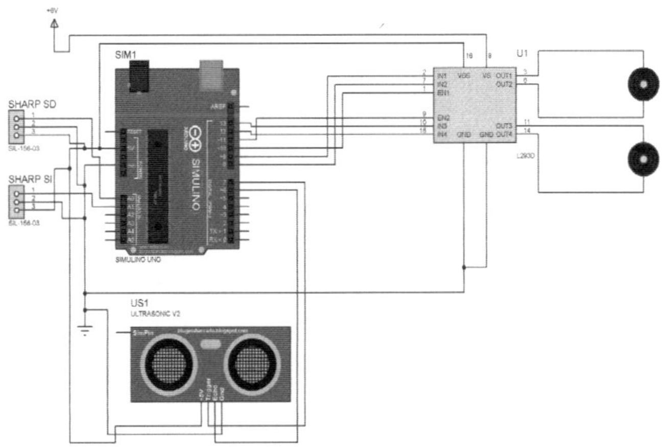

Fig. 9. Simulación del circuito

5 Resultados

En la Figura 10 se puede ver los sensores implementados a nuestro carro que consta de dos motores tanto derecho como izquierdo.

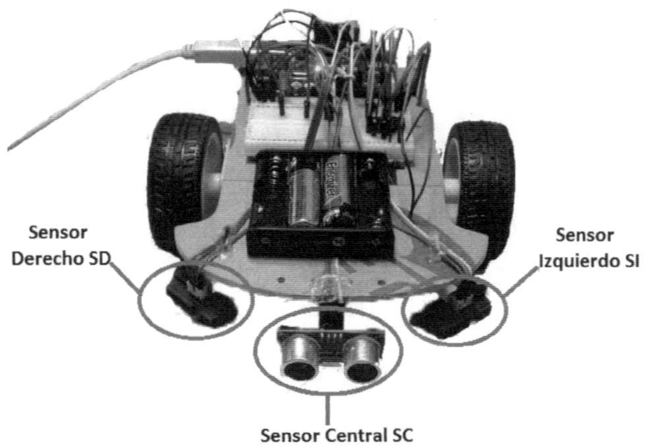

Fig. 10. Carro evita obstáculos implementado

En las figuras 11 y 12 se muestra una interfaz gráfica de usuario (GUI) para el motor derecho e izquierdo respectivamente, la cual permite una interacción sencilla con el control lógico fuzzy implementado en la aplicación, ya que no es necesario conocer ningún lenguaje de programación para ejecutar la misma. En la GUI se puede seleccionar el editor de reglas o visualizar reglas según las entradas es decir los sensores: SC, SD Y SI, también despliega las superficies de salida que indican el comportamiento de los motores.

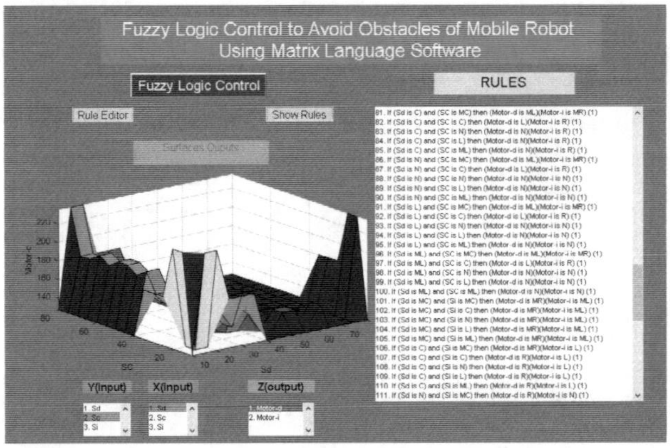

Fig. 11. GUI de parámetros del control Fuzzy Motor Derecho

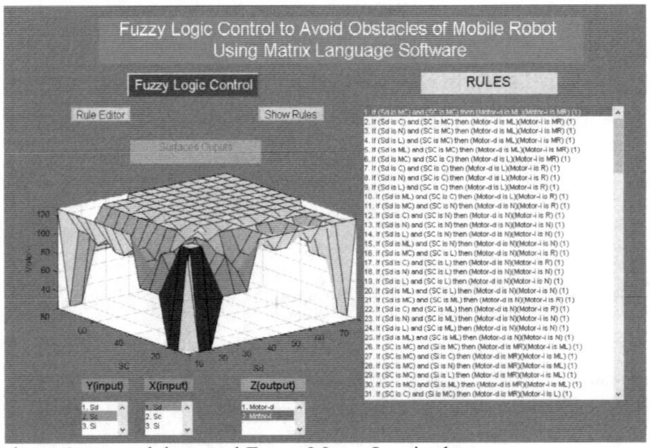

Fig. 12. GUI de parámetros del control Fuzzy Motor Izquierdo

6 Conclusiones

Mediante el uso del controlador de lógica difusa es posible trabajar a nivel grupal con entradas y salidas, ya que el mismo permite ingresar múltiples entradas y de la misma manera las salidas.

Las combinaciones de los diversos subconjuntos son de gran importancia ya que permiten generar las reglas para obtener como resultado un controlador correcto que cumpla con las condiciones requeridas.

En el trabajo se muestra la implementación de un controlador con lógica difusa que puede ser implementado para un robot que evite obstáculos.

Al obtener las entradas de los sensores ya sean estas las distintas combinaciones el controlador responderá según las reglas estipuladas en el programa. fis de Mathlab.

Referencias

1. K. WATANABE , Y. SHIRAISHI, S. G. TZAFESTAS, J. TANG y T. FUKUDA.: Feedback Control of an Omnidirectional. Journal of Intelligent and Robotic Systems, pp. 315–330, 2000.
2. B. Barry L. y S. Anthony , RAMMPS.: A Generalized Mission Planner for Multiple Mobile Robots In Unstructured Environments. International Conference on Robotics & Automation, pp. 1564-1571, 2000.
3. B. P. a. N. N. Zadeh.: GENETIC DESIGN OF FUZZY-LOGIC CONTROLLERIS FOR ROBOTIC MANIPULATORS. IEEE, pp. 267-272, 2000.
4. P. J. H. a. Y. J. P. Robert N. Lea.: Fuzzy Logic Based Robotic Arm Control. IEEE, pp. 128-133, 2001.
5. D. P. a. G.-A. C. Franck Betin.: Fuzzy Logic Applied to Speed Control of a Stepping Motor Drive. IEEE TRANSACTIONS ON INDUSTRIAL ELECTRONICS, vol. 47, nº 3, pp. 610-622, 2000.
6. P. Guillemin.: Fuzzy Logic Applied to Motor Control. IEEE TRANSACTIONS ON INDUSTRY APPLICATION, vol. 32, nº 1, 1996.
7. D. K. C. Sophia Mitchell.: Fuzzy Logic Decision Making for Autonomous Robotic Applications. University of Cincinnati, 2014.
8. S. Alessandro, R. Enrique H. y K. Kurt.: Using Fuzzy Logic for Mobile Robot Control. Practical Applications of Fuzzy Technologies, pp. 186-188, 2000.
9. H. A. Hagras.: A Hierarchical Type-2 Fuzzy Logic Control Architecture for Autonomous Mobile Robots. IEEE TRANSACTIONS ON FUZZY SYSTEMS, vol. 12, nº 4, pp. 524-539, 2004.
10. X. Li y B.-J. Choi.: Design of Obstacle Avoidance System for Mobile Robot using Fuzzy Logic Systems. International Journal of Smart Home, vol. 7, nº 3, pp. 321-328, 2013.
11. H.-X. L. a. S. Tong.: A Hybrid Adaptive Fuzzy Control for A Class of Nonlinear MIMO Systems. IEEE TRANSACTIONS ON FUZZY SYSTEMS, vol. 11, nº 1, pp. 24-34, 2003.
12. I. P. y. B. León.: Lógica difusa para principiantes: Teoría y práctica, Caracas. EDITORIAL TEXTO, C. A., 2007.
13. "Fuzzy Logic Toolbox 2 User's Guide". The MathWorks, Inc. COPYRIGHT 1995-2007.
14. J. L. E. N. P. E. R. Á. L. Rocha Morales Jesús Ángel.: Aplicaciones de la Lógica Borrosa al Control de un Dispositivo Robótico Didáctico de Evasión de Obstáculos y Buscador de Luz. La Mecatrónica, pp. 1-10, 2013.
15. T. L. A. G. a. C. M. Quintero.: Diseño de un Controlador Lógico Difuso para un sistema de calefacción. Fifth LACCEI International Latin American and Caribbean Conference for Engineering and Technology, Tampico, México, 2007.

Tele- Operation of a Sphere Mobile Robot Through a Web Application Developed in Linux

Santiago Pérez[1], Luis Proaño[2] and Víctor H. Andaluz[1,2]

[1]Universidad Técnica de Ambato, Ambato-Ecuador
ddsanty1992@gmail.com, victorhandaluz@uta.edu.ec

[2]Universidad de las Fuerzas Armadas ESPE, Sangolquí-Ecuador
vhandaluz1@espe.edu.ec, luis.e.proa@gmail.com.

Abstract. This paper describes a spherical mobile robot capable of navigating on two-dimensional surfaces with an external spherical shell of 245 mm diameter driven by the Internal Locomotion Unit based on the pendulum principle. The mobile robot is designed with a mechanical architecture and the development of advanced controls to satisfy with the planned and everything commanded from a web application that allows the management of the entire system through wireless communication using the 802.11x protocol.

Keywords: spherical mobile robot, linux, websocket, smart actuator, PID control

1 Introducción

Con la evolución de la ingeniería del software, ésta ha pasado no solo de estar en el sector empresarial administrativo, sino que ha logrado alcanzar todos los rincones en donde el mismo puede prestar un servicio y agilizar procesos. Por esta razón, con la integración de otras ramas de ingeniería es posible la creación de programas y sistemas de alta calidad, fiables y robustos, basados en la disciplina que caracteriza a la ingeniería en software [1]. No obstante, dentro de los dominios de aplicación del software se puede encontrar categorías cuya relevancia está dictaminado por el presente proyecto, es decir, solo se toma como referencia: *i) Aplicaciones web,* o web apps que son un conjunto de archivos de hipertexto vinculados que presentan información con uso de texto y gráficas limitadas integradas a las bases de datos y aplicaciones de negocios y por último *ii) Inteligencia artificial* se caracteriza por hacer uso de algoritmos no numéricos para resolver problemas complejos que no son fáciles de tratar computacionalmente o con un análisis directo utilizando aplicaciones como la robótica, sistemas expertos, reconocimiento de patrones (imagen y voz), redes neurales artificiales, demostración de teoremas y juegos [2].

En la literatura de los sistemas robóticos, el software desempeña un papel clave, pues representa el medio para incorporar la inteligencia en la máquina. Mediante éste es posible la percepción, la planificación, el control, el razonamiento y el aprendizaje de capacidades humanas que pueden reproducirse artificialmente en un sistema robótico computarizado como aplicaciones de software, los cuales implementan estructuras de datos y algoritmos diseñados en un amplio espectro de teorías [3].

Hoy en día, la robótica ha experimentado un gran crecimiento gracias al desarrollo de materiales y aplicaciones de software para diversos sectores productivos. En consecuencia, una de las áreas que está recibiendo especial atención es el software para programar robots, ya que existe una vasta literatura sobre la aplicación del mismo orientada a la ingeniería tecnológica [4]. La disponibilidad de hardware del robot humanoide conducirá a una creciente demanda de software y algoritmos útiles para mejorar la usabilidad y autonomía. Una importante área de necesidad será el software para una operación segura y autónoma en entornos humanos como hogares y oficinas [5]. Otro enfoque que los investigadores le han dado al software es el modelamiento aplicado en los robots móviles, que es útil para tareas de monitoreo y recopilación de datos adaptativos, especialmente en el contexto de misiones autónomas a largo plazo en las que las tareas programadas probablemente tengan utilidad limitada [6].

Por este motivo se han desarrollado robots esféricos que han tomado una atención significativa por parte de investigadores, empresarios, entre otros, ya que sus prestaciones de diseño ofrecen una movilidad omnidireccional, un amortiguamiento dinámico natural en las colisiones, así como una navegación de superficie bidimensional suave [7]. Independientemente del enfoque que posean este tipo de robots móviles, en investigaciones realizadas se ha encontrado que aparte de las consideraciones mecánicas y de diseño de estos prototipos esféricos, el software dictamina el comportamiento y las tareas que deben realizar, i.e.: El proyecto desarrollado por Harmo et al (2001) [8], presenta la implementación de un sistema de tele-presencia interactiva del movimiento ocular sobre internet con un robot móvil esférico, donde el software se encuentra plasmado en una interfaz de usuario con realidad aumentada y el acceso al sistema de forma remota, el propósito del sistema es brindar asistencia a personas dentro del hogar, así como la estimulación y enseñanza de la robótica. Seeman et al (2006) [9], se desarrolla un robot esférico autónomo con el nombre GroundBot para la ejecución de tareas de inspección de forma remota. A nivel de software, está compuesto por una arquitectura de control autónoma que adapta dinámicamente el grado de autonomía del robot en términos de control, percepción e interacción. Kaznov y Seeman (2010) [10], proponen la navegación al aire libre con un robot anfibio esférico con el nombre GroundBot cuyo algoritmo de programación está basado en Pure Pursuit (o seguimiento de trayectoria) el cual le permite al prototipo desplazarse con facilidad sobre tierra y agua, el enfoque del mismo está dirigido hacia la exploración de nuevos entornos. Calvo (2015) [11], propone una aplicación de aprendizaje básico mediante el manejo de forma inalámbrica de un robot esférico de la marca Sphero desarrollado por la compañía Orbotix, a través del cual los usuarios puedan iniciarse en el área de la programación y comprobar sus resultados con el dispositivo robótico mencionado.

Por lo anteriormente mencionado, el presente artículo se centra en la implementación de un sistema en el cual se adapta la robótica móvil y las comunicaciones avanzadas con el desarrollo de aplicaciones HTML, cuya labor es servir de mando inalámbrico para el manejo de un prototipo móvil esférico basado en péndulo con la incorporación de herramientas que permitan el uso de la tecnología táctil. Indistintamente al diseño de la interfaz de usuario, se genera un archivo.js ejecutable desde el lado del servidor en el cual se define el puerto de comunicación bi-direccional que actúa en tiempo real para el intercambio de datos, tanto de lectura como de escritura. Adicionalmente, se implementa un control PID para la estabilidad del prototipo a una reacción de una fuerza externa que trate de sacarlo de su estado de reposo. Finalmente, el sistema se caracteriza por ser de largo alcance, fácil manejo y compatible con el hardware y software existente.

Este trabajo se organiza en 6 Secciones incluidos la Introducción. La Sección 2 presenta la estructura del sistema; mientras que la Sección 3 muestra la construcción del sistema. El diseño de la interfaz de comunicación se presenta en la sección 4 a continuación en la Sección 5 se indica los resultados experimentales y se evalúa el desempeño del sistema. Finalmente, se exponen las conclusiones en la Sección 6.

2 Estructura del Sistema

El sistema desarrollado se basa en la arquitectura de interacción entre el usuario y el robot móvil por medio de una aplicación web, de tal manera, que el mismo pueda tener control sobre el prototipo con la mayor fluidez posible, haciendo uso de la tecnología táctil como Smart Phones, Tablets y ordenadores (joystick), con los cuales se podrá mejorar la experiencia al controlar el robot. Este sistema sigue protocolos los cuales permite establecer un puerto de comunicación bidireccional entre el servidor y el cliente mediante la plataforma Web Socket, el cual permite acceder a lugares de difícil acceso con la posibilidad de incorporar una cámara de video para el monitoreo, caracterizándose por movimientos flexibles en cualquier tipo de ambiente. Adicional, se adopta técnicas de control mecánicas y de diseño los cuales hacen al sistema capaz de realizar tareas y acciones según la necesidad del usuario de manera eficaz, eficiente y robusta manteniendo tiempos de coherencia en el proceso.

La Fig. 1 indica la estructura del sistema desarrollado donde el robot es programado para realizar tareas de forma autónoma mediante una tablet, smart phone o controles a través de aplicaciones de java (Web Socket) de tal manera que cumpla con lo requerido por el usuario. El sistema recibe la información a través de canales inalámbricos establecido por el estándar de comunicación IEEE 802.11x, para el manejo es necesario que el usuario se ubique de manera remota con el robot, con el objetivo de realizar exploraciones donde el sujeto no puede acceder por tamaño, peligros, dificultades medicas entre otros, la aplicación tendrá la capacidad de manipular los actuadores de conducción (delante, tras), disminuir o aumentar la velocidad de los mismos, así como también la activación de los motores de dirección (derecha, izquierda) y el monitoreo de las variables entregadas por los motores como son la temperatura, velocidad, voltaje.

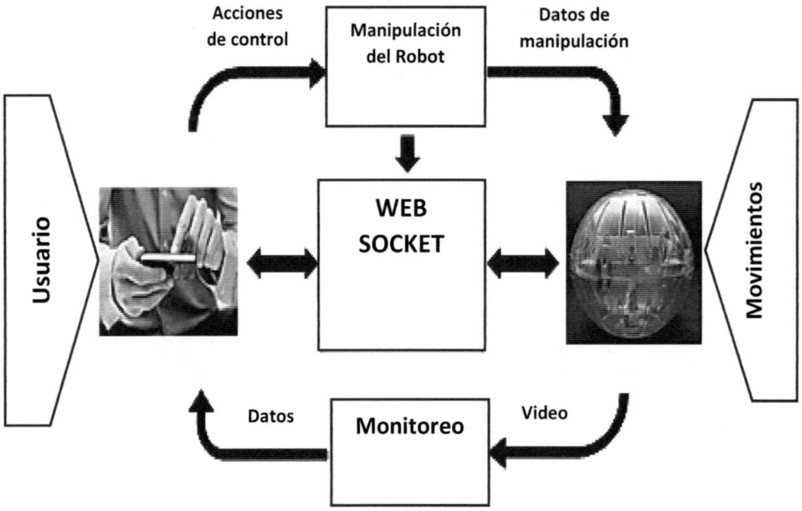

Fig. 1 Sistema de control del robot esférico

3 Construcción Control Abierto

3.1 Diseño electrónico

En la Fig. 2, se muestra el esquema de interconexión del sistema eléctrico del robot con sus componentes.

A. Módulo de comunicación inalámbrica: establece una comunicación punto multipunto donde el router se encarga de direccionar los datos de envío y recepción, para ello es necesario que todos los dispositivos que involucra el sistema estén dentro de la misma red, ya que no cuenta con la posibilidad de acceder desde cualquier punto remoto.

B. Motores de conducción: se encarga de controlador a los motores dinamyxel los cuales permiten la movilidad del robot para adelante y atrás.

C. Alimentación: Entrega el voltaje y corriente necesario para el robot por medio de baterías que son limitadas por medio de la tarjeta BUCK BOST que entrega y mantiene constante los parámetros de alimentación.

D. Tarjeta controladora: aloja el diseño web HTML para el envío y recepción de datos.

E. Motores de dirección y controlador PID: permite verificar y controlar el sentido en los tres ejes de robot Fig. 3 y el servo de dirección de derecha e izquierda mediante el principio físico del péndulo.

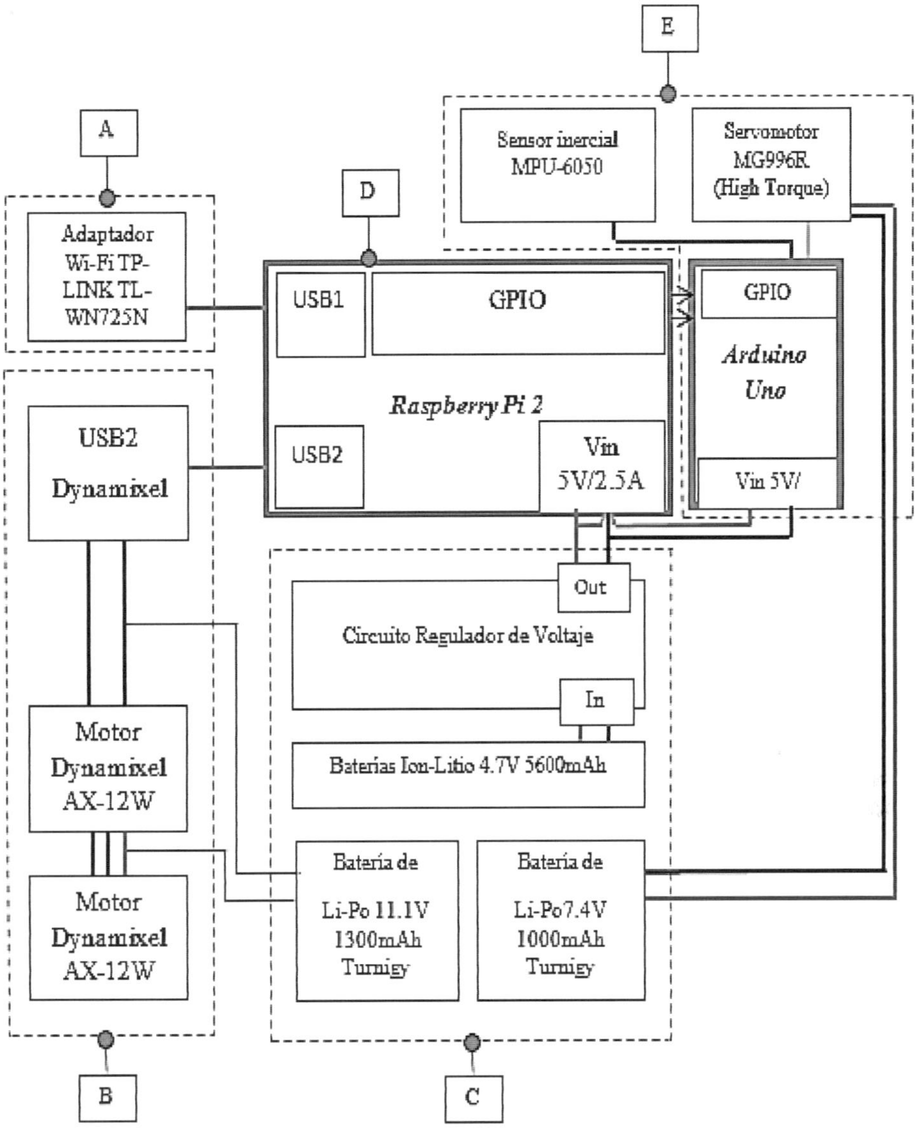

Fig. 2 Interconexión eléctrica de los componentes

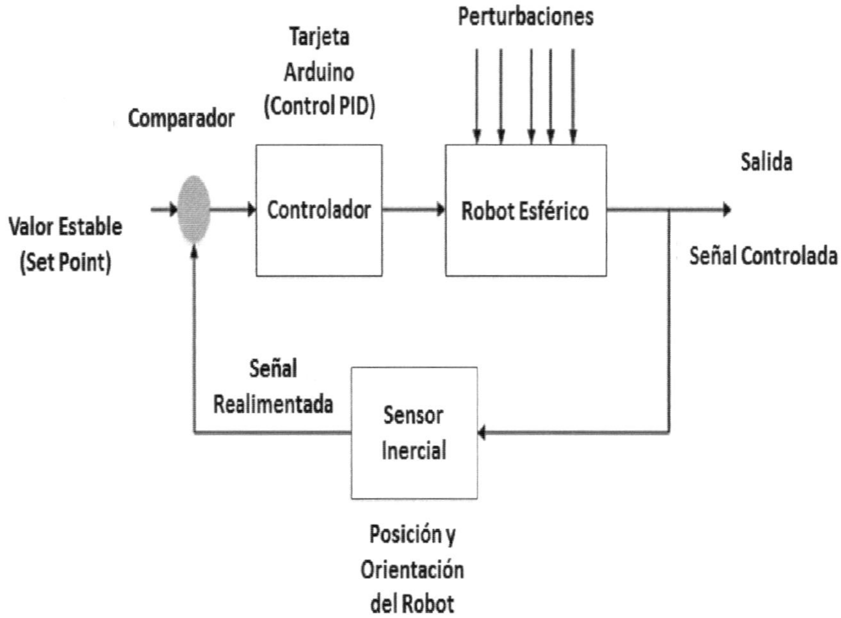

Fig. 3 Control del Robot Esférico

3.2 Diseño mecánico

En principio, para el diseño y fabricación del prototipo se consideró la utilización del software SolidWorks, ya que es una solución de diseño tridimensional con un entorno gráfico fácil de manejar y desde el punto de vista de diseño; intuitivo. Posteriormente, se valoró el mecanismo basado en Masa Pendular como UID (por sus siglas en inglés, Unit Internal Driving), proporcionando dos grados de libertad al robot esfera. El primer grado de libertad se ve reflejado en la tracción de la esfera el cual es un movimiento de rotación de 360º con respecto al eje central fijo. El segundo grado de libertad corresponde a la inclinación de la esfera cuyo propósito es darle dirección a la misma en torno a un diámetro perpendicular a dicho eje el cual varía desde $\pm 90^{o}$ en condiciones ideales.

De acuerdo con este análisis, involucra la creación de piezas soportes para los actuadores y la distribución de los elementos, de tal forma que encajen de manera precisa y se mantengan fijas en todo momento mediante la sujeción de tuercas y perno. Los componentes impresos en 3D incluyen el cuerpo interno, brazos para el péndulo, sujetadores o abrazaderas para los motores de dirección, bastidores o bases de soporte y la base que constituye al péndulo. La Fig. 4 muestra la configuración de hardware del robot esférico desde distintos puntos de vista.

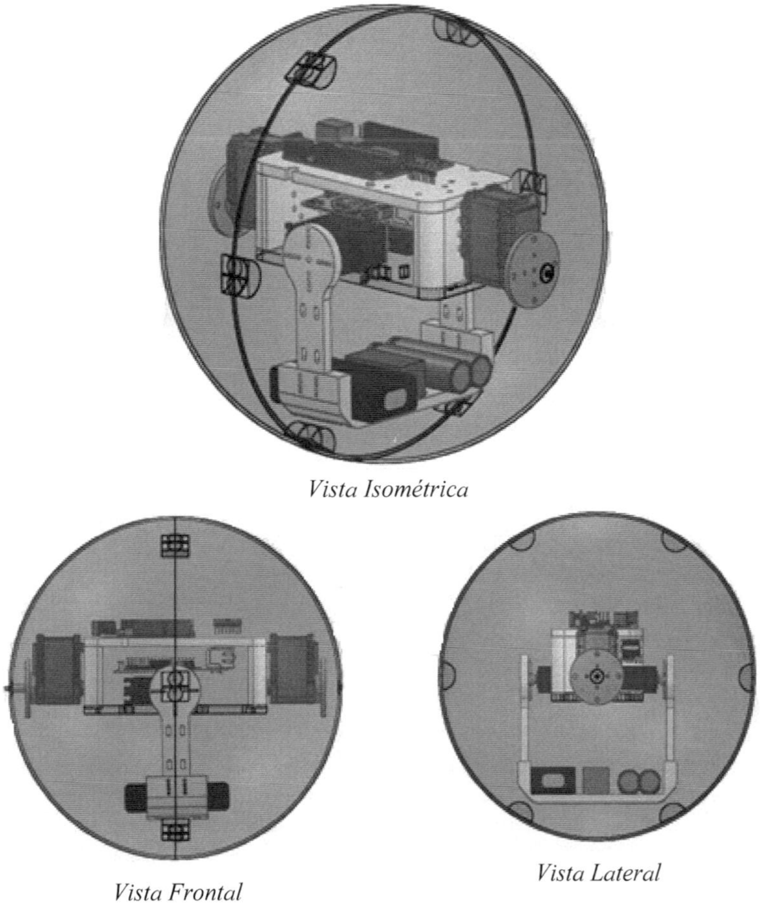

Fig. 4 Diseño mecánico del prototipo esférico basado en péndulo

4 Interfaz de comunicación WEB-HMI

La interfaz de control tiene como finalidad servir de intermediario para la ejecución de los movimientos sencillos del robot, como serían la marcha hacia adelante y hacia atrás, así como los giros derecha-izquierda mediante la combinación de botones. La interfaz táctil se compone de tres archivos principales, los mismos que se detallan a continuación: *i) InterfazTactil.html,* en este archivo se puede encontrar todo lo concerniente a la representación gráfica en 2D de los botones a través de la inclusión del elemento Canvas y mediante los cuales el usuario podrá comandar. A demás, integra todos los eventos enfocados con la parte táctil; *ii) index.js,* este archivo es el encargado de establecer una comunicación entre la InterfazTactil.html con el servody.py cada vez que se ejecuta; *iii) servody.py,* este archivo tiene como propósito la ejecución de los actuadores de conducción y/o dirección.

Cada uno de estos archivos se complementan entre sí, de tal forma que el usuario a cargo del manejo del robot esfera pueda hacerlo de manera intuitiva a través de una comunicación bidireccional entre el usuario y el prototipo. En la Fig. 5, se presenta la interfaz táctil.

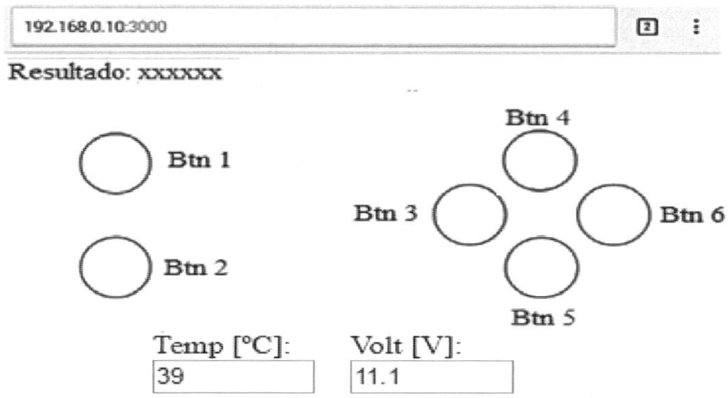

Fig. 5 Interfaz táctil en modo horizontal

La interfaz tiene la característica de detectar el sentido de orientación del dispositivo móvil. Esto quiere decir, que las áreas de mando o botones adaptan su funcionalidad ya sea de forma vertical u horizontal. Otras de las singularidades de esta interfaz, es que se ajusta a las dimensiones de pantalla de forma automática, así como también, se previno el zoom por defecto al realizar doble toque sobre la misma. Las funcionalidades de los botones se detallan en la Tabla 1.

Tabla 1: Descripción de la funcionalidad de los botones del mando táctil

Botones	Funcionalidad
Btn 1	Avance del robot esfera (punto de orientación)
Btn 2	Regreso del robot esfera (reversa desde el punto de orientación)
Btn 3	Desequilibra el centro de masa hacia la izquierda
Btn 4	Aumenta la velocidad de forma gradual de los motores de conducción (1 a 10)
Btn 5	Disminuye la velocidad de forma gradual de los motores de conducción (1 a 10)
Btn 6	Desequilibra el centro de masa hacia la derecha

5 Resultados experimentales

En esta sección, se realizan experimentos para verificar la fluidez de la interfaz HMI desarrollada en el presente proyecto de investigación a través de la actuación de un robot móvil esférico sobre el plano horizontal. A demás, se comprueba la labor del controlador de lazo cerrado PID cuya finalidad es corregir los grados de inclinación del robot actuador alcanzando su estado de reposo predefinido mediante software.

5.1 Prueba experimental de la HMI

Para poner en marcha este tipo de prueba experimental, inicialmente, se debe correr el servidor web o ejecutar el archivo *index.js*, mediante una Terminal en Linux Fig. 6.

Fig. 6 Ejecución del puerto de comunicación para el control inalámbrico.

En la Fig. 7, se presenta en la aplicación HTML en funcionamiento y simultáneamente la respuesta en consola del Script de Python (*servody.py*), con lo cual es posible corroborar la comunicación con los actuadores del prototipo y su activación.

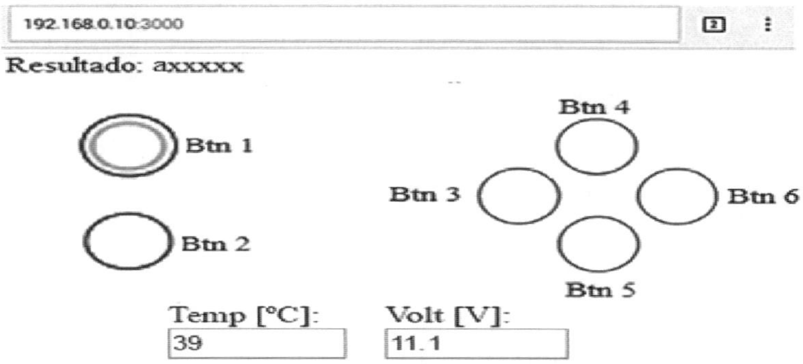

(a)

(b)

Fig. 7 (a) Captura de la aplicación web en Google Chrome (b) Monitoreo por consola de la ejecución de la aplicación web.

Donde, *js* representa la respuesta emitida por JavaScript a través del puerto 3000 definido para el WebSocket y *py* corresponde al resultado devuelta por el Script de Python.

5.2 Prueba experimental del controlador PID

Finalmente, mediante métodos de sintonización se consiguió dar valores a las constantes de sintonía del controlador, cuyas acciones se ajustan de tal manera que alcanzan el valor de consigna o SetPoint, el cual está establecido en un valor fijo correspondiente a 83, teniendo como resultado la estabilidad del prototipo como reacción a una fuerza externa que trate de sacarlo de su estado de reposo. Esta acción de corrección se la puede observar en la siguiente gráfica Fig. 8.

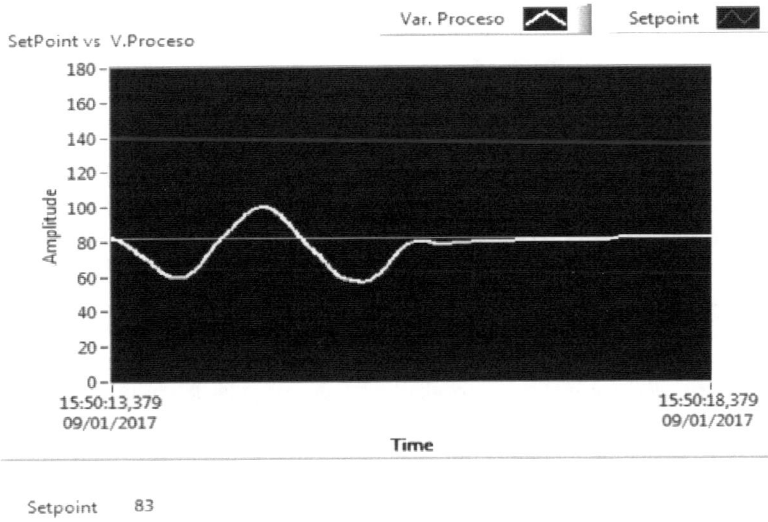

Fig. 8 Acción de corrección del controlador PID con SetPoint fijo

A continuación, se presenta la gráfica correspondiente a la señal de proceso escala de 0 a 100 %. (ver Fig. 9)

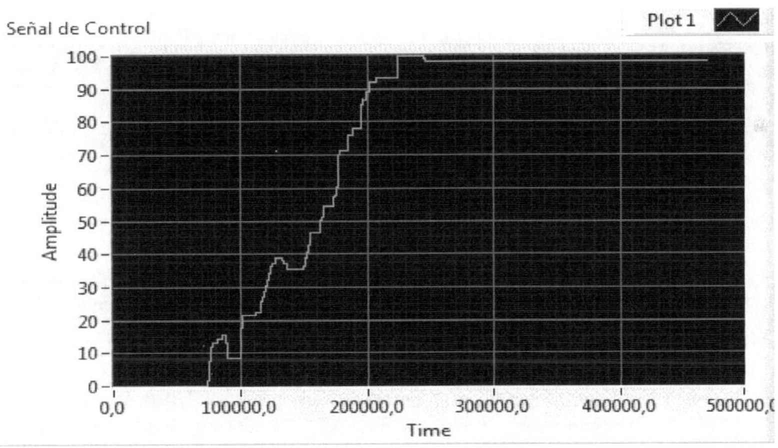

Fig. 9 Señal de control o variable controlada

5 Conclusiones

El control de operación inalámbrico del prototipo esfera, es más sensible debido a que la aplicación es en tiempo real por la inclusión del WebSocket. Sin embargo, a partir de este punto los actuadores toman un considerable tiempo de activación el mismo que se determinó de manera experimental y que bordea los 70 a 80 mseg, generando un cierto grado de complejidad en cuanto a maniobrabilidad. Es por ello que la incorporación del control de velocidad que ayuda relativamente al manejo del mismo. El diseño esférico del prototipo resultó ser capaz de moverse por ambientes que presenten cierto grado de complejidad, demostrando su capacidad de recuperación gracias a su principio de locomoción basado en péndulo siempre y cuando no se encentre atrapado. En cuanto a la estrategia de control empleada, hasta el punto en el que se ha desarrollado, ha demostrado ser útil, mejorando el comportamiento del mismo en caso de que experimente algún tipo de movimiento brusco externo.

Referencias

1. Brugali, D., and Prassler, E.: Software Engineering for Robotics. IEEE Robot. Autom. Mag., vol. 16, no. 1 (2009)

2. Pressman, R., and Troya, J.: Ingeniería del software: Un enfoque práctico, Séptima., Vol. 1. Connecticut. McGraw-Hill (2007)

3. Sommerville, I.: Ingeniería del software, Séptima. Madrid-Pearson Educación (2005)

4. DeLoach, S., Matson, E., and Li, Y.: Applying agent oriented software engineering to cooperative robotics. Proc, Fifteenth. Int. Florida Artif. Intell. Res. Soc. Conf., no. Flairs (2002) 396-401

5. Kuffner, J., Nishiwaki, H., Kagami, S., Inaba, M., and Inoue, H.: Motion Planning for Humanoid Robots, Vol. 12. Robot. Res (2002) 105-118

6. Girdhar, Y., and Dudek, G.: Modeling curiosity in a mobile robot for long-term autonomous exploration and monitoring, Vol. 40. Auton. Robots (2016) 1267–1278

7. Niu, X., Suherlan, A., Soh, G., Foong, S., Wood, K., and Otto, K.: Mechanical development and control of a miniature nonholonomic spherical rolling robot, 13th. Int. Conf. Control Autom. Robot. Vision, ICARCV (1997) 1923–1928

8. Harmo, P., Halme, A., Pitkanen, H., Virekoski, P., Halinen, M., and Suomela, J.: Moving Eye - interactive telepresence over Internet with a ball shaped mobile robot, Vol. 358. Telemat. Appl. Autom. Robot. 2001 (TA 2001). Proc. from IFAC Conf (1992) 481– 486

9. Seeman, M., Broxvall, M., Saffiotti, A., and Wide, P.: An autonomous spherical robot for security tasks, Vol. 2006. IEEE Int. Conf. Comput. Intell. Homel. Secur. Pers. Safety (2006) 51–55

10. Kaznov, V., and Seeman, M.: Outdoor navigation with a spherical amphibious robot. IEEE/RSJ 2010 Int. Conf. Intell. Robot. Syst. IROS 2010 - Conf. Proc (2010) 5113–

5118

11. Ruiz, J.: 5PHERO: Aplicación para el aprendizaje básico mediante el control de un dispositivo Sphero, (2015)

Escuela Superior Politecnica de Chimborazo
Panamericana Sur km 1 1/2
Riobamba - Ecuador
Postal Code: EC060155

Universidad de las Fuerzas Armadas, ESPE-L
Ecuador, Cotopaxi – Latacunga
Calle Quljano y Ordonez y Hermanas Paez

ISBN 978-1-5108-4396-7

9 781510 843967

CURRAN ASSOCIATES INC.
proceedings.com

56th American Association of Swine Veterinarians Annual Meeting 2025

Be The Pig's Champion

San Francisco, California, USA
1 - 4 March 2025